A TEST OF FAITH?

Throughout Europe, religion in the workplace is perceived as self-evident in some contexts, and as hugely problematic in others. The increasing number of legal scholars and practitioners who confront this issue, will find in this book numerous pathways along which to form their own legal opinion, and to help shape the as yet undecided legal approaches in many European countries.

Eva Brems, Ghent University, Belgium

Cultural Diversity and Law in Association with RELIGARE

Series Editor: Prakash Shah, Queen Mary, University of London, UK

RELIGARE is a project on Religious Diversity and Secular Models in Europe funded by the European Commission under the Seventh Framework Programme. The project brings together an interdisciplinary team of high profile researchers and 13 academic institutions to collaborate on examining how existing policy and practice is suited to the demands of religious diversity within Europe and what legal models can be recommended to accommodate such diversity in future. More details on the project can be seen at its website: http://www.religareproject.eu/. 'Cultural Diversity and Law in Association with RELIGARE' provides an outlet for the results of specific research undertaken within the RELIGARE project.

A Test of Faith?

Religious Diversity and Accommodation in the European Workplace

Edited by

KATAYOUN ALIDADI

MARIE-CLAIRE FOBLETS

JOGCHUM VRIELINK

Catholic University of Leuven, Belgium

Routledge
Taylor & Francis Group
LONDON AND NEW YORK

First published 2012 by Ashgate Publishing

2 Park Square, Milton Park, Abingdon, Oxon OX14 4RN
711 Third Avenue, New York, NY 10017, USA

Routledge is an imprint of the Taylor & Francis Group, an informa business

First issued in paperback 2016

British Library Cataloguing in Publication Data
A test of faith? : religious diversity and accommodation in
the European workplace. -- (Cultural diversity and law in
assocation with RELIGARE)
1. Religion in the workplace--Law and legislation--
European Union countries.
I. Series II. Alidadi, Katayoun. III. Foblets,
Marie-Claire, 1959– IV. Vrielink, Jogchum.
344.2'40125–dc23

Library of Congress Cataloging-in-Publication Data
A test of faith? : religious diversity and accommodation in the European
workplace / by Katayoun Alidadi, Marie-Claire Foblets and Jogchum Vrielink.
p. cm. -- (Cultural diversity and law in association with religare)
Includes bibliographical references and index.
ISBN 978-1-4094-4502-9 (hardback)
1. Religion in the workplace--Law and legislation--Europe. I.
Alidadi, Katayoun. II. Foblets, Marie-Claire, 1959– III. Vrielink, Jogchum.
KJC2945.R44T47 2012
344.401'25–dc23

2012006639

ISBN 978-1-4094-4502-9 (hbk)
ISBN 978-1-138-25605-7 (pbk)

Contents

Section II: New Player Joining In: The European Union and Religious Discrimination

PART II: IDENTITY, NEUTRALITY, SECULARISM: CASE STUDIES AND COMPARATIVE PERSPECTIVES

Section I: Country Studies: Turkey, France and Belgium

Section II: Comparative Perspectives in the Public and Private Workplace

Notes on Contributors

Katayoun Alidadi is a PhD candidate at the Catholic University of Leuven, Belgium, and a project researcher in the RELIGARE project, funded by the European Commission's Seventh Framework Programme. Her research focuses on religious freedom, anti-discrimination law and reasonable accommodations, in particular as it relates to the workplace. She holds a law degree from the Catholic University of Leuven and an LLM degree from Harvard Law School (2005).

Rim-Sarah Alouane is a PhD candidate in Public Law at the University Capitole in Toulouse, France, teaching assistant at the Jean-Francois Champollion University Center for Teaching and Research in Albi, France, and holds a Master's Degree in Comparative Public Law of Francophone Countries from the Faculty of Law of the University Capitole. Her thesis, "The judge and the protection of religious diversity in Canada, the United Kingdom and France," explores the practice of judges acting as "jurislators" with regard to the recognition and protection of cultural and religious specificities. Her main research interests are in the areas of civil liberties, cultural and religious diversity, and minority rights.

Amandine Barb is a PhD candidate at Sciences Po in Paris, France. Her dissertation focuses on Church–State relations in the United States since the 1980s. She holds a BA in Political Science and an MA in Comparative Politics from Sciences Po. Her Master's thesis was entitled "Non-believers in the United States or the limits of tolerance." She was a Fulbright visiting scholar at the Center for the Study of Democracy, Toleration and Religion at Columbia University (2009–2010).

Gabrielle Caceres is a PhD candidate at the Free University of Brussels, Belgium. She is also a law researcher at the Institute for European Studies of the Free University of Brussels, and has worked on the research project "Outsiders in Europe: The Foreigner and the 'Other' in the Process of Changing Rules and Identities" (2006–2011), coordinated by the Interdisciplinary Center "Migration, Asylum and Multiculturalism" (MAM) at the Free University of Brussels.

Marie-Claire Foblets is professor of law and of anthropology at the Universities of Leuven and Antwerp, Belgium. She is the Scientific Coordinator of the RELIGARE project (2010–2013), funded by the European Commission's Seventh Framework Programme. Since March 2012, she is also the director of the newly established Law & Anthropology department at the Max Planck Institute for Social Anthropology in Halle, Germany. She has held various visiting professorships both within and outside Europe. For several years she served as the head of the Department of Social and Cultural Anthropology at the Catholic University of Leuven. She has conducted extensive research and published widely on issues of migration law, including the elaboration of European migration law after the Treaty of Amsterdam, citizenship/nationality laws, compulsory integration, anti-racism and non-discrimination. In the field of anthropology of law, her research focuses on cultural diversity and legal practice, with a particular interest in the application of Islamic family laws in Europe, and more recently in the accommodation of cultural and religious diversity under state law.

Kristin Henrard is professor of minority protection at the Erasmus University of Rotterdam (EUR), the Netherlands, as well as associate professor of constitutional law. She studied law at the Catholic University of Leuven, Belgium, and obtained an LLM degree at Harvard Law School (1995). She holds a PhD degree from the Catholic University of Leuven (1999). She currently teaches human rights, comparative human rights, minority protection, constitutional law, introduction to public law and law pertaining to immigration (including refugee law). Her main publications pertain to the areas of human rights and minority protection. Themes she has been focusing on include the principle of equal treatment and the prohibition of (racial) discrimination, the freedom of religion and the accommodation of religious diversity, social rights and socio-economic participation. In 2008 she established the Minority Research Network. She is also editor of the *Netherlands International Law Review*, the *Global Review of Ethnopolitics* and the *International Journal on Group and Minority Rights*.

Titia Loenen is professor of legal theory at Utrecht University, the Netherlands. She studied history and law at Leiden University. She obtained a PhD at the same university with the topic "Difference in Equality." After having taught at the universities of Leiden and Utrecht, she was appointed as the second Professor of Gender and Law. Her research interest lies within the field of equality and law, human rights, gender and multicultural issues. She has published extensively on non-discrimination law and sex equality. She is also a member of the board of the Netherlands Institute of Human Rights and a member of the editorial board of the *Law, Democracy and Development Journal*.

Saïla Ouald Chaib is a PhD candidate at the Human Rights Centre of Ghent University, Belgium. In 2008 she obtained an LLM from Ghent University. She works on the project "Strengthening the European Court of Human Rights: More accountability through better legal reasoning." Her research consists of integrating a minority perspective in the case law of the European Court of Human Rights. She mainly focuses on religious and ethnic minorities and has a particular interest in cases concerning Muslims.

Julie Ringelheim is a researcher at the Belgian National Fund for Scientific Research (FNRS) and at the Center for Philosophy of Law of the Université Catholique de Louvain (UCL), Belgium. She also teaches international human rights law at UCL. She holds a PhD from the European University Institute in Florence, and an LLM from Cambridge University (Trinity Hall college). Her main publications are on human rights law, non-discrimination, minority protection, law and cultural diversity, and ethnic monitoring.

Yves Stox is a manager in employment services at Ernst & Young in Brussels, Belgium, and a voluntary researcher at the Free University of Brussels. He holds a law degree and a Master in Canon Law from the Catholic University of Leuven and a Master in Social Law from the Free University of Brussels. He is a member of the editorial board of the journal *Law, Religion and Society* (published by Larcier), and is the author of a book on discrimination and identity under Belgian and European labor law (*Discriminatie en identiteit—Identiteitsgebonden werkgevers in het Belgisch en Europees arbeidsrecht* (Larcier 2010)).

Hans-Martien ten Napel is a lecturer of constitutional law at Leiden University, the Netherlands, where he is also a research fellow at the Leiden Law School. From 1985 to 2000 he taught at the Department of Political Science. During most of 1992, he was a Post-Doctoral Fellow at the Minda de Gunzburg Center for European Studies at Harvard University. Since 2008 he has also been a senior researcher at the School of Human Rights Research. He has written extensively about Dutch political and parliamentary history and constitutional law. His current fields of expertise include Dutch parliamentary democracy, political rights, freedom of religion, the Dutch Constitution, and Church and State.

Efrat Tzadik is a PhD candidate at the Department of Anthropology of the Catholic University of Leuven, Belgium. She holds an MA in Anthropology from Bar Ilan University, Israel, where she was a research and teaching assistant, and an advanced MA in Anthropology from the Catholic University of Leuven. Her research focuses on the situation of Jewish women living in Belgium, with the main question centering on the identities of women within the context of social change.

Lucy Vickers is a professor of law at Oxford Brookes University, UK. Her main research area is the protection of human rights within the workplace and aspects of equality law. She has worked on issues relating to harassment at work, as well as religious discrimination and age discrimination. She is the author of *Freedom of Speech and Employment* (OUP 2002) and *Religious Freedom, Religious Discrimination and the Workplace* (Hart Publishing 2008). She is also the author of a report for the European Commission on *Religion and Belief Discrimination in Employment – The EU Law* (2007).

Jogchum Vrielink is a post-doctoral researcher at the Catholic University of Leuven, Belgium. Until 1 January 2012, he was the manager of the RELIGARE project, funded by the European Commission's Seventh Framework Programme. Since that date he works at the Research Centre on Equality Policies at the Catholic University of Leuven, coordinating research on anti-discrimination law. He holds a PhD in law from the Catholic University of Leuven (2010) and also studied anthropology and public administration in Belgium and in the Netherlands. His research areas include discrimination law, hate speech, freedom of speech, religion and religious freedom. He has published widely on these topics.

Mine Yıldırım is a PhD candidate at the Institute for Human Rights at Åbo Akademi, Finland, and a member of the Finnish Graduate School for Human Rights Research. She holds a BA in International Relations from Marmara University, Istanbul, Turkey, and an MA degree in Human Rights and Civil Liberties from Leicester University, UK. Her research concentrates on the collective dimension of religious freedom or belief, conscientious objections and international law, in particular as pertaining to Turkey.

Acknowledgments

A book such as this is by essence built on collaboration and is the result of joint efforts. As editors, we wish to warmly thank all those who contributed to its realization.

The starting point for this volume was an international symposium titled "Religious Diversity and the European Workplace," which was hosted at the Law Faculty of the Catholic University of Leuven on 13 January 2011. The chapters in this book are reworked and edited versions of selected papers presented there. The symposium itself was one of the various events organized within the frame of RELIGARE, an interdisciplinary European research project (2010–2013) funded by the European Commission under its Seventh Framework Programme. We are grateful to the Commission and, in particular, our Program Officer Louisa Anastopoulou for the generous support provided.

We are also indebted to all our contributors, with whom we had the pleasure of working and exchanging ideas over the course of 2011. Without their enthusiasm for and commitment to this joint endeavor, the volume simply could not have come to life. At various points, important developments and (un)expected judgments called for rewriting parts of chapters or refocusing debates, and we acknowledge that many contributors went above and beyond the call of duty to make sure this would not unduly delay publishing.

Thanks are also due to members of the RELIGARE project and the Institute for Migration Law and Legal Anthropology at the Catholic University of Leuven, many of whom participated in the January symposium. We are particularly grateful to Veit Bader and Prakash Shah, whose comments on individual chapters generated stimulating thoughts and important improvements.

Throughout the editing and publishing process, we had the good fortune to enjoy the support of Alison Kirk, Sarah Horsley, Elaine Couper and their colleagues at Ashgate Publishing, who were always available to answer our various queries along the way. Two anonymous reviewers offered useful comments and much-appreciated encouragements.

We also thank Karine Draeck for the secretarial support provided and Emily Waibel for assistance with the language review.

Last, but certainly not least, we are indebted to our families and friends, who gave encouragement and showed active interest in the progress of the book and thus, in their way, were instrumental in seeing this project to completion.

Katayoun Alidadi, Marie-Claire Foblets and Jogchum Vrielink
Leuven

List of Abbreviations

ACLU	American Civil Liberties Union
ADA	Americans with Disabilities Act (US)
CCPARDC	Consultation Commission on Accommodation Practices Related to Cultural Differences (Québec, Canada)
CEOOR	Centre for Equal Opportunities and Opposition to Racism (Belgium)
EAT	Employment Appeal Tribunal (UK)
EC Treaty	Treaty establishing the European Community
ECHR	European Convention on Human Rights
ECJ	European Court of Justice of the European Communities
EComHR	European Commission of Human Rights
ECtHR	European Court of Human Rights
EED	Employment Equality Directive
EEOC	Equal Employment Opportunity Commission (US)
ETC	Equal Treatment Commission (the Netherlands)
EU	European Union
HALDE	Haute Autorité de Lutte contre les Discriminations et pour l'Egalité (France)
ICCPR	International Covenant on Civil and Political Rights
NGO	Non-Governmental Organization
NSC	National Security Council (Turkey)
RED	Race Equality Directive
RFRA	Religious Freedom Restoration Act (US)
TCC	Turkish Constitutional Court
WRFA	Workplace Religious Freedom Act (US)

Introduction

Katayoun Alidadi, Marie-Claire Foblets and Jogchum Vrielink

In today's Europe, religion is increasingly discussed in a problematic tone and context. Indeed, "[t]he growing presence of other faith communities in general, and of the Muslim population in particular, is challenging some deeply held European assumptions."[1] In recent years, the issue of *religious* diversity in the various domains of social life has gained prominence amongst politicians, in academic circles and with the public at large in Europe. School administrators in the Netherlands, for example, are caught between requests from a growing Muslim student body for practical accommodations and eye-raising moves and pressures from right-wing politicians.[2] Debates on the wearing of *burqas* and other full-face covering veils in the public sphere are raging in parliamentary assemblies across Europe, and have already resulted in a number of local and country-wide "*burqa* bans."[3] These developments, signs of the contemporary European *zeitgeist*, cannot be overlooked when considering the topic of religious identity and diversity as it relates to the workplace, a crucial test case for policies of substantive or genuine equality in Europe.

As a potentially powerful element of personal identity, religion has already made its way into the amalgam of contemporary European workplaces, and with employees often belonging to minority religions or denominations, issues of accommodation of religious beliefs and practices have been raised before domestic courts and the European Court of Human Rights. Whether it be Muslim workers requesting time off to observe the Islamic Sugar Feast, pious Catholics seeking to wear visible crucifixes with their uniforms, or job seekers requesting state unemployment benefits after losing or leaving positions that contradict with their religious duties, issues of religious diversity and accommodation are receiving ample attention in the public arena. These examples—and the debates

1 G. Davie, "Is Europe an exceptional case?" *The Hedgehog Review*, Spring & Summer 2006, 32.

2 See, e.g.: X., "Vragen PVV aan minister over islamitische wasruimte op Hogeschool" [Questions of PVV (i.e. Partij voor de Vrijheid, Geert Wilders) to minister regarding Islamic washing cot at Institute for Higher Education], *De Telegraaf* 4 February 2011, available at www.telegraaf.nl.

3 M. Evans, "From Cartoons to Crucifixes: Current Controversies Concerning the Freedom of Religion and the Freedom of Expression before the European Court of Human Rights," 26 *J.L. & Religion* 345 (2011), 364–65. At the time of writing, *burqa* bans have entered into effect in France and Belgium, and similar proposals are being considered in the Dutch and Italian Parliaments, amongst others.

they spark—illustrate that the role and position of religion and religious identity in both the non-religious and the religious workplace is often controversial, contentious and constantly evolving. With one of its objectives being an attempt to better grasp what is currently going on in Europe, this edited collection brings together chapters[4] by legal scholars and social scientists on the many challenges created by (increasing) religious diversity in the European workplace.[5]

Together, the chapters provide a wealth of information on the legal responses across Europe to the situation of employees as well as employers who, to various degrees, face conflicts between professional and religious obligations. Divergent judicial decisions have been reached across Europe, with case law challenging the public perception of religion and religious conflicts in the context of labor relations. Because religious claims potentially conflict with other rights and interests in the workplace, a delicate balance must be struck between a multitude of interests, factors, perspectives and values. The case law of the European Court of Human Rights, the European Court of Justice, domestic experiences and comparative analyses can indicate trends, pinpoint "hard cases," and reveal established and innovative approaches alike. The chapters in this book aim to contribute to the debate concerning the proper scope of religious liberty and protection against religious discrimination in the workplace by addressing such divergent questions as:

- How has the stance of the European Court of Human Rights on religious freedom in the workplace evolved?
- How should we assess the hands-off approach by the European Court in this area, exemplified by the broad margin of appreciation for states?
- What about the right of employees not to be confronted with religious manifestation by co-workers, employers or the state in the workplace?
- How do various European states compare when it comes to the right of public school teachers to wear their religious dress?
- Should the high rates of unemployment amongst religious minorities be taken into account when debating the proper level of *de facto* or *de jure* accommodation in the workplace and, if so, how?
- What is the effect of a perceived proliferation and diversification of (Christian and non-Christian) faith-based companies across the European Union (EU)? Is their "privileged" exemption from aspects of discrimination law justified?

4 The papers were delivered at an international symposium on "Religious Diversity and the European Workplace," Leuven, Belgium on 13 January 2011. This symposium was organized under the umbrella of the EU-funded FP7 RELIGARE project (Religious Diversity and Secular Models in Europe—Innovative Approaches to Law and Policy), and hosted at the Law Faculty of the Catholic University of Leuven.

5 While the emphasis in this volume is mainly on Western Europe, specifically Belgium, France, and the Netherlands, it also includes a chapter on Turkey and—for comparative purposes—two chapters on the American experience.

- To what extent does the American experience, with more pro-active and affirmative approaches to diversity in the multi-religious workplace, offer perspectives for the European work landscape?

Within the broad field of labor relations and (religious) diversity, this volume brings together a number of European perspectives, comparative accounts and national case studies.[6] The volume approaches the issue of religious identity and diversity in the workplace from various perspectives, and it is our hope that it will be relevant for legal practitioners, researchers, lecturers and students interested in or working on human rights law, discrimination law, labor law and, generally, the intersection of law and religion. It should also spark the interest of national and EU-level policy-makers who venture into this thorny area of law and policy.

To a large extent, the chapter by Lucy Vickers can be read as an alternative introduction to the theme of this volume. Addressing an important factor that makes debates in this field so intricate, namely the various legal backgrounds of lawyers working in this field, Vickers identifies a range of perspectives from which the issues can be viewed, such as an equality perspective, a human rights perspective and the perspective of Church–State relations in this intersecting area of law. Each of these perspectives (or at least the dominant strands inside these, as an internal diversity cannot be denied)[7] comes with its particular ground rules, presuppositions and internal dynamic. Vickers illustrates how these different perspectives can lead to differing legal approaches to the central issues relating to religious diversity at work.

European components of the religion and workplace debate

The first part of this volume contains a number of chapters dealing with the case law of the European Court of Human Rights (ECtHR) on religious freedom in general, and as it applies to the workplace setting in particular, as well as on the current and prospective role of European Union law and the European Court of Justice (ECJ), specifically with regard to religious discrimination in employment.

The chapter by Saïla Ouald Chaib, ambitiously seeking to improve the legal reasoning of the European Court of Human Rights, provides a wide analysis and critique of the ECtHR's case law under Article 9 of the European Convention on Human Rights (ECHR) as applied to the rights of employees wishing to express their religious beliefs and practices in the workplace. She first explores the approach taken by the ECtHR in a number of cases where employees sought to reconcile their religious obligations with work schedules. The "freedom to resign"

6 A number of chapters offer both European and domestic perspectives, but have been placed in the respective parts of the volume based on their *predominant* focus.

7 Moreover, there is an important degree of overlap or concurrence, in practice, between each of the (ideal typical) perspectives.

argument, which under the jurisprudence figures prominently as the "ultimate guarantee of religious freedom," leads to these claims being considered—in the relevant terminology—manifestly ill-founded and thus inadmissible. A second set of analysed cases revolve around the wearing of religious attire, such as the headscarf, in the workplace. Here, the ECtHR has found interference with Article 9 of the Convention, but in the subsequent proportionality assessment gives limited weight to the employee's right to manifest religious identity. Ouald Chaib contrasts this to more generous approaches taken by the ECtHR in recent cases on family rights and the rights of prisoners, arguing that good practices derived from its own case law should help the Court move towards a more accommodating stance.

Kristin Henrard critically assesses the "margin of appreciation" doctrine of the ECtHR, and the ensuing broad state discretion in Church–State matters allowed under the ECHR, in the light of their compatibility with the existence of an international supervisory structure and general principles of legitimate limitations to human rights. Particular Church–State relations have an impact on the workplace as they can determine issues such as the choice of official holidays and the willingness towards accepting *de facto* reasonable accommodations. Henrard questions the hands-off approach taken by the ECtHR as being insufficiently in line with religion as a suspect class of differentiation, since this should trigger heightened scrutiny and a restricted margin of appreciation.

The next chapter, by Hans-Martien ten Napel, looks at the burning hot question, ignited by the *Lautsi v. Italy* case, of the government's ability to display religious symbols in a public (work)place, particularly crosses in public school classrooms. This case involves the negative aspect of religious freedom, namely the right *not* to believe or have a religion. Ten Napel offers an in-depth analysis and assessment of the ECtHR's opposite *Lautsi* rulings—on 3 November 2009 the Chamber held that crucifixes could not be displayed in Italian public schools, while on 18 March 2011 the Grand Chamber came to the opposite conclusion—in the light of the argument that the debate on the limits of the government's ability to display religious symbols in the public sphere is closely related to the issue of manifestations by citizens of religious symbols in public institutions.

Religious diversity issues can be addressed through freedom of religion and human rights as well as through an anti-discrimination perspective. In 2000, European Union law entered as a new player in the field of religion and the workplace with the Employment Equality Directive (2000/78/EC) prohibiting direct and indirect discrimination, the instruction to discriminate, harassment and victimization inter alia on the basis of religion or belief. However, in the 11 years since, the ECJ has not yet been offered the chance to render judgments to mediate between the widely divergent approaches in European countries to the accommodation of religious practices in the workplace related to religious discrimination. In her chapter, Titia Loenen notes that it is only a matter of time before the ECJ is called upon to decide on the sensitive issue of accommodation of religious practices in the workplace, such as the wish to wear a headscarf or a face-covering veil, or the refusal to shake hands with colleagues or clients of the opposite sex, and thus decide where EU law stands in this respect. Loenen continues by offering a fascinating account of dilemmas this diversity may create for the ECJ if, and when, it is called upon to decide how the various equality directives have to be interpreted and applied to such issues. She argues that the legal framing of the issues—e.g. as discrimination on grounds of religion, race/ethnic origin and/or gender—will, to a large extent, determine the ECJ's decision.

Another intersection, this time of discrimination and speech, is examined in the chapter by Jogchum Vrielink. In charting the intersections of speech and direct discrimination in the context of recruitment and hiring procedures in particular, Vrielink argues that even though discrimination is first and foremost thought of as a particular form of conduct, it is not exceptional for speech to either itself constitute, or provide evidence of the existence of, (direct) religious or racial discrimination. He identifies a number of categories of such speech, carefully attempting to delineate these from types of speech that should receive free speech protection.

Turning to an issue usually addressed from a Church–State perspective, Yves Stox takes on the topic of the complicated legal status of faith-based organizations, which he refers to as "expressive employers." While many employers may seek to realize a specific identity such as plurality or neutrality, the EU Employment Equality Directive only provides an exemption for employers whose ethos is based on religion or belief. Behind this provision lies a difficult political decision-making process that has led to the anything but straightforward and clear formulation of this exemption in the Directive. He illustrates how the formulations of this exemption under the Belgian Anti-discrimination Acts of 2003 and 2007 were also the result of political compromise that left the courts without clear guidelines, something which has been complicated even further by the case law of the Belgian Constitutional Court.

Identity, neutrality, secularism: Case studies and comparative perspectives

The focus in the second part of this volume is on particular case studies and comparative analyses. As far as the case studies are concerned, there is a general emphasis on working through legal sources and events, paying close attention to what actually happens in the application of the law while recognizing the need to locate particular developments in their broader context(s); for example, existing bans on headscarves for public servants in Turkey and the underlying concept of secularism.

Mine Yıldırım offers an internal perspective of the Turkish situation regarding religious dress in the public and private workplace. It is known that headscarves and other types of religious attire are prohibited for all Turkish public servants; however, the situation in the private workplace is far less clear. Yıldırım starts by offering the reader some background on the Turkish understanding of the constitutionally enshrined principle of secularism and its interpretation by the Turkish Constitutional Court. She argues that the application of this principle and its ensuing elaboration by the Turkish judiciary reflect a hierarchy between norms protecting secularism and norms protecting the freedom to manifest one's religion or belief, rather than a balanced and harmonized interpretation which she favors.

Turning to France, where the principle of *laïcité* forms the backbone of many debates on religion and secularism in the public space, Rim-Sarah Alouane evaluates the approach taken in France to religious symbols and practices in the workplace. The idea that religion is a private matter that has to be confined to the private sphere conflicts with the (new) French social reality where Muslims form an important and visible minority that assert their religious rights and interests. Through an examination of the case law and legal scholarship related to religion in the workplace, Alouane compares the situation in the public and private workplace. Interestingly, and in contrast to Yıldırım's analysis with regard to the Turkish judiciary, Alouane argues that French judges are becoming the voice of the religious pluralism that characterizes France on the ground.

An anthropological perspective is introduced into the debate by Efrat Tzadik who, on the basis of fieldwork and in-depth interviews with Jewish women in Brussels, offers us a privileged look into a largely inaccessible sphere. Through the personal accounts of Jewish and Israeli women, she highlights the interplay between Jewish identity and the workplace, with an emphasis on aspects of gender. In particular, she highlights a number of obstacles that Jewish women, and in particular orthodox Jewish women, experience in the Belgian workplace. For a number of women these barriers (or their prospects) have proven to be complete blockages, deterring or preventing them from participation in outside work while rendering the mother role even more appealing. In contrast, for other Jewish women these barriers have been triggers to finding "coping mechanisms" that allow them to function in workplaces even if they nonetheless often feel they are regarded as "the other."

While understanding local particularities and histories is crucial, a great deal is to be learned from comparisons of religious accommodation and management of diversity both inside Europe as well as beyond. Muslim women's dress continues to receive a large amount of public attention across Europe in various settings such as schools, public spaces and workplaces. Katayoun Alidadi's chapter addresses this topic, which lies at the intersection of gender, ethnicity and religion. Since religious dress is sometimes regarded as "unconventional" or "unprofessional," its presence in the workplace can challenge the policies of employers and companies that seek the services of "neutral-looking" staff. After discussing recent case law from the ECtHR and the situation under the EU Employment Equality Directive, the focus is on domestic case law from Belgium and the Netherlands. Noting marked differences between these two neighboring countries when it comes to the accommodation of Muslim dress in the workplace, the chapter draws attention to the fact that non-accommodation in the workplace entails consequences, in particular through the unemployment benefits system. Juxtaposing and comparing the approaches taken by domestic courts in workplace conflicts and in unemployment benefits proceedings has the potential to illuminate which signals and incentives are being sent out about what the acceptable and desirable position of Muslim women in society is. One danger that is not unimaginable is that the case law combined sends out unintended messages making Muslim women, and others with "unconventional dress" out of place or "redundant" when it comes to mainstream employment.

In many ways the American experience offers a strong contrast to Europe, and two chapters examine that experience in the light of the challenges faced in the European workplace. As such, the contributions by Gabrielle Caceres and Amandine Barb turn to perspectives from across the Atlantic and introduce a number of possible future routes for Europe, while reminding us that the current debate in Europe, which largely *problematizes* religion in the context of modernity and the mainstream workplace, should not be taken for granted. In particular, Caceres asks whether the concept of "reasonable accommodation" (the duty for private and public US employers under Title VII of the federal Civil Rights Act of 1964 to accommodate the religious observances and practices of their employees unless it results in undue hardship) could be "transposed" in Europe, particularly in the French secular context. She argues that considering the diverse constituencies in the US, it is understandable that the issue of religious diversity was more quickly tackled there. By contrast, the French model, with its secularist tradition of republican integration, as also addressed by Alouane, seems evidently more resistant to denominational pluralism. While Caceres illustrates that the wearing of signs or clothes expressing a religious affiliation or the ability to request time off for religious observance, in public services or private firms, are particularly sensitive in France, she notes "an embryonic right" to religious accommodations in the workplace, thanks to efforts by the former French equality body HALDE (*Haute Autorité de lutte contre les discriminations et pour l'égalité*, replaced in May 2011 by the *Défenseur de droits*) and French courts. However, she argues that much more needs to happen in order for "reasonable accommodations" to be accepted in the French employment context.

In contrast to the situation in France, a number of structural and societal preconditions and developments paved the way early on in the US for more *proactive and engaging* methods of handling religious diversity in the workplace. Barb analyses the emergence of the so-called "faith at work" movement since the 1990s in the US, under which managers have adopted such approaches. In the context of a steady rise in religious discrimination complaints, the main objective of this movement is to go beyond mere "reasonable accommodations" (as is addressed by Caceres) and to actively reassert the place and value of faith in American companies through the positive engagement with employees' diverse religious identities. The creation of Bible-study and other (inter)faith groups, the official acknowledgment of various holy days, the hiring of "corporate chaplains," a greater freedom of religious speech and a general emphasis on "spiritual well-being" are all signs of a move from more *reactive* attention to their employees' beliefs, with anti-discriminatory or accommodationist policies, to a more *affirmative* recognition of religious diversity. The debate again has to come down to the role of *context*. The high religiosity in the US contrasted with the continuing secularization amongst Europe's majority population forms one factor explaining why the "faith at work" movement is not as appealing and will most likely remain a marginal phenomenon in Europe, Barb argues. While a spontaneous transplantation of this new management model is unlikely, European managers can learn a number of things from this efficiency-driven and self-interested approach.

In the final chapter, Julie Ringelheim questions to what extent European law should play a role in (re)designing ways to approach or manage religious and other diversity as it is found in the workplace. While this closing chapter looks at a number of common themes and offers important future-oriented reflections on diversity, religion and labor relations, we want to conclude this introduction by addressing a few overarching concerns of our own.

Turning the tide?

Norms, practices, and sensitivities in Europe are not unwavering by any standard. While to a large extent the workplace produces and enforces rules of conduct of its own, there is room for the law to play a compass function towards creating a more tolerant society through impulses directed in the workplace. Within the EU, this process has already commenced with the adoption of the Employment Equality Directive in combating discrimination on grounds of religion or belief. However, both religious or belief-based discrimination as well as the freedom of thought, conscience and religion include open and necessarily vague notions that have arguably not entirely slipped into the European awareness just yet. So which factors are to be taken into account to effect social change, not only in case law but also on the "shop floor of social life"?[8] Since it is this setting that affects workers in their everyday work life, our concern should be for the use and impact of rules in that context. Turning the tide of societal pressures and misconceptions is the biggest challenge for the law.[9]

The idea that religion is first and foremost an issue of personal conscience explains part of the viewpoint that members of religious minorities are faced with in today's Europe. The religion–secular divide, which, to a large extent corresponds to the public–private divide, perseveres across Europe. Europe seems an exceptional place in this regard, as it is one of the few places where secularization is actually

8 See J. Griffiths, "The Social Working of Anti-Discrimination Law," in *Non Discrimination Law: Comparative Perspectives* (T. Loenen and P. R. Rodriguez, eds, Kluwer 1999), 314.

9 This is all the more challenging in this context as it appears that the position of the labor unions is divided on this issue. The typically individualized nature of religious accommodations often conflicts with the traditionally collective aspect of labor law. The laws of collective bargaining can appear of little use to the individual religious practitioner working in a factory or office subject to dominant norms and standards.

on the rise, at least amongst its majority population.[10] In many other parts of the world, religion does not have the problem status it has in twentieth-century Europe. The fact that religious practices are increasingly being brought to the attention of the judiciary, in the apparent absence of counterbalancing services to society, can confirm and strengthen this perspective. With the background being that "the Christian tradition has had an irreversible effect on the shaping of time and space in this part of the world,"[11] increasing diversity of religions and other convictions is transforming Europe into a new type of entity.[12] While several chapters in this volume provide perspectives on how to start turning the tide by identifying ways forward in responding to this challenge, a word of warning is appropriate: the approaches and perspectives offered throughout these chapters are mostly not miracle solutions, ready to be poured into legal or policy form. And even if some are ready to use, it is likely too optimistic to take for granted the capacities of the law to effect real social change in the short term, especially in the context of the workplace, where straying from social norms is often feared to lead to diminished competitiveness and profits.

A recent controversy that took place in Belgium offers a striking illustration of the way in which societal norms and practices tend to be tenacious, and even self-perpetuating. It concerned a case in which the employment contract of a female Muslim employee was not renewed by a large Dutch general store chain in the Belgian town of Genk, after the woman refused to take off the headscarf that she had started to wear on the job.[13] The striking thing about this case was that the same chain store is known in the Netherlands for its inclusive policy regarding the headscarf, e.g. even providing a headscarf as part of the company uniform to those who wish to wear it. In Belgium, however, it opted for prohibition. Following a media storm in which human rights NGOs and the Belgian equality body expressed their outrage over this case, the store responded with a statement that

---

10 G. Davie, "Is Europe an exceptional case?" *The Hedgehog Review*, Spring & Summer 2006, 23–34.

11 Ibid., 24.

12 The Framework which made the symposium and this present volume possible, the EU Seventh Framework Programme, also funds RELIGARE, "Religious Diversity and Secular Models in Europe: Innovative Approaches to Law and Policy" (2010–2013) which addresses the challenges of religious pluralism in contemporary Europe in the areas of the workplace, family law, the public space and financing of churches, and explains the forward-looking way of addressing the policy implications of the research. However, while the scholars were engaged in this exercise, the research itself was conducted largely without this concern in mind. For more information on RELIGARE, see www.religareproject.eu.

13 X., "Hema 'schikt zich naar gewoonten van het land'" [Hema is 'conforming itself to the customs of the country'], *De Standaard* 8 March 2011, available at www.standaard.be. In March 2012, the Belgian Centre for Equal Opportunities and Opposition to Racism announced that negotiation and mediation attempts had failed and it was pursuing the case in court, suing HEMA for discrimination on the basis of religion, see Y. Delepeleire, "Hema voor rechter na ontslag voor hoofddoek" [HEMA before the court after dismissal because of headscarf], *De Standaard* 6 March 2012.

it had only opted for the prohibition in response to a series of "negative customer comments," and that—more generally—it was "merely conforming to the customs of the country." Indeed, it is a little-noticed fact that one hardly ever encounters employees wearing headscarves in Belgian stores, especially in comparison with some surrounding countries. As it seems unlikely that this situation would be due to voluntary choices made by Muslim women, the main difference between most stores operating on the Belgian market and the Dutch one in Genk was that the latter was naive enough to make explicit that which most others do as well, albeit in a more covert or concealed fashion.

Of course, the fact that the religious freedom of employees is not a priority for employers is not a problem as such, as employers certainly have other priorities starting with staying in business. The issue becomes critical, however, if in a society (certain) religious practices become automatically equated with trouble and elicit resentment, and when—as a consequence—this negative perspective is (unquestioningly) copied into the norms and practices that govern the workplace. In such situations, most employers will seek to repress or avoid (conspicuous) expressions of religion at any cost, thereby "merely" following the trail of dominant customs with regard to religion's place in society. The challenge that we face is, as such, one for society as a whole, and not only for the national or European legislator. With an issue so complex, the means to turn the tide cannot be one-sided, let alone be limited to top-down (legal) approaches. Appropriate responses should benefit from a thorough understanding of the issues, contexts and interests at stake. This volume aims to contribute just that. What emerges from it—almost unanimously—is a call for a common and positive language to develop thoughtful, contextual and innovative ways to deal with the tensions that can arise with respect to religion at work.

Leuven

PART I
European Components of the Religion and Workplace Debate

Chapter 1
Religious Interests in the European Workplace: Different Perspectives

Lucy Vickers

Introduction

The relationship between religion and the workplace raises many complex and contested issues. Not only is the very definition of religion and belief contested, but a range of other tensions also exist, for example between the religious and the secular, and between the role of religion in the public and private sphere. Practical questions which arise at work include the extent to which religious interests such as religious dress should be accommodated in secular workplaces, and the extent to which organizations with a religious ethos should be allowed to require religious adherence from those they employ. The purpose of this chapter is not to provide single answers to these questions or resolution of these conflicts; rather, it is to explore a range of perspectives from which these debates can be viewed. In doing so, further insight into the difficulties involved in determining the scope of the relationship between religion and work should be provided.

The different perspectives from which the issue of religious diversity in the workplace can be viewed and which are explored further in this chapter include a Church–State based perspective, a human rights based perspective, an equality based perspective and a labor relations based perspective.[1] The different perspectives are both complementary and contradictory at times. They can be complementary in that each one adds weight to and strengthens the others' arguments. Equally, the different perspectives can cut across each other, and can be in tension or conflict with each other. Clearly, some of the tensions and conflicts

---

1 Of course there are likely to be different approaches within each perspective; for example, a range of meanings for equality exist within the literature (see, for example, S. Fredman, *Discrimination Law* (Oxford University Press 2002); C. Barnard and B. Hepple, "Substantive Equality," 59 *Cambridge Law Journal* 2000, 562) and so to explore an issue from an equality perspective could lead to a range of outcomes, depending on the exact equality perspective one takes. A full discussion of the range of meanings within each perspective is beyond the scope of this chapter, but to reflect the range of meanings which each perspective may encompass, the terms "equality based" or "human rights based" etc. are used in this chapter. It is acknowledged that this process involves using the terms in what may be viewed as their traditional or typical meanings.

are incapable of easy resolution, as they reflect different religious or political standpoints. However, while these issues remain to be debated in the theoretical realm, lawyers and human resources professionals need to deal with the cases which come before them in the workplace on a day to day basis. Thus a practical way forward has to be sought which allows for some sort of equilibrium or balance between these competing views of religion in the workplace.

Before considering some of the different perspectives, and possible ways forward, it is worth examining some of the practical problems that have faced European legal systems in dealing with the interaction of religion and the workplace. This chapter includes a particular focus on the position in the UK, but also contains comparative elements. It starts with some examples from case law of issues which have arisen in courts so far, to provide a practical backdrop to the discussion which follows. It then includes a brief discussion of the debates surrounding the definition of religion and belief, as well as an introduction to the main legal framework governing the relationship between law and religion at work, namely the Employment Equality Directive.[2] The chapter then moves on to examine the different perspectives (Church–State based, human rights based, etc.) and to consider the further light these different perspectives may throw on the interaction of religious interests with the European workplace.

Some examples from the case law

In one of the first religious discrimination employment cases in the UK, a classroom assistant, helping children for whom English was a second language, wanted to wear a face veil (*niqab*) when she was in the classroom with a male teacher.[3] When she refused to remove the veil she was suspended. She claimed that this was direct discrimination (less favorable treatment on grounds of religion), but was unsuccessful in her claim: the Employment Appeal Tribunal (EAT) confirmed that any teacher who covered his or her face at work would be subject to the same treatment. However, the EAT decided that the treatment could potentially amount to indirect discrimination, as the (neutral) requirement to have the face showing put Muslims at a disadvantage compared to others. However, in this case the discrimination was a proportionate way to achieve a legitimate aim, the aim being to enable the children to get the best education, and for this they needed to be able to see the teacher's face and expressions.[4]

2 Council Directive 2000/78/EC of 27 November 2000 Establishing a General Framework for Equal Treatment in Employment and Occupation, *OJ 303 L* 02/12/2000, 16–22.

3 *Azmi* v. *Kirklees Metropolitan Borough Council* [2007] ICR 1154.

4 *Azmi* v. *Kirklees Metropolitan Borough Council* [2007] ICR 1154.

Similarly, requirements to work on Saturdays have been allowed in the UK where necessary for business,[5] as have requirements to carry out civil partnership registrations, despite religious objections by a registrar.[6] A similar decision was reached by the Dutch Equal Treatment Commission (ETC; the Dutch equality body which issues non-binding opinions in discrimination cases) in its finding that civil servants cannot refuse to officiate at civil marriages between same-sex couples based on their religious beliefs.[7] A further Dutch example involves the suspension of a female Muslim teacher for refusing to shake hands on religious grounds. The ETC found this not to be justified and indirectly discriminatory.[8] However, this viewpoint was not followed by the civil courts and higher administrative courts.[9]

It is interesting to note a certain similarity in the issues which have come before the courts in different Member States. Equally similar in different states is the fact that the cases have not all been straightforward for courts to resolve, and have caused a deal of contention. At times states continue to act inconsistently, with differences in approach between ETC opinions and court rulings in the Netherlands, for example; and in the UK, the accommodation of staff who object to carrying out same-sex partnerships continues to be allowed in practice. A further example of the contentious nature of religious rights at work can be seen in the UK where interventions have been made from Christian leaders, asking for special courts to be set up to hear cases involving religion.[10] A full discussion of

---

5 *James* v. *MSC Cruises* 12 April 2006; case no. 2203173/05.

6 *Ladele* v. *Islington Borough Council* [2009] EWCA Civ 1357. It is worth noting however, that in its judgment the Court of Appeal did not criticize councils which had decided to accommodate requests not to perform civil partnerships for religious reasons.

7 Dutch Equal Treatment Commission opinion (hereafter "ETC opinion") 2008/40. All ETC opinions can be consulted at www.cgb.nl. Again, it is worth noting that the situation concerning civil servants with conscientious objections is not clear-cut in the Netherlands. There have, for instance, been previous opinions by the ETC with alternative outcomes. In opinions 2002/25 and 2002/26 the ETC accepted that (some) civil servants could invoke religious objections against carrying out marriages between same-sex couples.

8 ETC opinions 2006-220 and 2006-221.

9 Civil Court Utrecht 30 August 2007, LJN BB2648; Centrale Raad van Beroep 7 May 2009, LJL BI2240; see also the chapter by Titia Loenen in this volume (with regard to the issue of refusal by employees to shake hands with members of the other sex).

10 The suggestion was made by Lord Carey, former Archbishop of Canterbury, in evidence to the court in *McFarlane* v. *Relate Avon Ltd [2010] EWCA Civ B1*. The response from Lord Justice Laws is a robust refusal to countenance a separate court structure for religious cases, with such a move labeled "deeply inimical to the public interest." See further L. Vickers, "Religious Discrimination in the Workplace: An Emerging Hierarchy?" 12 *Ecclesiastical Law Journal* 2010, 280. The comment from Lord Carey may echo the speech by the current Archbishop of Canterbury (found at www.archbishopofcanterbury.org/1575 and discussed by P. Shah, "Transforming to Accommodate? Reflections on the Shari'a Debate in Britain," in *Legal Practice and Cultural Diversity* (R. Grillo et al., eds, Ashgate 2009), 73–92).

these disputes is beyond the scope of this chapter, but they illustrate the ongoing difficulties courts face in dealing with religious diversity in the workplace.

Definitions

Before considering the legal framework and the various perspectives from which the issues can be viewed, there is a preliminary issue which must be mentioned: from the outset, there is uncertainty about what exactly is meant by religion and belief. The Employment Equality Directive uses the term "religion and belief," and this echoes the European Convention on Human Rights (ECHR) which refers to religion and belief as part of "thought, conscience and religion." Adding the term "belief" to religion is helpful as it avoids some of the debate elsewhere in the world, such as in the US, about exactly what is a religion.[11] The broader term "belief" means that a wider range of beliefs can be included, including atheism and agnosticism. Yet this really just shifts the debate from the boundaries of the meaning of religion to a debate about what beliefs are covered. For example, the UK Employment Appeal Tribunal recently decided that a belief in climate change should be classified as a belief for the purposes of the UK Regulations.[12]

In terms of definition it is again worth considering the fact that it is not only religion and belief which is protected, but also a lack of religion or a lack of belief. This can sometimes create irreconcilable demands between those with religious beliefs and those whose beliefs or lack of them means they wish to have a religion-free public sphere.[13] It is sometimes argued that the right to religious freedom includes a right to be free from religion, although the scope of such a right is contested. Clearly improper proselytism can infringe a right to be free from religion, but this probably does not mean that atheists have a right never to be troubled by the sight of a religious symbol.

---

11 An alternative reading of the juxtaposition of religion with belief is that it has the effect of confining the term "belief" to those beliefs that are similar to religion, thus limiting the range of beliefs which are covered. For further discussion on the meaning of "belief" see L. Vickers, *Religious Freedom, Religious Discrimination and the Workplace* (Hart Publishing 2008), Chapter 2.

12 *Nicholson* v. *Grainger PLC* UKEAT/0219/09.

13 A. Lester and P. Uccellari, "Extending the Equality Duty to Religion, Conscience and Belief: Proceed with Caution," *European Human Rights Law Review* 567 (2008) at 570. Note that a belief in a secular public sphere is not limited to those who lack a religious belief. Those with a religious belief may well also support a secular public sphere.

The legal framework

The Employment Equality Directive,[14] with its protection against discrimination on a number of grounds, provides extensive protection for religious interests in the European workplace. Prior to its introduction, protection for religious rights could be found in international labor conventions, the International Covenant on Civil and Political Rights (ICCPR), the European Social Charter and the ECHR, but none of these were directly enforceable in the workplace. The implementation of local laws to comply with the Employment Equality Directive creates more significant protection as the local legislation can be applied by individual employees in Member States.

The Employment Equality Directive protects workers against direct and indirect discrimination on grounds of religion or belief, as well as protecting against harassment and instructions to discriminate.[15] The obvious beneficiaries of this protection are those who might have been denied work or promotion or other benefits at work because the employer objected to their religious beliefs. Such treatment is unlawful as it would amount to direct discrimination, and cannot be justified. Clearly there have to be some exceptions and, as with all equality grounds, there is an exception where being of a particular religion or belief is a genuine occupational requirement. To take an obvious example, refusal to employ a Hindu as a Catholic Chaplain would be justified.

The Employment Equality Directive also protects against indirect discrimination, and it is under this heading that the most common issues which arise at work will be dealt with. For example, requests to wear religious dress to work, requests for time off work for religious observance and the accommodation of refusal of work tasks for religious reasons are all dealt with as (potential) issues of indirect discrimination. This is because requirements not to wear religious dress, to work on Sundays, or to perform particular tasks at work tend to be adopted as "neutral" policies which nonetheless cause particular disadvantage to some religious groups. According to the Employment Equality Directive, such requirements must therefore be imposed for a legitimate aim, and must be proportionate in order to be considered lawful.

There are two main areas of contention that the legal provisions have to deal with: the first is the issue of religious workers in mainstream or "secular" organizations, who wish to have their religious practices accommodated in some way; the other involves the rights of non-religious or "secular" workers in organizations with a religious character ("religious-ethos organizations").[16]

---

14 Council Directive 2000/78/EC of 27 November 2000 Establishing a General Framework for Equal Treatment in Employment and Occupation, *OJ 303 L* 02/12/2000, 16–22 ("Employment Equality Directive").

15 Article 2, Employment Equality Directive.

16 The directive foresees exceptions being created for these organizations; see the chapter by Yves Stox in this volume.

In the first case, questions essentially relate to the extent to which the individual employee is protected by religious discrimination law.[17] Questions which arise include: to what extent can religious individuals expect an organization to accommodate religiously motivated requests? For example, can a religious individual ask for a uniform to be adapted by including long sleeves, or trousers, or by requesting to wear a headscarf? Can an employee ask for time off during work time for prayers? Can an employee expect space as well as time to be made available for prayers? When debating these questions, one has to consider how the religious interests of the individual worker interact with other interests at stake, such as the interests of the employer in running an efficient workplace. Moreover, does the employer have a competing interest in determining the ethos of the organization, so that the employer can remain religiously neutral? Further difficulties can arise if employees refuse to carry out aspects of their jobs for religious reasons, such as refusing to serve alcohol. An additional problem can arise in these cases where two equality grounds are in tension, for example a request to be exempt from providing services to gay clients, where the right of gay and lesbian service users to be given an equal service comes up against a claim from those with religious objections to have those objections respected.[18] Equally, issues relating to the headscarf have been said to raise issues of gender equality as well as religious equality.[19]

With regard to religious-ethos organizations, the issues relate to the extent to which equality law can or should be used to limit the freedom of religious organizations.[20] Questions concern religious organizations and their role as employers, and the extent to which religious employers should be bound by

17 See C. McCrudden, "Multiculturalism, Freedom of Religion, Equality, and the British Constitution: the JSF case considered," 9 (1) *International Journal of Constitutional Law* 200 (2011), 200–229.

18 See *Ladele* v. *Islington Borough Council* [2009] EWCA Civ 1357. See also the County Court case involving refusal of service to gay clients by Christian bed and breakfast owners, judgment available at www.judiciary.gov.uk/Resources/JCO/Documents/Judgments/hall-preddy-bull-judgment.pdf. See also *R (Eunice Johns and Owen Johns)* v. *Derby City Council and EHRC* [2011] EWHC 375 (Admin), a claim involving Christian applicants to foster children.

19 D. McGoldrick, *Human Rights and Religion: The Islamic Headscarf Debate in Europe* (Hart Publishing 2006).

20 See C. McCrudden, "Multiculturalism, Freedom of Religion, Equality, and the British Constitution: the JSF case considered," 9 (1) *International Journal of Constitutional Law* 200 (2011), 200–229, where he argues that in subjecting religious groups themselves to discrimination law, we have moved from promoting multiculturalism (in which religious and other minorities are protected against discrimination) to "post-multiculturalism" in which minority groups are required to adhere to the principles of the liberal state. See also M. Freedland and L. Vickers, "Religious Expression In the Workplace In the United Kingdom," 30 *Comparative Labor Law & Policy Journal* 2009, 597.

equality norms.[21] Clearly, the exception under the Employment Equality Directive allows some religious requirements to be imposed by employers, where there is a genuine and determining occupational requirement for the employee to have a particular religion or belief. So, to take an obvious example, a priest in the Catholic Church can be required to be Catholic. Less clear, however, is the extent to which the Directive's exception applies to broader categories of staff in religious-ethos organizations, those whose roles are not directly religious in nature. Examples of such staff include church cleaners or administrators, teachers in state funded or subsidized faith schools, and doctors in hospitals run by religious foundations.

Furthermore, how should the law respond if a requirement to adhere to a particular religion involves discrimination on other grounds? For example, a Catholic priest must not only be Catholic, but must also be male, so that a rule that an employee be a Catholic priest also involves gender discrimination. Moreover, according to orthodox Christian rules, homosexuality is sinful, so that Catholics in good standing with the Church should not form homosexual relationships. Could a religiously run hospital which requires senior staff to be Catholic also require such staff members not to be in a homosexual relationship?

As has been said earlier, the purpose of the chapter is not to provide legal answers to these questions, but rather to consider the range of perspectives from which the issues they present can be viewed.

Church–State based perspectives

Here one can see a number of different legal and cultural approaches in Europe. The separation of church and state is perhaps most strongly seen in France, which has a well-established principle of *laïcité* in public life,[22] but is also present in many EU Member States' constitutions. In contrast, some areas of Europe have established churches, again most notably England, which also has no written constitution.

Of course these formal differences may mask a greater unity in approach across Europe: after all, in the UK, constitutional conventions apply, and there is a well-established culture and tradition of religious neutrality in the courts, with an acceptance that in applying common law, courts must respect concepts such as religious freedom. This separation of church and state in Europe is underpinned by the ECHR, which protects freedom of religion under Article 9, and which binds the EU Member States, Council of Europe states, and the EU institutions.

A Church–State based perspective on religious equality leads to a clear understanding across Europe that the state and religion are largely separate zones of influence. The approach is taken that the state should not interfere with religious institutions and vice versa. But this also brings with it an assumption that religion is something apart from public life, and so it may also bring an equal assumption

21 See the chapter by Yves Stox in this volume.

22 See Loi du 9 décembre 1905 concernant la séparation des Églises et de l'État.

that the state should not be expected to protect religious interests of citizens. This approach of state neutrality may explain why employment protection against religious discrimination has been so long coming in Europe compared to other equality grounds.

With regard to the questions relating to the employment of staff by religious employers, then, this Church–State based approach would tend towards leaving religious-ethos organizations fairly free to organize themselves, and to set their own religiously inspired employment qualifications. The employment equality legislation could be viewed as a state interference with religious freedom in this regard. Thus, viewed from a Church–State based perspective, any discretion allowed by the law should be exercised in favor of allowing freedom to religious organizations to order their own affairs.

Taking a Church–State based perspective in the context of religious personnel in secular employment will lead to little sympathy being given to claims for religion to be accommodated at work, and this will be even more the case with regard to public sector employment. Church–State separation is likely to mean that public sector employment should be free from religious symbols, and free from an obligation to accommodate religious practices. Although this may not apply so strictly to private sector organizations, there may also be a view that religion is a private matter, and so little obligation will be imposed on the employer to accommodate religious requirements.

Human rights based perspective

A second perspective from which to view religious diversity and the workplace is from a human rights based perspective. Here the ECHR reminds us that freedom of religion is a fundamental human right, recognized not only in Europe but across the world.[23] Religious freedom is viewed as one of the foundations of a "democratic society," and as one of the "most vital elements that go to make up the identity of believers and their conception of life," and pluralism is viewed as indissociable from a democratic society.[24]

The reasons for protecting religious freedom are largely related to the role of religion in upholding individual autonomy and identity, although historically there is no doubt that there has also been a peace-keeping element.[25] But whatever the basis, the pedigree is a long one. Viewed as a human rights issue, there are

23 Freedom of religion is protected by the a range of Conventions and Charters including the ICCPR, the Universal Declaration of Human Rights, the African Charter on Human and Peoples' Rights and the American Declaration of the Rights and Duties of Man.

24 *Kokkinakis* v. *Greece* Series A no. 260-A, [1993] 17 EHRR 397 at para 31.

25 See, for example, J. Locke, *A Letter Concerning Toleration* (1698). See also R. McCrea, *Religion and the Public Order of the European Order* (Oxford University Press 2010), chapter 4.

again two dimensions. One is the importance of the individual human right of freedom of religion belief and conscience.[26] This does not necessarily require accommodation in the workplace, and indeed it has been made clear that Article 9 of the ECHR does not guarantee a right to religious freedom at work, but may instead be satisfied by a right to resign.[27] Nonetheless, viewed as a matter of human rights, we can see that the right will *not* be fully enjoyed if an individual is unable to work because of her beliefs.

Moreover, a further consequence of the recognition of a human rights based dimension to religious diversity is the recognition in human rights law of the group dimension of religious rights. Freedom of religion extends to a right to manifest religion *alone or in community with others*. This means that religious groups should be able to enter employment relationships in order better to organize or facilitate religious activity. Thus, restrictions on the freedom of religious groups, for example, to appoint a teacher, or a religious official, may interfere with the religious freedom of the group. Similarly, restrictions on the freedom of religious individuals to work with others as part of manifesting their religious commitment may also infringe their religious freedom. Thus both the accommodation of religious individuals in secular workplaces, and the freedom of religious organizations to discriminate on religious grounds can be shown to have a human rights based dimension.

One theme common to both the human rights based perspective and the Church–State based perspective is that they tend to wish to leave religious groups reasonably free to pursue their own ends, with minimal interference. There is an acceptance, for example, in the case law of the European Court of Human Rights (ECtHR), that has made clear that a "margin of appreciation" applies in this area, and that states' practice with regard to religious rights is an area in which there is legitimate variation.[28] Thus it is accepted that the issue of religion is one where there may be a range of legitimate, but different, views, and so a range of different practices may well be acceptable in human rights terms.

This legitimate variation in states' practice was confirmed most recently in the cases of *Obst* v. *Germany*[29] and *Schüth* v. *Germany*[30] in which churches wished to dismiss staff for failing to comply with religious teaching.[31] In both cases staff had been involved in extra-marital relationships; in *Schüth* the staff member was a church organist and in *Obst* it was the Director of European public relations for the Mormon Church. The cases were brought under Article 8 (privacy and family life)

26 *Kokkinakis* v. *Greece* Series A no. 260-A, [1993] 17 EHRR 397 at para 31.

27 *Stedman* v.*UK* (1997) 23 EHRR CD168. See the chapter by Saïla Ouald Chaib in this volume.

28 For a critical approach to the issue of "margin of appreciation" in this area, see the chapter by Kristin Henrard in this volume.

29 ECtHR 23 September 2010, *Obst* v. *Germany*, App. No. 425/03.

30 ECtHR 23 September 2010, *Schüth* v. *Germany*, App. No. 1620/03.

31 Also discussed in the chapters by Saïla Ouald Chaib and Yves Stox in this volume.

rather than Article 9 (religion and belief) of the ECHR. The ECtHR came down on different sides in the cases, with the claim of the Catholic organist upheld and the claim of the Mormon PR director rejected, but the reasoning was fairly technical and related to the extent to which privacy rights had been considered by the decision-makers in each case. In terms of the general approach, both cases referred to the need to give national courts a degree of discretion in deciding these cases,[32] given that there is no common practice across Member States, and since the issues involved religion and tradition. Thus using a human rights based perspective, the history of individual states is well respected with an acceptance that there can be more than one way to achieve proportionate protection for religious freedoms. This certainly seems a sensible way to approach such a sensitive issue. However, it could lead to inconsistent decision-making across Europe, with different outcomes on similar facts depending on the approach the state has, historically, taken on religious issues. So, outcomes could vary in England and Denmark, with their history of Church establishment, from France, with its history of strong *laïcité*.

Equality based perspectives

Whether such an approach is compatible with an equality based perspective may be open to question, however, and the issue of religious diversity in the European workplace clearly does have such an equality dimension which needs to be taken into account. The equality based perspective becomes clear when religion and the workplace is considered from a legal point of view, as the ground of religion or belief has been included in the Employment Equality Directive, and implemented across the EU into domestic legislation protecting against direct and indirect discrimination, victimization and harassment. However, it is also important to recognize that religion is a common ground of equality in most legal systems which include any form of equality protection. For example, in Canada and the US, equality protection has long included the ground of religion.

There is good reason for the inclusion of religion as an equality ground. There is evidence that religion is linked to disadvantage in the labor market. Research carried out in the UK before the employment protection against religious discrimination came into force showed that employment was one of the areas of life where religious individuals were most likely to experience unfair treatment.[33]

32 See also ECtHR 3 February 2011, *Siebenhaar* v. *Germany*, App. No. 18136/02, involving the dismissal of a member of the Universal Church/Brotherhood of Humanity who was dismissed from her post as a teacher in a kindergarten. The Chamber of the ECtHR found there to be no violation of Article 9 as the German Labor Court had undertaken an appropriate balancing exercise of the relevant interests in reaching their decision that the dismissal was fair.

33 P. Weller et al., *Religious Discrimination in England and Wales* (Home Office Research Study No. 220, 2001).

Examples included refusal to employ people because of their religious beliefs, refusal to accept a religious dress code, as well as some significant religious harassment at work. Moreover, there is also some evidence in the UK suggesting that Muslims earn less than other groups.[34]

Although it might be argued that religion and work should not be mixed, and that equal treatment can be achieved by excluding faith from work, it is clear on closer reflection that this approach is inadequate, especially given the evidence of disadvantage experienced by some religious groups. In the UK study,[35] unfair treatment was identified in the behavior of managers and colleagues as well as in the policies and practices of employers. Examples of discriminatory practices include being required to work on Saturdays or Sundays, being subjected to dress restrictions, suffering reduced promotion prospects and experiencing disrespectful attitudes towards religious customs. One example was of a Muslim woman who believed she was unsuccessful in a job application because she refused to shake hands with the interviewer at the end of the interview. Other examples include a Muslim woman who felt she was judged negatively because she would not drink alcohol at social work occasions; a Sikh woman who was moved from her work in a bakery for wearing a bangle, even though in tests it tested negative for bacteria; and Muslim women treated less favorably for wearing a headscarf.

One equality based approach is to accept some level of legal protection, but to limit it to formally equal treatment. Such an approach may provide formal equality, treating likes alike. For example, a rule that no religious dress can be worn to work is a formally equal rule, treating all religious groups equally, and may seem unobjectionable. However, such an approach ignores the developments in thinking about equality that have been made in relation to gender equality in particular, in which the difficulty of determining what groups are indeed "alike" has been highlighted.[36] A common example of the problem is the difficulty the courts experienced in deciding who was "like" a pregnant woman. It was quickly realized with regard to equality law that setting a neutral rule with which all should comply usually involves setting a "male" norm to which women have to comply. In the context of gender discrimination and pregnancy, an assumption that promotion will follow if you have 20 years' unbroken service by the age of 40, is treating everyone the same, but seriously disadvantages women. In the context of gender equality, then, it has long been established that "formal" equality is not enough.

---

34 See J. Lindley, "Race or religion? The impact of religion on the employment and earnings of Britain's ethnic communities," 28 *Journal of Ethnic and Migration Studies* 2002, 427.

35 P. Weller et al., *Religious Discrimination in England and Wales* (Home Office Research Study No. 220, 2001).

36 See P. Westen, "The Empty Idea of Equality," 95 *Harvard Law Review* 1982, 537; S. Fredman, *Discrimination Law* (Oxford University Press 2002), C. Barnard and B. Hepple, "Substantive Equality," 59 *Cambridge Law Journal* 2000, 562.

Moreover, it is clear that the "neutral" rules of the European workplace do mean setting a Christian "norm." For example, the traditional working year has holidays on Sundays, Christmas and Easter, which enable Christians time off for religious observance without having to make special requests; and Christians can, typically, comply with religious requirements in terms of dress code and daily prayers without any difficulty,[37] because they do not have any particular dress code, and they do not have to pray during the normal working day or week due to the working week revolving around a normal day of rest on a Sunday. A Muslim woman who feels obliged to wear a headscarf and to take time off for prayers in the day may not be able to do so without having to change rules or practices at work. It is clear that formally equal rules do not achieve *substantive* equality on grounds of religion any better than they achieve *substantive* gender equality.

Applying an equality based perspective to the scenarios of religious employees in the secular workplace and secular workers in the religious workplace will likely lead to different results from those found when taking either a Church–State or human rights based perspective. From an equality based perspective, it may seem quite reasonable to expect that substantial accommodations would be made to the secular workplace to enable substantively equal access to work for those from minority faith groups. For example, if evidence suggests that Muslims have difficulty gaining access to the workplace in comparison with Christians (for example because of a ban on headscarves), the equality based perspective might view this as resulting from indirect discrimination (the "neutral" requirement not to cover the head causing particular disadvantage to Muslim women). Allowing headscarves would improve access to work for Muslims and thereby achieve more equal treatment of this group. Equally, if a religious requirement is imposed on workers in a religious-ethos organization which indirectly discriminates on other grounds (for example, a requirement that indirectly discriminates on grounds of sex or sexual orientation), the equality based perspective would demand that the religious group should comply with equality norms, and avoid the indirect sex or sexual orientation discrimination unless it is absolutely necessary for the proper functioning of the job. Thus, given Catholic teaching on the priesthood, it may be proportionate to require priests to be male, but it would be unlikely to be proportionate to require teachers in a religious school to be heterosexual.[38]

Such an approach is compatible with an equality based perspective, guided by a need to address substantive inequality in society, to uphold individual dignity and

37 Although some Christians in the UK have faced restrictions when wanting to wear a cross visibly. See *Eweida* v. *British Airways* [2010] EWCA Civ 80.

38 For the approach of the UK courts on this issue see *R (on the application of Amicus – MSF and others)* v. *Secretary of State for Trade and Industry and others* [2004] IRLR 430 in which it was confirmed that the exception allowing sex and sexual orientation discrimination in the appointment of employment "for the purposes of an organized religion" would be acceptable in the case of clergy, but not in the case of teachers or other staff in religious-ethos organizations.

to redress disadvantage experienced by certain groups. However, this approach can be seen to be in conflict with the human rights and Church–State based perspectives, under which it was suggested that courts might leave employers (both religious and secular) a reasonable amount of freedom or discretion to determine the scope of the protection they would offer.

Difference in approach of the ECJ and the ECtHR

A further level of complexity in dealing with religious beliefs or practices at work arises from the fact that two different legal frameworks govern this area. First is the European Court of Justice (ECJ), which determines cases of religious discrimination under the Employment Equality Directive.[39] Secondly, the ECtHR determines cases involving religious human rights claims.[40] A case involving religious interests at work could be determined under either one of these legal systems, yet their approaches differ.[41] For example, the approach of the ECJ to gender equality is very strict: any requirement must have a legitimate aim, and the means chosen for achieving that objective must correspond to a real need on the part of the undertaking, must be appropriate with a view to achieving the objective in question and must be necessary to that end.[42] Economic cost or customer preference will not usually justify indirect sex discrimination. In contrast, in religion cases heard under the ECHR, the ECtHR is usually fairly respectful of the margin of appreciation, accepting that the practice of states may legitimately vary, according to each state's history and political situation.[43] It is difficult to imagine such an approach being taken if one takes an equality based perspective; after all, historically most of Europe has had well-established practices and traditions in which gender discrimination has flourished, with the historical and cultural place of women being as homemakers and child carers rather than senior executives and board members. Had a "margin of appreciation" approach been used in the context of gender discrimination in EU law, reflecting these historical norms, the extensive protection now available and generally accepted as correct would have been unlikely to have been established.

There is likely to be a difference in approach between these two legal systems for protecting religious interests. This clash may well be further complicated by the fact that under the Lisbon Treaty the EU can accede to the ECHR. Thus it

39 There has not yet been a case by the ECJ addressing religious discrimination under the Equality Employment Directive, but arguably this is only a matter of time.

40 These are mainly under Article 9 but some also involve Article 14, and so involve human rights and equality issues.

41 See the chapter by Titia Loenen in this volume.

42 *Bilka-Kaufhaus* v.*Weber von Hartz* [1986] ECR 1607–1631 [1986] ECR 1607.

43 See the chapter by Kristin Henrard in this volume.

would seem that the Employment Equality Directive will need to be interpreted to comply with the protection available under the ECHR.[44]

That there is a clash between these different perspectives is certainly clear; what is not yet clear is how this clash will be resolved. For example, from a Church–State perspective it seems clear that France expects to be able to continue with its policy of *laïcité*; but it is not clear from an equality based perspective this would be allowed: a rule banning head coverings clearly puts one religious group at a particular disadvantage as compared with others. The fact that it is a neutral rule works as a defense to direct discrimination, but indirect discrimination was created precisely to deal with such an issue. Of course, indirect discrimination can be justified, but any justification from France is likely to need to draw on established state practice and custom, issues which are not usually allowed to justify discrimination, at least not in relation to race or gender discrimination.[45]

If such indirect discrimination is to be justified, on the basis of legitimate variation in state practice, to reflect the different historical and political contexts, the result will be to reinforce a hierarchy as between equality rights,[46] given that such a justification would be unlikely to be accepted for other equality grounds such as sex or race. Such an approach would, effectively, accept that religious discrimination is different from other forms of discrimination. Indeed, it may be that this is the best resolution of this issue; any alternative risks gender and race discrimination principles being compromised because of problems with other discrimination grounds. However, such an approach will be a disappointment to those who argue that there should be no hierarchy as between different discrimination grounds;[47] and it may require further thought to work out why and to what extent such a hierarchy exists.[48]

44 W. Weiss, "Human Rights in the EU: Rethinking the Role of the European Convention on Human Rights after Lisbon," 7 *European Constitutional Law Review* February 2011, 64–95.

45 The ban on the *burqa* introduced in France in April 2011 has yet to be tested legally. Similar issues may well arise in Turkey.

46 M. Bell and L. Waddington, "Reflecting on Inequalities in European Equality Law," 28 *European Law Review* 2003, 349; M. Bell and L. Waddington, "More Equal Than Others: Distinguishing European Equality Directives," 38 *Common Market Law Review* 2001, 587; D. Schiek, "New Framework on Equal Treatment of Persons in EC law?" 8 *European Law Journal* 2002, 290.

47 See, for example, *Chacón Navas* v. *Eurest Colectividades SA* (2006) C-13/05, at para. 40.

48 See M. Bell and L. Waddington, "Reflecting on Inequalities in European Equality Law," 28 *European Law Review* 2003, 349. See also A. McColgan, "Class wars? Religion and (In)equality in the Workplace," 38 *Industrial Law Journal* 2009, 1; A. Lester and P. Uccellari, "Extending the Equality Duty to Religion, Conscience and Belief: Proceed with Caution," *European Human Rights Law Review* (2008), 567, all of whom suggest caution in treating religion equally to other equality grounds.

Thinking about hierarchy as between equality grounds leads on to further fascinating questions: where would religion fit in such a hierarchy? Is religion a chosen characteristic? How does an expectation that religion be kept in the private sphere square with the more recent acceptance that sexual orientation does not have to be kept in the private sphere?[49] Indeed, what these questions further demonstrate is that thinking about equality is itself highly contested, and arguably lacks clear theoretical underpinnings.[50] However, full discussion of these questions lies beyond the scope of this chapter, and will have to be discussed elsewhere.

Many of the questions raised here are, of course, intractable. They reflect an unresolved conflict between completely different approaches to fundamental questions, many of which have raged across Europe for centuries. It is interesting to see the broader difficulties which states have had in dealing with religion played out in the European workplace, perhaps a more peaceable context than earlier eras.

A labor relations perspective?

Nonetheless, real difficulties lie ahead for the courts to resolve, and this leads on to the final perspective from which this issue can be viewed, a labor relations perspective. This perspective reflects the practical reality that while legal theorists, political scientists, philosophers, theologians and sociology of religion scholars all work to create and debate theoretical resolutions of some of the intractable conflicts identified here, lawyers and human resources managers have to decide cases as they arise now. In order to do so, they will need to be pragmatic, and try to find some sort of equilibrium or "practical concordancy"[51] between the differing perspectives and differing interests that are in play in cases of religious discrimination and religious freedom.

It is suggested that the key to establishing this equilibrium between the conflicting approaches and rights is to focus on the notion of proportionality, a term which of course plays a role in all the perspectives noted above. Within the Employment Equality Directive, proportionality is the key issue, as it is the basis on which any justification of indirect discrimination will be judged, as well as being the basis on which any occupational exception to direct discrimination is judged. The notion of proportionality also appears in the case law of the ECtHR: restrictions on freedom to manifest religion are accepted when they are necessary for a legitimate aim, and to be necessary, a restriction must be proportionate.[52]

49 See C. Stychin, "Faith in the Future: Sexuality, Religion and the Public Sphere," 29 *Oxford Journal of Legal Studies* 2009, 729.

50 See C. O'Cinneide, "The Uncertain Foundations of Contemporary Anti-discrimination Law," 11 *International Journal of Discrimination and the Law* 2011, 7.

51 The phrase comes from German constitutional law: *German Classroom Crucifix* case, BVerfGE 93, 1, 1 BvR 1087/91.

52 *Handyside* v. *UK* (1981) 1 EHRR 737.

Making judgments based on proportionality enables the different interests to be weighed against each other: the right to religious freedom; the need to uphold equality on religious grounds and other grounds; to protect a freedom *from* religion; to protect other human rights such as privacy and freedom of speech. The assessment of proportionality can also take into account matters such as the nature and context of the job; the equality interests of service users; the freedom of religion of other members of staff or of the public; the interest in religious neutrality for customers and colleagues and for the employer. Where the balance lies in any proportionality equation may depend on the status of the employer: for example, whether it has a religious ethos, whether it is part of the public or private sector and whether it has a monopoly on providing particular types of employment. It may also depend on the religious and cultural traditions of the state. All these different interests can be taken into account in assessing proportionality, enabling a careful and responsive standard to develop for creating equilibrium between competing and conflicting interests.[53]

Although this may remain the best approach to providing a practical solution to otherwise intractable questions, it is certainly not perfect. For example, one limitation is that it leaves much to be determined by courts, and so from a labor relations point of view there is not much certainty, and outcomes of cases can be difficult to predict. Certainly the approach is very fact dependent, and therefore cannot lead to the development of clear and simple precedent. There remains no clear answer to a simple question such as "do employees in Europe have a right to refuse to work on Saturdays for religious reasons?" The answer to such a question depends on a variety of factors, which may be difficult to predict. It may be that those with legal training will be able to make a good prediction on how proportionality would be determined, but is likely to remain difficult for an employer or employee to determine without legal advice whether it is acceptable to refuse a request to miss work on a particular day, or to refuse to accommodate a request to adapt a work uniform for religious reasons. On the other hand, it would seem that any alternative to create greater certainty would probably lead to reduced protection for religious interests at work, with a corresponding reduction in equality for religious individuals. Although specifically enumerated rights would create certainty, it is unlikely that any legislature would wish to create an absolute right to time off for religious observance or an absolute right to adapt a uniform to comply with religious practice. Thus it is not surprising that religious discrimination rights have been created based on the idea of proportionality.

53 See further: L. Vickers, *Religious Freedom, Religious Discrimination and the Workplace* (Hart Publishing 2008), Chapter 7.

Conclusion

Much of the debate on religious interests at work takes place in the context of the particular perspectives discussed above. Thus the question of whether religious dress should be allowed in a public sector workplace may be answered by some in the negative because the question has been raised in the context of Church–State based debate; the fact that to do so may cause disadvantage to a minority religious group emerges as a problem once an equality perspective is also taken. Equally, those taking an equality based perspective may view with distaste the demands of a religious group to be allowed exemption from the equality norms in order to employ only those who comply with their religious teaching. Taking a human rights perspective allows one to view such demands with more tolerance, as they involve the right to religious freedom of a religious group. At a theoretical level, the debate between the different perspectives, and indeed within the different perspectives, can be heated as well as healthy. The danger can be, however, that the different groups merely "talk past each other" when trying to resolve practical problems which can arise in the workplace.

At a practical level, then, ways need to be found to resolve the various tensions between the interests of employers and employees in the work context. Developing a common language in which to discuss these issues is vital. The suggestion is that the notion of proportionality be used to help to develop that common language. "Proportionality" is one word which the different perspectives do have in common.[54] As mentioned above, proportionality is the key issue in determining the scope of protection under the Employment Equality Directive, as it provides the test of whether indirect discrimination is justified, and whether occupational exceptions are allowed. Equally, the notion of proportionality is central to the case law of the ECtHR, with freedom to manifest religion only limited where for a legitimate aim and proportionate.[55] Although human rights based perspectives and equality based perspectives may legitimately differ, then, they both speak the language of proportionality.

In assessing whether it is proportionate to protect religious interests, such as by allowing an exception to a neutral dress code for religious reasons, the question to be answered is whether the exception sought serves a legitimate aim and whether there is a proportionate relationship between the means used and the legitimate aim. In making that judgment, one can take into account a wide range of factors, and these might include the interests of the employer in having an efficient workforce, the interest in having a religiously neutral workplace, the interest of employer and employee in freedom of religion and freedom of expression, and the equality interest in removing barriers to participation in employment for minority

---

54 The usefulness of the notion of proportionality is, of course, itself contested. See J. Rivers, "Proportionality and Variable Intensity of Review," 65 *Cambridge Law Journal* 2006, 174, and D. Beatty, *The Ultimate Rule of Law* (Oxford University Press 2004).

55 *Handyside* v. *UK* (1981) 1 EHRR 737.

groups. Where the workplace forms part of the public sector, a factor may also be whether or not the wearing of religious apparel offends notions of the separation of Church and State.

Using the common language of proportionality enables those attempting to resolve disputes to ensure that they consider whether the aim can be realized using alternative means which impinge less on other interests. It also means that a wide range of factors are taken into account, including a consideration of the issue from the various different perspectives. Ensuring that a range of perspectives are included in any proportionality review should mean that better conclusions are reached, conclusions which reflect more completely the range of interests which are engaged in the debate over the interaction of religion with the workplace.

Of course, the interests being considered here are by nature incommensurable and so the notion of proportionality will be unable to solve with precision all the difficulties that may be faced by employers. However, the idea of proportionality may help us to navigate a more principled path through the maze of conflicting rights. The aim is to achieve some form of concordance or equilibrium between workers and employers, and the religious and secular sphere, by seeking to respond to the practical issues in a proportionate manner, giving due regard to the range of perspectives which may be brought to the issue.

Section I
Religion, Workplace Accommodations and the Case Law of the European Court of Human Rights

Chapter 2

Religious Accommodation in the Workplace: Improving the Legal Reasoning of the European Court of Human Rights

Saïla Ouald Chaib*

Introduction

Article 9 of the European Convention on Human Rights (ECHR) not only protects the right to hold or not to hold a religious belief, but also the right to manifest religious convictions.[1] In the workplace this manifestation will, for instance, take place when employees wear specific religious attire, such as the Sikh turban or the Islamic headscarf, or when they wish to observe religious days of rest, such as the Sabbath for Jews or Sundays for Christians. In these cases an exemption from a dress code or a readjustment of the work schedule could be requested.

How does the European Court of Human Rights (ECtHR or the Court) apply Article 9 in cases concerning religion in the workplace? Does an employer under this provision have to accommodate the religious needs of an employee on the work floor or does the employee simply have to change jobs when his contractual obligations do not fit with his religious obligation? To be sure, the issue is not that clear cut. The challenge in these kinds of cases is to find the right balance between the interests of the employer and the employee. The aim of this chapter is to examine how the ECtHR deals with this challenge and how it could deal with it in a better way.

* I am thankful to the editors of the book for their comments on a previous draft of this chapter. I am also thankful to my colleagues at the Human Rights Centre for the interesting discussions we had on this topic and I am particularly indebted to Eva Brems, Lourdes Peroni and Pieter Van den Heede for their insightful comments and suggestions. This contribution was made possible thanks to funding from the European Research Council for the project "Strengthening the European Court of Human Rights: More Accountability through Better Legal Reasoning".

1 C. Evans, *Freedom of Religion Under the European Convention on Human Rights* (Oxford University Press 2001) 103–33.

Extensive case law research[2] has shown that the ECtHR has been faced with mainly two kinds of cases concerning religious accommodation in the workplace: (1) cases concerning work schedules and (2) cases concerning the wearing of religious attire in the workplace. In this chapter both kinds of cases will be analyzed.

In the first section, the issue of work hours and religious holidays will be examined. In the second section, a closer look will be taken at the case law concerning religious attire in the workplace. In the third section, an attempt to suggest ways of improving the reasoning of the Court will be undertaken, with references to "good practices" derived from the case law of the ECtHR in other areas. The cases concerning religious accommodation in the workplace will be compared with a selection of cases concerning religion in spheres other than the workplace and cases concerning conflicts in the workplace related to other fundamental rights, such as the freedom of expression and the right to family life. Finally, some concluding remarks will be formulated.

I. Religion and work schedules in the workplace: No interference with the freedom of religion

Out of the—relatively rare—cases where the Court has been confronted with religious accommodation claims in the workplace, one category relates to employees requesting a work schedule adapted to their religious needs. Interestingly, these claims have been presented by members of minority religions as well as by individuals belonging to majority religions. For example, in *Stedman*[3] a Christian employee objected to working on Sundays, and the case of *X* v. *UK*[4] concerned a Muslim teacher asking for a readjustment of his work schedule so that he would be able to attend the Friday prayer in a mosque. Similarly, in *Konttinen*[5] a member of the Seventh Day Adventist church wanted to respect the Sabbath on Friday afternoons, which made it impossible for him to work after sunset on those days. Also, in *Kosteski* v. *the Former Republic of Yugoslavia*,[6] the applicant

2 A note on the methodology used: to examine whether an evolution has taken place since the well-known cases *X*, *Konttinen* and *Stedman*, an extensive case law analysis of Article 9 cases in the period 2000–2010 was undertaken. From selected cases concerning the workplace, only those concerning accommodation claims have been retained. Consequently, cases concerning conflicts due to the religious conviction as such of an employee, such as EComHR 1 July 1997, *Kalaç* v. *Turkey*, App. No. 20704/92, ECtHR 3 February 2011, ECtHR and ECtHR 12 April 2007, *Ivanova* v. *Bulgaria*, App. No. 52435/99, will not be discussed.

3 EComHR 9 April 1997, *Stedman* v. *United Kingdom*, App. No. 29107/95.

4 EComHR 12 March 1981, *X* v. *United Kingdom*, App. No. 8160/78 (also known as *Ahmad* v. *United Kingdom*).

5 EComHR 3 December 1996, *Konttinen* v. *Finland*, App. No. 2494/94.

6 ECtHR 13 April 2006, *Kosteski* v. *The Former Yugoslav Republic of Macedonia*, App. No. 55170/00.

complained about the refusal of his employer to grant him leave of absence to celebrate religious holidays.

In all these cases, the employees were dismissed or sanctioned by the employer, were forced to resign, or to opt for a part-time contract.

1. No interference with the freedom of religion

Except for *Kosteski*, none of the above-mentioned cases made it beyond the admissibility stage and the Strasbourg organs never found a clear interference with the right to freedom of religion. Two elements were important in this regard: the dubious position towards the question of whether or not a manifestation of religion was at stake (a), and the focus on the responsibility of the employee with the *freedom to resign doctrine* as well as the *contractual freedom* (b).

a. (No) manifestation of religious belief

Claims of religious accommodation in the workplace will mostly be dictated by the wish to *manifest* one's religious conviction or belief in the work sphere. Contrary to the cases concerning religious dress in the workplace,[7] the Strasbourg organs do not have a clear stance towards the question whether claims concerning work schedules could be considered as a manifestation of religion. In *X* v. *UK*, the now-defunct European Commission of Human Rights ("Commission") questioned whether the applicant "was required by Islam to disregard his continuing contractual obligations vis-à-vis the ILEA" following his transfer to a school nearby a mosque, and whether his religion requires from him "to attend the mosque during school time."[8]

The way the Commission narrows the question with regard to the manifestation of religion is problematic. The question should not be whether Islam requires *disregarding contractual obligations* or attending a mosque *during school time*, but whether attending collective prayers in a mosque on Friday could be seen as a manifestation of religion and, subsequently, whether this should be protected under Article 9 of the Convention. Moreover, by questioning whether Islam requires adherents to disregard contractual obligations, the Commission also seems to assume that if the applicant attends the Friday prayer, he would breach his contract and is thus in a preliminary stage of excluding the possibility that he can exercise his religion within the framework of his employment contract.

Also, in the case of *Kosteski*, the Court was "not persuaded" that the celebration of religious holidays was a manifestation of the applicant's belief. It considered the fact that

> while it may be that this absence from work was motivated by the applicant's intention of celebrating a Muslim festival it is not persuaded that this was a

7 Cf. *infra*.
8 EComHR 12 March 1981, *X* v. *United Kingdom*, App. No. 8160/78, par. 9.

> manifestation of his beliefs in the sense protected by Article 9 of the Convention or that the penalty imposed on him for breach of contract in absenting himself without permission was an interference with those rights.[9]

Although *Kosteski* differs from the other cases discussed in this section,[10] with this statement the Court appears reluctant to find that a certain claim consists of a manifestation of religion.[11]

The questioning position of the Court as to whether or not some claim relates to a manifestation of religion might be a dangerous exercise which places the Strasbourg judges in the role of theological scholars interpreting religious prescriptions.[12] Moreover, this would entail the risk that only one interpretation of a certain religious provision would be taken into account.[13] Therefore, an insider approach should be preferred.[14] This approach would take the motivation of the employee-believer into account when assessing whether a manifestation of religion was at stake in the particular case. Since the famous case of *Leyla Sahin*,[15] the Court has been inclined towards this insider approach.[16] In the case of *X* v. *UK*, for example, such an approach would mean that the Court should have taken

---

9 ECtHR 13 April 2006, *Kosteski* v. *The Former Yugoslav Republic of Macedonia*, App. No. 55170/00, par. 38.

10 The issue in *Kosteski* is not whether or not an employee is allowed to take leave of absence on religious holidays, since the Former Republic of Macedonia has a "Public Holidays Act" which not only recognizes Christmas and Easter as public holidays for all its citizens, but also recognizes the two Islamic holidays for citizens of Muslim faith. The underlying issue in this case is the fact that the applicant was not granted leave on these Holidays because—according to the employer—he did not prove he was of the Muslim faith. (The fact that the applicant never absented himself before on religious holidays, that he had also celebrated Christian holidays, that his parents were Christian and that his way of life and diet showed that he was of Christian faith made the national jurisdiction conclude that the applicant was "a self-proclaimed Muslim in order to justify his unjustified absence from work." See ECtHR 13 April 2006, *Kosteski* v. *The Former Yugoslav Republic of Macedonia*, App. No. 55170/00, par. 19.)

11 E. Bribosia, J. Ringelheim and I. Rorive, "Reasonable Accommodation for Religious Minorities: a Promising Concept for European Antidiscrimination Law?" 17 *Maastricht Journal of European and Comparative Law* 137 (2010), 154.

12 See also L. Vickers, *Religious Freedom, Religious Discrimination at the Workplace* (Hart Publishing 2008), 99–100.

13 P. Cumper, "The Accommodation of 'Uncontroversial' Religious Practices" in *Religious Pluralism and Human Rights in Europe: Where to Draw the Line?* (T. Loenen and J. E. Goldschmidt, eds, Intersentia 2007), 207.

14 E. Brems, "The Approach of the European Court of Human Rights to Religion" in *Die Rechtstellung des Menschen im Völkerrecht* (J.C.B. Mohr 2003), 8 (with reference in footnote 23).

15 ECtHR 10 November 2005, *Leyla Şahin* v. *Turkey*, App. No. 47774/98.

16 See, for example, ECtHR 7 December 2010, *Jakóbski* v. *Poland*, App. No. 18429/06 and ECtHR 4 March 2008, *El Morsli* v. *France*, App. No. 15585/06.

into account that the applicant himself considered it as his religious obligation to perform Friday prayer collectively.[17]

In *Konttinen* and *Stedman* the Commission avoided the question about the existence of a manifestation of religion by removing the case from the religious context. In *Konttinen*, the Commission found that the employee "as a civil servant of the State railways, had a duty to accept certain obligations towards his employer"[18] and that the dismissal of the applicant was not due to his religious convictions, but due to the fact that he refused to respect his work hours.[19] It further proceeds that:

> This refusal, even if motivated by his religious convictions, cannot as such be considered protected by Article 9 para. 1. Also, the applicant has not shown any pressure put on him to change religion or that he was prevented to manifest his religion.[20]

The latter statement of the Commission that "the applicant has not shown ... that he was prevented to manifest his religion" is a bit surprising. The cause of the conflict between the employee's religion and his contractual obligations lies precisely in the fact that he wanted to respect the Sabbath and thus wanted to manifest his religion. The Commission's reasoning might consequently be interpreted in such a way that it does not seem to recognize the Sabbath as a manifestation of religion. Likewise, the Commission observed in *Stedman* that "the applicant was dismissed for failing to agree to work certain hours rather than her religious belief as such."[21] Ignoring the element of religion in these cases seems like ignoring an elephant in a small room. Of course the applicants resigned or were dismissed because they did not agree with their work schedule, but the only reason they failed to agree with these conditions was because of their religious convictions.

If this reasoning were applied in other circumstances, claims of reasonable accommodation would virtually never be recognized by the Court. Imagine that a person with a disability is dismissed because he does not arrive on time at work, as the building is not easily accessible despite his multiple requests to adapt the building to his needs. Would it be logical if a judge accepts that the disabled employee was dismissed because of not respecting his contractual obligations to arrive on time at work and that the dismissal had nothing to do with the lack of accommodation? Or imagine the situation where an employee asks for a readjustment of her work schedule so that she might breastfeed her child at specific times during the workday. If she were dismissed or put in a situation where—for her—resignation is inevitable, could the Strasbourg judge hold that she is

17 In a mosque or in the school if there were other Muslims with whom he could pray. EComHR 12 March 1981, *X* v. *United Kingdom*, App. No. 8160/78, par. 19.

18 EComHR 3 December 1996, *Konttinen* v. *Finland*, App. No. 2494/94, par. 6.

19 *Id.* at par. 7.

20 *Id.* at par.7.

21 EComHR 9 April 1997, *Stedman* v. *United Kingdom*, App. No. 29107/95, par. 3.

dismissed only because of not being able to respect her contractual obligations and not because of her private life, with which no interference is consequently found?

In sum, it can be argued that in order to provide better reasoning in cases where an employee-believer is confronted with resignation or dismissal in the workplace because of a conflict related to a religious claim such as adapted work schedules, the religious motivation behind the employee's actions should be taken sufficiently into account. Moreover, when assessing whether a manifestation of religion is at stake, the insider approach of the applicant should be considered.

(b) Freedom to resign

The reluctance of the Strasbourg organs towards finding that a certain claim concerns a manifestation of religion was not the only element that led to not finding an interference. A second important element is the so-called *freedom to resign* doctrine. According to the Commission, in *X* v. *UK* the Inner London Education Authority (ILEA) was in principle entitled to rely on the terms of the employment contract with the employee, but "the question arises whether, under Article 9 of the Convention, the ILEA had to give due consideration to his religious position."[22] According to the Commission, "the applicant remained free to resign if and when he found that his teaching obligations conflicted with his religious duties."[23] Paradoxically, this position, where an employee has to make a choice between his full-time job and the manifestation of his religion, is the situation the applicant is complaining about:

> [It] would mean that a Muslim, who took his religious duty seriously, could never accept employment as a full-time teacher, but must be content with the lesser emoluments of part-time service, and would thus also be excluded from opportunities for promotion.[24]

In *Konttinen* the Commission went even further by stating that the freedom to resign is "the ultimate guarantee of his [the applicant's] right to freedom of religion."[25] This principle was also repeated in *Stedman*.[26]

In the three cases discussed above[27] it is clear that the "freedom to resign" doctrine could not really be perceived as a genuine *freedom* of choice by the employees. For the employee in *X* v. *UK*, for instance, stepping over to a part-time contract meant a lot of disadvantages concerning pay and career opportunities.[28] Resigning would, for him, also carry heavy consequences. The argument of the Commission

22 EComHR 12 March 1981, *X* v. *United Kingdom*, App. No. 8160/78, par. 13.
23 *Id.* at par. 15.
24 *Id.* at par. 32.
25 EComHR 3 December 1996, *Konttinen* v. *Finland*, App. No. 2494/94, par. 7.
26 EComHR 9 April 1997, *Stedman* v. *United Kingdom*, App. No. 29107/95, par. 3.
27 *X* v. *United Kingdom*, *Konttinen* v. *Finland* and *Stedman* v. *the United Kingdom*.
28 EComHR 12 March 1981, *X* v. *United Kingdom*, App. No. 8160/78, par. 16.

that resigning is the ultimate guarantee to the freedom of religion can therefore be highly criticized since it places before the applicant-employees a difficult dilemma between job and religion. Because of his or her religion and the manifestation of it, an individual will not be able to exercise the profession he or she wants, or will have to make extra efforts to find a job that suits his or her religious needs. It is clear that what the Commission considers to be a freedom will not be experienced by every employee in the same way, especially when an employee belongs to a minority religion and lives in a country where the state system—including official holidays and days of rest—is largely organized along the precepts of a majority religion. In this case, the employee is, under the case law of the Commission, more burdened than employees belonging to the majority religion.[29]

A second element that is closely linked to the freedom to resign of the employee is the idea of his or her own free will when entering into a contractual relationship with an employer. Here, the question arises whether an employee distances himself from his rights by signing a contract with his employer. This is not the case, since the ECtHR still keeps the right to assess whether a contractual restriction of a fundamental right is proportionate.[30] A different position would lead to an undermining of the fundamental rights guaranteed by the Convention. In other words, the fact that an applicant by his or her own free will places him or herself in this particular situation by signing a contract should not be a reason to deny *a priori* that an interference with his or her freedom of religion took place. This approach "casts the applicant … as the author of their own misfortune, and sees the remedy as lying in their own hands."[31]

Furthermore, putting all the responsibility on the side of the employee by stating that he or she should bear the consequences of the contract he signed by his own free will, starts from the assumption that he had a full choice about all the aspects of the contract. In *X* v. *UK*, for instance, the Commission observed that the applicant "of his own free will, accepted teaching obligations under his contract." One could then argue that the applicant should bear the consequences of the contract he signed and should thus follow the regular work schedule like the other employees, or quit his job. This argument, however, ignores the fact that an individual who voluntarily signs a contract does not always have a say in its terms. Caroline Evans argues that "[i]n these types of situations, the Commission

29 See also R. Gavison and N. Perez, "Days of Rest in Multicultural Societies: Private, Public, Separate?" in *Law and Religion in Theoretical and Historical Context* (P. Cane, C. Evans and Z. Robinson, eds, Cambridge University Press 2008), 186–213 and M. Nussbaum, *Liberty of Conscience* (Basic Books, 2008), 119. See also *infra.*

30 L. Vickers, *Religious Freedom, Religious Discrimination at the Workplace* (Hart Publishing 2008) 93–94. See *mutatis mutandis* ECtHR 23 September 2010, *Obst* v. *Germany*, App. No. 425/03 and ECtHR 23 September 2010, *Schüth* v. *Germany*, App. No. 1620/03.

31 M. Evans, "Freedom of Religion and the European Convention on Human Rights: Approaches, Trends and Tensions" in *Law and Religion in Theoretical and Historical Context* (P. Cane, C. Evans and Z. Robinson, eds, Cambridge University Press 2008) 296.

talks about people having a choice or making a 'voluntary' decision in a context where they may only have a range of unpalatable choices."[32] The Court ignores completely the fact that the applicant belongs to a minority religion and thus does not always freely make choices as we would like him to do.[33] Or to put it in the words of Seglow:

> matters are not so simple because, while we can hold Mr Ahmad[34] responsible for his beliefs, we cannot hold him responsible for the fact that in the UK Friday is a work day.[35]

Certainly, the freedom to resign doctrine and the argument of the applicant's free will to sign a contract should not be referred to in the light way of the Commission. If the Court would like to use this argument, that an employee remains free to resign and take into account that he entered into a contractual relationship by his own free will, this could at most be used during a proportionality analysis, but should certainly not lead to not finding an interference.[36] This way of reasoning at the level of interference creates a disequilibrium disadvantaging the employee-believer.

It is strongly suggested that as the Court proceeds to a proportionality analysis in cases concerning claims of religious accommodation in the workplace, all the interests of both the employee and employer could and should be taken into account. On the side of the employee, the real-life consequences of a dismissal and subsequent search for an alternative position should be taken into account.[37] On the side of the employer, the feasibility of the accommodation claim should be examined. The existence of an alternative which is less restrictive on the employee's rights is also one of the elements that could be examined.[38] Vickers has proposed several other elements such as the nature of the job, the content of

---

32 C. Evans, *Freedom of Religion Under the European Convention on Human Rights* (Oxford University Press, 2001) 131.

33 See also J. Ringelheim, *Diversité culturelle et droits de l'homme. La protection des minorités par la Convention européenne des droits de l'homme* (Bruylant 2006) 162.

34 Ahmad is the name of the applicant in the case *X* v. *UK* (1981).

35 J. Seglow, "Theories of Religious Exemptions" in *Diversity in Europe. Dilemmas of Differential Treatment in Theory and Practice* (Gideon Calder and Emanuela Ceva, eds, Routledge 2011), 55.

36 See also S. Knights, "Approaches to Diversity in the Domestic Courts: Article 9 of the European Convention on Human Rights," in *Legal Practice and Cultural Diversity* (R. Grillo et al., eds, Ashgate 2010) 291.

37 See *mutatis mutandis* ECtHR 26 September 1995, *Vögt* v. *Germany*, App. No. 17851/91, *infra*.

38 E. Brems, "Human Rights: Minimum and Maximum Perspectives," 9 *Human Rights Law Review* 349 (2009), 360. See also E. Bribosia, J. Ringelheim and I. Rorive, "Reasonable Accommodation for Religious Minorities: A Promising Concept for European Antidiscrimination Law?" 17 *Maastricht Journal of European and Comparative Law* 137 (2010), 151.

the religious claim and the nature of the restriction.[39] An additional element which can play a role in the proportionality analysis is whether the employee belongs to a minority religion.

Such an approach would give more attention to the situation of the employee. To date, the Strasbourg judges have placed the contractual obligations central in their reasoning. In the cases cited above, the interpretation of Article 9 of the ECHR was governed by these contractual obligations rather than by the religious duties of the employee.[40] A proportionality analysis would offer a more genuine balance between the several interests at stake.

2. No discrimination on the ground of religion[41]

All the applicants in the above-mentioned cases alleged a discrimination on the ground of their religion. However, in *X* v. *UK*, *Konttinen*, *Stedman* as well as in *Kosteski*, the Strasbourg organs did not find that the measures taken (or not taken) were violating Article 14 in conjunction with Article 9 of the ECHR.

In *X* v. *UK* the Commission observed that the applicant did not show that he was treated differently than, for instance, Jewish teachers, and declared the claim manifestly ill-founded. The Commission apparently found no need to compare the applicant's situation with teachers belonging to a majority religion or with teachers not having a religion. It made a very interesting statement concerning this issue:

> in respect of the general question of religious and public holidays, ... that, in most countries, only the religious holidays of the majority of the population are celebrated as public holidays. Thus Protestant holidays are not always public holidays in Catholic countries and vice versa.[42]

The Commission thus not only recognized but also normalized the fact that in most countries only the religious holidays of the majority are celebrated as public holidays.[43] In *Konttinen* the Commission unsuccessfully tried to soften this stance somewhat by on the one hand acknowledging the fact "that the Finnish legislation on work hours provides that the weekly day of rest is usually Sunday," but on the other

---

39 See also L. Vickers, *Religious Freedom, Religious Discrimination at the Workplace* (Hart Publishing 2008), 102–107. Vickers adds two categories: nature of employer, relationship between the religious expression and applicant's job.

40 P. Cumper, "The Accommodation of 'Uncontroversial' Religious Practices" in *Religious Pluralism and Human Rights in Europe: Where to Draw the Line?* (T. Loenen & J. E. Goldschmidt, eds, Intersentia 2007) 198.

41 This part is only discussed briefly, since the focus of this chapter is on the Article 9 case law. However, the element of discrimination could not be omitted from the chapter.

42 EComHR 12 March 1981, *X* v. *United Kingdom*, App. No. 8160/78, par. 28.

43 See also E. Bribosia, J. Ringelheim and I. Rorive, "Reasonable Accommodation for Religious Minorities: a Promising Concept for European Antidiscrimination Law?" 17 *Maastricht Journal of European and Comparative Law* 137 (2010), 153.

hand it observed that this legislation does not contain any provision "which would guarantee to members of a certain religious community an absolute right to have a particular day regarded as a holy day."[44] In other words, in this case, the Commission rejected the discrimination argument by referring to the formally non-discriminatory character of the Finnish legislation. However, the effect of this legislation is that religions which do not have Sunday as a holy day, which is the case for most of the minority religions, are less accommodated in the workplace.[45] It is exactly because the applicants have to undergo the same employment system organized along the (religious) needs of the majority that they are restricted in the exercise of their freedom of religion. When a certain measure is general in application and in principle neutral, but causes particular hardship for certain people, the question of "indirect discrimination" may arise.[46] Thus, applied to the cases discussed above it can be concluded that the applicants in *X* v. *UK* and *Konttinen* v. *Finland* are indirectly discriminated against on the basis of their (minority) religion.

Hence, in the landmark case *Thlimmenos* v. *Greece*, the Court also recognized that

> The right not to be discriminated against in the enjoyment of the rights guaranteed under the Convention is also violated when States without an objective and reasonable justification fail to treat differently persons whose situations are significantly different.[47]

According to this reasoning, minorities could claim exceptions to general rules unless the state has a reasonable and objective justification for not allowing this exception. In the case of *X* v. *UK* this would mean that the Court would have to examine whether the refusal to adapt the applicant's work schedule was proportionate to the legitimate aim.[48] To date, in the field of religious claims in the workplace this principle has not been applied. However, the Court recently applied religious accommodation in a prison context.[49]

---

44 EComHR 3 December 1996, *Konttinen* v. *Finland*, App. No. 2494/94, par. 7.

45 See also L. Vickers, *Religious Freedom, Religious Discrimination at the Workplace* (Hart Publishing, 2008), 92 and J. Ringelheim, *Diversité culturelle et droits de l'homme. La protection des minorités par la Convention européenne des droits de l'homme* (Bruylant 2006), 325–326.

46 P. Bosset and M.-Cl. Foblets, "Accomodating Diversity in Quebec and Europe: Different Legal Concepts, Similar Result?" in *Institutional Accommodation and the Citizen: Legal and Political Interaction in a Pluralist Society* (Council of Europe Publishing 2009), 37, 61.

47 ECtHR 6 April 2000, *Thlimmenos* v. *Greece*, App. No. 34369/97, par. 44.

48 J. Ringelheim, *Diversité culturelle et droits de l'homme. La protection des minorités par la Convention européenne des droits de l'homme* (Bruylant 2006), 332.

49 See *infra*, ECtHR 7 December 2010, *Jakóbski* v. *Poland*, App. No. 18429/06.

Although these principles of indirect discrimination and differential treatment could be seen as "principal tools that may be used to guarantee respect for minority cultures,"[50] they still remain unrealized in the field of employment.

II. Religious attire in the workplace: Interference with but no violation of the freedom of religion

Until now, the issue of religious attire in the workplace was only raised before the ECtHR by Muslim women wearing an Islamic headscarf.[51] However, it seems that the Court will be confronted with other religious claims in the near future, since a case has recently been communicated concerning a British Christian woman wanting to wear a cross on the work floor.[52] Under this section three cases will be discussed. *Dahlab* v. *Switzerland* involved a Swiss primary school teacher, while *Kurtulmus* v. *Turkey* and *Kavakçi* v. *Turkey* concerned, respectively, a university professor and a parliamentarian in Turkey.

1. Interference with the freedom of religion

Contrary to the adjudication concerning work hours, the Court did find that an interference with the right to freedom of religion occurred in the cases of *Dahlab*, a primary school teacher, and in *Kurtulmus*, a university professor, both being prohibited from wearing a headscarf in their workplace.[53] Moreover, the Court seems to have adopted a more insider approach when assessing whether a manifestation of religion is at stake. Although the Court in the case of *Dahlab* did not explicitly acknowledge that the headscarf is a manifestation of religion,[54] the Court proceeds in *Kurtulmus* that

---

50 E. Brems, "Human Rights as a Framework for Negotiating/Protecting Cultural Differences: an Exploration in the Case-law of the European Court of Human Rights" in *Cultural Diversity and the Law. State Responses from Around the World* (M.-Cl. Foblets et al., eds, Bruylant 2010), 667–668.

51 At the domestic level other religious groups issued claims concerning this matter. See, for example: S. Ouald Chaib, "About Crucifixes and Headscarves in Dutch Jurisprudence. Is There a Difference Between Both?" *Strasbourgobservers.com* 2010. See also the chapters by Katayoun Alidadi and Rim-Sarah Alouane in this volume.

52 ECtHR 12 April 2011, *Nadia Eweida and Shirley Chaplin* v. *UK*, App. No. 48420/10 and 59842/10.

53 The third case discussed in this section, *Kavakçi* v. *Turkey*, was not examined under Article 9 of the Convention. See *infra*.

54 In *Dahlab* v. *Switzerland* the Court did not explicitly state that the headscarf was a manifestation of a religious belief, but it can indirectly be assumed to be the case, since it examined the case under Article 9. Moreover, the Court mentioned the following principle: "The pluralism indissociable from a democratic society, which has been dearly won over the centuries, depends on it. While religious freedom is primarily a matter of individual

> on the basis that the rules on dress for public servants constituted interference with her right to manifest her religion, *as she considered that Muslim women have a religious duty to wear the Islamic headscarf*.[55]

This very personal approach of the Court contrasts with the position of the Commission in, for instance, *X* v. *UK* where the necessity of performing the Friday prayer during work hours was questioned. Here the Court attaches particular importance to the question whether in the specific case the motivation to wear the headscarf is driven by the religious belief of the applicant. By applying this insider approach in this case and thus accepting that the underlying issue concerned a manifestation of religion, the Court accepts that a headscarf ban in the workplace entails an interference with the freedom to manifest one's religion.

The cases discussed under this section clearly show the importance of recognizing that a manifestation of religion was at stake, since the Court proceeds to a proportionality analysis. However, the fact that the case has reached this phase does not guarantee that the reasoning under this proportionality analysis will be satisfactory, whatever the outcome of the case will be.

In the next part a closer look will be taken at the Court's reasoning in the cases of *Dahlab* and *Kurtulmus* where the Court did not find a violation, and *Kavakçi* where a violation was found, but not concerning the applicant's freedom of religion.

2. Dahlab and Kurtulmus: Manifestly ill-founded

Lucia Dahlab was a Swiss woman who converted to Islam after working for almost two years in a public primary school in Switzerland. After her conversion she started wearing the headscarf, and wore it while working in the school for approximately four years, and this without any objections from the school management, the parents or the pupils. It was only after these four years that the education board prohibited her from wearing a headscarf at school.

Dahlab's claim that the prohibition imposed on her against wearing a headscarf during her school activities consisted of a violation of her freedom of religion guaranteed by Article 9 of the ECHR was declared manifestly ill-founded and thus inadmissible.[56] Referring to the margin of appreciation in this field,[57] the Court concluded that the prohibition on wearing the headscarf was not unreasonable. It

---

conscience, it also implies freedom to manifest one's religion. Bearing witness in words and deeds is bound up with the existence of religious convictions."

55 ECtHR 24 January 2006, *Kurtulmus* v. *Turkey*, App. No. 65500/01, at par. 5 (own emphasis).

56 For an excellent analysis of this case see also C. Evans, "The 'Islamic scarf' in the European Court of Human Rights," 7 *Melbourne Journal of International Law* 52 (2006), 52–73.

57 See also the chapter by Kristin Henrard in this volume.

observed that the national authorities took the personal conviction of the applicant sufficiently into account and that they amply balanced the applicant's freedom of religion against the principle of state neutrality. The Court attaches particular importance to the protection of the rights of others, in this case the young pupils, by stressing that the headscarf could have a proselytizing effect on children:

> It cannot be denied outright that the wearing of a headscarf might have some kind of proselytizing effect, seeing that it appears to be imposed on women by a precept which is laid down in the Koran and which, as the Federal Court noted, is hard to square with the principle of gender equality. It therefore appears difficult to reconcile the wearing of an Islamic headscarf with the message of tolerance, respect for others and, above all, equality and non-discrimination that all teachers in a democratic society must convey to their pupils.[58]

This part of the Court's reasoning can be contrasted with its observation that for several years the applicant has been teaching with a headscarf

> without any action being taken by the head teacher or the district schools inspector or any comments being made by parents. That implies that during the period in question there were no objections to the content or quality of the teaching provided by the applicant, who does not appear to have sought to gain any kind of advantage from the outward manifestation of her religious beliefs.[59]

In other words, Mrs Dahlab had been teaching for approximately four years with her headscarf and no complaints about pressure towards the pupils were formulated, nor was it reported that pupils were being indirectly influenced. The reasoning applied by the Court is thus confusing and contradictory. On the one hand it recognizes that the applicant performed a good job as a teacher but on the other hand it depersonalizes the issue by first stating that the headscarf as such could have a proselytizing influence on the children—which is factually proven to be untrue—and secondly by stating that the wearing of the headscarf is difficult to reconcile with "the message of tolerance, respect for others and, above all, equality and non-discrimination that all teachers in a democratic society must convey to their pupils"—which is also proven to be untrue by the above-mentioned observation. Consequently, a more pragmatic approach would be more appropriate in this case, especially since the Court claims to balance the right of the teacher to manifest her religion against the need to protect pupils by preserving religious harmony. The balancing exercise the Court is trying to make in its reasoning is also incomplete. A more complete and fair proportionality analysis would have included the uncontested conduct of the applicant and the

58 ECtHR 15 February 2001, *Dahlab* v. *Switzerland*, App. No. 42393/98, par. 14.
59 *Id.* at par. 13.

consequences a headscarf ban might have for her.[60] Instead, the case was declared manifestly ill-founded and inadmissible, which is a paradoxical conclusion considering the complexity of the case.

The same "manifestly ill-founded" conclusion was reached in *Kurtulmus* v. *Turkey*. Contrary to *Dahlab*, where the argument of state neutrality plays only a marginal role in the Court's reasoning, the central line of reasoning used by the Court in *Kurtulmus* is that of secularism.

Mrs *Kurtulmus*, a Turkish university professor who wore a headscarf, was suspended from her duties and eventually dismissed on the ground that she had failed to comply with the dress code applicable to state officials. As in *Dahlab*, the applicant had already been wearing the headscarf for some time on the job before she received her first "warning."

In this case also, the Court granted a wide margin of appreciation to Turkey and accorded particular attention to the principle of state neutrality. Instead, the Court put forward the Turkish Kemalistic principle of secularism. The Court states that it is

> that principle, and not objections to the way a person dresses as a result of his or her religious beliefs, that is the paramount consideration that is underpinning the rules.[61]

This part of the Court's reasoning shows similarities with the reasoning in *Konttinen* and *Stedman*,[62] where the Commission did not find that the employee was dismissed because of his religion and the manifestation of it, but because of the failure to respect his contractual duties.[63] Moreover, similarly to the work schedule cases discussed in the previous section, the Court emphasized that Mrs Kurtulmus had "assumed the status of a public servant of her own free will" and that

> as a university lecturer, and thus a person in authority at the university and a representative of the State, she could not have been unaware of the rules requiring her not to express her religious beliefs in public in an ostentatious manner.[64]

The emphasis on free will and on facing the consequences of the "choice" made, indirectly places the employee before a dilemma. Mrs Kurtulmus can indeed make the choice between being a professor and not being a professor. But since the dress code is a general rule applicable in all the public universities, this

60 See *mutatis mutandis* ECtHR 26 September 1995, *Vögt* v. *Germany*, App. No. 17851/91, discussed below.

61 ECtHR 24 January 2006, *Kurtulmus* v. *Turkey*, App. No. 65500/01, par. 6.

62 See *supra*.

63 See *supra*.

64 ECtHR 24 January 2006, *Kurtulmus* v. *Turkey*, App. No. 65500/01, par. 6.

"choice" hides the dilemma between manifesting one's religion on the one hand and pursuing a career as an academic and public servant on the other. In other words, wearing a headscarf *a priori* restricts freedom of choice of profession and career opportunities in Turkey,[65] which is exactly the issue the applicant is contesting before the Court. It cannot be denied that the principle of secularism is fundamental in Turkish society.[66] The question should be whether the measure taken is proportionate in attaining this aim. Taking into account that the applicant teaches adult students, that she was allowed to obtain her PhD with a headscarf and that she has been teaching for two years with a headscarf without getting any complaint, the proportionality of the ban is highly debatable. However, in cases against Turkey in the field of religious freedom the principle of secularism plays a major role.[67]

The Court concluded that the claim is manifestly ill-founded, referring to the reasoning used in the case of *Dahlab*, namely neutrality *and* the tender age of the children. Interestingly, the latter element, the age of the students taught by the applicant, was not taken into account in the reasoning of *Kurtulmus*.. If the Court had been consistent in its case law, it would at least have touched upon this issue. As a university professor, the applicant teaches adult students who cannot be considered as vulnerable as primary school children. Moreover, contrary to *Dahlab*, the Court did not mention the fact that Mrs Kurtulmus had been teaching for two years with a headscarf before any issue arose. Consequently, in *Kurtulmus*, the Court has taken the perspective of the applicant even less into account, while it accorded the principle of secularism an almighty weight in the balance.

3. Kavakçi: Headscarf at the parliament

In *Kavakçi* v. *Turkey*,[68] the Court was again confronted with the headscarf in a workplace setting. Mrs Kavakçi was elected as a member of parliament.[69] When she wanted to take the oath, she was forced to leave the parliament following protests about her Islamic headscarf. She was a member of the party *Fazilet Partisi* which openly advocated for the right to wear the headscarf. The party was subsequently dissolved by the Turkish Constitutional Court on the basis that it was a "centre of activities contrary to the principle of secularism."[70] The conduct of

65 J. Maclure and C. Taylor, *Laïcité é liberté de conscience* (La Découverte 2010), 58.

66 See the chapter by Mine Yıldırım in this volume.

67 See also, for example, ECtHR 10 November 2005, *Leyla Şahin* v. *Turkey*, App. No. 47774/98.

68 ECtHR 5 April 2007, *Kavakçi* v. *Turkey*, App. No. 71907/01. See also the chapter by Mine Yıldırım in this volume.

69 For a detailed description of the facts and the context see K. Shively, "Religious Bodies and the Secular State: The Merve Kavakçi Affair," 1 *Journal of Middle East Women's Studies* 46 (2005), 46–72.

70 ECtHR 5 April 2007, *Kavakçi* v. *Turkey*, App. No. 71907/01, par. 42.

certain leaders and members of the party, including the applicant's conduct, were taken into account in reaching this conclusion. The Turkish Constitutional Court stripped two parliamentarians, including the applicant,[71] of their status of Member of Parliament and prohibited five members of the party, including the applicant, from becoming founding members, ordinary members, leaders or auditors of any other political party for five years.[72]

Mrs Kavakçi claimed under Article 9 and Article 3 of Protocol 1 to the Convention that she was sanctioned because of her religious convictions and because of the fact that she manifested her religion by wearing the headscarf.

The Court opted for examining the case solely under Article 3 of Protocol 1 which guarantees the right to free elections. It noted that the temporary political sanctions following the dissolution of the party aimed to preserve the secular character of the Turkish political regime. Subsequently, it found the aim pursued to be legitimate. In its proportionality analysis, the Court observed that the legislation concerning the dissolution of political parties had a very wide scope since all the actions and statements made by party members could be taken into consideration to conclude that a party had to be dissolved, irrespective of the level of involvement of that member. In this case, the Court observed that the president and the vice-president of the party did not suffer the same sanctions as the applicant, despite the fact that they were in a comparable situation to the applicant. Subsequently, the Court concluded that the measures taken towards the applicant were not proportionate to the aim pursued and thus that they had been violating the applicant's freedom to participate in free elections; the Court did not find it necessary to examine her dismissal as a parliamentarian as such.

Although the outcome in this case was favorable for the applicant, some remarks can be made with regard to the line of reasoning followed by the Court. The most striking element in the reasoning is the absence of an assessment of a possible violation of the freedom of religion of the applicant. Although there was a strong link between the applicant's religious freedom and the political sanctions imposed on her, which is also implicitly recognized by the Court through the acceptance of the Turkish principle of secularism as a legitimate aim, the Court clearly avoided entering into this discussion.[73] The question whether a parliamentarian who is democratically elected can be prevented from taking up her function because of her headscarf remains unanswered.[74] It is not clear whether the Court refrained

71 It is unclear whether the political activities of the applicant formed the basis of this sanction or whether this was due to another discussion concerning the applicant's nationality.

72 ECtHR 5 April 2007, *Kavakçi* v. *Turkey*, App. No. 71907/01, par. 23.

73 The Court did not even mention the word "headscarf" once in its reasoning.

74 See also A. Barras, "A Rights-based Discourse to Contest the Boundaries of State Secularism? The Case of the Headscarf Bans in France and Turkey," 16 *Democratization* 1237 (2009), 1249.

from answering this question because it knew beforehand that it was a lost battle or because it did not come to a consensus on this issue.

A first conclusion that can be drawn from the cases discussed above is the inconsistency in the reasoning of the Court. While in the first case much weight is given to the rights of others—*in casu* the children—this element is not mentioned in *Kurtulmus* where the principle of secularism is the main and only argument. Subsequently, in the third case, the Court neglects the argument linked to the headscarf, while this was the main argument of the applicant. A second related observation is the lack of a pragmatic and employee/applicant friendly approach of the Court. Similar to the work schedule cases discussed in the previous section where it has been argued that more attention is paid to the contractual obligations and the responsibility of the applicant, the Court is also giving less weight to the interests of the applicant in the cases concerning religious attire in the workplace.

III. Improving the Court's legal reasoning: "Good practices" in the case law of the ECtHR

The title of this chapter reveals an ambitious and audacious aim: improving the legal reasoning of the Court in cases concerning religious accommodation in the workplace. The cases discussed above revealed several opportunities for improvement in the Court's reasoning.

It is first observed that the Court shows a reluctance to find an interference in cases concerning religious claims in the workplace. Insofar as it found that the claims concerning work scheduling are related to a manifestation of a religious conviction, the Court does not find an interference with the freedom of religion and holds the opinion that the employee remains free to leave his job. Consequently, the case does not reach the proportionality test and the several interests at stake are not balanced. Secondly, in the cases concerning religious attire in the workplace, the Court accepts that the headscarf is a manifestation of a religious conviction and finds an interference with the freedom of religion. Nevertheless, at the level of the proportionality assessment it does not sufficiently weigh the several interests at stake.

In this section, a closer look will be taken at the legal reasoning of the Court in other fields than the freedom of religion in search of "good practices" within the case law of the Court itself. The cases have been selected on the ground of factual similarities that can be found with the cases discussed in the previous sections. The first kind of cases concern employees who have been dismissed or have resigned because of reasons related to their political ideas or facts related to their private or family life. Next, a comparison will be drawn with cases where religious accommodation claims were raised in context other than a workplace setting.

1. Looking over the fence of Article 9

a. Freedom of expression in the workplace

The landmark case *Vögt* v. *Germany*[75] shows several factual similarities with the cases discussed in the previous sections, but at the level of reasoning the different approaches taken with these cases is remarkable. Mrs Vögt was a teacher in a German public school, where she taught French and German courses. She was also a member of the DKP, a communist political party. When she became actively involved in this party, she was dismissed from her job as a teacher. The authorities argued that she failed to comply "with the duty to uphold the free democratic system of the country."[76]

The Court found that the dismissal interfered with the applicant's freedom of expression but agreed that a duty of loyalty could be expected from a civil servant, so as to protect national security, prevent disorder and protect the rights of others. Subsequently, the Court examined whether the measure was necessary in a democratic society, meaning relevant and sufficient. The way in which the Court proceeds in this necessity test is very interesting. The Court notes that

> there are several reasons for considering dismissal of a secondary-school teacher by way of disciplinary sanction for breach of duty to be a very severe measure. This is firstly because of the effect that such a measure has on the reputation of the person concerned and secondly because secondary-school teachers dismissed in this way lose their livelihood, at least in principle, as the disciplinary court may allow them to keep part of their salary. Finally, secondary-school teachers in this situation may find it well nigh impossible to find another job as a teacher, since in Germany teaching posts outside the civil service are scarce.[77]

Thus in this case the Court adopts a very inclusive and sensitive approach towards the personal situation of the employee. The Court even goes a step further by stating that

> [c]onsequently, they will almost certainly be deprived of the opportunity to exercise the sole profession for which they have a calling, for which they have been trained and in which they have acquired skills and experience.[78]

This approach can first be contrasted to the cases where the Court states that the freedom to resign is the ultimate guarantee of one's freedom of religion. In fact, despite the factual similarities between the cases discussed above, the Court at no point mentions the possibility of the applicant resigning, nor does the Court refer

---

75 ECtHR 26 September 1995, *Vögt* v. *Germany*, App. No. 17851/91.
76 *Id.* at par. 44.
77 *Id.* at par. 60.
78 *Id.* at par. 60.

to the fact that the applicant entered in this contract by her own free will. On the contrary, the Court notes the consequences the termination of the contract would have on her. Why the Court applies the freedom to resign doctrine in Article 9 cases and not in Article 10 cases is not clear, but the reasoning in *Vögt* shows that leaving out this doctrine gives room for a proper proportionality analysis, while its application in the freedom of religion cases means that claims are blocked at the interference level.[79] Secondly, in this proportionality analysis the Court puts the applicant in a central position by taking due regard of the consequences of a dismissal and the particularities of the profession.[80]

A more specific comparison can be drawn between *Vögt* and *Dahlab* v. *Switzerland.* In *Dahlab* the Court acknowledges on the one hand that no critique can be leveled on the conduct of the applicant, but still uses the argument of indoctrination of the children as a red thread in its reasoning. In *Vögt*, we clearly see that the ECtHR is adopting a more pragmatic approach. Here the Court acknowledges, on the one hand, that there could be a risk of indoctrination of the pupils, but it notes, on the other hand, that "no criticism was leveled on [the applicant] on this point."[81] "On the contrary, the applicant's work at school had been considered wholly satisfactory by her superiors and she was held in high regard by her pupils, their parents, and her colleagues."[82] The Court also observes that a teacher is a figure of authority to pupils which implies a responsibility outside the school building. But in this case, no evidence was brought before the Court of such conduct. Finally, since the political party to which the applicant belongs was not banned, her activities were not illegal as such. The Court concluded that the arguments put forward by the government were relevant to the aim pursued, but not sufficient. Consequently, the dismissal of the applicant was found to be disproportionate. Balancing all the elements, the Court found that it was not sufficiently shown that the applicant in practice was causing any harm while exercising her rights guaranteed by Article 10 of the Convention.

In sum, from *Vögt* several "good practices" can be deduced for cases concerning religious accommodation in the workplace. Instead of focusing on the contractual obligations and integrating a "freedom to resign" argument in its reasoning, thereby placing all the responsibility on the shoulders of the employee, the Court should also take the situation of the applicant into account. This leads to a more balanced reasoning of the several interests at stake, of both the employer and the employee. With this approach the cases concerning the accommodation of work schedules would at least have been examined under a proportionality analysis. A second good practice in *Vögt* is the pragmatic approach of the Court. While in *Dahlab* and *Kurtulmus* the Court is following a principled approach—based on secularism and

79 *X* v. *United Kingdom*, *Konttinen* v. *Finland* and *Stedman* v. *the United Kingdom*.

80 For example, the fact that she was a teacher would make it more difficult to find a workplace where she would be accepted with her political ideas.

81 ECtHR 26 September 1995, *Vögt* v. *Germany*, App. No. 17851/91, par. 60.

82 *Id.* at par. 60.

a possible proselytizing effect of the headscarf—in *Vögt* the Court is looking at the de facto conduct of the employee, even though it also recognizes the potential indoctrinating effect of her political ideas. A more pragmatic approach would also lead to a more genuine balancing of the interests of the parties involved.

b. The right to a family life and the workplace

b.1 The church as employer All the cases discussed above concerned private employers or the State as employer. A special situation occurs when a church is the employer of an individual. Here the religious freedom of the Church-employer could enter into conflict with the fundamental rights of their employees, such as their freedom of religion or their right to private life.[83] The Court and the Commission have on a number of occasions had the opportunity to review such cases. In *X* v. *Denmark*[84] a clergyman was faced with resignation from the church when he would not abandon his practice whereby he obliged parents to follow five religious lessons before being able to christen their child. In *Karlsson* v. *Sweden*[85] the applicant was found not to be qualified for the job as vicar since he did not want to work together with clergywomen. Similarly, in *Williamson* v. *UK*[86] a priest complained that he was faced with dismissal since he did not agree with the new policy of the church allowing women to enter the priesthood. In all these cases, the Commission declared the cases inadmissible and referred to the freedom to leave the office. In fact, the arguments which the Commission later used in the cases concerning work hours were used for the first time in cases where the church was the employer:

> Their individual freedom of thought, conscience or religion is exercised at the moment they accept or refuse employment as clergymen, and their right to leave the church guarantees their freedom of religion in case they oppose its teachings.[87]

However, it seems that the Court is embarking on a new line of reasoning when it comes to cases involving Church-employers. Recently, the Court issued two judgments, *Obst* v. *Germany*[88] and *Shüth* v. *Germany*,[89] involving respectively the Mormon Church and the Catholic Church as employers.[90] The two cases show a number of similarities but are distinct nonetheless, both in the facts and in the ruling of the Court. Mr Obst, a member of the Mormon Church and director of the public

83 See the chapter by Yves Stox on religious-ethos employers in this volume.
84 EComHR 8 March 1976, *X* v. *Denmark*, App. No. 7374/75.
85 EComHR 12 April 1989, *Karlsson* v. *Sweden*, App. No. 12356/86.
86 EComHR 17 May 1995, *Williamson* v. *United Kingdom*, App. No. 27008/95.
87 EComHR 8 March 1976, *X* v. *Denmark*, App. No. 7374/75.
88 ECtHR 23 September 2010, *Obst* v. *Germany*, App. No. 425/03.
89 ECtHR 23 September 2010, *Schüth* v. *Germany*, App. No. 1620/03.
90 See also the chapters by Lucy Vickers and Yves Stox in this volume.

relations department of the Church for Europe, was dismissed after admitting to an extra-marital sexual relationship. Mr Shüth, organist and chief of the choir, was dismissed when the Church that employed him discovered that he was expecting a child with a woman other than his wife, from whom he was separated. Both employees complained before the ECtHR about a lack of protection accorded by the State in their relationship with their employers. Both cases were dealt with under Article 8 of the ECHR.

In *Obst* v. *Germany* the Court found that the decisions of the national jurisdictions which confirmed the dismissal of the applicant were not unreasonable since it balanced the several interests at stake. This balancing exercise required that the seriousness of the facts (sexual relationship with another woman while still living together with his wife), the important position of the applicant (director of a public relations department at a European level) and the enhanced duty of loyalty linked to his post were taken into account.

Contrary to *Obst*, in *Shüth* v. *Germany* the Court did find a violation of Article 8 of the ECHR. It observed that the several interests at stake were not sufficiently balanced by the national judicial body and that a more thorough examination was needed. The Court also acknowledges that a Church may impose a duty of loyalty upon its employees, but the several interests at stake must be taken into account, such as the nature of the post. This balancing exercise was not undertaken by the national jurisdictions. Moreover, the Court refers to the limited possibilities of finding a new job,[91] taking into account the specific training of Mr Shüth. According to the Court, it would be difficult, if not impossible, for him to find a new job outside the Church. The Court concludes that the national jurisdictions "did not balance the rights of the applicant and those of the church-employer as is required by the Convention."[92]

Although the different outcomes in the cases can lead to discussions,[93] several "good practices" can be observed with regard to the reasoning. First, the Court does not drop the case at the interference level, but allows room to examine the issues more profoundly at the proportionality level. The argument that employees working for a Church remain free to leave the church is not used here. Moreover,

91 ECtHR 23 September 2010, *Schüth* v. *Germany*, App. No. 1620/03, par. 73: "Or, aux yeux de la Cour, le fait qu'un employé licencié par un employeur ecclésial ait des possibilités limitées de trouver un nouvel emploi revêt une importance particulière." [However, in the eyes of the Court, the fact that an employee who is dismissed by a church-employer has limited possibilities of finding a new job should be accorded particular importance].

92 ECtHR 23 September 2010, *Schüth* v. *Germany*, App. No. 1620/03, par. 74. Own translation.

93 See, for example, G. De Beco, "Le droit au respect de la vie privée dans les relations de travail au sein des societiés religieuses—L'approche Européenne des droits de l'homme," 86 *Revue trimestrielle des droits de l'homme* 375 (2011), 390. [The right to family life and private life in work relations in religious societies—The approach of the European Court of Human Rights].

as in *Vögt*, the Court also takes the situation of the applicant into consideration, although the reasoning in *Shüth* is more elaborate than in *Obst* in this regard. In my opinion, the Court does not convincingly show that the several interests are well balanced in *Obst*. The arguments raised in this case concern mainly the interests of the employer, namely the work ethics and the importance of the job. However, in this case the consequences of the dismissal, such as the likelihood of the applicant finding another job, were not taken into account. Whether or not this might lead to another outcome, it is at least inconsistent with the reasoning in *Shüth* where the Court firmly argues that the national jurisdictions did not balance the rights of the applicant and those of the Church-employer as is required by the Convention. This leads us to a second particularly interesting point in these cases. Even though not consistently applied, the way the Court stresses the importance of balancing the several interests of the employer and the employee at stake is, taking into account the previous case law involving the church as employer, striking.

This line of reasoning is continued in a later case involving the Protestant church as employer, *Siebenhaar* v. *Germany*. Mrs Siebenhaar was dismissed from her job in a day care centre ran by the protestant church after the church found out that she was an active member of another religious group, the Universal Church. Thus a conflict arose between the freedom of religion of the church-employer and the believer-employee, respectively. In its reasoning the Court took, similarly to *Vögt*, several aspects of the applicant's life into account such as her age, the nature of the job and the possibility of finding another job.[94]

In sum, a positive evolution can be found in the Court's case law where a Church is the employer. The focus lies in balancing the interests of the employer and the employee respectively, whereby special attention is paid to the consequences of a possible dismissal for the employee.

b.2 The "freedom to resign" in 2010 In a recent case, *Konstantin Markin* v. *Russia*,[95] the applicant, an army serviceman, claimed discrimination in the workplace on the ground of gender because he was not awarded parental leave on the same terms as his female colleagues. The applicant had lost his case at the national level. The Russian Constitutional Court inter alia argued that "[if] the serviceman decides to take care of his child himself, he is entitled to early termination of his service for family reasons."[96] Although formulated in a more

94 However, in light of the arguments that were raised in the case of Vögt, some critique can also be uttered. The Court namely refers to the possible influence the applicant can have on the children she is educating. However, no proof of proselytizing behavior is put forward in this case, making the fear of "of influence on the children by an educator who is a member of a belief that is contradictory with the principles of the Protestant church" ungrounded. See ECtHR 3 February 2011, *Siebenhaar* v. *Germany*, App. No. 18136/02, par. 44 (translation by the author).

95 ECtHR 7 October 2010, *Konstantin Markin* v. *Russia*, App. No. 30078/06.

96 *Id.* at par. 19.

subtle manner than, for instance, *Konttinen* v. *Finland*, this statement of the Russian Court is similar to the freedom to resign argument used by the ECtHR in the freedom of religion cases discussed in this chapter. However, the Strasbourg Court surprisingly reacted as follows:

> The Court is particularly struck by the Constitutional Court's intimation that a serviceman wishing to take personal care of his children was free to resign from the armed forces. Servicemen are thereby forced to make a difficult choice between nursing their new-born children and pursuing their military career, no such choice being faced by servicewomen.[97]

The Court criticizes in this case the same kind of reasoning which it adopted itself, namely the argument that one remains free to resign when one's job conflicts with one's freedoms guaranteed by the Convention. Here the Court also acknowledges that this argument puts a "difficult choice" in front of the applicant-employee. Moreover, referring to the unique nature of the armed forces, the Court also takes the consequences of a possible resignation into account:

> It is therefore clear that, if they choose to resign from military service to be able to take care of their new-born children, servicemen would encounter difficulties in obtaining civilian posts in their areas of specialisation which would reflect the seniority and status that they had achieved in the armed forces.[98]

Consequently, this case is also an example of a "good practice." Not only does the Court criticize the freedom to resign approach, but it also takes the particular situation of the applicant into account in a well-weighted proportionality analysis. The question arises whether, after taking this firm stance against a freedom to resign approach, the Court would still apply the freedom to resign doctrine in future cases in the field of the freedom of religion.

2. Looking over the fence of the workplace: Religious accommodation in prison

Claims of prisoners who wish to exercise their religion during their detention have come before the ECtHR on a number of occasions.[99] These claims mostly concern visits by a minister, dietary rules and the observance of prayer in prison.

---

97 *Id.* at par. 58.

98 *Id.* at par. 58.

99 See, for example, ECtHR 9 November 2010, *Ali* v. *Romania*, App. No. 20307/02 (2010); ECtHR 13 November 2007, *Schiavone* v. *Italy*, App. No. 65039/01; ECtHR 30 November 2006, *Igors Dmitijevs* v. *Latvia*, App. No. 61638/00; ECtHR 24 October 2006, *Vincent* v. *France*, App. No. 6253/03 and ECtHR 23 September 2004, *Enea* v. *Italy*, App. No. 74912/01.

In *Jakóbski* v. *Poland*[100] the Court dealt with a very interesting example of religious accommodation. Mr Jakóbski, detained in a Polish prison, asked on several occasions to be served meat-free meals in order to follow the religious dietary rules required by his Mahayana Buddhist religion. For a few months he was provided a "PK diet"—a diet that contains no pork—upon doctor's orders, but thereafter he was put back on the general prison non-meat-free diet to which he objected on religious grounds.

The Court first examined whether a manifestation of a religious belief is involved. Contrary to the government, the Court did not enter into the discussion of whether or not vegetarianism is really a religious dietary prescription. The Court held that the case fell within the scope of Article 9:

> without deciding whether such decisions are taken in every case to fulfil a religious duty ... in the present case the Court considers that the applicant's decision to adhere to a vegetarian diet can be regarded as motivated or inspired by a religion and was not unreasonable.[101]

This part of the reasoning is in line with the case of Leyla Sahin.[102] Thus the Court does not judge in general whether a certain claim is related to a manifestation of a religious conviction, but makes the experience of the applicant central. As already argued, this insider approach should also be favored in cases where religious accommodation claims occur in the workplace.

In this case the Court concluded that the refusal of the authorities to accommodate the applicant's religious claim interfered with the applicant's freedom of religion. The Court was not convinced by the argument of the Polish government that providing each detainee with special food would entail too many technical and financial difficulties:

> Unlike in the latter case, he was not offered any alternative diet, nor was the Buddhist Mission consulted on the issue of the appropriate diet. The Court is not persuaded that the provision of a vegetarian diet to the applicant would have entailed any disruption to the management of the prison or to any decline in the standards of meals served to other prisoners.[103]

Jakóbski v. *Poland* has the potential to become a landmark case in the field of freedom of religion. It is the first time the Court actually accepted reasonable accommodation of a religious claim. The context of a prison is of course different to the context of employment, since in the situation of a prison, a detainee completely relies on the authorities. Yet the balancing exercise the Court

100 ECtHR 7 December 2010, *Jakóbski* v. *Poland*, App. No. 18429/06.
101 *Id.* at par. 45.
102 *Supra.*
103 ECtHR 7 December 2010, *Jakóbski* v. *Poland*, App. No. 18429/06, par. 52.

handled in this case could be applied to cases in the field of the workplace as well, especially for complaints concerning work schedules. Both the interests of the authorities and the prisoner were taken into account. The Court admitted that special arrangements for one prisoner may have financial implications for the custodial institution, but the nature of the claim was not as such that this is an insurmountable problem as the prisoner "merely asked to be granted a vegetarian diet excluding meat products." This reasoning can be compared with the "undue hardship" test used by the US Supreme Court[104] or the Canadian Supreme Court. If the Court followed the same line of reasoning in workplace cases, the feasibility of accommodating a particular religious claim would have to be taken seriously during the proportionality assessment, which would also lead to a more genuine balancing of the several interests at stake in that context.

Conclusion

Through the application of the "freedom to resign" doctrine, the Commission has always concluded that no interference with the freedom of religion occurs when an employer refuses to adapt work schedules to the religious needs of the employee. In these cases it was held that no discrimination on the basis of religion took place. This reasoning of the Commission shows a lack of recognition for the vulnerable position of members of minority religions towards an employment culture that is adapted to precepts of the majority religion. Also, contrary to cases in other fields than the freedom of religion, the Court does not take the possible consequences of a dismissal into account. A first step forward in a case concerning work hours and religious holidays would be to abandon the "freedom to resign" argument and to submit the case to a proportionality analysis, as the Court seems to move towards in the *Konstantin Markin* case. Under this proportionality test the Court should balance the several interests at stake. On the side of the applicant this would mean that the nature of his employment would be taken into account, and that the existence of a less restrictive alternative should be examined. Also, an important element in this analysis could be whether the employee belongs to a minority or a majority religion. Finally, the feasibility for the employer of the accommodation of the claim should be examined seriously. In a second part, under Article 14 of the ECHR in the light of the *Thlimmenos* judgment, the existence of indirect discrimination should be verified.

In the second kind of cases analyzed, namely the cases concerning religious attire in the workplace, the Court has accepted that the headscarf is a manifestation of a religious belief and has found an interference with but no violation of the applicants' freedom. It has been argued that the Court should adopt a more individual and more pragmatic approach towards the applicant, taking into account the personal conduct of the employee.

---

104 See also the chapter by Gabrielle Caceres in this volume.

In cases where other freedoms protected under the Convention are at stake, the Court is applying the proportionality test more thoroughly, taking on a more pragmatic approach that is more sensitive to the individual situation and conduct of the applicant. And in the very recent case of *Jakóbski* v. *Poland*, the Court showed more willingness to accommodate a religious claim of a member of a minority religion. Although this case does not concern the workplace but a prison, the question arises whether this case will be followed in all fields where individuals are claiming accommodation for their religious needs. In *Niemietz* v. *Germany*[105] the Court stated that "[i]n the course of their working lives ... the majority of people have a significant, if not the greatest, opportunity of developing relationships with the outside world." The religious identity of an employee should not close this crucial window on the world, especially not when that employee belongs to a (religious) minority.

105 ECtHR 16 December 1992, *Niemetiez* v. *Germany*, App. No. 13710/88, par. 29.

Chapter 3

A Critical Appraisal of the Margin of Appreciation Left to States Pertaining to "Church–State Relations" under the Jurisprudence of the European Court of Human Rights

Kristin Henrard

Introduction

When talking about religious diversity, and state obligations concerning religious diversity, what comes immediately to mind is freedom of religion and the related state obligations. In Europe the most central reference point concerning fundamental rights is undoubtedly the European Convention on Human Rights (ECHR) and the related jurisprudence of the European Court of Human Rights (hereafter ECtHR or the (European) Court). The Court is one of the most prominent international courts dedicated to the protection of human rights. Its reputation is even such that it is also referred to by national courts outside the remit of the Council of Europe, the South African Constitutional Court being a prominent example.[1] Notwithstanding this status, one regularly finds critical assessments of particular judgments of the Court and also articles that express more fundamental concerns about some of its jurisprudential lines, one of which pertains to the margin of appreciation that is granted to states.[2]

The jurisprudence of the European Court on the freedom of religion may not be very extensive, but it is characterized by a very well-known and steady line of jurisprudence following which states tend to be granted a wide margin of appreciation concerning questions of Church–State relations. This wide margin of appreciation would be in order when no common European standard can be

1 See also R. K. M. Smith, *Textbook on International Human Rights* (OUP 2009), 93.

2 Inter alia G. Letsas, "Two Concepts of the Margin of Appreciation," 26 *Oxford Journal of Legal Studies* 705 (2006); R. St. J. Macdonald, "The Margin of Appreciation," in *The European System for the Protection of Human Rights* (R. St. J. Macdonald et al., eds, Martinus Neihoff Publishers 1993); O. Gross and F. Ni Aolain, "From Discretion to Scrutiny: Revisiting the Application of the Margin of Appreciation Doctrine in the Context of Article 15 of the ECHR," 23 *Human Rights Quarterly* 625 (2001).

detected in the matter. Indeed, when comparing the Member States of the Council of Europe in this regard a great diversity in systems emerges. While the Court immediately adds that this margin goes hand in hand with European supervision, the question then is whether this supervision is "adequate." As it relates to religious diversity in the workplace, the question becomes how the Court's supervision plays out for the protection of religious diversity (in the workplace).

This chapter starts with an identification and appraisal of problems with the margin of appreciation doctrine in general. Subsequently, the particular problems with the margin of appreciation doctrine as applied to Church–State relations will be focused upon. Thirdly, further zooming in, the special position of secularism and the protection of secularism as a legitimate aim of restrictions to the freedom to manifest one's religion will be highlighted. Fourthly, a connection will be made with duties of reasonable accommodation on grounds of religion in terms of the prohibition of discrimination (and the lack thereof in the jurisprudence of the Court so far). Finally, an appraisal will be made of potential future developments or hope for the future in this respect.

I. Problems with the margin of appreciation doctrine in general as conceptualized (and used) by the European Court of Human Rights

Prior to setting out the different tensions surrounding the margin of appreciation doctrine, it is essential to clarify the meaning of this doctrine, and what it refers to.

a. State discretion and margin of appreciation

There are several ways in which states are entitled to some discretion pertaining to the way in which they fulfill their human rights obligations[3] in addition to under the ECHR. First of all, human rights obligations of states can be considered as obligations of results. A particular result needs to be achieved, but there is a choice of means.[4] There are often a variety of ways in which particular human rights obligations can be satisfied, especially when it concerns positive state obligations. The negative obligations of non-interference, that used to be focused upon in terms of the ECHR and other civil and political rights conventions, seem to be rather straightforward in the sense that there is only one way to deal with this: not to interfere or not to undertake particular actions. Still, over time the European Court has steadily expanded the range of positive state obligations incumbent on state parties to the ECHR. There exists a rather extensive jurisprudence underscoring the vital importance of positive obligations in order to achieve an

3 See also J. Rivers, "Proportionality and Variable Intensity Review," 65 *Cambridge Law Journal* 174 (2006), 191–201.

4 This can be compared with the state obligations concerning EU directives.

effective protection of the fundamental rights concerned.[5] The focus is then on the effective protection of fundamental rights, and it is readily understandable that the ways of fulfilling these positive obligations do not need to be identical in all countries. Secondly, human rights are generally considered to impose a bottom line, a minimum threshold. States cannot sink below this minimum, but various degrees or levels of compliance can be envisaged, including some that are rather minimal in approach. In other words, human rights do not require states to adopt the highest level of protection, as long as what they do is "good enough."[6]

While these two "forms" of state discretion pertaining to human rights obligations seem entirely acceptable, that is less evidently the case for the third form of discretion, more particularly the margin of appreciation doctrine of the Court. Following this doctrine, the Court leaves states some discretion in determining whether a particular limitation of a human right amounts to either a legitimate and thus proportionate limitation or to a violation of the human right concerned.

Most human rights are not absolute and states are allowed to limit the enjoyment of these rights under certain conditions. When these conditions are met, the limitation is "legitimate" and does not amount to a violation of the right concerned. While in principle in the ECHR one has to have regard for the limitation clause of the particular right concerned,[7] a certain "system" emerges across the limitation clauses:[8] in addition to a certain base in national law for the limitation, the latter also needs to be proportionate to a particular legitimate aim. The proportionality requirement[9] tends to be the one that receives most attention, the one that plays the most prevalent role in the evaluation of the legitimacy of the limitation. The

---

5 Inter alia A. R. Mowbrai, *The Development of Positive Obligations Under the European Convention on Human Rights by the European Court of Human Rights* (Hart Publishing 2004).

6 Y. Arai-Takahashi, *The Margin of Appreciation Doctrine and the Principle of Proportionality in the Jurisprudence of the European Court of Human Rights* (Intersentia 2002), 237; P. Mahoney, "Marvelous Richness of Diversity or Invidious Cultural Relativism?" 19 *Human Rights Law Journal* 1 (1998), 3.

7 Some national and international human rights documents/instruments work with a general limitation clause instead: inter alia the Universal Declaration of Human Rights (article 29, 2) and the South African Bill of Rights (section 36).

8 By the way, although in principle only applying to negative obligations arising from those rights which contain limitation clauses, the doctrine of legitimate limitations has also come to play a part regarding positive state obligations—*mutatis mutandis*: in the end a "fair balance" test applies. See also K. Henrard, *Mensenrechten vanuit internationaal en nationaal perspectief* (BJU 2008), 194–200 (and references therein).

9 It is possible to distinguish different dimensions of the proportionality principle (see also R. Alexy, A *Theory of Constitutional Rights* (OUP 2001), 397) but the one that is mostly used by supervisory bodies is the requirement of a reasonable relationship between limitation on the one hand and legitimate aim on the other: inter alia Y. Arai, "The System of Restrictions," in *Theory and Practice of the European Convention on Human Rights* (P. Van Dijk, F. Van Hoof, A. van Rijn and L. Zwaak, eds, Intersentia 2006), 341; J.H. Gerards,

margin of appreciation doctrine is "attached" as it were to that requirement. In other words, states are granted a certain level of discretion to determine whether or not a particular limitation is proportionate to the legitimate aim invoked.[10]

Importantly, this margin of appreciation is used for both negative and positive state obligations. In terms of the negative state obligations the question is whether the state has gone too far; while for positive state obligations the question is whether the state has done enough. In view of the above statement about different legitimate ways of fulfilling one's positive state obligations, it will not come as a surprise that the ECtHR tends to leave states a wide(r) margin concerning positive state obligations.[11]

This doctrine of the margin of appreciation is related to the supposed fact that national authorities are better placed to make the proportionality assessment because of their exposure to and "knowledge of local particularities."[12] When tying this doctrine to the idea of human rights as minimum threshold, the margin of appreciation concerns the delineation in particular cases of this minimum threshold. To some extent this seems acceptable, in that the evaluation of whether a particular limitation is disproportionate or not depends on all relevant circumstances of the case, hence these "local particularities" and the supposed knowledge of these particularities do matter (in this respect).

When the Court grants a wide margin of appreciation, it quickly adds that this goes hand in hand with European supervision.[13] In other words, the Court itself indicates that the supervisory role of the ECtHR is supposed to be meaningful. The question is now whether this supervision is indeed meaningful, and how this translates in terms of the protection and promotion of religious diversity in the workplace.

b. Critique of the margin of appreciation doctrine of the ECtHR

The ECtHR is the international court that has most prominently and most explicitly developed and used a margin of appreciation doctrine. Other supervisory bodies are hesitant to use it or even explicitly reject it, like the Human Rights Committee supervising the International Covenant on Civil and Political Rights (ICCPR). Over the years several strands of critique have been formulated against the margin of appreciation doctrine as developed and used by the ECtHR. Here we

---

"Gelijke Behandeling en het EVRM: van krachteloze waarborg naar norm met tanden," 30 *NJCM Bulletin* 167 (2004), 180.

10 See also J. H. Gerards, "Pluralism, Deference and the Margin of Appreciation Doctrine," 17 *European Law Journal* 80 (2011), 106.

11 J. Van de Lanotte and Y. Haeck (eds), *Handboek EVRM: Algemene Beginselen* (Intersentia 2005), 101. See also J. Schokkenbroek, "The System of Restrictions," in *Theory and Practice of the European Convention on Human Rights* (P. van Dijk, F. van Hoof, A. van Rijn and L. Zwaak, eds, Intersentia 2006), 349.

12 Inter alia Gerards, *supra* note 10, 110.

13 ECtHR (Grand Chamber) 18 March 2011, *Lautsi* v. *Italy*, App. No. 30814/06, par. 70; ECtHR (Grand Chamber) 10 November 2005, *Leyla Sahin* v. *Turkey*, App. No. 44774/98, par. 110.

will primarily focus on the more fundamental problems with thinking in terms of a margin of appreciation for states, so as to argue for a reduced "use" and importance of this doctrine, while in the end also touching on problems regarding the (inconsistent and non-principled) application of this doctrine.

Granting states a margin of appreciation involves two interrelated tensions: one in terms of having an international supervisory system, the other in terms of basic principles concerning legitimate limitations to human rights.

b.1 First tension: in terms of having an international supervisory system

On the one hand it needs to be acknowledged that by ratifying the Convention states accept a system of international supervision and allow the ECtHR to supervise their actions and inactions for compliance with the Convention. In other words, contracting state parties accept that the ECtHR has the final word in this respect.[14] The preamble of the Convention also clearly envisages an increasing convergence between the contracting parties.[15] This would seem to imply that it is accepted and expected of the ECtHR to take the lead in terms of the delineation of states' human rights obligations. This means at least that the supervision needs to be meaningful. Supervision should not be the exception but rather the rule, and should definitely not be reduced to virtually no supervision.

On the other hand, total uniformity is neither a necessity nor a possibility. The exact parameters of state obligations differ between countries in view of the "local" context and particularities.[16] Consequently, a measure of flexibility is essential and it is important to leave some discretion to states so as to determine what is needed in their particular context. The margin of appreciation doctrine tends to be justified on the basis of "subsidiarity" in the sense that the international supervisory mechanisms are subsidiary to the national ones.[17] This in turn implies that the primary responsibility to respect fundamental rights lies with the states.[18]

Both views are intuitively "right," at least to some extent. So the crucial question is where to draw the line for the respective spheres of "authority"? In which respects and to what extent is state discretion concerning human rights

14 In the words of Yutaka Arai: "the Court has consistently emphasized that it is for the Court to give the final ruling on whether the limitations as applied are compatible with the Convention" (Y. Arai, "The System of Restrictions," in *Theory and Practice of the European Convention on Human Rights* (P. Van Dijk et al., eds, Intersentia 2006), 341.

15 ECHR, preambular paragraphs 4–5: "considering that the aim of the Council of Europe is the achievement of greater unity between its Members … reaffirming their profound belief in those Fundamental Freedoms which are the foundational of justice and peace in the world and are best maintained … on the other by a common understanding and observance of Human Rights upon which they depend."

16 See also Mahoney 1998, *supra* note 6, 12.

17 See in particular ECtHR 7 December 1976, *Handyside* v. *UK*, App. No. 5493/72, par. 48.

18 Inter alia G. Letsas, *A Theory of Interpretation of the European Convention on Human Rights* (OUP 2007), 83.

acceptable? This in turn requires one to consider what exactly subsidiarity is about, and what does it mean that the international supervisory system is subsidiary to the national system and that the primary responsibility for respecting human rights falls to the national system?

It means that the national authorities should not violate these rights themselves; and that there should be redress at the national level in case of an unjustified infringement.[19] However, this all presumes political will to respect fundamental rights as well as a flawless system where no mistakes are made. Reality tends to be different. Hence it is important, even essential, that there is a system of international supervision that kicks in and assesses the situation "objectively." Indeed, the primary responsibility in relation to the respect of human rights lies with the states. But it is exactly that, the primary responsibility, not the ultimate one. Allowing the last word to the states themselves would defeat the purpose of having an international supervisory system at all. The fact that national authorities are "closer" to the local particularities, the circumstances and emotions on the ground, might also make them more prone to be influenced by "the illusion of the day" (and the related pressures).[20] Put differently, concerning sensitive situations and questions, it would be equally justifiable to say that these are better decided—or supervised—at a more "remote" level, exactly because of the distance from local public opinion and the related "change in societal circumstances."[21]

What does seem acceptable in terms of subsidiarity or what are acceptable implications of the subsidiarity rationale? It is beyond the confines of this chapter to be exhaustive in this respect, but a good example seems to be that the establishment of the facts is for the national authorities, at least by way of starting point. Similarly, it makes sense to have consideration for the weighing process that has been conducted by the national authorities: to the extent that this has been done meticulously and with regard to all relevant interests, there appears good reason to grant states a considerable margin of appreciation.[22] Still, in the end and notwithstanding the margin of appreciation for states, the ECtHR's weighing of all the relevant interests at stake might be such that the interference is considered disproportionate.

---

19 This is also reflected in one of the admissibility requirements of a claim before the ECtHR: the need to have exhausted all national remedies (see Article 35 of the ECHR).

20 This is a translation of an expression often used in Dutch: *de waan van de dag*.

21 These words are used by the ECtHR in one of its steady line of jurisprudence following which the ECHR is a living instrument which needs to be interpreted in line with present-day conditions: see inter alia G. Letsas, *A Theory of Interpretation of the European Convention on Human Rights* (OUP 2007), 58–79; S. C. Prebensen, "Evolutive Interpretation of the European Convention on Human Rights," in *Protecting Human Rights: The European Perspective* (P. Mahoney and R. Rysdal, eds, Heymans 2000), 1127–1137. See also *infra*.

22 The ECtHR generally requires the national courts to show in their argumentation that they have carefully weighed the conflicting interests *in concreto*: see inter alia ECtHR 25 May 1993, *Kokkinakis* v. *Greece*, App. No. 14307/88, par. 49; ECtHR 6 February 2001, *Tammer* v. *Estonia*, App. No. 41205/98, par. 69.

b.2 Second tension: The value of human rights as fundamental rights and the related doctrine of legitimate limitations to human rights

The second tension involved with the granting of a margin of appreciation to states concerns the implications of leaving national authorities a margin of appreciation to determine when a limitation amounts to a violation of the human right concerned. The other side of the coin is that this actually implies a reduction of the level of scrutiny or the intensity of review by the Court itself. Indeed, the margin of appreciation is not always equally extensive or wide. In the words of the Court: "the scope of the margin of appreciation will vary according to the circumstances, the subject matter and its background."[23] Clearly, the more extensive the margin of appreciation, the lower the level of scrutiny and thus the lower the actual protection offered by the ECtHR. However, this implication of the margin of appreciation doctrine seems difficult to reconcile with one of the basic principles pertaining to legitimate limitations to human rights and the underlying recognition of the essential value of human rights as fundamental rights.

It was already pointed out that limitations are only legitimate when they comply with the conditions imposed in the respective limitation clauses. Notwithstanding the variety among limitation clauses that can be noted, there is not only a certain system that can be identified but also general principles that apply to all limitation clauses and their application. The one that is particularly relevant here is that exceptions or grounds for legitimate limitations to human rights need to be interpreted restrictively;[24] this as opposed to the scope of application of fundamental rights which needs to be interpreted broadly. It is indeed not difficult to understand that the rationale of a system of protection of human rights considers protection of human rights as a baseline, while limitations are the exception. In other words, the starting point is that once something falls within the scope of application of a fundamental right, it needs to be protected; and when public authorities limit the enjoyment of these rights, they need to have good reasons and have to put forward specific, concrete reasons why they would be allowed to limit the enjoyment of a fundamental right.[25]

In terms of supervision this arguably implies that supervision of human rights is the baseline, and does not leave a margin of appreciation to states. It was already highlighted that there are different types of state discretion, several of which are acceptable, as there is indeed no need for uniformity. However, the determination of the "bottom line" should be kept in check, and in this respect supervision by the ECtHR should not be made insignificant. Put differently, granting states a margin of appreciation concerning the minimum threshold seems to be antithetical to the

23 Inter alia ECtHR 27 March 1998, *Petrovic* v. *Austria*, App. No. 20458/92, par. 38.

24 Inter alia N. Jayawickrama, *The Judicial Application of Human Rights Law: National, Regional and International Jurisprudence* (CUP 2002), 184.

25 Inter alia T. Loenen, *Geloof in het geding: Juridische grenzen van religieus pluralisme in het perspectief van de mensenrechten* (Sdu 2006), 41; G. Pitt, "Religion or Belief: Aiming at the Right Target?" in *Equality Law in an Enlarged European Union: Understanding the Article 13 Directives* (H. Meenan, ed., CUP 2007), 209.

entire idea that human rights are enshrined in an international convention and their protection is supervised by an international supervisory mechanism.

It should also be noted that in other respects the Court is willing to adopt particular interpretative devices that denote a more pro-active and demanding stance. Particularly relevant in this regard is the doctrine according to which the concepts in the ECHR have an autonomous meaning, and do not necessarily mirror the meaning that these concepts have in the national legal systems of the contracting parties.[26] This obviously reduces the scope for national particularities.

Similarly, the living instrument doctrine[27] paves the way for progressive developments in the jurisprudence, in which the ECtHR takes up a more guiding, directive role, de facto narrowing the margin of appreciation of states. On the one hand this doctrine seems to confirm the subsidiarity principle in that it concerns the need for the standards to be in tune with the "present day situations" in the Member States. This appears to say that the states and sentiments of the national populations determine the reference point for the meaning of the convention standards. However, it is still the ECtHR which decides when the "turn" is made, and those states that have not yet developed to that extent will just have to follow suit. Hence, in the end it is the ECtHR which takes control and sets the stage.

The preceding argumentation is meant to corroborate that, in line with the central interpretative principle of human rights, the emphasis should be on the supervision by the international supervisory body, while the margin of appreciation (and judicial self restraint) should be the exception, meriting a narrow construction. Indeed, regardless of how extensive the margin of appreciation left to states, the international control exercised should still be meaningful, and even dominant.

Furthermore, from a human rights and a related "rule of law" perspective it also needs to be remarked that allowing states a margin of appreciation regarding the way in which they implement human rights carries the risk of negating the need for uniformity and the related concerns of legal certainty, as well as predictability.[28] This actually ties in with criticisms of the way in which the margin of appreciation doctrine is applied: as it stands, the case law of the Court does not provide clear guidelines as to the limits of this margin of appreciation and how it monitors these supposed limits.[29] The Court does recognize that this margin is not always

26 Inter alia Letsas, *supra* note 2, 42–43.

27 For a nice analysis of the jurisprudence of the ECtHR in this respect see inter alia Prebensen, *supra* note 21, 1127–1137 and Letsas, *supra* note 2, 58–79.

28 See inter alia on the importance of the rule of law: T. Bingham, *The Rule of Law* (Penguin 2010), 3–9.

29 S. Greer, "Balancing and the European Court of Human Rights: A Contribution to the Habermas-Alexy Debate," 63 *Cambridge Law Journal* 412 (2004), 423–425; P. Mahoney, "Marvelous Richness of Diversity or Invidious Cultural Relativism?" 19 *Human Rights Law Journal* 1 (1998), 1; J. Schokkenbroek, "The Basis, Nature and Application of the Margin of Appreciation Doctrine in the Case Law of the European Court of Human Rights," 19 *Human Rights Law Journal* 30 (1998), 36.

equally extensive, and certain factors are even singled out as being relevant in this respect.[30] However, because these factors are not consistently, or in any event not systematically, applied, the margin of appreciation doctrine is on uneasy terms with these basic values of the rule of law.

II. Problems with the broad margin of appreciation the European Court of Human Rights grants states when Church–State relations are in play

While the preceding argumentation focused on the margin of appreciation doctrine in general, the following analysis will zoom in on the use of this doctrine in relation to Church–State relations. Following a succinct introduction about the concept of "Church–State relations," the way in which the Court addresses these Church–State relations is discussed. Subsequently, the role of the common European standard in this respect is analyzed. Further, the problematic nature of a broad margin of appreciation for a matter which is intimately linked to the freedom of religion is denounced. Finally, the relevance of the prohibition of discrimination on the basis of religion is addressed.

a. The concept "Church–State relations"

It is important to remark that Church–State relations is a matter which is not confined to (the implications of) the separation of church and state,[31] but also refers to more substantive ideals pertaining to the content of state policy, the duty of state neutrality pertaining to religions being key. Church–State relations is thus a broad concept, although it does not cover just any matter pertaining to religion, as will be discussed further.

b. Limits to the margin of appreciation regarding Church–State relations: European control to what effect?

What does the Court mean when it underscores that the broad margin of appreciation left to states concerning Church–State relations goes hand in hand with European supervision? Strikingly, according to the Court, this wide margin of appreciation would imply that even a system of a state church would not necessarily violate state parties' duties in terms of the ECHR. The bottom line seems to be the rather vague criterion that the freedom to manifest one's religion should be enjoyed by adherents of all religions present in the state or the requirement that the necessary

30 See also Gerards, *supra* note 10, 107–108.

31 According to Wibren van der Burg (*Het ideaal van de neutrale staat. Inclusieve, exclusieve en compenserende visies op godsdienst en cultuur* (BJU 2009), 18) the legally, historically and philosophically most appropriate perspective considers this to concern the institutional relationship between church and public authorities/government.

guarantees should be in place to ensure that the freedom of others to have or change a religion is respected.[32] What is in any event not possible is coercion by the state to adopt a particular religion or to refuse someone the right to leave the church.[33]

In other words, the Court acknowledges that the freedom of religion imposes some constraints on the states' freedom to adopt a particular system of Church–State relations. The questions raised here are: is this supervision in terms of the freedom of religion done in a complete and appropriate way (d) and are there other criteria that should be used but have been passed over (avoided) by the Court (e)? These questions are preceded by a critical analysis of the impact of a (perceived) common European standard on the determination of the extent of the margin of appreciation in particular cases (c).

c. The "common European standard" and the margin of appreciation for states

Prior to discussing the identification as well as implications of a common European standard pertaining to Church–State relations, some more general critical remarks about the way in which the Court uses the common European standard are equally relevant.

c.1 In general

It has already been mentioned that the margin of appreciation is not always equally extensive. The Court has identified in its jurisprudence factors that influence the extent of the margin of appreciation in particular instances. The Court does not use these factors in any systematic way though. Hence it is not surprising that the exact categorization of the distinctive factors and sub-factors by various academics is not identical.[34] However, the following criteria are commonly enumerated: 1) the existence of a common European standard; 2) the nature (the particular importance) of the fundamental right concerned; 3) the type of legitimate aim pursued by the state; 4) the prevalence of general policy choices (financial implications); and 5) whether a case concerns conflicting rights.

Zooming in on the common European standard, when a firm common European standard exists for a particular matter and a particular state has a markedly lower or incongruent standard, this is indeed suspect and requires closer scrutiny. However, a fundamental critique seems justified when it comes to the position of the Court that the absence of a common European standard should lead to granting a broad margin of appreciation to states. After all, from a human rights protection point of view it can be argued that exactly in circumstances where there is no consensus,

---

32 C. Evans, *Freedom of Religion under the ECHR* (OUP 2001), 50.

33 ECtHR 23 October 1990, *Darby* v. *Sweden*, App. No. 1581/85, par. 45. See also ECtHR 25 May 1993, *Kokkinakis* v. *Greece*, App. No. 14307/88, par. 46–50; ECtHR 29 August 1996, *Manoussakis* v. *Greece*, App. No. 18748/91, par. 36.

34 See Gerards, *supra* note 10, 107 and 108, and the references to other authors found there.

the international supervisory mechanism should give direction and guidance and "oblige" the dissenters to follow suit. To the extent that it does not do so, it neglects non-dominant, disadvantaged groups, like minorities, by allowing, confirming and even strengthening the dominant position (the status quo). While it may be disproportionate and inappropriate to force all states to adopt a uniform approach, a narrow margin of appreciation need not require the adoption of one particular model. It definitely seems possible to provide more guidelines, and to identify boundaries that should not be crossed in terms of human rights obligations.[35]

c.2 As applied to Church–State relations

When comparing the countries that are members of the Council of Europe there is indeed a great variety as to the relations between church(es) and states. The preceding paragraphs have argued that the absence of a common European standard should not necessarily lead to granting states a broad margin of appreciation.

In addition, it needs to be underscored that while there may be a great diversity between the Member States of the Council of Europe, at the same time there is a clear, albeit slow, trend to move away from state churches, and a trend towards the reduction of the relative weight of state churches and towards granting more extensive rights to other religions. This tendency has been most notable in Sweden, Finland, Italy, Spain and Portugal, while also in other Scandinavian countries the forces calling for the abolishment of the state church, or at least abandoning former privileges of the National Church so as to place them on an equal footing with the other churches and religions, are becoming stronger.[36] In other words there does

35 See also K. Henrard, *The Ambiguous Relationship between Religious Minorities and Fundamental (Minority) Rights* (BJU 2011).

36 C. Evans and C. A. Thomas, "Church-State Relations in the European Court of Human Rights," 31 *Brigham Young University Law Review* 699 (2006), 706 and J. Temperman, *State-Religion Relationships and Human Rights Law: Towards a Right to Religiously Neutral Governance* (Martinus Nijhoff 2010), 61, who points out that "in Europe alone since the late 18th century, dozens of churches and religions have been disestablished, the disestablishment of the Church of Sweden in January 2000 being the most recent example." See also the contributions by O. Einar Dorum ("The State and Church Moving towards Dissolution in Norway") and Ingemund Hägg ("Sweden – Secular Population and Non-secular State") in *Separation of Church and State in Europe with Views on Sweden, Norway, the Netherlands, Belgium, France, Spain, Italy, Slovenia and Greece* (F. de Beaufort, I. Hägg and P. van Schie, eds, European Liberal Forum 2008). See also, for a more general perspective, G. Ercolessi and I. Hagg, "Towards Religious Neutrality of Public Institutions in Europe: Introduction," in *id.*, 1–16. See also L. Bloss, *European Law of Religion – Organizational and Institutional Analysis of National Systems and their Implications for the Future European Integration Process*, Jean Monnet Working Paper 13/03, 67–68, where she points out furthermore that even despite considerable differences between the various models that still exist, a closer analysis allows one to detect significant similarities too.

seem to be an (emerging) common European standard that state churches are not compatible with the obligations under the ECHR.[37]

While there is no need for uniformity, and a degree of diversity pertaining to Church–State relations is acceptable, there in fact does seem to be an emerging common European standard about one bottom line, namely that a state church (at least) would not be acceptable (in terms of human rights obligations). In the following paragraphs, this is further argued in terms of limits that flow from the freedom of religion in itself and in combination with the prohibition of discrimination.

d. Problems with a broad margin of appreciation in Church–State relations related to the freedom of religion

The Court describes the freedom of religion in a steady line of jurisprudence as a cornerstone or one of the foundations of a democratic society,[38] which is the reference point for the ECHR system. This arguably points towards a narrow margin of appreciation for the states concerning the freedom of religion. This narrow margin is further corroborated by the fact that the limitation clause of the freedom of religion accepts very few "legitimate aims" in comparison with the other rights (e.g. the right to respect for privacy). A narrow margin of appreciation concerning the freedom of religion can be argued to require implications for the discretion left to states when they make choices about the relations between church and state. In any event, the importance of the freedom of religion seems to call for

37 This remark about an alleged emerging common European standard can be related to several other problems pertaining to the way in which the ECtHR decides on the existence or absence of a common European standard. The ECtHR has not established clear criteria, let alone a consistent approach for the determination of a European consensus. The term itself would denote a comparative investigation among European states, but the ECtHR in some cases pays more attention to the developments on the world level, by considering the existence of international (or regional) courts, or even the practice in a particular non-European country (like the US). In any event, whether or not there is a common European standard is often a question of interpretation without a conclusive answer. Consequently, it is not surprising that marked differences of opinion exist about the existence versus absence of such a European consensus. The dissenting opinions in some of the judgments of the ECtHR are telling in this respect. To the extent that the dissents tend to criticize the denial of a common European standard, this gives the impression that the ECtHR is too demanding in this respect. More problematically, this in turn gives the impression that the ECtHR prefers to give states a wide margin of appreciation (and thus to abdicate to some extent its supervisory role). This also seems to be confirmed by those instances where the ECtHR starts by accepting a European consensus about a certain theme, only to immediately add that this consensus does not reach as far as to concern the particular question at issue in the case.

38 Inter alia ECtHR 3 May 2007, *case of 97 Members of the Gldani Congregation of Jehovah's Witnesses and 4 others* v. *Georgia*, App. No. 71156/01, par. 130.

a strict scrutiny of the implications for this fundamental right of choices pertaining to Church–State relations.

However, the Court chooses to focus on the fact that there is no common European standard pertaining to the delicate question of relations between church and state in order to justify granting states a wide margin of appreciation. This can be argued to amount to an abdication (to some extent) of its own supervisory role. Several judgments indeed give the impression that the Court does not want to second-guess the assessment and choices of the national authorities in this respect (be it for strict separation or for a state church). Excellent examples of this are the cases pertaining to prohibitions of wearing the headscarf in the education sphere, where the Court was swayed by vague and general allegations of threats to public order (a secular legal order) to accept these far-reaching limitations as legitimate.[39] The Court's steady line of jurisprudence, according to which having a state church would not necessarily be contrary to the Convention, is similarly difficult to reconcile with the freedom of religion, and more particularly the related duty of state neutrality.[40] As will be more fully argued *infra*, the acceptance of a state church system is also problematic in view of the prohibition of discrimination on the basis of religion.[41]

A related point is the jurisprudence pertaining to positive state obligations under Article 9 of the ECHR which is remarkably poor in comparison with the vast and rich body of positive obligations the Court has identified in terms of other Convention Articles (like Article 8). Positive obligations under Article 9 of the ECHR have been more or less confined to the sphere of protection against acts of intolerance by public authorities and private parties.[42] The importance of these

39 See also T. Loenen and A. Terlouw, "Het EVRM en het Turkse verbod: de zaak van Leyla Sahin vs. Turkije" [The ECtHR and the Turkish Prohibition: the Case of Leyla Sahin v. Turkey], 32 *NJCM Bulletin* 213 (2006), 228–230.

40 Inter alia K. H. Ladeur and I. Augsberg, "The Myth of the Neutral State: The Relationship Between State and Religion in the Face of New Challenges," 8 *German Law Journal* 143 (2007), 143 and 146. See also D. H. Davis, "The Evolution of Religious Freedom as a Universal Human Right: Examining the Role of the 1981 United Nations Declaration on the Elimination of All Forms of Intolerance and of Discrimination based on Religion or Belief," 27 *Brigham Young University Law Review* 217 (2002), 217.

41 Inter alia P. G. Danchin, "Suspect Symbols: Value Pluralism as a Theory of Religious Freedom in International Law," 33 *Yale Journal of International Law* 1 (2008), 13; P. Cumper, "The UK and the UN Declaration on the Elimination of Intolerance and Discrimination based on Religion and Belief," 32 *Emory International Law Review* 13 (2007), 24.

42 See also Ministerie van BZK, *Nota Grondrechten in de Pluriforme Samenleving* [*Report on Fundamental Rights in a Pluriform Society*], (2004), 8, which identifies a certain degree of positive duties of care on the part of the government concerning the facilitation of religious manifestations, especially in relation to persons under a special regime like prisoners.

De Jong discusses in his overview of positive state obligations in respect of the freedom of religion or belief only duties of due diligence to prevent, punish, investigate or redress the harm caused by acts of private persons or entities: see D. de Jong, "The Legal Obligations of State and Non-State Actors in Respect of the Protection of Freedom

positive obligations for the effective enjoyment of the freedom of religion is also on point for duties to actively and positively accommodate[43] the needs of religious groups (often religious minorities).[44] These duties of positive accommodation would seem to be just as important to realize religious pluralism and an effective enjoyment of the freedom to manifest one's religion. However, also pertaining to the positive obligation side of state obligations under Article 9 of the ECHR, the Court tends to leave the contracting states a wide margin of appreciation. Here also it can be argued that the central importance of the freedom of religion for the convention system, and the importance of positive state obligations for the effective enjoyment of fundamental rights, should imply that positive accommodation (of religious manifestations)[45] should follow unless there are strong policy considerations not to do so.[46] This more welcoming attitude towards positive accommodation would in turn appear to constrain states' discretion concerning Church–State relations.

---

of Thought, Conscience or Religion or Belief," 3 *Religion and Human Rights* 1 (2008), 7–10. See also M. T. Parker, "The Freedom to Manifest Religious Belief: an Analysis of the Necessity Clauses of the ICCPR and the ECHR," 17 *Duke Journal of Comparative and International Law* 91 (2006), 98.

43 See also *infra* on duties of positive accommodation in terms of the right to equal treatment.

44 See also K. Boyle, "Freedom of Religion in International Law," in *Religion, Human Rights and International Law: A Critical Examination of Islamic State Practice* (J. Rehman and S. C. Bréau, eds, Martinus Nijhoff 2007), 29.

45 See also P. Bosset, *Reflections on the Scope and Limits of the Duty of Reasonable Accommodation in the Field of Education* (Cat. 2.120-4.20.2, February 2005), 4–5. For an analogous argument regarding the US religion clause, see inter alia B. Diniz de Ayala, "Church-State Relations, Religious Human Rights, Pluralism and Equality," 17 *ERPL/REDP* 77 (2006), 94.

46 See inter alia B. Tahzib-Lie, "Interdiction of Religious Discrimination: Problems that Members of Minority Religious and Belief Communities Experience in the Exercise of their Freedom of Religion or Belief," in *International Protection of Religious Freedom* (J. F. Flauss, ed., Bruylant 2002), 60; D. Shelton, "Conscientious Objection and Religious Groups," in *International Protection of Religious Freedom* (J. F. Flauss, ed., Bruylant 2002), 194–195, and the contributions of Javaid Rehman ("A Clash of Civilisations and a Conflict of Cities," 189–194) and Peter Cumper ("The Accommodation of Uncontroversial Religious Practices," 205–209) in *Religious Pluralism and Human Rights in Europe: Where to Draw the Line?* (M. L. P. Loenen and J. E. Goldschmidt, eds, Intersentia 2007). See also Veit Bader's ideal of the associative democracy, since this (inter alia) requires or presupposes the maximal accommodation of religious practices/manifestations of religions: V. Bader, *Secularism or Democracy: Associational Governance of Religious Diversity* (Amsterdam University Press 2007), 20, 27 and 84. According to Bader, liberal democracy requires some flexible (not absolute) accommodation of religious practices, see inter alia Bader 2007, 136, 138, 140, and especially 164.

e. Broad margin of appreciation in Church–State relations and the prohibition of discrimination on the basis of religion

Choices made concerning Church–State relations tend to entail differential treatment between religions. Hence this needs to be scrutinized in terms of the prohibition of discrimination on the basis of religion. Especially when particular religions get a special status which goes hand in hand with privileges and advantages, and even when it only concerns a symbolic status, this sends out signals of insiders and outsiders, of first and second class religions. It is common knowledge that the prohibition of discrimination does not prohibit every differentiation. Notwithstanding the specificities of each non-discrimination regime, the criteria of "reasonable and objective justification" reflect a common baseline.[47] This in turn can be broken down in two requirements: there needs to be a legitimate aim, and the differential treatment needs to be proportionate to that legitimate aim. Following steady jurisprudence, the ECHR supervisory bodies traditionally did not scrutinize differentiations very strictly. Over time, particular grounds were qualified as "suspect" and would trigger heightened scrutiny resulting in a presumption of illegality. The protection against instances of invidious discrimination on a particular ground would thus be stronger when that ground is considered to be a suspect class.

Grounds are considered suspect when they concern characteristics that are *in se* irrelevant for someone's functioning in society, and/or innate characteristics or ones that are so intimately connected to one's identity that one should not be expected to change that in order to be treated equally and fairly, and/or there has been a history of discrimination on the basis of that ground.[48] Grounds that are generally considered to be suspect include race and gender. Religion arguably also fulfills the criteria of "suspect class."[49] Furthermore, it is generally recognized that there is an extensive overlap between religion on the one hand and race-ethnicity on the other.[50]

47 See also HRC, General Comment no 18, par. 13 and M. Bell, "Direct Discrimination," in *Cases, Materials and Text on National, Supranational and International Non-Discrimination Law* (D. Schiek, L. Waddington and M. Bell, eds, Hart 2007), 269–271.

48 See inter alia J. H. Gerards, *Rechterlijke Toetsing aan het Gelijkheidsbeginsel* (Sdu 2002) 85–91.

49 D. J. Sullivan, "Advancing the Freedom of Religion or Belief through the UN Declaration on the Elimination of Religious Intolerance and Discrimination," 82 *American Journal of International Law* 487 (1988), 488 and 508.

50 Inter alia E. Darian Smith, *Religion, Race, Rights: Landmarks in the History of Modern Anglo-American Law* (Hart 2010), 36–41. This is also noted by the Advisory Committee of the Framework Convention for the Protection of National Minorities in its evaluations of state reports, for example in Georgia (2009), par. 75; it in fact seems to be the case that religious identity is increasingly associated in the public perception with national identity.

However, there are several indications that religion is not generally—not full-heartedly—accepted as such a suspect class. Religion may be one of the grounds of prohibited discrimination that tends to be enumerated explicitly in Article 14 of the ECHR, but that is not in itself conclusive.[51] It is, in any event, striking that it took over 20 years to achieve consensus within the UN on a Declaration on the Elimination of all Forms of Intolerance and of Discrimination based on Religion or Belief, while this was virtually immediately realized for race. Furthermore, the not legally binding Declaration on Racial Discrimination was equally swiftly followed by the 1965 Convention on the Elimination of all forms of Racial Discrimination. Notwithstanding several calls to develop a legally binding convention for religious discrimination, this is clearly not on the cards for the foreseeable future.[52]

Furthermore, the jurisprudence of the ECtHR does not fully confirm this suspect status of religion.[53] Arguably the court recognized this suspect status of religion in *Hoffmann* v. *Austria*, a 1993 case pertaining to Jehovah's witnesses. In *Hoffmann*, where a custody decision had been decided negatively for the mother, the ECtHR held that "a distinction based essentially on a difference in religion alone is not acceptable."[54] This seems indeed an indication that according to the Court differentiations on the basis of religion are suspect. However, until recently the Court has not repeated this statement, or used its more common "very weighty reasons" language, and thus not clearly confirmed the suspect status of religion. This was especially noticeable in cases with more or less the same factual background as *Hoffmann*,[55] or other cases in which discrimination on the basis of religion was a key component.[56] While in several of these cases the Court *de facto* scrutinized rather strictly, this is not always the case. For example, in *Ismaelova*

51 Indeed, several of the explicitly enumerated grounds in article 14 of the ECHR have not (yet) been considered as suspect class, like political opinion, social status and property. On the other hand, grounds not enumerated have been qualified as suspect, like sexual orientation.

52 Inter alia C. Evans, "Religious Freedom in European Human Rights Law: The Search for a Guiding Conception," in *Religion and International Law* (M. W. Janis and C. Evans, eds, Martinus Nijhoff Publishers 1999), 387; J. Temperman, "25th Anniversary Commemoration of the Adoption of the 1981 UN Declaration on the Elimination of Intolerance and Discrimination Based on Religion or Belief: A Report," 2 *Religion and Human Rights* 19 (2007).

53 See also C. Evans and C. A. Thomas, "Church-State Relations in the European Court of Human Rights," 31 *Brigham Young University Law Review* 699 (2006), who underscore that the Court has taken a generous approach to state claims of an objective and reasonable basis for making a distinction between religions.

54 ECtHR 23 June 1993, *Hoffmann* v. *Austria,* App. No. 12875/87, par. 36.

55 For example, ECtHR 16 December 2003, *Palau-Martinez* v. *France*, App. No. 64927/01.

56 D. De Prins, S. Sottiaux and J. Vrielink, *Handboek Discriminatierecht* (Kluwer 2005), 30–31. There was not even a hint at this special status of religion as ground of differentiation in the more recent Gldani case where discriminatory aspects were key.

v. *Russia*,[57] a case with a similar factual background to *Hoffmann*, the majority of the Chamber does not appear to adopt a demanding level of scrutiny at all, which is vigorously criticized by a dissent of three judges.

Especially in view of the *de facto* high scrutiny in several cases of invidious discrimination on the basis of religion, the Court's avoidance of qualifying religion explicitly as a suspect ground appears to be triggered by its need to hold on to its jurisprudence that states have a wide margin of appreciation pertaining to their choice as to the relationship between church and state.[58] Unfortunately the Court has so far not acknowledged the tension its position concerning Church–State relations creates in relation to other essential lines of jurisprudence pertaining to the freedom of religion and the prohibition of discrimination. Hence it has not made an effort to provide further guidelines on how much support a state can give a particular religion without this resulting in inappropriate pressure on others to also join that religion or in appropriate disadvantages for non-adherents.

Whether or not religion is accepted as a suspect class, a state-church model seems difficult to square with the prohibition of discrimination on the basis of religion, in the sense that there does not seem to be a reasonable and objective justification to elevate the standing of one religion over others in the public domain in a democratic society, characterized by pluralism.[59] What is more, by leaving the states a wide margin of appreciation and thus "refusing" to take a position in controversial matters, the Court actually does take a position. Accepting the decisions of the national authorities implies leaving intact *de facto* preferences given to or acquired by the culturally embedded, prevailing, majority religions, thus *de facto* disadvantaging or solidifying the disadvantages of the minority religions and their adherents.

In sum, granting states a broad margin of appreciation may in general not be a good idea, and moreover is not in line with some of the fundamental principles of human rights. This is especially problematic regarding Church–State relations, as there are additional tensions with the basic tenets of particular fundamental rights, the freedom of religion and the prohibition of discrimination on the basis of religion more specifically.[60]

---

57 ECtHR 29 November 2007, *Ismailova* v. *Russia*, App. No. 37614/02.

58 Evans and Thomas also confirm this as they put forward that the focus of the Court is very much on religious freedom (and its doctrine of a broad margin of appreciation concerning Church–State relations) while non-discrimination only plays a minor role: Evans and Thomas, *supra* note 36, 721. See also *Id.* at 723–724 where they favor a more searching scrutiny of the differential treatment between religions implicated in questions that are said to pertain to Church–State relations.

59 M. C. Nussbaum, *Liberty of Conscience: In Defense of America's Tradition of Religious Equality* (Basic Books 2008), 9, 11, 21.

60 This ambiguity concerning religion and religious rights is actually repeated in several other international jurisdictions/organizations, including the EU. The EU indeed leaves the Member States total freedom as to the choices made pertaining to Church–State relations: inter alia L. Christoffersen, "Religion as a Factor in Multi-Layered European

III. Secularism as constitutional value triggers an even wider margin of appreciation for states?

Secularism is arguably intrinsically related to state choices pertaining to Church–State relations, and according to the Court it is (supposed to be) in line with a democratic society and the values underlying it. The jurisprudence of the ECtHR seems to indicate that when a state adopts secularism as a constitutional value, this will entail an even broader margin of appreciation for that state concerning its Church–State relations in the broad sense.[61] This secularism line of jurisprudence was first of all visible in the seminal case *Refah Partisi*, pertaining to the dissolution of a political party by the Turkish Constitutional Court.[62] While the previous case law of the Court had been very critical of dissolutions of political parties in Turkey, in this case it concluded that there had not been a violation of Article 11. According to the Government, the party at stake would have implied a threat to secularism, one of the founding values of Turkey. The Court went along with the Government as it attached special weight to the alleged goal of safeguarding secularism as legitimate aim for the limitation of a fundamental right.

Subsequently, this line of argumentation has also featured prominently in cases pertaining to headscarves in education. In several of these cases the Court even appears to say that an attitude which would not be in line with the principle of secularism would not necessarily be protected by Article 9, as if such an attitude would not even fall within the scope of application of the freedom of religion.[63]

Union Legislation," in *Law and Religion in Multicultural Societies* (R. Mehdi et al., eds, Djof Publishing 2008), 114–125. For an emphasis on the potential of the non-discrimination arsenal at the disposal of the Union, see I. Rorive, "Religious Symbols in the Public Space: In Search of a European Answer," 30 *Cardozo Law Review* 2688 (2009), 2688–2693. Similarly, it may now have competence to regulate discrimination on the basis of religion, but it has chosen not to expand reasonable accommodation duties to this ground of differentiation. Overall there seems to be heightened sensitivity concerns in terms of sovereignty and national identity when religion is concerned. See also Z. Enyedi, "Conclusion: Emerging Issues in the Study of Church-State Relations," 26 *West European Politics* 218 (2010), 233, where it is underscored that "national identity, particularly on the peripheries of Europe, is often built around religious values and is linked to Church-State regimes as well. … The links between nation and religion are often recognized, but the implications of these links for Church-State relations must be more fully taken into account. These links mean that the logic of nationalism and national identity formation may have a direct impact on Church-State relations."

61 See also N. Nathwani, "Islamic Headscarves and Human Rights: A Critical Analysis of the Relevant Case Law of the European Court of Human Rights," 25 *Netherlands Quarterly of Human Rights* 221 (2007), 234.

62 ECtHR (Grand Chamber) 13 February 2003, *Refah Partisi and others* v. *Turkey*, App. No. 41340/98; 41342/98; 41343/98.

63 ECtHR (Grand Chamber) 10 November 2005, *Leyla Sahin* v. *Turkey*, App. No. 44774/98, par. 116; repeated in the cases mentioned in the following footnote.

While initially these cases concerned Turkey, more recent case law has clarified that the Court extends this line of reasoning also to France, seemingly accepting that secularism is also a key value for the French legal system.[64]

Be that as it may, the explicit references to the special value attached to secularism in the countries where it allows secularism seemingly to encroach further on the effective enjoyment of fundamental rights, would at least provide the possibility for the Court to go a different route in countries where this principle is less central. The Court seems to announce such a development by underlining in both *Dogru*[65] and *Aktas*[66] that secularism is a constitutional core value for Turkey, France and Switzerland (and thus *a contrario* not for the other Member States of the Council of Europe).

IV. Case law: Focus on religious diversity in the workplace

How does this line of jurisprudence pertaining to the margin of appreciation of states, especially concerning Church–State relations, play out in the workplace? It is first of all imperative to note that the supervisory bodies of the ECHR do not always use explicit margin of appreciation language in the employment sphere. Still, they are similarly not willing to second-guess positions taken by a national government.

The former European Commission on Human Rights had a steady line of jurisprudence revealing that it was unwilling to provide protection against dismissals of persons because employees came to work late or left early regularly in order to comply with a prescript of their religion. While several cases indeed concern Jews or Muslims, they are not confined to these religions, but, for example also concern the Seventh Day Adventist Church or "regular" Christians, albeit from minority denominations.[67] According to the Commission the refusal to respect working hours even if it is motivated by religious convictions cannot be protected

64 ECtHR 4 December 2008, *Dogru* v. *France*, App. No. 27058/05, par. 72; ECtHR 30 June 2009, *Aktas* v. *France*, App. No. 43563/08.

65 ECtHR 4 December 2008, *Dogru* v. *France*, App. No. 27058/05, par. 72.

66 ECtHR 30 June 2009, *Aktas* v. *France*, App. No. 43563/08.

67 ECommHR 3 December 1996, *Konttinen* v. *Finland*, App. No. 24949/94 concerned a man working at the state railways who joined the Seventh Day Adventist Church. That religion has Sabbath duty from sunset on Friday to Saturday. On a few Fridays during winter this meant that he had to leave early from work. His dismissal for these unauthorized absences did not even raise issues under article 9(1) as these absences were not accepted as manifestations of his religion. In *Stedman* v. *UK* a private sector employer dismissed an employee who did not want to work on Sunday. The Commission relied on its *Kontinnen* reasoning and concluded that *a fortiori* unauthorized absences from work for religious reasons are not protected in relations between private persons (there would not be a positive obligation for the state to ensure that private employers would accept this behavior from their employees).

by Article 9, paragraph 1: the dismissal would not be because of an employee's religious convictions, but for having refused to respect working hours.[68]

This line of reasoning also ties in with the restrictive approach adopted towards what qualifies as a manifestation of religion.[69] However, by denying a particular act as a manifestation of religion, the Commission (and later also the Court) substitutes its own assessment for that of the adherents of the religion. This tends to be difficult to reconcile with the interpretative restraint which is due in theological matters, since this only allows state judges to intervene in exceptional cases where the absence of religious motive is manifest.[70]

Alternatively, the Commission holds that a dismissal related to absences from work to fulfill religious observances does not amount to an interference: the person concerned had accepted the position knowing that the work schedule would prove incompatible with fulfillment of particular religious observance.[71] In other words, the Commission was not amenable to identify duties of reasonable accommodation, a line of jurisprudence which has been confirmed by the Court in the more recent judgment in *Kosteski*.[72] In its inadmissibility decision in *Dahlab* v. *Switzerland*,[73] the Court was not ready to identify duties of reasonable accommodation concerning religious dress and dress code in a particular employment setting. In this case the Court was willing to accept far-reaching restrictions on the freedom to manifest one's religion for public school teachers. *Dahlab* was not allowed to wear the headscarf in order to ensure the denominational neutrality of the state education system, and also out of concern for the potential interference with the religious beliefs of the pupils (of a rather young age). However, there had been no complaints from parents about undue pressure on the children, nor any other complaints on the content or quality of her teaching.[74] While the Court does not use the protection of secularism language (as in the headscarf cases against Turkey and France), the reasoning in the decision is rather similar to that in the latter cases, while Switzerland was indeed the third country the Court had identified in *Dogru*[75] and *Aktas*[76] as a country for which secularism is a central constitutional value.

68 Inter alia ECommHR 3 December 1996, *Konttinen* v. *Finland*, App. No. 24949/94.

69 The supervisory bodies of the ECHR tended to require that a manifestation be intimately linked to religion: inter alia Evans 1999, 394.

70 Dissenting Opinion of judges Bratza, Fischbach, Thomassen, Tsatsa-Nikolovska, Pantiru, Levits en Traja in *Cha'are Shalom Ve Tsedek* v. *France*, 27 June 2000, App. No. 27417/95. See also Evans, *supra* note 32, 120.

71 ECommHR 12 March 1981, *Ahmad* v. *UK*, App. No. 22954/93.

72 See *infra* for more information on duties of reasonable accommodation, as well as on the *Kosteski* judgment.

73 ECtHR 15 February 2001, *Dahlab* v. *Switzerland*, App. No. 42393/98.

74 ECtHR 15 February 2001, *Dahlab* v. *Switzerland*, App. No. 42393/98, par. 1.

75 ECtHR 4 December 2008, *Dogru* v. *France*, App. No. 27058/05, par. 72.

76 ECtHR 30 June 2009, *Aktas* v. *France*, App. No. 43563/08.

Unfortunately, in so far as complainants also raised an issue in terms of Article 14, because a country adopts the day of rest of one particular religion as the official day of rest for the entire country, thus disadvantaging adherents to religions with other Sabbath days, the Commission considered also that complaint manifestly ill-founded. Instead of focusing on the relationship between the dominant and the minority religions, and the related disproportionate impact of having one religion determine the day of rest and the religious holidays, the Commission totally bypassed that problem (of indirect discrimination) and merely stated that the national legislation does not provide an absolute right for members of a religious community to have a particular day regarded as their holy day:

> Nor is there any appearance on the facts as submitted by the applicant, that she was treated in any way differently from employees of any other religious conviction. In these circumstances the Commission considers there is no appearance of any discriminatory treatment of the applicant.[77]

In this way, the Commission ignored the differential treatment which results from the apparently neutral rule of having one and the same weekly day of rest for all, irrespective of religious persuasion, and hence not accommodating religiously inspired commitments on alternative Sabbath days.

V. Duties of reasonable accommodation in terms of the prohibition of discrimination

Duties of reasonable accommodation have fairly recently been developed as a specific, additional dimension of the equality principle. The underlying rationale of duties of reasonable accommodation is that one needs to deal with hurdles experienced by particular groups or persons to fully participate in public life, and have genuinely equal access to employment and services. The goal of this differential treatment is clearly realizing substantive or genuine equality and can actually be considered as a special type of "duties of differential treatment."[78] While duties of reasonable accommodation were originally conceived in the US and Canada exactly to deal with religious diversity, as it further developed and spread to other countries, and even the UN and the EU, the focus shifted markedly to persons with a disability.[79] The kind of measures that have been

---

77 ECommHR 9 April 1997, *Stedman* v. *UK*, App. No. 29107/95, par. 3.

78 There is furthermore a close parallel to indirect discrimination and positive action: K. Henrard, *Equal Rights versus Special Rights: Minority Protection and the Prohibition of Discrimination* (European Commission 2007), 25–31.

79 P. Bosset, *Reflections on the Scope and Limits of the Duty of Reasonable Accommodation in the Field of Religion* (Commission des droits de la personne et des droits de la jeunesse 2005), 2; J. Cromwell, "Cultural Discrimination: The Reasonable

discussed in Canada and recognized by the Canadian Supreme Court pertaining to religious diversity include exactly dress code, break policies, religious leaves and recruitment procedures. Uniforms that do not have health or safety rationales (such as school uniforms) can be easily altered to accommodate the individual and in any event some efforts to accommodate the employee in some manner will be required. When one's religion requires religious observances at certain times during the day, this can be accommodated by a modified break policy or flexible working hours, of course each time depending on the circumstances.[80]

Considering the ratio and the kind of measures envisaged here, these duties of reasonable accommodation can be considered the counterpart of a particular type of positive state obligations in relation to substantive rights. It seems that the ECtHR's hands-off approach regarding sensitive questions that have to do with religion and Church–State relations in the broad sense[81] and the limited range of positive state obligations it has identified in terms of Article 9 of the ECHR (as discussed *supra*), also limits the development of duties of reasonable accommodation in terms of the prohibition of discrimination. This is unfortunate, especially as thinking in terms of duties of reasonable accommodation has been theoretically prepared by the *Thlimmenos* judgment, and the reasoning developed there about duties to differentiate, in 2000. In *Thlimmenos*, the Court agreed that someone who is convicted for being a conscious objector, while he was exercising his freedom to manifest his religion, could not be treated the same as someone who had committed another type of conviction unrelated to the exercise of fundamental rights. Duties of reasonable accommodation are also intrinsically related to the prohibition of indirect discrimination, as is the case for duties to differentiate more generally. Indeed, in order to avoid finding a disproportionate negative impact and thus indirect discrimination, differential treatment of some kind might be necessary.

However, it was already noted that the ECtHR has struggled a long time with the notion of indirect discrimination, also after the *Thlimmenos* judgment.[82]

Accommodation of Religion in the Workplace," 10 *Employee Responsibilities and Rights Journal* 155 (1997), 156–159; J. Goldschmidt, "Reasonable Accommodation in EU Equality Law in a Broader Perspective?" 8 *ERA Forum* 39 (2007), 45; L. Waddington and M. Bell, "More Equal Than Others: Distinguishing European Union Equality Directives," 38 *Common Market Law Review* 587 (2001), 597.

80 P. A. Neena Gupta, "The Employer's Duty to Provide Religious Accommodation," *HRinfodesk* (June 2004), available at www.hrinfodesk.com.

81 As was shown *supra*, the Court is critical about outright invidious discrimination or the imposition of criminal sanctions for the exercise of religious beliefs (as in *Thlimmenos*).

82 While the Court initially had severe problems even acknowledging the concept of indirect discrimination, the Grand Chamber judgment in *D. H. et al.* v. *Czech Republic* arguably signals an important breakthrough (ECtHR (Grand Chamber) 13 November 2007, *D. H. et al.* v. *Czech Republic*, App. No. 57325/00). See also K. Henrard, "De Verhouding tussen de concepten redelijke aanpassing, indirecte discriminatie en proportionaliteit," in *De nieuwe federale antidiscriminatiewetten* (C. Bayart et al., eds, Die Keure 2008), 269–270.

Furthermore, the *Thlimmenos* line itself has not been used in very creative or innovative ways to identify positive obligations to adopt differential treatment. In so far as the Court has used the *Thlimmenos* rationale in other cases related to ethnic or national minorities, the results have been rather modest, in general.[83] The main achievement until now is the recognition of the special duty on state authorities "to take all reasonable steps to unmask any racist motive and to establish whether or not ethnic hatred or prejudice may have played a role in the events."[84] However, the Court initially even missed the opportunity to extend this line of jurisprudence to instances of violence inspired by religious discrimination in its judgment pertaining to *97 members of the Gldani Congregation of Jehovah Witnesses and 4 others* v. *Georgia* (3 May 2007). Fortunately this anomaly has been redressed in the more recent *Milanovic* v. *Serbia*[85] judgment.

One particular type of differential treatment that could be necessary in order to avoid a finding of indirect discrimination, namely exemptions from laws of general application, have been rejected outright by the supervisory system.[86] So far the issue of exemptions has only featured in older jurisprudence, pre-2000, and hence the influence of the *Thlimmenos* reasoning has not yet been tested. In the older case law, requests for exemptions were formulated in relation to laws on taxation, pension schemes, compulsory vaccination, rules about the way in which animals should be slaughtered, etc., because these laws would have a disproportionate impact on the adherents of a particular religion. In terms of the freedom of religion as such, the Court and the Commission seemed reluctant to even identify an interference with the freedom of religion, because the norms were neutral and did not have any religious connotation.[87] In terms of the prohibition of discrimination, this would have similarly led to a finding that there was not even a differential treatment.

The extremely careful and thus slow development of duties of differential treatment may also reflect the unease of the Court with this line of thinking and the flawed incorporation in the jurisprudence, as is also visible in the fact that there are still cases in which the Court glosses over instances of indirect discrimination.

83 See also L. Baillie, "Protection of Religious Minorities in Europe: The Council of Europe's Successes and Failures," 23 *American University International Law Review* 617 (2008), 620.

84 While this principle was formulated the first time in ECtHR 26 February 2004, *Nachova* v. *Bulgaria*, App. Nos. 43577/98 and 43579/98, par. 158, it has been confirmed many times since: inter alia ECtHR 13 December 2005, *Bekos and Koutropoulos* v. *Greece*, App. No. 15250/02, par. 73; ECtHR 23 February 2006, *Ognyanova and Choban* v. *Bulgaria*, App. No. 46317/99, par. 148.

85 ECtHR 14 December 2010, *Milanovic* v. *Serbia*, App. No. 44614/07, par. 96.

86 Either because the challenge to the neutral law was considered manifestly unfounded (and thus inadmissible) or because the restriction by this general and neutral law is considered justified: see inter alia C. Evans, *Freedom of Religion under the European Convention on Human Rights* (OUP, 2001), 179–186, and the case law discussed there.

87 ECommHR 13 May 1980, *X* v. *UK*, App. No. 8416/79.

Overall, it is thus not so surprising that duties of reasonable accommodation have not yet featured (let alone prominently) in the jurisprudence of the Court. This has definitely led to missed opportunities in the workplace, and exactly pertaining to the issues enumerated above as ones that have been developed in Canada: flexible working hours in order to attend Friday prayers for Muslims, time off during religious days of rest and the like.

As the preceding analysis of the case law of the supervisory organs of the ECHR in terms of Article 9 of the ECHR has shown, their apparent reluctance to identify state duties to accommodate religious diversity at work[88] is visible in all stages of the determination process. Denying something the status of religion or manifestation of religion may be the most radical approach, denying an interference as a close second, but the end result is a rather marked lack of accommodation of religious diversity. The Court confirmed in *Kosteski* v. *the Former Yugoslav Republic of Macedonia*[89] that it, like the former Commission, is not willing to establish an explicit duty of reasonable accommodation of religious differences which would require the state to take reasonable measures to ensure the effective enjoyment of the freedom to manifest one's religion, also by members of religious minorities.[90]

Unfortunately, the Court has so far not been called upon to investigate whether a lack of reasonable accommodation amounts to a violation of Article 14 following the *Thlimmenos* principle. A full expansion of the latter line of jurisprudence, in combination with a more thorough grounding for the prohibition of indirect

88 This can be nicely contrasted with the "older" judgment of the ECJ in *Vivien Prais* v. *Council* concerning the complaint that the date for written tests of the competition to enter the service of the EU was set on a date when she could not take the tests because of religious reasons. The Court held that in so far as a candidate informs in good time the appointing authority about religious reasons which make particular dates impossible for him, this should be taken into account in fixing dates for tests. While there would not be an absolute obligation to avoid such dates, it should in any event be endeavored (par. 16–18).

89 ECtHR 13 April 2006, *Kosteski* v. *the Former Yugoslav Republic of Macedonia*, App. No. 55170/00. Note that in ECtHR 2 October 2011, *Pichon and Sajous* v. *France*, App. No. 49853/99, the Court adopted a similar restrictive approach in relation to the professional activities of pharmacists who refused to distribute contraceptive pills because of their religious convictions. According to the Court the complaint was inadmissible because in their capacity as pharmacists they are not entitled to express their religious conviction in this way which amounts to an imposition of their religious beliefs on others. While it seems reasonable that the Convention does not protect such expressions of religious convictions in the professional sphere, it is problematic that the Court's reasoning is somewhat fuzzy. It seems both to deny that this refusal would amount to a manifestation of religion and to hold that the conviction for refusal to sell did not amount to an interference with the exercise of the rights guaranteed by Article 9.

90 J. Ringelheim, *Diversité Culturelle et droits de l'homme, L' emergence de la problematique des minorities dans le droit de la Convention Europeenne des Droits de l 'Homme* (Bruylant 2006), 169.

discrimination in the case law, could still spark the emergence of a jurisprudential line embracing duties of reasonable accommodation in terms of the prohibition of discrimination (as well).

Conclusion: Hope for the future?

While the Court still tends to use the language of a broad margin of appreciation for states concerning Church–State relations, in several contexts the margin is de facto reduced.[91] Already in older case law it was visible that the state is not allowed to meddle with religious leadership and possible schisms within a religion. Allegations of possible dangers for public security and order are not easily accepted in the sense that precise proof is required.[92] The Court has become increasingly demanding about the requirements that registration and recognition schemes need to fulfill: the criteria need to be non-discriminatory in themselves and as applied, while the procedures used need to be transparent and adequately swift.[93] Similar remarks can be made pertaining to criteria and procedures in order for religious communities to obtain legal personality. The Court correctly intimates that legal personality is often a critical precondition for many activities based on collective manifestation.[94]

A few cases can be mentioned that signal a more critical scrutiny of a preferential status of one particular religion, first in the educational sphere, and public education more specifically. The European Commission on Human Rights had accepted in a

91 See also C. Evans and C. A. Thomas, "Church-State Relations in the European Court of Human Rights," 31 *Brigham Young University Law Review* 699 (2006), 699–670; A. Nieuwenhuis, "An Analysis of the Margin of Appreciation as Used in the Case of Leyla Sahin of 29 January 2004," 1 *European Constitutional Law Review* 495 (2005), 502–503.

92 ECtHR 14 December 1999, *Serif* v. *Greece*, App. No. 38178/97; ECtHR 17 October 2002, *Agga* v. *Greece*, App. No. 37439/97.

93 Inter alia ECtHR 13 December 2001, *Metropolitan Church of Bessarabia and others* v. *Moldova*, App. No. 45701/99. See also ECtHR 10 June 2010, *Jehovah's Witnesses of Moscow* v. *Russia*, App. No. 302/02 (in which the Court does not accept the reasoning of the Russian courts, de facto relying on prejudices about Jehovah's Witnesses): protection against loss of status as registered religious organization (with legal personality and all those rights).

94 ECtHR 16 December 1997, *Canea Catholic Church* v. *Greece*, App. No. 25528/94, par. 40–41; ECtHR 13 December 2001, *Metropolitan Church of Bessarabia and others* v. *Moldova*, par. 118; ECtHR 1 October 2009, *Kimlya and others* v. *Russia*, App. No. 76836/01; ECtHR 31 July 2008, *Religionsgemeinschaft der Zeugen Jehovas and Others* v. *Austria*, App. No. 40825/98, par. 66 (par. 78–80: related positive obligation (not of the kind of positive accommodation) to keep the time during which the organization had to wait for conferment of legal personality reasonably short).

case against Sweden[95] that education about religions in public education focuses on a particular religion without amounting to religious indoctrination. According to Evans this evaluation was hard to understand and she warned about an increased danger that the course would lead to proselytism and the marginalization of people who think differently.[96] Fortunately, the Grand Chamber reversed that line of thinking in *Folgero* v. *Norway*.[97] While it acknowledged that parents do not have the right to keep their children in the dark about other religions, it also noted that the class concerned de facto has a predominant focus on Christianity. Notwithstanding the grant of a wide margin of appreciation, and remarks that in itself a disproportionate attention to one particular religion would not amount to indoctrination,[98] the Court de facto adopted a strict scrutiny approach and pursues a detailed evaluation of all aspects of the case. This detailed weighing process led the Court to conclude that, all in all, the quantitative and qualitative differences between Christianity and the other religions amount to a failure to provide the requisite education in public education.

Secondly, and still concerning public education, the Chamber judgment in *Lautsi* v. *Italy* of 3 November 2009 clearly circumscribed the possibility of having a religious symbol in a classroom of a public school. According to the Chamber the predominant meaning and connotation of the cross would be religious.[99] This powerful symbol would exert pressure on the pupils, especially those of young age.[100] The Court attached due weight to the fact that this cross in a public

95 ECommHR 3 December 1986, *Angeleni* v. *Sweden*, App. No. 10491/83. It needs to be acknowledged that *Angeleni* v. *Sweden* turned on Article 9 and not the second article of the first additional protocol because Sweden had filed a reservation in relation to the latter article. Nevertheless, the Commission holds that Article 9 also prohibits indoctrination in education. According to the Commission there would not be religious indoctrination, notwithstanding the fact that de facto the instruction about religions focused on Christianity.

96 C. Evans, *Freedom of Religion under the ECHR*, (OUP, 2001), 94.

97 ECtHR 29 June 2007, *Folgero* v. *Norway*, App. No. 15472/02. It should be noted that the Human Rights Committee pronounced on a case about the same facts but in relation to different parents (*Leirvag et al.* v. *Norway*, 3 November 2004). While neither the Committee nor the Court pronounce explicitly on the legitimacy of partial exemptions as category, they both seem to question that legitimacy to a great extent (see also C. Moe, "Religious Human Rights and Religion in Schools," paper presented at the international conference *Religion in Schools: Problems of Pluralism in the Public Sphere* (Montenegro 2005)). The Committee is clearly more sensitive and realistic about the context in which the exemption takes place by taking into account the loyalty issue for pupils and the chilling effect on parents (of having to scrutinize closely the content of the education system).

98 ECtHR 29 June 2007, *Folgero et al.* v. *Norway*, App. No. 15472/02, par. 89. An analogue argumentation can be found in the more recent judgment ECtHR 9 October 2007, *Hasan en Eylem Zengin* v. *Turkey*, App. No. 1448/04, where the Court also takes into consideration that Islam is the majority religion in the country (par. 63).

99 ECtHR 3 November 2009, *Lautsi* v. *Italy*, App. No. 30814/06, par. 51.

100 *Id.* at par. 50.

classroom represents an official recognition and state support of one particular religion.[101] According to the Chamber the state had not met its duties of neutrality.[102] Finally, *Arslan et al.* v. *Turkey*[103] even seems to denote a limit to the wide state discretion pertaining to the regulation of religious dress, also when this limitation is allegedly crucial to the maintenance of secularism. *In casu* it did not concern a setting or a building where concerns of state neutrality are in order. To the contrary, the case concerned the prohibition for every person of wearing religious clothes and a Turban in the public space in general. The reasoning of the Court clearly shows that Turkey did not enjoy a wide margin of appreciation in this matter.

How do these developments translate in terms of hope for the future? While the first two remarks pertain to rather solid and welcome trends in the jurisprudence, unfortunately several of the latter cases do not yet constitute steady lines of jurisprudence. When considering the important shift in *Folgero*, one also needs to acknowledge that there have been later cases in which the Court did not adequately factor in de facto pressures regarding religious education in the same way as it identified de facto dominance of one religion in the curriculum. For example, in *Grzelak* v. *Poland* of 15 June 2010, the Court remained oblivious to the stigmatization flowing from the absence of a mark for religion/ethics in school reports which was due to the fact that the applicant did not want to follow a course on religion while the ethics class was not provided. The Grand Chamber's judgment in *Lautsi* v. *Italy* of 18 March 2011 reversed the Chamber judgment in crucial respects. While the Grand Chamber confirmed the state's duty of neutrality and impartiality, and also that the crucifix is above all a religious symbol, it argued that "there is no evidence before the Court that the display of a religious symbol on classroom walls may have an influence on pupils so it cannot reasonably be asserted that it does or does not have an effect on young persons whose convictions are still in the process of being formed."[104] The emphasis is clearly put on the broad margin of appreciation due to states concerning the content of the curriculum as well as the place of religion in society. Concerning the limit of indoctrination,[105] the Grand Chamber opined that a regulation prescribing the presence of crucifixes in state-school classrooms may confer a preponderant visibility to that majority religion in the school environment, but this would not be sufficient to denote a process of indoctrination.[106] A crucifix on a wall would be an essentially passive symbol,[107]

---

101 *Id.* at par. 53.

102 *Id.* at par. 56.

103 ECtHR 23 February 2010, *Arslan et al.* v. *Turkey*, App. No. 41135/98, par. 49–51.

104 ECtHR (Grand Chamber) 18 March 2011, *Lautsi and others* v. *Italy*, App. No. 30814/06, par. 66.

105 *Id.* at par. 62 and 69.

106 *Id.* at par. 71.

107 *Id.* at par. 72.

and it is not accompanied with compulsory teaching about Christianity,[108] while Italy would open its school environment in several respects to other religions.[109] The Grand Chamber therefore concluded that Italy has acted within the limits of its margin of appreciation.[110]

Overall, it is impossible to formulate a conclusion with a truly hopeful message concerning a solid trend towards a marked reduction of the margin of appreciation of states, which could have positive implications for state duties to protect religious diversity in the workplace. So far, there have only been a few glimmers of hope.

108 The Court gives a startling reading of its own *Folgero* judgment, arguably rewriting that judgment as if it would not have considered it problematic that the larger share of a multi-religious syllabus was reserved for one particular religion in paragraph 71.

109 *Id.* at par. 74.

110 *Id.* at par. 76–77.

Chapter 4

Beyond *Lautsi*: An Alternative Approach to Limiting the Government's Ability to Display Religious Symbols in the Public Workplace

Hans-Martien ten Napel

Introduction

The topic of religious symbols in the public workplace has at least two dimensions. The present chapter will look into the first dimension of the government's ability to display religious symbols in the public sphere, particularly crosses in public school classrooms. The European Court of Human Rights (ECtHR or the Court) recently had to rule on this issue for the first time in its Chamber and Grand Chamber judgments in *Lautsi* v. *Italy* (2009 and 2011, respectively).[1]

The Chamber did not consider restriction of the two rights at stake, namely the freedom of religion or belief and the freedom of education in accordance with the religious and philosophical beliefs of the parents, to be justified. According to the unanimous Chamber judgment, this restriction was incompatible with the duty of the State to observe philosophical neutrality in the exercise of its public service, particularly in the field of education.

The Grand Chamber, to the contrary, ruled by a 15-2 majority that the decision to display crosses in public school classrooms in principle falls within the margin of appreciation granted to the State Parties. In light of the facts that, among other things, the crucifix did not imply that there was any compulsory teaching about Christianity and that Italy had opened up its school system to other religions and beliefs, there had been no violation of the rights involved.

The two opposite rulings illustrate that a case like *Lautsi* is difficult, not least because the negative freedom of religion of employees in and around the public workplace may also be involved.

The second dimension of the topic of religious symbols in the public workplace concerns the question of how judges should deal with the manifestation of

1 ECtHR 3 November 2009, *Lautsi* v. *Italy*, App. No. 30814/06; ECtHR (Grand Chamber), 18 March 2011, *Lautsi* v. *Italy*, App. No. 30814/06.

religious symbols by citizens in public institutions.[2] In the light of the important role of human rights in our legal and political system, I contended elsewhere that the freedom of religion or belief ought to be central to the approach of the courts.[3] As human rights should only be limited in a democratic society if this is strictly unavoidable, courts should grant individuals and groups maximum protection under the freedom of religion or belief. The main conclusion on that occasion was that, in a comparative perspective, the ECtHR has addressed the second dimension of the problem of religious symbols in the public workspace on several occasions and thus far does not live up to this standard.[4]

One of the central ideas underlying the current chapter is that the questions regarding the limits of the government's ability to display religious symbols in the public sphere, and how judges should deal with the manifestation by citizens of religious symbols in public institutions, are closely interrelated. First, the Chamber and Grand Chamber judgments in the *Lautsi* case and several related cases in the Italian context will be discussed. Next, two prototypical reactions will be described: one (Mancini's) agreeing with the Chamber judgment; the other (Weiler's) agreeing with the Grand Chamber judgment. Finally, after a brief comparison with US case law, an alternative approach inspired by the concept of positive secularism is sketched as a possible way out of this deadlock. This concept has recently been defended in the report of The Consultation Commission on Accommodation Practices Related to Cultural Differences (CCPARDC), which was responsible for analyzing the challenges posed by a new migratory situation in Québec, Canada, among others. According to the report,

> [a] more rigid form of secularism allows for greater restriction of the free exercise of religion in the name of a certain interpretation of State neutrality and the separation of political and religious powers, while open secularism defends a model centred on the protection of freedom of conscience and religion and a more flexible conception of State neutrality.[5]

The chapter ends with a conclusion.

---

2 See also the chapters by Mine Yıldırım, Katayoun Alidadi and Rim-Sarah Alouane in this volume.

3 H.-M. Th. D. ten Napel and F. H. Karim Theissen, "The European Court of Human Rights on Religious Symbols in Public Institutions—A Comparative Perspective: Maximum Protection of the Freedom of Religion through Judicial Minimalism?" in *Law and Religion in the 21st Century. Relations between States and Religious Communities* (S. Ferrari and R. Cristofori, eds, Ashgate 2010), 313–321.

4 *Id.*

5 G. Bouchard and C. Taylor, *Building the Future. A Time for Reconciliation. Report* (Commission de Consultation sur les Pratiques d'Accommodement Reliées aux Différences Culturelles 2008), 137.

1. *Lautsi* v. *Italy* and related cases in the Italian context

The facts of the *Lautsi* case can now be considered well known. Therefore, a brief summary suffices here. The complainant, Mrs Soile Lautsi, holds Italian citizenship and lives in Northern Italy. In the public school that her children aged 11 and 13 years attended in the years 2001–2002, a crucifix hung on the wall in all classrooms. Mrs Lautsi considered this contrary to the principle of secularism with which she wished to raise her children. The national administration of justice brought no solution. On 15 December 2004, the Constitutional Court declared itself incompetent, as the obligation to hang crucifixes in classrooms was based on Royal Decrees from 1924 and 1928 and therefore not on legislation. On 13 February 2006, the Italian Council of State, in turn, rejected the complaint. According to the Council, the crucifix was no longer exclusively religious in nature but rather had become part of the secular values of the Italian Constitution and represented the general civic values.

In her complaint submitted before the European Court on 27 July 2006, Mrs Lautsi argued, partly on behalf of her children, that the display of crucifixes in her children's public school violated the right to education in accordance with the religious and philosophical beliefs of the parents laid down in Article 2 of the First Protocol to the European Convention on Human Rights (ECHR). She also claimed that her freedom of religion or belief, guaranteed in Article 9 of the ECHR, had been infringed.

According to the Chamber, the State had the obligation to refrain from the imposition, albeit indirectly, of beliefs in places where citizens are dependent on the State and especially where they are particularly vulnerable. The education of children is an example of such a sensitive sector, because children are not considered sufficiently mentally robust. The crucifix as a symbol has a multitude of meanings, but the religious meaning dominates. With respect to Mrs Lautsi's concerns about the impact that the display of the crucifix might have on her children, the Court stated:

> Negative freedom of religion is not restricted to the absence of religious services or religious education. It extends to practices and symbols expressing, in particular or in general, a belief, a religion or atheism. That negative right deserves special protection if it is the State which expresses a belief and dissenters are placed in a situation from which they cannot extract themselves if not by making disproportionate efforts and acts of sacrifice.[6]

Affixing a cross in a public school classroom cannot be justified by the request of other parents who wish for education in accordance with their religious and philosophical beliefs, nor—as the government originally argued—by the need for a compromise with Christian-inspired political parties. The State should observe

6 ECtHR 3 November 2009, *Lautsi* v. *Italy*, App. No. 30814/06, par. 55.

philosophical neutrality in the context of public education where presence is required regardless of religion and where the aim should be to teach the students to think critically. The Chamber did not see how the placing of a symbol that can reasonably be associated with Catholicism in the premises of public schools contributed to the pluralism in education that is essential for the maintenance of a "democratic society" as mandated by the Convention. Thus, the Court unanimously found that Article 2 of Protocol 1, examined in conjunction with Article 9 of the ECHR, had been violated.

Like the Chamber, the Grand Chamber considered the crucifix to be primarily a religious symbol. It could therefore imagine why Mrs Lautsi saw in the display of the cross in State school classrooms an infringement of the right to have her children educated and taught in accordance with her philosophical convictions as a parent. Yet, according to the Grand Chamber:

> Be that as it may, the applicant's subjective perception is not in itself sufficient to establish a breach of Article 2 of Protocol No. 1.[7]

The government, in turn, referred to the fact that the country's historical development had also at least partly turned the display of crucifixes in public school classrooms into a tradition symbolizing the values upon which western civilization in general and the Italian political and legal order in particular were founded, and which they wished to continue. In reaction to this position, the Grand Chamber stated that:

> the decision whether or not to perpetuate a tradition falls in principle within the margin of appreciation of the respondent State. The Court must moreover take into account the fact that Europe is marked by a great diversity between the States of which it is composed, particularly in the sphere of cultural and historical development.[8]

In addition, what was important to the Grand Chamber was that a cross was "an essentially passive symbol," which "cannot be deemed to have an influence on pupils comparable to that of didactic speech or participation in religious activities."[9]

The question of the limits on the government's ability to display religious symbols in the public sphere is not restricted to children and their parents, but is also potentially relevant for the workplace. In Italy, for example, there have been several other lawsuits on this issue. Thus, in 1991–1992, primary school teacher Angelo Lazzarini removed the crucifix from his classroom during lessons several times, as he wanted to familiarize pupils with the symbols of all religions.

---

7 ECtHR (Grand Chamber) 18 March 2011, *Lautsi* v. *Italy*, App. No. 30814/06, par. 66.

8 *Id.*, par. 68.

9 *Id.*, par. 72.

Lazzarini was then ordered by the head of the school to put the crucifix back in the classroom, an order that he challenged before the Administrative Tribunal. However, the Tribunal dismissed his claim that the order infringed both his freedom of teaching and the principle of State secularism.[10] In addition, there is the case of Franco Coppoli, teacher of a third-year history class. Although the Royal Decrees of 1924 and 1928 do not apply to high schools, the head of the school allowed some of the pupils to hang a crucifix in the classroom upon their request. Coppoli, who objected, used to remove the crucifix from the wall during his lessons. During a subsequent class assembly, a majority of the pupils voted in favor of displaying the crucifix during history lessons, a decision confirmed by the class board. As Coppoli protested, disciplinary proceedings were started against him. In 2009, the National Council of Public Education found him guilty of insubordination and suspended him from his job and salary for one month. At the same time, a Tribunal where Coppoli had filed a lawsuit ruled that he had not been discriminated against by the head of the school.[11]

In Italy, crucifixes are displayed not only in primary and middle schools, but also in courtrooms. In 2009, Tribunal judge Luigi Tosti, who had declined to hold several hearings because of the presence of the crucifix in the courtroom, was eventually acquitted by the Court of Cassation after having been convicted previously by two lower courts. His refusal to perform an official duty had not actually caused any disruption, as he had been replaced by colleagues. However, the Disciplinary Division of the Superior Council of the Judiciary subsequently removed him from office because he had continued his noncompliance after a courtroom without a crucifix had been made available to him.[12]

On the other hand, in 2000, a secretary by the name of Marcello Montagnana, who refused to perform his duties at a polling station because of the display of crucifixes in polling stations (that are often set up in public schools), was acquitted by the Court of Cassation. Although no crucifix was affixed in the actual polling station assigned to him, the Court reasoned that his duty had been conferred to him based on a draw and that an infringement on his freedom of conscience was a sufficiently serious reason for him to decline the appointment. Moreover, as the freedom of conscience is an indivisible entity, the right applied to all polling stations in the country.[13]

---

10 Administrative Tribunal of Lombardy (Division of Brescia) Ruling No. 603 of 22 May 2006, as discussed in: C. Panara, “Lautsi v. Italy: The Display of Religious Symbols by the State,” 17 *European Public Law* 139 (2011), 154–155.

11 Tribunal of Terni (Civil Division) Order of 24 June 2009, as discussed in: *Id.*, 155–156.

12 Court of Cassation (Sixth Criminal Division) Ruling No. 28482 of 10 July 2009 and Disciplinary Division of the High Council of the Judiciary Decision of 22 January 2010, as discussed in: *Id.*, 160–161.

13 Court of Cassation (Fourth Criminal Division) Ruling No. 4273 of 1 March 2000, as discussed in: *Id.*, 156–157.

2. Reception of the (Grand) Chamber judgment(s) in the case of *Lautsi* v. *Italy*

In several articles on the Chamber judgment in the *Lautsi* case, Susanna Mancini has expressed concern that European legislators and courts in general, and the ECtHR in particular, tend to interpret religious symbols in a way that reflects the prejudices of what still constitutes the majority of the population. As a result,

> crucifixes may be displayed in the public schools because secularized Christianity represents a structural element of the western constitutional identity, while the wearing of Islamic symbols is either banned or restricted because it represents values and practices that are cast as illiberal and undemocratic.[14]

Mancini has not hesitated to call this phenomenon a "new form of cultural racism."[15] She therefore wholeheartedly welcomed the Chamber judgment in the *Lautsi* case, in that to her it seemed to strengthen the counter-majoritarian role of the ECtHR.[16] At the same time, however, she realized that this "remarkable shift" caused certain risks for the Court in terms of its likelihood to provoke populist resentment among European citizens.[17] Of course, it may be possible, at least in part, to explain the Grand Chamber judgment in the *Lautsi* case precisely as an attempt to prevent this from continuing any further and thereby safeguarding the authority of the Court for the time being.

The Chamber judgment in the *Lautsi* case has also met with fierce criticism, however, notably by Joseph H. Weiler who also intervened in the case for ten States Parties objecting to the Chamber judgment. According to Weiler, the ECHR protects not only the individual freedoms of and from religion, but also

> a second *collective*, *identitarian*, Freedom, conceptually stemming from self-determination, namely the freedom of nations/states to include in their self-definition, in their self-understanding and in their national and statal symbology, a more or less robust entanglement of religion and religious symbols.[18]

Moreover, like the freedom of religion, the freedom from religion is not absolute, and sometimes needs to be balanced against precisely this collective, identitarian

14 S. Mancini, "The Power of Symbols and Symbols as Power: Secularism and Religion as Guarantors of Cultural Convergence," 30 *Cardozo Law Review* 2629 (2009), 2631.

15 S. Mancini, "The Crucifix Rage: Supranational Constitutionalism Bumps Against the Counter-Majoritarian Difficulty," 6 *European Constitutional Law Review* 6 (2010), 18.

16 *Id.*, 8.

17 *Id.*, 24, 27.

18 J. H. H. Weiler, "State and Nation; Church, Mosque and Synagogue—the Trailer," 8 *International Journal of Constitutional Law* 157 (2010), 158.

freedom of religion.[19] In failing to do so, the judgment by the Chamber in the *Lautsi* case was "not an expression of the pluralism manifest by the Convention system, but an expression of the values of the laïque State."[20] Although the Chamber may well have regarded its position to be a neutral one, as Weiler pointed out,

> [s]ecularity, *laïcité* is not an empty category which signifies absence of faith. It is to many a rich world view which holds, inter alia, the political conviction that religion only has a legitimate place in the private sphere and that there may not be any entanglement of public authority and religion. ... It is legally disingenuous to adopt a political position which splits our society, and to claim that somehow it is neutral.[21]

It was perfectly clear to Weiler that, given the traditional diversity within Europe in the field of Church–State relations, the Chamber ought to have realized that "there cannot be one solution that fits all Members, all classrooms, all situations."[22]

3. Comparison with US case law

According to Weiler, in attempting to impose precisely this one-size-fits-all solution, the Chamber judgment led to "the Americanization of Europe":

> Americanization in two respects: First a single and unique rule for everyone, and second, a rigid, American style, separation of Church and State, as if the people of those Members whose State identity is not laïque, cannot be trusted to live by the principles of tolerance and pluralism.[23]

Yet, specifically with regard to the issue of the limits of the government's ability to display religious symbols in the public workplace, the case law of the US Supreme Court has not been as clear-cut as this citation suggests.

Thus, in the case of *Stone* v. *Graham*,[24] the US Supreme Court was presented a law that required Kentucky public schools to show the Ten Commandments in classrooms. Like the Italian Government in *Lautsi*, Kentucky tried to show a "secular legislative purpose" in an attempt to justify this by stating that schools were obliged to write below the image in lowercase letters: "The secular application of the Ten Commandments is clearly seen in its adoption as the fundamental legal code of Western Civilization and the Common Law of the

19 *Id.*, 160.
20 *Id.*, 163.
21 *Id.*, 164.
22 *Id.*, 165.
23 *Id.*, 163.
24 *Stone* v. *Graham*, 449 US 39 (1980).

United States." The Supreme Court was not convinced and ruled with five votes against four that the measure constituted support of religion by the government, and thus was unconstitutional. According to the Supreme Court, the law violated the Establishment Clause of the first amendment, which prohibits the government to found a religion, or to advantage one religion over another or to advantage religion in general over nonreligious beliefs. One of the "dissenters," Chief Justice Rehnquist, warned, however, that "[t]he Establishment Clause does not require that the public sector be insulated from all things which may have a religious significance or origin."[25]

Moreover, four years later, the Supreme Court ruled in *Lynch* v. *Donnelly*[26] that a Nativity scene placed on a municipal square by the city of Pawtucket in Rhode Island was constitutionally allowed. The Court stated that the stall only expressed the historical origin of the feast day, which had both a secular and a religious significance. Under these circumstances, the placing of the stall could not reasonably be regarded as an attempt by the State to promote Christianity.

Since these two judgments from the 1980s, the US Supreme Court has given several other partly conflicting and inconsistent rulings, such as *County of Allegheny* v. *ACLU*,[27] *Capitol Square Review Board* v. *Pinette*,[28] *McCreary County* v. *ACLU of Kentucky*[29] and *Van Orden* v. *Perry*.[30] Each time it granted the necessary weight to the specific history and context of the relevant symbol. The resulting lack of clear guidelines reflects the deep divisions within the Supreme Court in this area.[31]

Nevertheless, according to at least one observer, following the Grand Chamber judgment in the *Lautsi* case, the ECtHR now holds at least six teachings in common with the US Supreme Court with respect to limiting the government's ability to display religious symbols in the public workplace. These points include the eventual acknowledgment that neither the positive nor the negative aspect of religious freedom requires the secularization of society:

> The United States Supreme Court became famous for its image of a "high and impregnable wall of separation between church and state," that left religion hermetically sealed from political life and public institutions. But the reality today is that the Court has abandoned much of its strict separatism and now allows religious and non-religious parties alike to engage in peaceable public activities, even in public schools. The European Court of Human Rights likewise

25 *Id.*, 45–46.

26 *Lynch* v. *Donnelly*, 465 US 668 (1984).

27 *County of Allegheny* v. *ACLU*, 492 US 573 (1989).

28 *Capitol Square Review Board* v. *Pinette*, 515 US 753 (1995).

29 *McCreary County* v. *ACLU of Kentucky*, 545 US 844 (2005).

30 *Van Orden* v. *Perry*, 545 US 677 (2005).

31 See I. C. Lupu et al., *Religious Displays and the Courts* (The Pew Forum on Religion and Public Life 2007).

> became famous for promoting French-style laïcité in public schools and public life, striking down Muslim headscarves and other religious symbols as contrary to the democratic "message of tolerance, respect for others, and equality and non-discrimination." Lautsi suggests a new policy that respects the rights of private religious and secular groups alike to express their views, but allows government to reflect democratically the traditional religious views of its majority.[32]

Although the observer in question, John Witte Jr., without doubt has a point, two remarks here are in order. First, the new policy of the ECtHR has yet to materialize in the field of the manifestation by citizens of religious symbols in public institutions. Second, in the event that this occurs sooner or later, it would at least theoretically give the Court the opportunity to become slightly stricter toward countries such as Italy with respect to the limits of the government's ability to display religious symbols in the public workspace. In doing so, the Court could draw inspiration from the concept of open secularism, to which the next section will be dedicated.[33]

4. An alternative approach

In the past, in cases concerning the admissibility of restrictions on the wearing of a headscarf by students in public educational institutions, the Court awarded a very wide margin of appreciation to France and Turkey. It has done so because the constraint was motivated by constitutionally protected secularism.[34] Among others, Henrard has raised the question of whether the margin previously granted to France and Turkey has not been too broad, as in this way, a supervisory body threatens to deny itself the chance to monitor seriously the degree to which religious freedom is actually protected in these countries.[35] For the same reason, it can be argued

---

32 J. Witte Jr., "Lift High the Cross? Religion In Public Spaces," *The Huffington Post*, 27 March 2011.

33 According to Veit Bader, secularism is a mystifying concept. Although I find myself in agreement with several of Bader's arguments, I still believe that contrasting radical (or rigid) and open secularism—even if loosely defined as in what follows—can be illuminating in debates between proponents of different types of Church–State relations. See V. Bader, "Constitutionalizing Secularism, Alternative Secularisms or Liberal–Democratic Constitutionalism? A Critical Reading of Some Turkish, ECtHR and Indian Supreme Court Cases on 'Secularism'," 6 *Utrecht Law Review* 8 (2010).

34 ECtHR 29 June 2004, *Leyla Sahin* v. *Turkey*, *EHRC* 2004/80, with note L. F. M. Verhey; ECtHR (Grand Chamber) 10 November 2005, *Leyla Sahin* v. *Turkey*, *EHRC* 2006/15, with note L. F. M. Verhey; ECtHR 4 December 2008, *Dogru* v. *France*, *EHRC* 2009/8, with note A. Woltjer; ECtHR 30 June 2009, *Aktas* v. *France*, *EHRC* 2009/114, with note K. Henrard.

35 K. Henrard, "Case Note—ECtHR 30 June 2009, *Aktas* v. *France*," *EHRC* 2009/114, at 10.

from a substantial point of view that the ECtHR ought to impose human law limits on the degree of secularism, as practiced in France and Turkey. Thus, as I have argued elsewhere, a bold judgment would be required to grant believers, finally, to what they are entitled under Article 9 of the European Convention: maximum and effective protection of their religious liberty.[36]

Given the fact that the Court does not yet live up to the standard of granting individuals and groups maximum protection under the freedom of religion or belief in the field of manifestation by citizens of religious symbols in public institutions, the ruling of the Grand Chamber in the *Lautsi* case is clearly to be preferred over the Chamber judgment. By granting France and Turkey what it begrudged Italy, and therefore refusing to honor complaints from the first category of symbol issues (the manifestation by citizens of religious symbols in public institutions) while honoring complaints from the second category (the government's ability to display religious symbols in the public sphere), the Chamber once again raised the question of whether it is in favor of a model of Church–State relations in which radical secularism is the measure of all things. Radical secularism is defined in the Canadian report referred to earlier as "[a] form of secularism aimed at banishing all religious expression from State institutions or in the public sphere overall and confining such expression to the private sphere."[37]

In the Canadian report, Gérard Bouchard and Charles Taylor argue that in the divided and multicultural societies of our time, states must remain neutral not just with respect to the various religions but also with regard to their secular equivalents:

> Indeed, a system that replaces religion as the foundation of its action by a comprehensive moral and political philosophy makes those who embrace any sort of religion second-class citizens since their fundamental reasons are not enshrined in the officially recognized philosophy.[38]

---

36 H.-M. Th. D. ten Napel and F. H. Karim Theissen, "The European Court of Human Rights on Religious Symbols in Public Institutions—A Comparative Perspective: Maximum Protection of the Freedom of Religion through Judicial Minimalism?" in *Law and Religion in the 21st Century. Relations between States and Religious Communities* (S. Ferrari and R. Cristofori, eds, Ashgate 2010), 322.

37 G. Bouchard and C. Taylor, *supra* note 5, 289. See also Z. R. Calo, "Pluralism, Secularism and the European Court of Human Rights," 26 *Journal of Law and Religion* 261 (2010), 266; M. D. Evans, "From Cartoons to Crucifixes: Current Controversies Concerning the Freedom of Religion and the Freedom of Expression Before the European Court of Human Rights," 26 *Journal of Law and Religion* 345 (2010), 360.

38 G. Bouchard and C. Taylor, *supra* note 5, 134–135. Fundamental reasons are defined in the report as "[r]easons or motives stemming from world views or conceptions of good that enable individuals to understand the world around them and to give a meaning and a direction to their lives." *Id.*, 286.

For the authors, secularism in general comprises four fundamental elements. The first two elements deal with the ends secularism seeks to achieve, i.e. recognition of the equivalent moral value of each individual, and freedom of conscience and religion, respectively. The other two principles concern the institutional means of realizing these goals, i.e. State neutrality toward all religions and beliefs, and the separation of Church and State.[39] The more open kind of secularism they themselves defend is "a model centred on the protection of freedom of conscience and religion and a more flexible conception of State neutrality."[40] The system "favours equal access to public institutions both by users and employees by refocusing the analysis of State neutrality on the State's acts rather than on employees' and users' appearance."[41]

Specifically with respect to the topic of this chapter—the government's ability to display religious symbols in the public workspace—the report leaves open the possibility that such a symbol, although originating in the religion of the majority, does not genuinely restrict the behavior of individuals not belonging to this majority. Yet a symbol that clearly identifies the State with a particular religion, such as the crucifix hanging above the president's chair in the National Assembly of Québec, must not be kept in place because it currently appears to have only heritage value. Or, to quote two sentences that *mutatis mutandis* appear equally applicable to crosses in Italian public school classrooms: "It seems preferable for the very place where elected representatives deliberate and legislate not to be identified with a specific religion. The National Assembly is the assembly of all Quebecers."[42]

Interestingly, the alternative approach to the question of the limits of the government's ability to display religious symbols in the public workplace suggested above resembles the one defended by Mancini and Rosenfeld whose "ideal conditions" nevertheless differ significantly from those of the CCPARDC:

> [i]n terms of religious symbols, this translates into refraining from official imposition of majority ones and greater acceptance of minority ones so long as they are not proven to pose a threat to the survival of pluralist secularism itself—a very high threshold indeed.[43]

Their "ideal conditions" include "a conception of secularism that is truly *areligious* and that neither favors nor disadvantages any religion or the non-religious" and "a

---

39 *Id.*, 135.

40 *Id.*, 137.

41 *Id.*, 148.

42 *Id.*, 152.

43 S. Mancini and M. Rosenfeld, *Unveiling the Limits of Tolerance: Comparing the Treatment of Majority and Minority Religious Symbols in the Public Sphere*, Benjamin N. Cardozo School of Law, Jacob Burns Institute for Advanced Legal Studies, September 2010, Working Paper No. 309, 34.

public sphere that is clearly and firmly delimited from the private sphere and that is entirely amenable to the rule of areligious secularism."[44]

The Canadian report, to the contrary, consciously limits the requirement of neutrality to public institutions. This is because imposing the same duty on individuals when they enter public space in general and public institutions in particular assumes a complete isolation of public life and private life that is untenable in practice: "In a free society such as ours, religion can simply not be confined within the strict limits of the home and places of worship."[45]

Conclusion

Recently it was pointed out that it is likely that every possible decision regarding the public display of religious symbols will appear non-neutral to some of the citizens.[46] The concept of open secularism makes it theoretically possible to prevent this from happening once one accepts the consequences of the sociological shifts that are visible worldwide, which suggest that pluralism is on the rise virtually everywhere. These consequences include

> a need to recognize that [the] idea of the secular state should not be thought of as an end in itself, but as an instrumental means toward creations of states that can help different worldviews—even deeply divided ones—to find peaceful ways to live together.[47]

When applied to the case at hand, the notion of open secularism leads to the conclusion that the Chamber was probably right in finding a violation in *Lautsi* v. *Italy*. In the light of the same concept, however, the course followed by the Court regarding the manifestation by citizens of religious symbols in public institutions cannot fully satisfy. Until the ECtHR remedies that situation, the Grand Chamber judgment in the *Lautsi* case is to be preferred over the Chamber judgment, even though it fails to provide maximum protection to employees and others in the public workspace, such as Lazzarini, Coppoli, Tosti, and Montagnana.

Had the Court forbidden Italy to display crosses in public school classrooms, while granting countries such as France and Turkey a margin of appreciation in banning, for example, headscarves in State schools and universities, it could easily have been accused of pursuing a hidden agenda of advancing radical secularism

44 *Id.*, 24.

45 G. Bouchard and C. Taylor, *supra* note 5, 142–143.

46 J. Martínez-Torrón and W. Cole Durham, Jr., "Religion and the Secular State," in *Religion and the Secular State: National Reports* (J. Martínez-Torrón and W. Cole Durham, Jr., General Reporters, The International Center for Law and Religion Studies (2010)), 1–56, at 49.

47 *Id.*, 56.

or laicism.[48] This type of secularism is fundamentally flawed, however, in so far as it is based on the wrongful assumption that private life and public life can be completely separated and that religion ought to play no role whatsoever in the latter. Open secularism, to the contrary, stresses the importance of the duty of neutrality of the State in divided and multicultural societies, but limits it to public institutions. In so doing, it offers precisely the middle ground that in possible future cases regarding the government's ability to display religious symbols in the public workplace could make the ECtHR run fewer risks in terms of its authority.

---

48 This fact appears to be overlooked by P. Ronchi, "Crucifixes, Margin of Appreciation and Consensus: The Grand Chamber Ruling in *Lautsi* v. *Italy*," 13 *Ecclesiastical Law Journal* 287 (2011), 287–297, according to whom not the Chamber but the Grand Chamber ruling "shows an incoherent approach of double standards on the issue of religious symbols" (at 296).

Section II

New Player Joining In: The European Union and Religious Discrimination

Chapter 5
Accommodation of Religion and Sex Equality in the Workplace under the EU Equality Directives: A Double Bind for the European Court of Justice

Titia Loenen

Introduction

Accommodation of religion in the workplace is a sensitive issue in many EU countries, especially when it comes to non-Judeo-Christian religions that have arrived and settled in Europe with immigration from non-European countries. Islam is the most prominent example. In this immigration context the question whether to accommodate or not becomes intertwined with discussions on integration, social cohesion and national identity. The resulting controversies over this subject are exacerbated when, in addition, accommodation engages the position of women and potentially infringes on notions of sex equality.

This specific context may explain why discussions on allowing or prohibiting all kinds of practices inspired by Islam in the workplace, such as the wish to wear a headscarf, a face-covering veil or the refusal to shake hands with colleagues or clients of the opposite sex, receive so much public and scholarly attention. These issues have become focal points for some of the dilemmas involved in accommodating religiously inspired practices in the workplace.

Interestingly, different EU countries have taken on widely divergent approaches towards these issues. France is well known for its very strict policies. State employees are not allowed to wear any religious symbols in the workplace, whether they function as judges or cleaners. Students in primary and secondary education are not allowed to wear any ostentatious religious symbols in public schools. In 2010 France adopted a general *burqa*[1] ban. This law prohibits face-covering

1 In the media the term *burqa* is generally used as a generic term for all face-covering veils. In this article I will also use it in this way, though arguably a difference could be made between a face-covering veil which still shows the eyes through a small slit (*niqab*) and a face-covering veil that hides even the eyes behind gauze.

veils anywhere in public.[2] The UK, on the other hand, is very accommodationist. Police officers can don a turban or headscarf and Rabinder Singh was the first Sikh judge to sit with a turban.[3] Other countries move somewhere in between these two approaches. Thus, in the Netherlands public school teachers and students are allowed to wear a headscarf in class. Police officers and judges, on the other hand, are not allowed to do so. Other controversies that are debated in the Netherlands concern the question of whether an employer has to accept the religiously inspired wish of an employee not to shake hands with a person of the opposite sex (for instance clients and colleagues), though this contravenes Dutch greeting conventions and may be perceived as offensive and an act of sex discrimination.

So far, the European Court of Justice (hereafter ECJ or the Court) has not rendered any judgments on this type of issue, but no doubt it will be just a matter of time as three directives regarding non-discrimination cover at least some of the issues mentioned. This is specifically the case for those issues that arise in an employment context.[4] This means that the ECJ will eventually have to decide where EU law stands in this respect. This begs the question which direction the Court will or should take. This chapter does not intend to give specific advice, but to provide an analysis of some of the difficult choices to be made and the dilemmas involved for the Court. I limit myself to three.

First, the legal framing of the issues referred to above as either involving discrimination on grounds of religion, race/ethnic origin[5] and/or sex will be addressed (§1). In this respect I confine myself to three examples in the employment context that have raised considerable debate in several EU countries: the refusal by an employer to accommodate the religiously inspired wish to wear a headscarf at work, the refusal to allow a face-covering veil and the refusal to hire someone who is unwilling to shake hands with colleagues, clients or other persons of the opposite sex. In the following I will refer to these examples as "the issues." If we take a look at the practices in the Member States, we can discern quite different and sometimes even contradictory ways of framing these issues in terms of discrimination on grounds of religion, sex and/or race.

Second, I explore the interpretation and application of the concept of indirect discrimination in this context (§2). To what extent can non-accommodation be

2 The law is effective as of 11 April 2011. See, for more information, http://articles.cnn.com/2011-03-04/world/france.burqa.ban_1_burqa-ban-full-face-veil?_s=PM:WORLD.

3 See www.sikhiwiki.org/index.php/Rabinder_Singh.

4 See for discrimination on grounds of race or ethnic origin: Directive 2000/43/EC of 29 June 2000, *OJ 180 L*, 19/7/2000, 22 (Race directive); for sex discrimination: Directive 2006/54/EC of 5 July 2006, *PJ 204 L*, 26.7.2006, 23 (Recast directive) and for discrimination on grounds of (amongst others) religion: Directive 2000/78/EC of 27 November 2000, *OJ 303 L*, 2/12/2000, 16 (Employment Equality Directive).

5 In this chapter I use "race" and "ethnic origin" interchangeably, following the broad approach to race discrimination in the (standard setting) International Convention on the Elimination of all Forms of Racial Discrimination.

challenged by invoking the prohibition of indirect discrimination as guaranteed by the EU directives? Dutch case law shows it can be interpreted as requiring far-reaching accommodation of religious practices. I will present a selection of cases decided by the Dutch Equal Treatment Commission (ETC) to illustrate this and discuss some of their implications, especially where the position of women is involved.

Finally, the degree of uniformity EU law requires in accommodating religion in the workplace in all Member States will be discussed (§3). How much discretion will be left to the Member States to decide such issues? Of special relevance in this respect is the question whether the ECJ will leave a similarly wide margin of discretion to the Member States as the European Court of Human Rights (ECtHR) so far has accorded under the European Convention on Human Rights (ECHR).[6]

I will round off with some concluding remarks.

1. Framing the issues as discrimination on grounds of religion, sex and/or race

The issues discussed in this chapter, that is the refusal by an employer to accommodate the religiously inspired wish to wear a headscarf at work, the refusal to allow a face-covering veil and the refusal to hire someone who is unwilling to shake hands with colleagues, clients or other persons of the opposite sex, involve the intersection of religion, sex and race. This may complicate matters for the ECJ, as EU law has put in place different equal treatment directives for each ground that may provide for different ways of reviewing potential discrimination on those grounds. In the following I will deal briefly with each ground, discussing the likelihood of framing the issues as discrimination on that ground and trying to assess the consequences of different framing for assessing the compatibility with the applicable EU directive.[7]

1.1 Religion

Framing the issues in terms of potential discrimination based on religion is the most obvious way, as the refusal to accommodate a religiously inspired practice is in fact what is at stake for the employee involved. Depending on the specific way in which accommodation is denied, direct or indirect discrimination could be at stake. Direct discrimination on grounds of religion could occur where a refusal to accommodate targets the symbols of a specific religion only (for instance only targeting headscarves or *burqas*, but not turbans). Similarly, the specific targeting

---

6 See the chapter by Kristin Henrard in this volume.

7 The latter is based on my analysis in T. Loenen, "The Headscarf Debate: Approaching the Intersection of Sex, Religion and Race Under the ECHR and EC Equality Law in European Union Non-discrimination Law," in *Comparative Perspectives on Multidimensional Equality Law* (D. Schiek and V. Chege, eds, Routledge-Cavendish 2009), 313–328.

of any religious expression, as opposed to other expressions of belief (for instance political) could constitute direct discrimination.

More commonly, however, refusals to accommodate headscarves or *burqas* stem from neutral dress codes or policies that by implication prohibit certain religious expressions. In those instances the potential claim is one of indirect discrimination.[8] In order not to complicate matters too much, in this chapter I will start from the premise that the prohibitions involved are part of such neutral measures, unless otherwise indicated. So they would fall in the realm of potential indirect discrimination, not direct.[9]

As Roseberry showed, establishing a disparate impact in headscarf cases[10] could amount to a first potential bottleneck for a claim of indirect discrimination because of the intersectionality problems involved.[11] It is often mostly Muslim women who are adversely affected by dress codes banning head coverings or religious symbols more generally, not Muslims as such (Muslim men generally are not affected). However, legal practice in the Netherlands shows this need not be a barrier to claims based on indirect discrimination on grounds of religion.[12]

If the barrier of showing disparate impact is successfully passed, the thrust of the review under the EU directive will be whether the dress code can be objectively justified. The outcome of this test will depend very much on the strictness of review. I will get back to this point when discussing the Dutch (quasi-)case law (§2).

8 In addition, if an employer were to use a neutral dress code to hide his intent to exclude headscarves or *burqa*s this could be approached as direct discrimination.

9 For purposes of the Employment Equality Directive it can be argued that the difference between direct or indirect discrimination may be of limited importance, as the Employment Equality Directive allows for an open assessment of justifications put forward for both direct and indirect discrimination. In EU law this possibility of open assessment is generally not accepted for direct discrimination, but Article 2 Section 5 of the Employment Equality Directive provides that the directive "shall be without prejudice to measures laid down by national law which, in a democratic society, are necessary for public security, for the maintenance of public order and the prevention of criminal offences, for the protection of health and for the protection of the rights and freedoms of others." The equality directives regarding sex and race discrimination do not contain such a general limitation clause.

10 The same would hold true for face-covering veils, but not for the "shaking hands" issue. The latter is a practice shared by certain groups of both Muslim men and women.

11 L. Roseberry, "Religion, Ethnicity and Gender in the Danish Headscarf Debate in European Union Non-discrimination Law," in *Comparative Perspectives on Multidimensional Equality Law* (D. Schiek and V. Chege, eds, Routledge-Cavendish 2009), 329–351.

12 In fact many such claims have been successful, see for an overview the yearly publication on the opinions of the Dutch Equal Treatment Commission: *Gelijke behandeling: oordelen en commentaar* [Equal treatment: opinions and comments] (Kluwer). Regrettably no overview is available in English.

1.2 Sex

Challenging non-accommodation of the issues that are central to this chapter as sex discrimination seems much less common, though it certainly is not far-fetched. Where dress codes by implication prohibit headscarves or face-covering veils, the disparate impact of such dress codes on Muslim women seems obvious. Multiple discrimination grounds are at work here and intersect. In fact, in Norway the *Ombud* upheld a claim by a Muslim woman that a dress code which prohibited her from wearing a headscarf at work constituted indirect sex discrimination.[13]

This Norwegian framing seems to be in stark contrast with approaches that would regard wearing a headscarf and/or face-covering veil as *incompatible* with the principle of sex equality. As far as face-covering veils are concerned, the latter seems to be the dominant view in European jurisdictions. As president Sarkozy said when explaining the reasons for introducing a general ban on face-covering veils in France, a *burqa* is "a sign of subservience and debasement," which is contrary to the principle of sex equality.[14] In the same vein, a parliamentary commission of inquiry on the wearing of the *burqa*, which published its report in January 2010, considers that wearing it is a practice that contradicts the fundamental values of the French Republic, especially the freedom and dignity of women. The ban has been upheld by the Constitutional Council.[15] Whatever the merits of this position, it seems to express a general mood towards *burqas*.

In regards to *headscarves* the legal mood is much more mixed. Sex equality played a clear role in the French discussions on banning ostentatious religious symbols in public schools. Many regarded the ban necessary to protect girls from being pressured into wearing a symbol of their inferiority.[16] In this respect, the French find themselves in respectable company. The ECtHR expressed several times that wearing a headscarf is "hard to square" with sex equality.[17] In several other countries such as the Netherlands and the UK, the notion of sex equality is hardly referred to in the case law, so apparently wearing

---

13 For a description of the case and its outcome see H. Skjeie, "Headscarves in Schools: European Comparisons," in *Religious Pluralism and Human Rights in Europe: Where to Draw the Line?* (M. L. P. Loenen and J. E. Goldschmidt, eds, Intersentia, 2007), 129–145.

14 See, for example, J. Galbraith-Marten, "Religious Beliefs and the UK Courts," *The Times* (UK) 16 September 2010, available at www.timesonline.co.uk.

15 M. McKee, "France Constitutional Court Approves Burqa Ban," *Jurist* 7 October 2010, available at http://jurist.org.

16 See, for example, the report of the Stasi Commission, which advised the French Government on a ban on religious symbols: Commission de réflexion sur l'application du principe de laïcité dans la République, *Rapport au président de la République*, 11 December 2003, available at http://lesrapports.ladocumentationfrancaise.fr/BRP/034000725/0000.pdf.

17 ECtHR 15 February 2001, *Dahlab* v. *Switzerland* (decision on admissibility), App. No. 42393/98 and ECtHR 10 November 2005, *Sahin* v. *Turkey* (Grand Chamber), section 111, App. No. 44774/98.

a headscarf is not considered to be incompatible with it. In Germany the *Bundesverfassungsgericht*, the Constitutional Court, specifically warned against interpreting the headscarf in this way. In 2003 it decided that a prohibition for a teacher in a public school to wear a headscarf must have a basis in law and that it is up to the legislatures of the states to decide whether valid reasons exist to do so. At the same time, it explicitly stated that such a decision could not be based on the presumption that wearing a headscarf is symbolic of women's oppression. The *Bundesverfassungsgericht* referred to recent research which shows that young women often start wearing a headscarf to lead self-chosen lives without foregoing their culture of origin.[18]

The unwillingness to hire someone because (s)he refuses to *shake hands* is not likely to be framed as potential sex discrimination instead of discrimination on grounds of religion. First of all, within Muslim groups practicing it, both men and women adhere to it and no clear indications of a particular disparate impact on either group exist. Moreover, the person not willing to shake hands with someone of the opposite sex is by many perceived as discriminating him- or herself on grounds of sex. So how could Muslims who practice this then avail themselves of a prohibition of sex discrimination to be allowed to act as such?

Where indirect sex discrimination in employment is potentially at stake, the objective justification test to be applied under the applicable EU directive would generally be strict. Though the ECJ case law seems to show an increasing leniency in assessing the objective justification put forward by Member States, especially in social security and social policy cases, the standard in relation to employers is strict.[19] If so, not many exceptions will be allowed, and probably fewer than are allowed right now in several European countries. As Roseberry remarks when commenting on a Danish headscarf case in which religion-based discrimination was the focus and a prohibition to wear a headscarf was upheld: "Applying the stricter burden of proof required by the law on sex discrimination could have resulted in a different outcome."[20] Of course, we will have to wait and see what the Court's approach will be when it is asked to decide on this issue.

---

18 *Bundesverfassungsgericht*, 24 September 2003, *Ludin*, 2BvR 1436/02: "Die Forschungsergebnisse zeigen jedoch, dass die Deutung des Kopftuchs nicht auf ein Zeichen gesellschaftlicher Unterdrückung der Frau verkurzt werden darf. Vielmehr kann das Kopftuch für junge muslimische Frauen auch ein frei gewähltes Mittel sein, um ohne Bruch mit der Herkunfstkultur ein selbstbestimmtes Leben zu führen." (Section 52).

19 Cf. D. Schiek, L. Waddington and M. Bell (eds), *Cases, Materials and Texts on National, Supranational and International Non-discrimination Law* (Hart Publishing 2007), 443–451, and C. Tobler, *Indirect discrimination. A Case Study into the Legal Development of the Concept of Indirect Discrimination under EU law* (Intersentia 2005), 245–246.

20 L. Roseberry, "Religion, Ethnicity and Gender in the Danish Headscarf Debate in European Union Non-discrimination Law," in *Comparative Perspectives on Multidimensional Equality Law* (D. Schiek and V. Chege, eds, Routledge-Cavendish 2009), 337.

1.3 Race/ethnic origin

As the great majority of Muslims have a non-western immigrant background, framing the issues in terms of discrimination on grounds of race also seems feasible.[21] In fact, for quite a few women the choice to wear a headscarf may spring rather from a wish to express their cultural background and identity than from a specific interpretation of religious prescriptions. The headscarf emphasizes this identity as something to be proud of in reaction to negative or hostile attitudes by majority groups and as a statement against pressures to dissolve into the dominant culture.[22] This fits with the fact that the issues discussed in this chapter play an important part in the much larger public debate on the integration of immigrant groups. Should they assimilate or should Western societies opt for a multiculturalist future? The debate has become even more sensitive and complex because the issues have been taken up and seem to me in some way to be "hijacked" by right-wing groups who are generally known for hostility towards non-western immigration and for promoting nationalist sentiment. Therefore, the issues figure prominently on their agenda. Thus, persons endorsing very different political views who may also be critical of some Islamic practices may feel they are unwillingly supporting this agenda.

Given this background, the interpretation by the ECJ of the concept of race and ethnic origin discrimination in the EU directive is of crucial importance. Again, legal practice in the Member States may vary in its approaches. In the Netherlands, for instance, race discrimination is conceived broadly to include color, descent, or national or ethnic origin.[23] Yet so far none of the issues dealt with in this chapter have been assessed in terms of discrimination on grounds of race or ethnic origin. Most are handled as cases involving discrimination based on religion. In the UK, race discrimination is defined broadly as well and includes discrimination against a group of persons defined by reference to color, race, nationality or ethnic or national origins. The prohibition of race discrimination has been used to challenge dress codes that disadvantage certain religious minorities.[24] Thus Sikhs have brought successful claims of race discrimination against the prohibition of wearing a turban. Sikhs are considered to constitute a distinct ethnic group in addition to a religious one and so could claim the protection of legislation combating discrimination on grounds of race.[25] Muslims, however, have not been considered

21 *Id.*, 333.

22 See more extensively on the position and identity of Islamic groups in Western Europe, including the position of women: S. Ferrari and A. Bradney (eds), *Islam and European legal systems*, (Ashgate 2000) and S. Vertovec and C. Peach (eds), *Islam in Europe. The Politics of Religion and Community* (Macmillan Press 1997).

23 This approach is based on the Convention on the Elimination of All Discrimination on the basis of Race that embraces a broad definition as well (Article 1, Section 1).

24 See, for an overview, S. Poulter, "Muslim Headscarves in School: Contrasting Legal Approaches in England and France," 17 *Oxford Journal of Legal Studies* 1997, 43–74.

25 *Mandla* v. *Dowell Lee* [1983] 2 AC 548 (HL).

as such because their backgrounds are considered too diverse. The difficulties involved in thus separating religion and ethnic origin are manifold.[26]

Generally speaking, race discrimination is considered to be particularly offensive. This suggests that the existence of a link between discrimination on grounds of religion and race will make the former even more onerous and less easy to justify, and met with stricter scrutiny by reviewing courts, including the ECJ. The case law of the European Court of Human Rights provides an interesting example. According to this court, race discrimination is a "particularly invidious kind of discrimination" that merits very strict review indeed: "Where the difference in treatment is based on race, colour or ethnic origin, the notion of objective and reasonable classification must be interpreted *as strictly as possible* [emphasis added]."[27]

2. Indirect discrimination and accommodation of religion

The second major decision to be made by the ECJ regards the question whether, and if so to what extent, the application of the concept of indirect discrimination requires accommodation of religion. In this respect the Dutch experiences provide some very interesting examples of the potential scope of the concept of indirect discrimination. I will illustrate this by giving a sample of the opinions of the Dutch ETC, in which it concluded that the refusal to accommodate the religious wishes of the complainant constituted indirect discrimination.[28] Interestingly, the ETC explicitly developed its jurisprudential line on the basis of the ECJ's approach to indirect discrimination on grounds of sex (or perhaps rather: on its interpretation of that approach). Though the Equal Treatment Commission cannot give legally binding decisions, its opinions are adhered to in the majority of cases. As access to the ETC is easy and inexpensive, it handles several hundred equal treatment and non-discrimination claims each year and has built up a considerable body of (quasi-judicial) "case law."

2.1 Accommodation of religious days of rest and worship

A first line of cases concerns the accommodation of employees' wishes to be free on their religious day of rest and to have time off for attending to their prayers.

---

26 See S. Fredman, "Equality: a New Generation?" 30 *Industrial law Journal* 145 2001, 145–168.

27 ECtHR (Grand Chamber) 13 November 2007, *D. H.* v. *Czech Republic*, App. No. 57325.

28 For an overview of Dutch anti-discrimination law and the supervising role of the Equal Treatment Commission see J. Goldschmidt, "Anti-discrimination Law in the Netherlands: A Specific Legal Patchwork, Normative System and Institutional Structure," in *Taking Employment Discrimination Seriously: Chinese and European Perspectives* (Y. Li and J. Goldschmidt, eds, Martinus Nijhoff 2009), 239–260.

Two judgments of the ETC are illustrative of its reasoning in such cases. The first concerned a devout Christian who was refused as lockkeeper because he would not be available for work on Sundays.[29] He claimed this treatment amounted to indirect discrimination on grounds of religion. The ETC considered the requirement to be available for work on all days of the week to have a disparate impact on workers such as complainants who, for religious reasons, do not wish to work on their Sabbath day. This amounts to indirect discrimination on grounds of religion, unless the employer can put forward an objective justification. To be objectively justified the treatment has to pursue a legitimate aim and the means employed have to be appropriate and necessary to achieve it. In many, if not most, cases the objective justification test will turn on the "necessity" element. To decide about the necessity of the measure the ETC assesses whether the aim cannot be achieved by other, less problematic means (i.e. a subsidiarity test) and whether the means chosen are proportionate (i.e. a proportionality test). Applied to the case at hand the ETC concluded the requirement of necessity was not met. The employer had not been able to provide a convincing argument why the accommodation of a single lockkeeper who does not wish to work on Sundays would give rise to problems in servicing the locks in the district concerned. Though this judgment leaves room for a different outcome in other cases, depending on the actual possibilities for the employer to accommodate the wishes of an employee without running into problems, the message is clear: a worker has a presumptive right to be accommodated in his wish to respect his religious day of rest. An employer who cannot put forward compelling reasons for not accommodating this wish discriminates on the grounds of religion.

In the second case a Muslim applicant was refused for the job of social counselor because he would not be fully available on Friday afternoon as he wished to attend Friday prayer in the mosque.[30] To do so he needed an extension of his lunch break by about an hour. The employer did not want to allow this, as all counselors were expected to be present on Friday afternoon to meet their clients. No exceptions were made, be it for employees who would also prefer to be free on Friday afternoon to take care of their children or, as in this case, go for their prayers. Again the ETC considered the employer's aim in itself legitimate, but the means chosen lacked the required necessity. As the extra time needed to attend Friday prayer was very limited, the refusal to employ the applicant for not being available all Friday afternoon was not necessary to make sure clients are able to meet their counselors on Friday afternoon.

---

29 ETC opinion 2006-147. All opinions are available at www.cgb.nl, but are in Dutch only.

30 ETC opinion 1999-49.

2.2 Accommodation of wearing religiously inspired dress

A second line of cases has clarified how the concept of indirect discrimination protects workers who wish to wear a headscarf or other religiously inspired symbols at work. As in the cases described in the previous section, the starting point is the obligation of the employer to accommodate the wishes of the employee unless this cannot be reasonably required, or, in terms of the objective justification test: unless the reasons for the employer's refusal to accommodate serve a legitimate aim and the means employed are appropriate and necessary to achieve it. Generally speaking, where headscarves are concerned a very limited number of justifications have been accepted so far. Again, the ETC interprets the requirement of the means being "necessary" in a very strict way. Safety and security can indeed provide a justification, but not, for instance, the wish not to offend clients or to protect the image of an enterprise. In the latter cases the ETC often requires employers to adapt their dress codes to include matching headscarves instead of prohibiting them altogether.[31] In the context of public employment, the ETC has been reluctant to accept the argument of state neutrality to prohibit religiously inspired dress. So far, this argument has not been accepted in the case of public school teachers[32] and has met with a rather critical approach in relation to police officers.[33] Regarding judges, however, the ETC is likely to accept the argument.[34]

The approach to banning face-covering veils from the workplace will probably be quite different. In a case dealing with a student who challenged a ban on face-covering veils the ETC endorsed arguments that focus on the impediments such veiling poses to communication and/or safety.[35] This would seem to hold equally true for the workplace.

Interestingly, the ETC has been much more protective of face-covering veils where clients are concerned. Though not involving employment, the cases are interesting to mention here because of the far-reaching obligation to accommodate religiously inspired practices the ETC derives from the concept of indirect discrimination. In one of the cases a school director asked the ETC whether his

31 See for an overview the guidelines the Equal Treatment Commission has formulated on employment, religion and equal treatment: Commissie Gelijke Behandeling, *Advies Commissie Gelijke Behandeling inzake arbeid, religie en gelijke behandeling*, 12 August 2004, available at www.cgb.nl.

32 ETC opinion 1999-18.

33 ETC opinion 2006-30.

34 This can be derived from a case concerning a law clerk (ETC opinion 2001-53). Though the refusal to accommodate her wish to wear a headscarf in the courtroom during sessions of the court was held to infringe the equal treatment act, the wording of the decision indicates that the Commission would have arrived at a different conclusion if she had been a judge. This case gave rise to considerable debate. The actual practice did not change and the overall consensus seems to be that state neutrality requires judges not to show their religious or other convictions by wearing any such symbols in court.

35 ETC opinion 2003-40.

behavior towards the mother of a potential future pupil had been legitimate.[36] When the mother came for a meeting to register her child, the director had refused to talk to her because she was wearing a face-covering veil which she did not want to remove during the interview. Because of this, she had not been able to register her child for the school. The director did not mind if parents did not want to shake his hand or were unwilling to look him in the eyes, but he did not want to accept talking to someone wearing a full veil. To justify his action the director pointed to the difficulties such veils pose for proper communication and to the difficulties this parent would pose if she were to participate in all kinds of school activities. Other parents would certainly object to her veil and he had to take that into account as well. The ETC held that the director's actions violated the General Equal Treatment Act, as they constitute indirect discrimination on the basis of religion. According to the ETC, in this case no objective justification existed for the treatment. First, it was considered that the director could have received the necessary information, which was in fact not very extensive, notwithstanding the woman wearing the veil. Alternatively, he could have fetched a female colleague to talk to the woman instead. Besides, the results of his refusal, that the mother could not register her child, was disproportionate taking into consideration the limited meaning of the interview: hardly ever was a child rejected as a pupil. As far as the second argument of the director was concerned, the ETC considered that the question whether the director could legitimately refuse a mother to participate in all kinds of school activities because she wears a face-covering veil would have to be decided on a case-by-case basis and cannot be decided in the abstract.

A second case concerned an organization that gives socially vulnerable people advice on all kinds of financial and other issues.[37] The organization employed both male and female social counselors who helped clients on a first-come, first-served basis during fixed consultation hours. Thus clients did not have their "own" counselor if they visited more than once. The policy of the organization was not to speak with women wearing face-covering veils, unless they remove the veil during the interview with the social counselor, whether this person be a man or a woman. This was motivated by the need for good communication. Facial expressions were considered to be very important to be sure whether the client had understood everything (many clients being very poor in Dutch). If the client refused to uncover her face during the interview, she would be sent away.

The ETC did not accept that this argument fulfilled the required test of an "objective justification" and considered the policy to constitute indirect discrimination on the basis of religion. Though the Commission acknowledged that the aim of the policy, that is guaranteeing good communication, was legitimate, the means did not meet the test of subsidiarity: as in the case of the school director, the Commission pointed to the fact that the social counselors had enough women

36 ETC opinion 2004-95.
37 ETC opinion 2005-86.

available to allocate veil-wearing women to female counselors, in whose presence they would feel comfortable removing the veil.

Both cases involving face-covering veils show how the concept of indirect discrimination again works as an instrument to create a presumptive *right* to accommodation of religion.

2.3 Accommodation of religiously inspired objections to perform certain acts

A third line of cases worth mentioning here concerns religiously inspired wishes to refrain from performing certain acts that are considered part of the job or normal functioning in the workplace. Also in this type of case the ETC expects employers to do their very best to accommodate such wishes. Thus a Muslim employee in a home for old age pensioners successfully claimed accommodation of her wish not to be involved in serving alcoholic beverages to the clients.[38] Similarly, a trainee at a medical centre was justified in refusing to vaccinate children because of her religiously inspired conscientious objection to vaccination.[39]

In most cases dealing with employees who refused to shake hands with persons of the opposite sex, the ETC has been similarly strict for employers. Interestingly, however, in several of these cases the Dutch courts that rendered legally binding decisions in the subsequent procedures came to different conclusions. The first case concerned a Muslim man who was denied a job as a customer manager at the Social Services Department of the city of Rotterdam because of his refusal to shake hands with women.[40] The municipality stated in defense that they had to protect women against sex discrimination by a civil servant. The ETC held that the protection of women against discrimination constituted a legitimate aim, but that the municipality had failed to seek alternative ways of showing respect to both male and female clients equally, as the applicant had offered to refrain from shaking hands with both men and women and greet everyone respectfully in some other way. The District Court of Rotterdam, however, considered that a customer manager is an important contact person between the local authorities and the citizens. The Court ruled that the city of Rotterdam has the right to choose "to observe the usual rules of etiquette and of greeting customs in the Netherlands." As a result, the Court considered it necessary and proportional to reject a candidate for the specific position who is not willing to observe those rules of etiquette.[41]

---

38 ETC opinion 2000-75. A recent German case was decided in a similar way: an employer has to accommodate the wish of a Muslim shelf stocker in a supermarket not to stock alcohol if this is practically feasible. See X., "Muslim Shelf Stockers Can Refuse to Handle Alcohol," *Spiegel Online* 25 February 2011, available at www.spiegel.de/international.

39 ETC opinion 2001-89.

40 ETC opinion 2006-202.

41 District Court of Rotterdam 6 August 2008, *LJN*: BD9643, available at www.rechtspraak.nl.

The second case concerned a female teacher in a public school, who decided no longer to shake hands with male persons and was subsequently dismissed. The ETC considered this to constitute indirect discrimination on the ground of religion for similar reasons as in the first case. The teacher was prepared to greet everyone in the same (sex neutral) way and in a polite manner, but without shaking hands.[42] In subsequent legal procedures however, the Central Board of Appeal considered that the school had a legitimate aim in requiring their teachers to shake hands irrespective of sex, as they wanted to comply with prevailing customs in Dutch society. This was deemed particularly important, as the school had many pupils and teachers of multi-ethnic descent. Pupils have to be prepared for a society in which shaking hands is the prevailing custom for greeting and showing respect. The dismissal of the teacher was judged lawful as it pursued a legitimate aim and the dismissal was deemed necessary and proportional.[43]

The diverging conclusions of the ETC and the courts in this type of case shows the crucial role the objective justification test plays. More specifically, the difference in outcome seems to stem from the far stricter approach of the ETC towards the requirement that the policy or measure is indeed "necessary" to achieve a legitimate aim. The ETC gives almost absolute status to the subsidiarity test, that is the test whether the same aim could have been achieved with less restrictive means.

Elsewhere I have been very critical of the way in which this approach may lead to endorsing claims for accommodating all kinds of sex-segregated practice, as the cases concerning the face-covering veils show.[44] To fulfill both the religiously inspired wish of some Muslim women not to speak to men unveiled *and* to guarantee good communication, the school and the social counselors were supposed, if not required, to provide sex-segregated services to the women concerned. It seems only a small step from here to requiring employers to similarly accommodate the wishes of some Muslim women and men not to work closely together with persons of the opposite sex, not to share a working room or canteen facilities and so on. As in many instances it will no doubt be quite easy for employers to arrange for separate facilities without compromising the work to be done. How can an employer pass the objective justification test if it is applied as strictly as by the ETC? I would regard this as highly problematic considering the history of "separate spheres" that has been a barrier to the emancipation of women for such a long time. In fact, I would submit that accommodation of sex-segregated practices that are solely based on (religiously or otherwise) inspired perceptions of the proper relationship between men and women is incompatible with the demands of equal treatment and non-discrimination on grounds of sex.

42 ETC opinion 2006-220.

43 Central Board of Appeal 7 May 2009, *LJN*: BI2440, available at www.rechtspraak.nl.

44 T. Loenen, 2006. "Gezichtsbedekkende sluiers: toestaan of beperken?" 31 *NJCM-Bulletin* 984 (2006), 984–996.

More recently the ETC itself seems to have become worried about the far-reaching consequences of its very strict approach. In several cases it has voiced its qualms about accommodating religiously inspired wishes that lead to sex segregation in an *obiter dictum*. One of these concerned the way in which an institute of higher education accommodated a student who did not wish to have physical contact with persons of the opposite sex. The student was not just allowed to refrain from shaking hands, but in addition he was provided with examiners of the same sex. This measure was intended to prevent any doubts with regards to the examiners' impartiality towards him. The ETC warned the institute that this kind of accommodation is undesirable and even incompatible with the object and purpose of the equal treatment legislation.[45]

2.4 Conclusions on the potential of indirect discrimination review

The Dutch experience shows the potential role of the concept of indirect discrimination in supporting claims for accommodation of religion in the workplace. It will be up to the ECJ to decide whether this approach is to be followed under the EU directives, or whether Dutch law is providing more than is required. In this respect it will first of all be crucial how the ECJ will approach the link between the disparate impact suffered by certain employees and their specific religious convictions. Is any practice which is inspired by religion and is adversely affected by an employer's policy or measure able to set off a claim of indirect discrimination on grounds of religion, which can only be refuted if it passes the (supposedly strict) objective justification test? As shown above, the ETC is very generous in accepting almost any practices claimed by complainants to be a manifestation of religion as such. Even the refusal to serve alcohol (not having to drink it yourself) and a refusal to vaccinate patients (not being forced to receive a vaccination yourself) were accepted as a religious expression that needs to be respected to prevent indirect discrimination on grounds of religion. If so, potentially any act in daily life could be argued to constitute a religious manifestation. It should be noted that the European Court of Human Rights has not been as deferential in accepting what individuals themselves perceive as manifestations of religion that merit protection under the ECHR.[46] Secondly, it will be crucial how strict the ECJ will be in applying the objective justification

---

45 ETC opinion 2009-1, Section 3.16.

46 See, for example, the analysis of the Court's case law on this subject in C. Evans, *Freedom of Religion Under the European Convention on Human Rights* (Oxford University Press 2001), and for subsequent case law see, for example, the decision of the ECtHR 2 October 2001, *Pichon and Sajous* v. *France*, App. No. 49853/99. In this case two pharmacists complained about being obliged by French legislation to sell contraceptives in contravention of their religious objections. The Court did not consider this requirement to engage their right to freedom of religion as guaranteed under the Convention.

test. Here again I hope to have shown the far-reaching potential of the concept of indirect discrimination if it is applied as strictly as in the opinions of the ETC.

3. Uniform application of EU equality law versus national discretion

The importance of the strictness of the test to be applied points to a third major choice to be made by the ECJ: how much discretion will the ECJ leave to the national authorities to implement and apply the non-discrimination provisions of the equality directives in this sensitive area? A strict interpretation could entail far-reaching obligations to accommodate religion in the workplace that may not be acceptable to all Member States. The Dutch interpretation of non-discrimination law, for instance, which does not allow for a refusal to employ a Muslim woman as a public school teacher because she wishes to wear a headscarf in class, would appear unacceptable for France. How is the ECJ to decide in this sensitive area? Generally speaking, though EU directives may leave the forms and methods chosen to the discretion of the Member States, the results to be achieved are binding. This suggests a more or less uniform outcome of discrimination claims across Europe should be achieved, at least as far as minimum standards are concerned.

In the area of sex discrimination this seems to be the case. The ECJ's case law has provided a set of rather detailed rules and principles that govern the interpretation and transposition of the directives in all Member States. They ensure that the levels of protection against discrimination to be derived from EU law are similar between countries.[47]

As the widely diverging approaches to the sensitive issues discussed in this chapter show, in the area of discrimination on grounds of religion or belief this kind of uniformity may be a much more controversial goal to pursue for political reasons. In this respect the approach by the European Court of Human Rights may be telling.

The ECtHR leaves the states party to ECHR a wide margin of appreciation to regulate relationships between state and religion and to limit manifestations of religion accordingly, at least outside the private sphere. The ECtHR considers the *forum internum* to constitute the core of the right to freedom of religion that is protected by Article 9 of the ECHR. Individual *manifestations* of religion receive much less protection. The ECtHR has shown itself particularly deferential in its case law concerning headscarf bans in public education. In the landmark case *Sahin* v. *Turkey* it has elaborated its approach.[48] This case concerned a university student who objected to the dress regulations of a Turkish state university. The regulations contained a ban on all religious attire being worn in the university.

---

47 For an overview of sex discrimination case law see, for example, E. Ellis, *EU Anti-Discrimination Law* (Oxford University Press 2005).

48 ECtHR (Grand Chamber) 10 November 2005, *Leila Sahin* v. *Turkey*, App. No. 44774/98.

The ECtHR held the ban to be compatible with the rights enshrined in the ECHR. In its decision the ECtHR kept its distance and emphasized the margin of appreciation to be left to the states party to the Convention:

> where questions concerning the relationship between State and religions are concerned, on which opinion in a democratic society may reasonably differ widely, the role of the national decision-making body must be given special importance.[49]

The ECtHR accorded particular importance to the lack of a common ground between the states party to the Convention regarding the regulation of wearing religious symbols in public education. Consequently the Turkish government was given a significant margin of appreciation to decide whether it is indeed "necessary" in the Turkish context to prohibit wearing religious symbols in teaching institutions. The ECtHR accepted the arguments put forward by the government, especially those that referred to the specific Turkish history of secularism, and the strong political significance of wearing a headscarf in Turkey connected with the growing influence of extremist political movements in that country. As a result Turkey was allowed to prohibit not just teachers, but also grown-up students from wearing religious symbols in educational institutions. In a way this is all the more remarkable, as even in France, well known for its strict *laïcité*, this is not the case. For students, the legal ban introduced in 2004 extends only to primary and secondary education, not to universities. In fact, one may wonder whether in the specific context of university education a "common ground" was indeed lacking in European countries.[50]

Though the different context in which the ECtHR operates should be kept in mind, a deferential approach would be politically attractive for the ECJ as well. As has been pointed out by Bell, the EU often tries to avoid getting involved in moral controversies. He refers to the transnational (non-)recognition of same-sex partnerships as an example. In this context the ECJ has taken pains to stay away from imposing a specific position. As Bell remarks: "This is perhaps best described as a form of 'moral subsidiarity,' which regards issues of cultural or moral sensitivity as best left to national discretion."[51] If the ECJ follows this approach where headscarf bans are at stake, this would mean the directives will provide women challenging such bans with procedural safeguards, but only by requiring national legal bodies to assess whether they serve a legitimate aim and are appropriate and necessary to that end in the specific national context, and

49 ECtHR (Grand Chamber) 10 November 2005, *Leila Sahin* v. *Turkey*, App. No. 44774/98, par. 109.

50 Cf. the dissenting opinion of judge Tulkens in the *Sahin* judgment.

51 M. Bell, *Anti-discrimination Law and the European Union* (Oxford University Press 2002), 120.

without formulating more detailed and uniform European criteria to guide such an assessment.

Though politically understandable, such an approach has considerable setbacks. To start with, it may leave vulnerable minority groups with less human rights protection than majority groups. The German experience may provide an example of how this may turn out. As mentioned before, in Germany the *Bundesverfassungsgericht* was confronted with the question of whether it was constitutional for a public school to prohibit a Muslim teacher to wear a headscarf in the class room. The Court held that this issue should be decided through the democratic process and that any restriction would have to be based on a formal act of the legislatures of the German states. Subsequently, several states adopted such legislation restricting the right to manifest religion through certain forms of dress. These restrictions will predominantly affect members of minority religions such as Muslims. Several German states even introduced legislation which more or less explicitly bars Muslim religious symbols, leaving the wearing of Christian attire untouched. In fact, in some states this was for the explicit purpose of allowing nuns or monks to teach in public schools while wearing their habit. The difference in treatment was sometimes justified by the argument that Christian symbols are to be perceived as religiously neutral as they have become part of the Western cultural tradition. As such the legislation was presented as not privileging one religion over another, but as just protecting a neutral educational setting. So far, such regulations have not been struck down by German courts as incompatible with equality and non-discrimination.[52]

A second setback of a deferential approach by the ECJ could be that it potentially leads to widely diverging outcomes of transposing the equality directives in this area: they may come to mean entirely different things in different countries. This is perhaps all the more problematic as some of the issues clearly engage potential sex discrimination, an area where the ECJ traditionally has been strict in not allowing widely diverging practices between states. One wonders whether a relaxation of the standards regarding non-discrimination on grounds of sex in one area could lead to a relaxation in other areas as well. In addition, condoning widely diverging practices concerning headscarf bans may affect the free movement of female workers. In France, for instance, no public employment is available to Muslim women wearing headscarves. How many women from countries not having headscarf bans will be discouraged from moving to France for this reason?

52 For an overview of the German developments see U. Sachsofsky, "Religion and Equality in Germany. The Headscarf Debate from a Constitutional Perspective," in *European Union Non-discrimination Law. Comparative Perspectives on Multidimensional Equality Law* (D. Schiek and V. Chege, eds, Routledge/Cavendish 2009), 353–370.

Concluding remarks

In this chapter I explored some of the difficult choices awaiting the ECJ when it is called upon to assess the Member States' obligations to accommodate religious practices that have raised considerable controversy. Where EU countries sometimes have diametrically opposite approaches (which they often cherish) the Court faces a double bind. In particular, the different perceptions of Islamic practices in relation to women's equality are highly problematic from the point of view of the EU equality directives. In some countries, wearing a headscarf as a manifestation of Islamic faith is perceived as incompatible with the notion of sex equality, whereas in other jurisdictions Muslim women faced with a prohibition of wearing it at work can bring a claim of indirect sex discrimination.

We will have to wait and see how the ECJ will deal with this situation. Will it impose a uniform standard on all Member States in such controversial cases or leave them wide discretion? On the one hand the directives would seem to call for the former. Although Member States may choose the means to implement the non-discrimination standards laid down in the equality directives, they are bound to achieve an equal outcome, that is guarantee an equal level of protection against discrimination on grounds of religion, sex or race. Yet it is hard to conceive of a substantively uniform level of protection that would be politically acceptable to all EU countries. Approaches in the UK and France, to name only two, are worlds apart. In this context a hands-off approach focusing on some procedural safeguards only may be inevitable. If this is the case, one wonders though why we would have EU directives that cover this type of issue to start with.

Chapter 6

Silence is Golden? Charting the Intersections of Speech and Direct Discrimination under EU Law with a Special Focus on Racial and Religious Discrimination in Recruitment

Jogchum Vrielink*

Introduction

Discrimination inter alia on the grounds of race and religion is prohibited in the European workplace.[1] Speech,[2] be it of a religious or any other nature, is considered to be free unless specific restrictions apply. Individuals have a fundamental right to speak, even if the messages they convey are unpopular, insulting or misleading.[3] So what happens when speech and discrimination collide or intersect in the context of the workplace?

Cases abound of such collisions, involving the entire cast of workplace actors. Even though discrimination is most often thought of as a form of conduct, it is not exceptional for it to in fact be realized or evidenced by means of speech, as much human activity and decision-making in particular takes place by means of speech. In many cases these situations will not raise significant free speech concerns, since

* This work was supported by the RELIGARE project, which received funding under the European Commission's Seventh Framework Programme (Socio-economic Sciences and Humanities) under grant agreement number 44635. The author thanks Christian Bayart, Marie-Claire Foblets and Stefan Sottiaux for their insightful suggestions.

1 As in many other, non-European, contexts, of course. However, the European workplace constitutes the focus of this chapter, in the light of the focus of the symposium that gave rise to it, and due to the—more or less—uniform (minimum) norms that exist throughout the whole of the EU region, in enactment of the relevant directives (*infra* §1).

2 Speech, for the purposes of this chapter, is understood as anything a person says, writes or does that is intended to convey a message that could reasonably be expected to be understood by others. The emphasis, however, is on verbal and written utterances.

3 Or, as the mantra of the European Court of Human Rights (ECtHR) would have it, "freedom of expression ... is applicable not only to 'information' or 'ideas' that are favourably received or regarded as inoffensive or as a matter of indifference, but also to those that offend, shock or disturb the State or any sector of the population" (ECtHR 7 December 1976, *Handyside* v. *United Kingdom*, App. No. 5493/72, par. 49).

often such "communicative efforts do not seriously implicate the values that lie behind freedom of speech."[4] The employer that tells a candidate that he or she will not be hired or promoted because of his or her sex, ethnicity, religion or belief, sexual orientation, age or handicap may technically be engaging in speech, but he or she will thereby (generally) be discriminating as well. It is doubtful that even the most hardened free speech absolutists would deny this. Likewise, so-called smoking gun statements—expressing outward discriminatory animus, and followed by a negative decision regarding the applicant—are commonly accepted as evidence in discrimination cases.

The situation can also be less clear-cut however, with the conflation or evidentiary bond between discrimination and speech being more ambiguous. What if, for instance, an employer publicly engages in discriminatory—e.g. racist or anti-religious—speech or even announces his intention to discriminate, but there are no other signs that a discriminatory act took place? And to what extent does discrimination law also restrict the types of questions that an employer can ask or more generally the things he can say during a job interview? More controversial still is the issue of "discriminatory"[5] workplace harassment: can jokes, posters, or even playing certain types of music amount to a hostile work environment violating someone's dignity, and therefore amount to discrimination? In these and many other cases in which speech and discrimination law collide, it must be decided whether the expression deserves free speech protection, or whether it really amounts to (evidence of) a prohibited form of discrimination.

At present, such situations remain fundamentally under-analyzed, which, especially in the light of their frequent occurrence, can be deemed problematic, since it is liable to pave the way for arbitrary decisions both within and across EU Member States. So far, the only aspect of this issue that has received systematic attention in the literature is the tension between the prohibition of harassment and free speech principles.[6] While the latter issue has been debated vigorously, the

4 K. Greenawalt, *Speech, Crime, and the Uses of Language* (Oxford University Press 1989), 3 (speaking not specifically about speech and discrimination in the workplace, but more generally about the issue of why "many acts of communication have never been thought to raise free speech problems"). Compare F. Schauer, *Free Speech: A Philosophical Enquiry* (Cambridge University Press 1982), 13.

5 EU discrimination law defines harassment based on protected grounds as a manifestation of discrimination (*infra* §1).

6 And even such, mostly for the North-American context. For a selection, see: J. M. Balkin, "Free Speech and Hostile Environments," *Columbia Law Review* 2295 (1999); K. R. Browne, "Title VII as Censorship: Hostile-Environment Harassment and the First Amendment," 52 *Ohio State Law Journal* 481 (1991); J. B. Gerard, "The First Amendment in a Hostile Environment: A Primer on Free Speech and Sexual Harassment," 68 *Notre Dame Law Review* 1003 (1993); E. Volokh, "Freedom of Speech and Workplace Harassment," 39 *UCLA Law Review* 1791 (1992); E. Volokh, "How Harassment Law Restricts Free Speech," 47 *Rutgers Law Review* 563 (1995); E. Volokh, "What Speech Does 'Hostile Work Environment' Harassment Law Restrict?" 85 *Georgetown Law Journal* 627 (1997);

extent to which other manifestations of discrimination that fall within the scope of EU discrimination law—such as direct discrimination, indirect discrimination, and the instruction to discriminate—can also be realized or evidenced by means of speech, and if so what criteria the content and context of that speech has to meet without unduly restricting the freedom of speech, has been a neglected area.[7]

A general treatment of this vast and complicated topic exceeds the reach and ambitions of the current chapter. Instead, I will focus on one single category of overlap or tension between speech and discrimination: that of direct discrimination[8] by means of (or evidenced by) speech in the context of hiring procedures in private employment,[9] with a special focus on racial and religious discrimination.

The chapter starts with a brief overview of some of the key aspects of EU legislation prohibiting direct discrimination in employment and the workplace, which are relevant for the current purposes (§1). Subsequently, the chapter goes on to examine the extent to which direct discrimination in the context of hiring procedures, on the basis of race and/or religion in particular, can be realized or evidenced by means of speech (§2). I will conclude with a review of my main points, and with some closing thoughts (§3).

N. Strossen, "The Tensions Between Regulating Workplace Harassment and the First Amendment: No Trump," 71 *Chicago-Kent Law Review* 701 (1995). Specifically on the European context, see, for example: L. Vickers, "Is All Harassment Equal? The Case of Religious Harassment," 65 *Cambridge Law Journal* 579 (2006); I. Bacik, "Harassment," in *Equality in Diversity, The New Equality Directives* (C. Costello and E. Barry, eds, Irish Centre for European Law 2003), 151–176; J. Vrielink and S. Sottiaux, "Banning Sexism: How Harassment Law May Threaten Freedom of Expression and Undermine Antidiscrimination Policies," 10 *International Journal of Discrimination and the Law* 263 (2008).

7 This can be explained firstly due to the fact that the tension between harassment and free speech is prima facie most apparent. An additional reason for this one-sided attention arguably has to do with the "default" focus in both discrimination law and labor law analyses, which tends to be respectively on the victims and employees, and on their rights and freedoms, and much less so on those of the decision-makers in this context. This also explains why harassment is the only manifestation of discrimination that has regularly been analyzed from a (free) speech angle, since employees can engage in harassment vis-à-vis each other, while they—generally speaking—cannot (or are far less liable to) commit any of the other manifestations of discrimination.

8 The reasons for focusing on direct (rather than indirect) discrimination are related to the fact that—after intimidation—most cases in which speech is dealt with under discrimination law concern direct discrimination. An analysis of these types of cases would therefore seem to be the most relevant from a practical point of view. At the same time, this focus facilitates drawing on a significant number of non-fictitious illustrations.

9 The exclusive focus on hiring for *private* employment is due to the specific nature of speech restrictions and responsibilities that hold regarding (hiring for) the civil service. However, one could see Hans-Martien ten Napel's chapter in this volume as dealing with a particular aspect of this issue, i.e. that of symbolic religious speech by public employers.

1. EU framework concerning direct racial and religious discrimination in employment

The EU legal framework concerning the prohibition of discrimination on the grounds of race and religion in the area of employment is founded on Article 13 of the Treaty establishing the European Community ("EC Treaty"), which authorizes the Council to adopt measures to combat discrimination based on sex, racial or ethnic origin, religion or belief, disability, age or sexual orientation.[10]

In 2000, two directives were adopted pursuant to Article 13 of the EC Treaty: the so-called Race Equality Directive (RED)[11] and the Employment Equality Directive (EED).[12] The EED introduced minimal standards of non-discrimination on the grounds of religion or belief, disability, age and sexual orientation in all aspects of employment, including (decisions about) hiring, promoting, compensating and firing employees. The RED—offering protection only to discrimination on the basis of race and ethnic origin—covers employment as well, while also extending to other areas of public life, such as social protection, health care, education and access to goods and services.

In doing so, the directives aim at ensuring access to important opportunities for the full participation of all persons in society—inter alia in the workplace—irrespective of their protected grounds, in order that they might realize their potential.[13] The Council believes furthermore that discrimination based on the protected grounds "may undermine the achievement of the objectives of the EC Treaty," and in particular "the attainment of a high level of employment and social protection, raising the standard of living and the quality of life, economic and social cohesion and solidarity, and the free movement of persons."[14]

Both the EED and the RED prohibit a number of manifestations of discrimination, i.e. direct discrimination, indirect discrimination, harassment and

10 Article 13 reads as follows: "1. Without prejudice to the other provisions of this Treaty and within the limits of the powers conferred by it upon the Community, the Council, acting unanimously on a proposal from the Commission and after consulting the European Parliament, may take appropriate action to combat discrimination based on sex, racial or ethnic origin, religion or belief, disability, age or sexual orientation. 2. By way of derogation from paragraph 1, when the Council adopts Community incentive measures, excluding any harmonisation of the laws and regulations of the Member States, to support action taken by the Member States in order to contribute to the achievement of the objectives referred to in paragraph 1, it shall act in accordance with the procedure referred to in Article 251."

11 Council Directive 2000/43/EC of 29 June 2000 implementing the principle of equal treatment between persons irrespective of racial or ethnic origin, *OJ 180 L* 19/07/2000, 23–27.

12 Council Directive 2000/78/EC of 27 November 2000 Establishing a General Framework for Equal Treatment in Employment and Occupation, *OJ 303 L* 02/12/2000, 16–22.

13 Preamble §12 RED; Preamble §9 EED.

14 Preamble §9 RED; Preamble §11 EED.

the instruction to discriminate.[15] Direct discrimination "shall be taken to occur where one person is treated less favourably than another is, has been or would be treated in a comparable situation," and such "on the grounds of" one of the protected characteristics.[16] As such, four elements need to be present in order for direct discrimination to be established: a less favorable treatment (1), of a person (2), than another person is, has been or would be treated in a comparable situation (3) and such on the grounds of inter alia race, religion or belief (4).[17] Crucial in direct discrimination is that the unfavorable treatment is directly predicated on the protected ground, in the sense of it being the *cause* or the *motive* (although this should be distinguished from intent, which is not required).[18]

Although not the topic of this text, the definition of indirect discrimination will nonetheless be relevant in the remainder of this chapter as well.[19] Indirect discrimination under both the EED and the RED occurs "where an apparently neutral provision, criterion or practice would put persons" of a certain racial or ethnic origin or of a particular religion or belief "at a particular disadvantage compared with other persons unless that provision, criterion or practice is objectively justified by a legitimate aim and the means of achieving that aim are appropriate and necessary."[20] Like direct discrimination, indirect discrimination therefore also requires the presence of four elements: there needs to be an

15 The EED also includes an obligation to make reasonable accommodations for persons with a handicap (Art. 5 EED), but does not, strictly speaking, define the refusal to make such accommodations as a manifestation of discrimination (see L. Waddington and A. Hendriks, "The Expanding Concept of Employment Discrimination in Europe: From Direct and Indirect Discrimination to Reasonable Accommodation Discrimination," 18 *International Journal of Comparative Labour Law and Industrial Relations* 403 (2002)). Some Member States do, however, in their implementation legislation of the Directive, explicitly include the refusal to make reasonable accommodations in the concept of discrimination.

16 Article 2 (2a) EED and RED.

17 See extensively M. J. Busstra, *The Implications of the Racial Equality Directive for Minority Protection Within the European Union* (Eleven International Publishing 2010), 148–156. See also: M. Ambrus, *Enforcement Mechanisms of the Racial Equality Directive and Minority Protection* (Eleven International Publishing 2010), 24–25.

18 R.A. Sedler, "The Role of 'Intent' in Discrimination Analysis," in *Non-Discrimination Law: Comparative Perspectives* (T. Loenen and P. Rodrigues, eds, Kluwer 1999); M. J. Busstra, *The Implications of the Racial Equality Directive for Minority Protection Within the European Union* (Eleven International Publishing 2010), 146; M. Ambrus, M. J. Busstra and K. Henrard, "The Racial Equality Directive and Effective Protection Against Discrimination: Mismatches Between the Substantive Law and Its Application," 3 *Erasmus Law Review* 165 (2010), 171; C. Bayart and C. Deiteren, "Direct en indirect onderscheid," in *De Nieuwe Federale Antidiscriminatiewetten* (C. Bayart, S. Sottiaux and S. Van Drooghenbroeck, eds, die Keure 2008), 195; E. Ellis, *EU Anti-Discrimination Law* (Oxford University Press 2005), 103; M. Ambrus, *Enforcement Mechanisms of the Racial Equality Directive and Minority Protection* (Eleven International Publishing 2010), 24–25.

19 Mainly in distinguishing and delineating it from direct discrimination.

20 Article 2 (2b) EED and RED.

apparently neutral provision, criterion or practice (1); that would put persons with the protected characteristics at a particular disadvantage (2); compared to other persons (3); unless that provision (etc.) is objectively justified by a legitimate aim and the means of achieving that aim are appropriate and necessary (4).[21]

In order for discrimination to be established under the directives, a two-phased model applies.[22] The applicant first needs to make (at least) a prima facie case of discrimination (§1.1). If successful, the burden of proof will shift so that it is subsequently for the respondent to demonstrate that no discrimination has taken place (§1.2).

1.1. First phase: prima facie case of discrimination

As mentioned, the applicant needs first to establish facts from which it may be presumed that discrimination took place. Both directives provide that the burden of proof—more specifically the burden of persuasion[23]—in (most)[24] discrimination cases will shift when complainants "establish, before a court or other competent authority, facts from which it may be presumed that there has been direct or indirect discrimination."[25]

As such, a presumption of discrimination is made on the basis of the facts, but the facts do not themselves constitute the presumption: the presumption results from drawing inferences from the facts.[26] Furthermore, the facts that are to be

---

21 See extensively M. J. Busstra, *The Implications of the Racial Equality Directive for Minority Protection Within the European Union* (Eleven International Publishing 2010), 203–231.

22 See extensively M. Ambrus, *Enforcement Mechanisms of the Racial Equality Directive and Minority Protection* (Eleven International Publishing 2010), 35–56.

23 In general evidence law two forms of the burden of proof tend to be distinguished: first an evidential or subjective burden of proof (burden of production), and secondly a legal or objective burden of proof (burden of persuasion). The burden of production concerns the duty upon parties in a legal proceeding to introduce sufficient evidence, or counter-evidence, relating to assertions of fact to have an issue be considered by the fact-finder rather than it being summarily dismissed or decided. The burden of persuasion concerns the duty upon a party to *persuade* the fact-finder to decide for that party on an assertion of fact. While the former burden tends to shift back and forth in (most) legal procedures, the latter is usually allocated at the beginning of a procedure, the onus remaining on the same party throughout the process. See extensively J. Kokott, *The Burden of Proof in Comparative and International Human Rights Law: Civil and Common Law Approaches with Special Reference to the American and German Legal Systems* (Kluwer Law International 1998).

24 Both directives exclude criminal procedures from this measure (Art. 8 (3) RED; Art. 10 (3) EED), and Member States are also not required to apply Art. 8 (1) RED or Art. 10 (1) EED to proceedings in which it is for the court or competent body to investigate the facts of the case (Art. 8 (5) RED; Art. 10 (5) EED).

25 Article 10 (1) EED; Article 8 (1) RED.

26 C. Tobler, *Indirect Discrimination. A Case Study into the Development of the Legal Concept of Indirect Discrimination under EC Law* (Intersentia 2005), 43; H. Collins,

established do not, by themselves, have to lead to the conclusion that there was an act of unlawful discrimination, i.e. that an unjustified less favorable treatment on the protected grounds did in fact take place. The directives do not provide further information on either the nature of the (initial) burden on the complainant, or on the facts that can or will be regarded as relevant. However, it does seem clear that this burden was intended to be rather minimal.[27]

1.2. Second phase: refutation of discrimination

Once an applicant has established facts from which the presumption of (direct or indirect) discrimination can be inferred, the burden of proof shifts to the respondent, who will then have "to prove that there has been no breach of the principle of equal treatment."[28] This can be done, either by negating causality (§1.2.1) or by claiming that the prima facie discrimination falls under a legally permissible exception and/or that it is justified (§1.2.2).

1.2.1. Negation of causality

In order to discharge his burden of proof, the respondent can first attempt to negate the causal link between the harm that the "less favourable treatment" resulted in and the protected ground. In direct discrimination the causality of the harm is based on the adverse treatment being predicated on the protected ground (*supra* §1).[29] As such, a respondent—in order not to be found guilty of direct discrimination—can attempt to demonstrate, on the balance of probabilities, that the treatment was not predicated on the prohibited ground(s). He can, in other words, attempt to negate the prima facie causality that appeared to emerge from the facts established by the applicant, by challenging the link between the protected ground and the harm.

If the respondent does not succeed in doing so, the court—or other competent authority—will find that the respondent unlawfully discriminated, *unless* the respondent is able to justify the unequal treatment and/or if it falls under an exception included in the directives (*infra* §1.2.2).

1.2.2. Exceptions and justifications

When a respondent is unable to prove a lack of causality, the exceptions and justifications available under the RED and EED may still be invoked to demonstrate why an adverse treatment, based on a protected ground, should not in

"Discrimination, Equality and Social Inclusion," 66 *Modern Law Review* 16 (2003), 32; S. Fredman, *Discrimination Law* (Oxford University Press 2002), 96–100.

27 J. Gerards, *Judicial Review in Equal Treatment Cases* (Martinus Nijhoff 2005), 78–79; M. Ambrus, *Enforcement Mechanisms of the Racial Equality Directive and Minority Protection* (Eleven International Publishing 2010), 41.

28 Art. 10 (1) EED; Art. 8 (1) RED.

29 M. Ambrus, *Enforcement Mechanisms of the Racial Equality Directive and Minority Protection* (Eleven International Publishing 2010), 50–52.

a given case be regarded as (prohibited) discrimination. Under both directives, the concept of direct discrimination—as opposed to that of indirect discrimination—does not allow for justifications or exceptions of a general nature, but only offers specific, and limited, justification clauses.[30] Under the RED, and in the context of employment, these are limited to the genuine and determining occupational requirement and positive action. The EED, like the RED, also allows for these justifications, and additionally provides several "ground-specific" justifications. As far as religion is concerned, the EED contains (the option of)[31] an additional, specific type of occupational requirement for churches and other public and private organizations based on a religious ethos.[32]

1.2.2.1. Positive action Both directives offer the possibility of positive action, as an exception or justification[33] for unequal treatment of a direct (or indirect) nature, "with a view to ensuring full equality in practice."[34] The relevant provisions stipulate that "the principle of equal treatment shall not prevent any Member State from maintaining or adopting specific measures to prevent or compensate for disadvantages linked to" any of the discrimination grounds.

The case law of the European Court of Justice of the European Communities (ECJ) on this issue—having been developed in cases of sex discrimination[35]—is

30 On a side note: the directives offer neither any exceptions to the prohibition of harassment, nor opportunities to "justify" it. As far as the instruction to discriminate is concerned, it remains somewhat unclear to what extent it can be justified. The directives offer no explicit guidance on this issue, but most commentators assume that in this context the systems of justification for the other manifestations of discrimination should be applied *mutatis mutandis*, depending on the type of discrimination the instruction to which was given.

31 Implementation of Article 4 (2) EED is optional, and several Member States have not included it in their legislation, at least not expressly (CEJI and ENAR, "Religious Discrimination and Legal Protection in the European Union," *Fact Sheet* (2007), 19).

32 Regarding positive action on the basis of religion, the EED contains an additional, specific provision for Northern Ireland, excluding the recruitment into the police service (including its support staff) and that of teachers from the strict prohibitions of (religious) discrimination that the Directive entails, as long as the relevant recruitment programmes "are expressly authorised by national legislation" (Article 15 EED).

33 One can argue over whether positive action should properly be regarded as an exception to the prohibition of discrimination, or rather as a justification for unequal treatment (or even as a necessary component of equal treatment), depending on whether one attaches greater weight, respectively, to a formal or to a substantive ideal of equality and non-discrimination. The ECJ by and large sees it as an exception to the principle of equal treatment.

34 Article 7 (1) EED; Article 5 RED.

35 Although it is not entirely certain that these principles will also be applied to positive action involving other grounds than sex, commentators by and large agree that there do not, at present, appear to be indications that this will *not* be the case. First, the explanatory memorandum to the EED expressly indicates that the principles of the existing case law of the ECJ are to be employed to assess the permissibility of every form of positive

quite restrictive, and by and large entails the following criteria.[36] First, positive action is only admissible as long as groups really are in a significantly under-represented position.[37] Secondly, rules that guarantee the disadvantaged group an absolute and unconditional preference or priority for appointment or promotion overstep the limits of permissible positive action, and are disproportional to any given aim.[38] Thirdly, all applications should be subjected to an objective and transparent assessment, taking into account the individual situation of all candidates.[39] And finally, preference may only be granted provided that a candidate from a disadvantaged group at least possesses (substantially) equivalent merits.[40] All of this excludes far-reaching measures such as so-called hard quota.

---

action, even if it is not based on sex, but on grounds such as religion, handicap, age or sexual orientation (see, for example, A. Haquet, "L'action positive, instrument de l'égalité des chances entre hommes et femmes," 37 *Revue trimestrielle de droit Européen* 305 (2001), 307–308). An analogous line of reasoning can be followed with regard to the RED (see, for example, T. Jones, "The Race Directive: Redefining Protection from Discrimination in EU Law," 5 *EHLR* 515 (2003), 522–524). Secondly, the EED itself—as mentioned in footnote 32—includes a specific provision for positive action on the basis of religion in Northern Ireland, limited to the recruitment of teaching personnel and the police service: arguably (the need for) this express "exception to the rule" would indicate *a contrario* that more generally (in other Member States and/or domains) the restrictive rules for positive action are to remain in force, at least for the criteria included in the EED. Compare: D. De Prins, S. Sottiaux and J. Vrielink, *Handboek discriminatierecht* (Kluwer 2005), 106.

36 See more extensively on positive action in EU law, for example: D. Caruso, "Limits of the Classic Method: Positive Action in the European Union after the New Equality Directives," 44 *Harvard International Law Journal* 331 (2003); D. Schiek, "Positive Action in Community Law," 25 *Industrial Law Journal* 239 (1996); C. Tobler, "Positive Action Under the Revised Second Equal Treatment Directive," in *L'égalité entre les femmes et les hommes et la vie professionnelle–le point sur les développements actuels en Europe* (Association Française des Femmes Juristes and European Women Lawyers Association, eds, Dalloz 2003), 59–92; R. Badinter, "Les discriminations positives dans l'Union européenne," in *Les droits de l'homme au seuil du troisième millénaire, Mélanges en hommage à Pierre Lambert* (Bruylant 2000), 37–49; O. De Schutter and B. Renauld, "Egalité de traitement. L'action affirmative devant la Cour de justice de Communautés Européennes. A propos de l'arrêt "Kalanke" du 17 octobre 1995," *JTT* 125 (1996); S. Fredman, "Affirmative Action and the European Court of Justice: A Critical Analysis," in *Social Law and Policy in an Evolving European Union* (J. Shaw, ed., Hart Publishing 2000), 171–195; D. Schiek, "Sex Equality Law After Kalanke and Marschall," 4 *European Law Journal* 148 (1998).

37 See, for example, Case C-450/93, *Kalanke* v. *Freie Hansestadt Bremen* [1995], ECR I-3051; Case C-158/97, *Georg Badeck and others* [2000], ECR I-1875.

38 See, for example, Case C-450/93, *Kalanke* v. *Freie Hansestadt Bremen* [1995], ECR I-3051; Case C-409/95, *Marschall* v. *Land Nordrhein-Westfalen* [1997], ECR I-6363.

39 See, for example, Case C-158/97, *Georg Badeck and others* [2000], ECR I-1875; Case C-407/98, *Abrahamsson and Anderson* v. *Fogelqvist* [2000], ECR I-5539.

40 See, for example, Case C-407/98, *Abrahamsson and Anderson* v. *Fogelqvist* [2000], ECR I-5539.

1.2.2.2. Occupational requirements As for the occupational requirements, both the EED and the RED allow Member States "to provide that a difference of treatment, which is based on a characteristic related to" one of the protected grounds "shall not constitute discrimination where, by reason of the nature of the particular occupational activities concerned or of the context in which they are carried out, such a characteristic constitutes a genuine and determining occupational requirement."[41] Such an occupational requirement, in order to be legitimate, needs to be justified by a legitimate aim (i.e. not being itself discriminatory or otherwise illegal), and be proportionate in the light of that aim. However, the preambles of both directives indicate that this justification applies to "very limited circumstances,"[42] which is commonly interpreted as indicating that a high level of scrutiny must be applied.[43]

In addition to this general provision on occupational requirements, the EED also includes a more specific one concerning professional activities of "churches and other public or private organisations the ethos of which is based on religion or belief." Member States may allow that "in the case of occupational activities within" such organizations "a difference of treatment based on a person's religion or belief shall not constitute discrimination where … a person's religion or belief constitute a genuine, legitimate and justified occupational requirement, having regard to the organisation's ethos," again taking into account either "the nature of these activities" or "the context in which they are carried out."[44] As such—and contrary to the general provision regarding occupational requirements—the requirement referred to in Article 4 (2) EED need not be determining, though it must be genuine, legitimate and justified, and have regard to an organization's ethos.

The provision goes on to state that it "should not justify discrimination on another ground," thereby (again) emphasizing that it potentially only warrants a difference in treatment on the basis of religion or belief, and not on other grounds, such as sexual orientation.

The concluding section of Article 4 (2) EED states that the directive "shall thus not prejudice the right of churches and other public or private organisations, the ethos of which is based on religion or belief … to require individuals working for them to act in good faith and with loyalty to the organisation's ethos."[45]

---

41 Article 4 (1) EED; Article 4 RED.

42 Preamble §18 RED; Preamble §23 EED. Adding, moreover, that "[s]uch circumstances should be included in the information provided by the Member States to the Commission."

43 See, for example, M. J. Busstra, *The Implications of the Racial Equality Directive for Minority Protection Within the European Union* (Eleven International Publishing 2010), 160; S. Sottiaux, "De rechtvaardigingsgronden in het federale antidiscriminatierecht," in *De nieuwe federale antidiscriminatiewetten* (C. Bayart, S. Sottiaux and S. Van Drooghenbroeck, eds, Die Keure 2008), 243.

44 Article 4 (2) EED.

45 See also Preamble §24 EED: "The European Union in its Declaration No 11 on the status of churches and non-confessional organisations, annexed to the Final Act of the

Debate rages in the literature as to a number of issues with regard to Article 4 (2) EED, such as the types of organizations that are entitled to invoke it; the types of occupational activities within those organizations that it can legitimately be invoked for; the extent of the differential treatment it may justify; and the problem of how exactly to interpret the formal restriction that the provision cannot justify discrimination on other grounds than religion or belief. The answers to most of these questions remain relatively uncertain, in the absence of case law of the ECJ to settle them.[46]

2. Direct discrimination or the presumption thereof through speech in the context of hiring[47]

What do these general rules imply as far as speech is concerned? In regulating direct discrimination the directives at no point explicitly prohibit speech. However, as with many (or even most) prohibitions of conduct,[48] regulating direct discrimination also has an indirect or incidental impact on certain types of speech.[49] That is the case, first since speech can realize (or can be used to realize) many actions, including discrimination as defined in the directives. As such, some speech can by itself amount to direct discrimination (§2.1). Secondly, speech that is de facto relevant does not conceptually have to constitute unlawful direct discrimination in and by itself: under the directives it would suffice when the speech leads to a presumption thereof (*supra* §1.1) in order for the burden of proof to shift (§2.2).

Amsterdam Treaty, has explicitly recognized that it respects and does not prejudice the status under national law of churches and religious associations or communities in the Member States and that it equally respects the status of philosophical and non-confessional organisations. With this in view, Member States may maintain or lay down specific provisions on genuine, legitimate and justified occupational requirements which might be required for carrying out an occupational activity."

46 On these and other issues see the chapters by Yves Stox and Amandine Barb in this volume.

47 This paper is conceptual in nature. Examples from case law that are provided in this section are used mainly to elucidate the analytical distinctions that are being made. They are predominantly derived from Dutch and Belgian case law.

48 Innumerable legal restrictions of conduct also impair people's ability to express themselves the way they want. For a general and thoughtful treatment of this topic (albeit limited to criminal infractions), see K. Greenawalt, *Speech, Crime, and the Uses of Language* (Oxford University Press 1989).

49 Arguably this would seem to be the case with discrimination law even more so than with many other forms of conduct regulations, since discrimination tends to be highly "expressive" conduct—see, for example, E. Chemerinsky and C. Fisk, "The Expressive Interest of Associations," 9 *William & Mary Bill of Rights Journal* 595 (2001).

In employing this conceptual distinction, it should be kept in mind that from a procedural or practical point of view—in the light of the two-phased model of establishing discrimination (*supra*)—all an applicant *has* to do, and perhaps more importantly all he *can* (initially) do, is to create a presumption of discrimination. The directives do not provide for something as a "complete" proof of discrimination, which would preclude attempts by the respondent to dispute the factual evidence brought forward, or to negate or justify the alleged discrimination. In that regard the distinction between speech that may itself constitute direct discrimination, and speech that may (only) lead to a presumption thereof, will, in practice, be one of degree rather than of kind. Nonetheless, the distinction seems relevant both conceptually and practically as it points to an important difference in what one aims to establish (and conversely what the respondent has to discharge or disprove): in the former case this concerns whether the speech itself took place, whereas in the latter situation one not only has to demonstrate the likelihood of the speech having taken place, but also that it is sufficiently indicative of an underlying act of discrimination not coinciding with the speech itself.

2.1. Speech that can amount to direct discrimination

In order for speech to amount to direct discrimination under EU discrimination law, it must itself constitute a form of less favorable treatment on the grounds of race or religion (without there being any exception or justification available). In the following it will be argued that at least three such, partially overlapping, categories of speech can be identified. The first category is speech that directly and unmediatedly *excludes* or *disadvantages* persons from opportunities on a discriminatory basis (§2.1.1). Secondly, direct discrimination can arguably also be realized by speech that is (highly) likely to *deter* applicants from continuing to pursue opportunities on a discriminatory basis. Finally, and closely related to the latter, speech can also amount to direct discrimination when it is (highly) likely to *mislead* applicants from continuing to pursue opportunities on a discriminatory basis (§2.1.2).

2.1.1. Speech that (directly and unmediatedly) excludes or disadvantages persons from opportunities on a discriminatory basis

Both in the EED and the RED the prohibition of direct discrimination in the context of employment is mainly aimed at (discriminatory) decisions or other conduct of employers and others with the power to control access to important opportunities. Regulated actions include decisions about hiring, promoting, compensating and firing employees. Many of these acts are or may be taken by means of speech, either verbal or written; this is the case particularly in the phase of hiring.

As such, one of the most obvious ways in which speech can constitute direct discrimination in the context of hiring is when it itself amounts to a decision or an act that directly and unmediatedly excludes one or more persons from important workplace opportunities, on the basis of discriminatory considerations.

This in effect concerns transactional speech that carries out an "ordinary" direct discrimination by means of communicating, unequivocally committing the listener or the speaker or both to action.

Examples of this include the situation mentioned in the introduction, in which someone is told during a job interview that he will not be hired because he is of foreign origin or because he is a Muslim. Other types of example could involve letters or other written forms of communication that expressly exclude someone from a hiring procedure due to being an atheist or on the basis of his ethnicity or skin color, as in a striking Belgian case in which a black applicant was rejected with the (written) remark "My dog does not tolerate this person: risk of dog bites due to the applicant's skin color."[50]

Examples in relation to other discrimination grounds are plentiful as well. To provide but one illustration: in a case from the Netherlands, a contractor said the following while rejecting a (male) candidate: "Do you have a male partner, as your e-mail address seems to indicate? Then we really cannot work together. This conflicts too much with my principles."[51]

This first category of speech that amounts to direct discrimination is generally accepted—or rather taken for granted—both in case law as well as in literature. The fact that such manifestations of discrimination in fact also concern "speech" is rarely even explicitly addressed, either in the literature or in case law, precisely because it is considered so self-evident.

This is unproblematic from a free speech point of view, as long as the conflation or coincidence between direct discrimination and speech is sufficiently complete and unmediated. In those cases, the mere fact that a discriminatory exclusion is realized by means of speech indeed does not imply that it enjoys heightened protection on the basis of free speech: there are no exemptions from legal conduct regulations in general—or from discrimination law specifically—for people who manage to violate it by means of verbal or written communication, i.e. speech in the technical sense of the word. This is the case even in criminal law, where carrying out an ordinary criminal purpose by communicating is no less punishable than doing it by any other means. The fact, for instance, that a homicide is carried out "by telling a blind companion on a mountain path that he can safely step to the right, while wanting to cause his death and knowing that a 2000-foot drop lies

50 All translations are my own, unless otherwise indicated.

51 Tribunal of Arnhem, 23 September 2010, *LJN*: BN8113. It concerned a criminal case and the defendant argued that his freedom of speech and especially his freedom of religion precluded his statements from being regarded as discrimination. The judge ruled that the defendant was free to lead his life and to conduct his business in accordance with his beliefs, but that this freedom reached its limits in the discriminatory exclusion of individuals that the statements entailed. Cf. *infra* §2.2.2 for the (hypothetical) situation in which the contractor had only posed his initial query concerning sexual orientation or another protected characteristic (followed by a negative decision), without explicitly stating that a particular answer to the question would lead to exclusion.

to the right,"[52] does not result in this communication being protected under free speech principles.

In the case of direct discrimination of course it need not even be proved or demonstrated that a person wanted to discriminate by means of his statements, since intent is not required. What *is* required for this particular type of (unprotected) speech to occur without raising free speech issues is that the speech meets at least three conditions. First, it should originate from persons who are in fact in a position to discriminate, being decision-makers in hiring procedures. Generally this would concern either the employer or the head of human resources, or other authorized parties. If this is not the case, the speech cannot itself amount to a direct discrimination of this category, although it might still give rise to a presumption of discrimination (*infra* §2.2.1). Secondly, there should be a direct connection between the speech and a concrete hiring procedure, and finally the speech should unequivocally exclude or disadvantage one or more specific and identifiable persons in relation to the hiring procedure on the basis of their protected characteristics.

If speech corresponds with these conditions, and assuming it can be proven, it will generally come down to direct discrimination, since very few exceptions or justifications will hold. To begin with, negating the discrimination will in any case be practically impossible, save by disputing the available proof. What will be possible in some cases—just as in other cases of adverse treatment directly based on a protected ground—is to claim a justification or exception. Justifications for this type of speech will generally be limited to occupational requirements, and will as such be quite rare in the context of race and religion. In exceptional cases positive action might constitute a justification as well, but generally this would not seem to merit categorical exclusions or disadvantages of the sort that are at issue here.

2.1.2. Speech that is likely to deter or mislead applicants from continuing to pursue important opportunities on a discriminatory basis

The second and third categories of speech that can amount to direct discrimination in the context of hiring will be dealt with together, since they are closely related. It concerns speech that has the effect of either (significantly) deterring or misleading applicants from continuing to pursue opportunities, on a discriminatory basis. Both categories of speech would include certain statements, advertisements, announcements, signs or other expressions containing a (discriminatory) preference or dispreference by decision-makers for applicants of a certain race, religion or belief.

Here, the "less favourable treatment" that results from such speech—and as such the reason for qualifying it as a direct discrimination—is not quite as unmediated as in the first category of speech that was discussed. In that sense it would not seem correct—as is often done in cases such as these—to approach them in the same manner, for instance by arguing that a sign "saying that 'Turks cannot

52 K. Greenawalt, *Speech, Crime, and the Uses of Language* (Oxford University Press 1989), 6. See also: B. Means, "Criminal Speech and the First Amendment," 86 *Marquette Law Review* 501 (2002).

enter' involves a direct causal link, because there is no intermediary circumstance necessary to ascertain that there is a connection between being Turkish and the disadvantage of not being able to enter."[53] In reality there are intermediate circumstances in such cases: a sign that says "Turks cannot enter" does not in fact impair someone's very *ability* to enter. It does however render it highly likely that someone of Turkish origin or nationality would not enter,[54] since the sign gives them reasonable cause, at the very least, to believe they are not welcome, and will subsequently be excluded (or worse) anyway.

As such, a more accurate argument for qualifying such speech in itself as "a less favourable treatment" consists in the fact that it is highly likely to de facto screen or skew the population that will apply for (or further pursue) an available position, in a discriminatory manner. When people have good grounds to think that they will not stand a chance if they apply for or continue to pursue a particular (job) opportunity, they cannot reasonably be expected to do so. As such, they will be either *deterred* from applying or further pursuing (job) opportunities, or, if the effect was unintentional, they will at the very least be *misled* into doing this.[55]

2.1.2.1. The Feryn case The most prominent illustration from case law in which this type of speech is being grappled with, and that by and large offers the above line of reasoning, comes from the case law of the ECJ, and concerns the case of *Centrum voor Gelijkheid van Kansen* v. *Firma Feryn* (hereafter "*Feryn*").[56] Analyzing this case in some detail can serve to identify criteria, including those of a contextual nature, for the second and third categories of directly discriminatory speech.

---

53 M. J. Busstra, *The Implications of the Racial Equality Directive for Minority Protection Within the European Union* (Eleven International Publishing 2010), 139.

54 Or conversely: it makes it very unlikely that someone of Turkish origin or nationality would enter.

55 Though it does fall within the scope of this chapter, one should note that certain statements, advertisements, signs, etc. can also be *indirectly* discriminatory, following the same line of reasoning. Some case law also explicitly does this, an interesting example being provided by a ruling of the tribunal of Huy (Belgium) in which it had to rule on a restaurant that put up a sign at its entrance prohibiting any form of head covering (Court of First Instance of Huy, 26 May 2010, nr. 09/928/B). A woman wearing a headscarf for medical reasons (due to hair loss as a result of chemotherapy) entered the restaurant, but was subsequently confronted with the headgear policy. An employee asked her to remove her headscarf. When the woman explained her situation she was told the policy applied regardless of circumstances. The woman subsequently left the restaurant but did file a complaint for (indirect) discrimination on the basis of "state of health" (a protected characteristic under Belgian discrimination law). The judge not only accepted her claim of indirect discrimination on the basis of state of health, but also found the sign to be indirectly discriminatory on the basis of *religion*, arguing that the sign (likely) deters women wearing a headscarf from entering the restaurant, thereby having an indirectly discriminatory effect.

56 Case C-54/07, *Centrum voor gelijkheid van kansen en voor racismebestrijding (Centre for equal opportunities and combating racism)* v. *Firma Feryn NV* [2008], ECR I-5187.

The *Feryn* case concerned a private employer (a producer and installer of sectional doors), who had, amongst other things, made public statements in the press—after putting up a conspicuous job vacancy notice—that he did not and would not hire persons of Moroccan origin, since allegedly his customers were unwilling to accept them.[57] The case was brought as an injunction procedure by the Belgian equality body, the Centre for Equal Opportunities and Opposition to Racism (CEOOR).[58] The Brussels Labor Tribunal ruled that such speech did not itself constitute discrimination. It acknowledged that discrimination legislation could imply de facto restrictions on speech, but that such requires "that the claimant demonstrates that the reproached 'hiring policy,' that is only substantiated with public statements to the press, also constitutes an act, namely is based on acts":

> *In casu* it is neither demonstrated nor is the presumption established that so much as one single candidate mechanic of foreign origin has applied, and that he or she was not hired on account of his or her ethnic origins. A press article can neither supply this proof, nor the presumption thereof.[59]

The Tribunal did accept that the speech could lead to a *presumption* of (potential) direct discrimination vis-à-vis subsequent hiring decisions, but it believed this presumption to be sufficiently negated or redressed by the fact that the defendant had distanced himself from his former statements in later press releases and statements in the media:

> Since the discriminatory behaviour was established by means of the media, subsequent press statements also constitute a sufficient redress. No discrimination … can either be established or feared any longer.[60]

---

57 On 28 April 2005, newspapers published interviews with Mr. Pascal Feryn, one of the firm's directors, in which he was quoted to have said that his firm did not and would not recruit persons of Moroccan origin for the available position: "Apart from Moroccans, no one else has responded to our notice in two weeks … but we aren't looking for Moroccans. Our customers don't want them. They have to install … doors in private homes, often villas, and those customers don't want them coming into their homes … I must comply with my customers' requirements. If you say 'I want that particular product or I want it like this and like that', and I say 'I'm not doing it, I'll send those people,' then you will say 'I don't need that door.' Then I'm putting myself out of business. We must meet the customers' requirements. This isn't my problem. I didn't create this problem in Belgium. I want the firm to do well and I want us to achieve our turnover at the end of the year, and how do I do that?—I must do it the way the customer wants it done!"

58 Centrum voor gelijkheid van kansen en voor racismebestrijding / Centre pour l'égalité des chances et la lutte contre le racisme, see www.diversite.be. On the history and chronology of the *Feryn* case, see I. Aendenboom (CEOOR), "The Feryn case," 30 June 2009, Equinet Seminar.

59 Brussels Labor Tribunal 26 June 2006, available at www.diversite.be.

60 Ibid.

The Labor Court of Appeals subsequently asked the ECJ for a preliminary ruling regarding a number of issues. The ECJ had to decide first whether speech—in the form of public statements made by an employer during a selection procedure—could itself constitute direct discrimination, without particular complainants having come forward contending that they had been victims of discrimination.[61] A number of other questions concerned the character of facts from which it may be presumed that there has been direct or indirect discrimination, including whether the aforementioned statements were sufficient to presume the existence of a (continued) directly discriminatory recruitment policy.[62]

In relation to the first question the ECJ ruled that

> the fact that an employer states publicly that it *will not* recruit employees of a certain ethnic or racial origin constitutes direct discrimination in respect of recruitment ... such statements being likely strongly to dissuade certain candidates from submitting their candidature and, accordingly, to hinder their access to the labour market.[63]

---

61 The relevant question being: "(1) Is there direct discrimination within the meaning of Article 2(2)(a) of Council Directive 2000/43/EC of 29 June 2000 implementing the principle of equal treatment between persons irrespective of racial or ethnic origin where an employer, after putting up a conspicuous job vacancy notice, publicly states: 'I must comply with my customers' requirements. If you say "I want that particular product or I want it like this and like that," and I say "I'm not doing it, I'll send those people," then you say "I don't need that door." Then I'm putting myself out of business. We must meet the customers' requirements. This isn't my problem. I didn't create this problem in Belgium. I want the firm to do well and I want us to achieve our turnover at the end of the year, and how do I do that?–I must do it the way the customer wants it done!'?" The UK and Irish government intervened in the case, arguing that there could be no direct discrimination where an employer had not demonstrably acted on his discriminatory statements. Additionally, the governments argued that, in the absence of one or more identifiable victims, a public equality body (like the CEOOR) should not be allowed to bring a claim before the courts.

62 The relevant questions being: "(4) What is to be understood by 'facts from which it may be presumed that there has been direct or indirect discrimination' within the terms of Article 8(1) of Directive 2004/43? How strict must a national court be in assessing facts which give rise to a presumption of discrimination? (a) To what extent do earlier acts of discrimination (public announcement of directly discriminatory selection criteria in April 2005) constitute 'facts from which it may be presumed that there has been direct or indirect discrimination' within the terms of Article 8(1) of [Directive 2000/43]? (b) Does an established act of discrimination in April 2005 (public announcement in April 2005) subsequently give rise to a presumption of the continuation of a directly discriminatory recruitment policy?"

63 Case C-54/07, *Centrum voor gelijkheid van kansen en voor racismebestrijding (Centre for equal opportunities and combating racism)* v. *Firma Feryn NV* [2008], ECR I-5187, §28 (emphasis in original).

Regarding the second (cluster of) questions, the ECJ accepted that such public statements

> are sufficient for a presumption of the existence of a recruitment policy which is directly discriminatory.[64]

The Court went on to state that "[c]onsequently, given such presumption, the employer concerned will have to prove that there was no breach of the principle of equal treatment and non-discrimination, for example by showing that the employer's actual recruitment practice does not correspond to those statements."[65]

The latter passage has given rise to some puzzlement and criticism in the literature. Several commentators have interpreted it as entailing a tension or even a contradiction with the acceptance of dissuasive or deterrent speech as a form of direct discrimination: on the one hand the ECJ accepts public statements announcing a discriminatory hiring practice as constituting discrimination in itself, while on the other hand it considers such speech as a mere presumption of discrimination, allowing the defendant the possibility to demonstrate that his recruitment policy in fact does not correspond to his statements.[66]

This alleged contradiction can be explained away, however, by looking at the distinct questions that the ECJ sought to answer in the respective passages, combined with the facts in the national case that gave rise to it: whereas the former passage in the ruling concerns the situation in which an employer makes certain public statements in an ongoing hiring procedure, the latter passage arguably

64 Ibid., §34.

65 Ibid., §34.

66 See, for example, Ambrus, Busstra and Henrard: "The ECJ … increased the confusion [about how a finding of discrimination is related to the establishment of a presumption of discrimination] by qualifying a public statement revealing a discriminatory recruitment policy both as a presumption of discrimination and as prohibited discrimination in itself without explicitly applying the review model and without explaining the respective qualifications in this context. In paragraph 28 of its judgment, the ECJ explicitly states that 'the fact that an employer states publicly that it will not recruit employees of a certain racial or ethnic origin constitutes direct discrimination in respect of recruitment within the meaning of Article 2(2)(a) of Directive 2000/43' … The Court subsequently stipulates in paragraph 31 that the statements concerned 'may constitute facts of such a nature as to give rise to a presumption of a discriminatory recruitment policy' … Hence, what a few paragraphs earlier is said to constitute direct discrimination, is now possibly merely a presumption of discrimination" (M. Ambrus, M. J. Busstra and K. Henrard, "The Racial Equality Directive and Effective Protection Against Discrimination: Mismatches Between the Substantive Law and Its Application," 3 *Erasmus Law Review* 165 (2010), 175). See also M. J. Busstra, *The Implications of the Racial Equality Directive for Minority Protection Within the European Union* (Eleven International Publishing 2010), 150–151 (concluding that the Court "clearly hinged on two thoughts, and that it remains to be seen whether it will in the future unambiguously include statements in its interpretation of 'treatment'").

is concerned only with the question of whether such (previous) speech can still be taken into account (as amounting to a presumption of discrimination) when it concerns subsequent or future procedures. Specific in the *Feryn* case was the fact that the CEOOR did not *immediately* go to court following Feryn's public statements. Rather, the CEOOR had initially opted for mediation, and trying to get the firm to adopt diversity measures. This extra-legal approach was abandoned, however, because Feryn failed to respect promises made concerning the implementation of diversity training and plans. By that time, the vacancy that had given rise to the issue was no longer available, but other vacancies were. In order for the aforementioned injunction procedure to still offer adequate redress,[67] the court had to ascertain to what extent such ongoing and future facts were implicated by the previous speech of the defendant as well, i.e. by (still) being demonstrative or presumptive of an ongoing directly discriminatory recruitment *policy*.[68]

In this reading the ECJ offers relatively clear, consistent and workable criteria for when dissuasive, deterrent or misleading speech can be said to itself constitute discrimination (§2.1.2.2), and when such speech merely amounts to a presumption of discrimination (*infra* §2.2.1).

2.1.2.2. Criteria, negation and exceptions/justifications Based in large part on the *Feryn* ruling, one can conclude that a number of requirements should be fulfilled in order for this type of speech to occur, and be accepted as direct discrimination, without unduly infringing upon the freedom of speech. First, the speech must originate from and be directly attributable to a decision-maker in recruitment procedures. Secondly, the relevant speech must also be temporally related to a concrete and ongoing hiring procedure. If this is not the case, such speech might still be said to have a certain dissuasive effect on future hiring procedures, but it cannot conceptually be deemed actionable discrimination—i.e. actual adverse treatment, which necessarily should relate to specific (job) opportunities—in itself, at the time when the statements are made. Naturally such statements by an employer *outside* an ongoing hiring procedure can nevertheless constitute a reason to pay close attention to future hiring procedures, and they might also amount to

67 Due to its future-oriented nature, the injunction procedure is particularly relevant where it concerns ongoing and future facts.

68 This reading of the ECJ's preliminary ruling in *Feryn* is also followed consistently in the ruling by the Brussels Labor Court of Appeal, which first unequivocally accepts that "the aforementioned public statements made by Feryn constitute direct discrimination in respect of recruitment on the grounds of race or ethnic origin," and secondly goes on to consider whether said statements and the events, additionally, "*afterwards* constitute a presumption of *continued* discrimination in the recruitment policy of Feryn" (emphasis added), accepting that only in relation to the latter can Feryn "adduce evidence, among other things, that the actual recruitment practice of the undertaking does not correspond to those statements" (Labor Court of Appeals Brussels, 1 September 2009).

facts from which a presumption of discrimination can be inferred in future such cases (*infra* §2.2.1).[69]

These first two criteria invalidate overly broad interpretations that the *Feryn* ruling has given rise to concerning the equation of certain types of speech with discrimination, such as the general claim that "saying that one will discriminate, is discrimination" without having (explicit) regard to the transactional context of the speech and the identity of the speaker,[70] or even by extending the reasoning of the ECJ to situations in which politicians "merely" propose exclusionary policy measures aimed at minorities.[71] The latter readings clearly ignore the specificities of the *Feryn* case, and the required (contextual) characteristics of this category of directly discriminatory speech more generally.

A final requirement, closely related to the second one, that this category of speech must fulfill in order to be regarded as a form of direct discrimination, is that it should *significantly* or *unequivocally* deter or mislead applicants, i.e. doing so to an extent that the latter would reasonably believe the further pursuit of the opportunity to be pointless or unwise. In assessing this it should be the ordinary listener's or reader's perception of a message—rather than the decision-maker's intent or the subjective reading by the plaintiff—that is taken as dispositive in determining this.[72] If the deterring or misleading effect is insufficiently clear or strong by such a reading, one cannot regard the speech by itself as a form of direct discrimination, since qualifying it as a form of adverse treatment would then be excessively hypothetical. Again, this would not preclude such speech from being used as facts from which a presumption of discrimination may be inferred (*infra* §2.2.1).

As for possibilities of demonstrating that this type of discrimination did *not* take place, it would again seem unlikely that it could be negated, save by disputing the available proof. In any case, if the employer's public statements announcing or advertising a discriminatory recruitment policy are done during an ongoing hiring procedure, this cannot be negated by claiming the actual hiring criteria did not correspond with the speech (cf. *supra* §2.1.2.1), since the discrimination consists of the (likely) deterrent or misleading effect that the speech gave rise to.

---

69 That can be rebutted, for instance by demonstrating that subsequent recruitment practices do not (any longer) correspond to those statements (cf. *supra* §2.1.2.1 and *infra* §2.2.1).

70 See CEOOR, "Zaak-Feryn: zeggen dat men zal discrimineren is discriminatie" [Feryn-case: saying that one will discriminate, is discrimination"], *Press release*, 10 July 2008. Compare: A. Eriksson, "European Court of Justice: Broadening the Scope of European Nondiscrimination Law," 7 *ICON* 731 (2009), 748.

71 See, for example, I. Aendenboom (CEOOR), "The Feryn case," Brussels, June 30th 2009, Equinet Seminar.

72 Compare H. Norton, "You Can't Ask (or Say) That: The First Amendment and Civil Rights Restrictions on Decisionmaker Speech," 11 *William & Mary Bill of Rights Journal* 727 (2003), 729. Based on US case law, Norton describes the ordinary reader as "neither the most suspicious nor the most insensitive of our citizenry."

However, with the conclusion of whether this type of speech amounts to discrimination being significantly dependent on the likelihood of the effect, negation could hypothetically consist of showing that the speech was insufficiently likely to dissuade, deter or mislead; for instance by arguing or showing that the message was ambiguous in its potential effects, or perhaps even by demonstrating that despite the allegedly dissuading or deterrent speech, large numbers of applicants from the allegedly disadvantaged groups did apply.[73]

Regarding exceptions and justifications, occupational requirements, of either a general or a religious nature (cf. *supra* §1.2.2.2), could of course be successfully invoked, if the job legitimately requires it. As such, stating a preference for a Christian or for someone of a certain skin color is lawful when the nature of the particular occupational activities or the context in which they are carried out necessitates this, with the requirement being justified by a legitimate aim, and it being proportionate in the light of that aim.

The same goes for speech that announces positive action, under the condition that the criteria for that exception are respected (cf. *supra* §1.2.2.1). One should note, however, that this implies that speech announcing measures such as hard quota with regard to a certain hiring procedure, would in principle also amount to this form of direct discrimination, just as the actual practice of such measures does.[74] When the criteria for positive action are clearly transgressed in public statements or announcements, there would, after all, seem to be no legally relevant difference between the effects of such speech, and other speech that deters potential applicants from opportunities on a discriminatory basis.[75] In order for this effect to occur and for the announcement of illegitimate "positive action" to actually itself constitute direct discrimination, it does require, however, that the criteria be quite *flagrantly* transgressed. If this is not the case, the misleading or deterrent effect will not be sufficiently likely to occur in order to qualify the announcement itself as direct discrimination.[76] To give an example: in a Dutch case, an employer had mentioned in a job advertisement that he would give preference to a homosexual candidate "in case of equal qualifications."[77] The actual practice of such positive action is clearly not allowed by Dutch discrimination law, which only offers the possibility

73 And, moreover, were not discriminated against in the subsequent procedure.

74 Cf. *supra* §1.2.2.1 on the requirements and criteria that positive action has to fulfill under EU discrimination law in order to be considered lawful.

75 That which is allowed will strongly depend on the local implementation of rules concerning positive action, which vary significantly from Member State to Member State (in accordance with the leeway provided on this point by the Directives that *allow for* but do not *oblige* positive action).

76 Although it might still amount to a presumption thereof: *infra* §2.2.1.

77 The relevant part of the advertisement read as follows: "[X] is a professional organization that strives to attain diversity. Both men and women are invited to apply, in case of equal qualifications we will give preference to a homo[sexual]."

of positive action for women, ethnic minorities and persons with a disability.[78] However, the announcement would itself seem insufficient to fulfill the definition of direct discrimination, since the way in which the (legally illegitimate) preference is formulated seems unlikely to significantly dissuade other applicants. In order for this to occur, the employer's preference, as expressed in the announcement, arguably would have had to be of a "higher degree," for instance by stating that heterosexuals need not apply or that their applications would only be taken into account if and when no homosexual candidates were minimally qualified.

2.2. Speech that creates a presumption of direct discrimination

The previous section dealt with speech that conceptually amounts to direct discrimination. The current section concerns speech that does not fulfill the definition of direct discrimination, but that nonetheless contributes or amounts to facts from which the *presumption* of direct discrimination can be established. As mentioned, neither the directives nor EU law in general provide much clarity on the kinds of facts that are liable to give rise to such a presumption. One can, as such, only (re)turn to the concept of direct discrimination itself—entailing a causal link between a harm and a protected ground—in order to identify potentially relevant indicators for a presumption of discrimination,[79] while bearing in mind that the initial burden for the complainant to establish such a presumption was intended to be minimal (cf. *supra* §1.1).

In the following, two main categories of speech from which a presumption of discrimination may be inferred will be discussed. The first is speech that indicates that the disadvantaging or the exclusion of persons from important opportunities on a discriminatory basis likely took place (§2.2.1). The second category concerns speech that is liable to facilitate discriminatory decision-making (§2.2.2).

2.2.1. Speech that indicates the occurrence of direct discrimination

The first category of speech from which a presumption of discrimination might be inferred in hiring procedures is all speech that reliably indicates that the disadvantaging or the exclusion of persons from important opportunities on a discriminatory basis took place, or might have taken place; combined of course with a particular adverse decision or treatment vis-à-vis a claimant. In practice, this can concern a wide variety of speech, and the following examples should not be regarded as being exhaustive.

78 Art. 2.3 Equal Treatment Act (Algemene Wet Gelijke Behandeling) and Art. 3.1c Disability or Chronic Disease Equal Treatment Act (Wet Gelijke Behandeling op grond van Handicap of Chronische ziekte). See also: Equal Treatment Commission, opinion 2006/61.

79 M. Ambrus, M. J. Busstra and K. Henrard, "The Racial Equality Directive and Effective Protection Against Discrimination: Mismatches Between the Substantive Law and Its Application," 3 *Erasmus Law Review* 165 (2010), 176.

To begin with, one could think of all speech from which a pattern of adverse treatment might be inferred; as was the case for the statements made in the *Feryn* case, regarding future or subsequent hiring procedures (cf. *supra* §2.1.2.1). An employer will then subsequently have to show that his current hiring practices do not in fact correspond with the presumption that was established on the basis of said speech, or argue that the general exceptions and justifications apply.

Often this type of speech will also come in the form of overheard, accidentally forwarded, intercepted or leaked communications showing that discrimination took place. An interesting example of this occurred in Belgium some time ago. A man of Turkish origin had applied for a sales function at a security company. Soon afterwards he received a standard message through email, saying that he would not be selected. Attached to that email however was an internal mail from the responsible HR manager saying: "Could you please get rid of this person? A foreigner selling security: now that's something I haven't seen before." This type of speech could clearly lead to shifting the burden of proof, as in fact it did in this case, resulting in a conviction, since the security company representatives were unable to show that the decision to exclude the Turkish applicant was taken on non-discriminatory grounds.[80] Likewise, in a Dutch case a large supermarket chain urgently required additional personnel for their branches in several cities. Those in charge had included, in writing and via an email exchange, in the internal recruitment requirements (that were subsequently leaked) that persons of Moroccan origin were not to be considered as candidates: "No Moroccans!"[81] Again, it seems that such speech should be construed as, among other things,[82] amounting to a presumption of direct discrimination.

Furthermore, one could think of so-called "smoking gun statements," i.e. expressions of outward discriminatory animus. When such statements are accompanied or followed by a negative decision regarding the applicant, they will normally give rise to a presumption of discrimination. An example of this would be the case in which a Muslim employer states his opinion, during a job interview

80 Labor Court Ghent, 26 March 2007. In a comparable—albeit slightly more veiled—case from the Netherlands, a job seeker received an email refusing him for a job; attached to the message was an additional mail saying that the employer was (only) looking for "a Jansen or a Smith" (typically Dutch names) (Equal Treatment Commission, opinion 2010-93 of 17 June 2010).

81 As it concerned a criminal case the burden of proof could not be shifted on the basis of these statements, but the recruitment requirement combined with the fact that all Moroccan applicants were rejected did lead to a conviction for criminal discrimination (Court of The Hague, 11 October 2010).

82 Aside from this, one might note that this type of speech—at least in the examples that were provided here—also arguably by itself concerns a manifestation of discrimination, namely that of an instruction to discriminate (cf. *supra* §1).

with a woman wearing an Islamic headscarf, that Muslim women do not belong in the workplace, followed by a decision not to hire the applicant.[83]

Likewise, the use of discriminatory slurs, terms or code words by decision-makers can provide a presumption that an employment decision was motivated by race or religion, since such speech could be regarded as prima facie proof of discriminatory intent. Albeit outside the context of hiring, an example of this occurred in Belgium, where an employer offered the following "justification" for firing a black employee in a dismissal letter: "Cannot adjust himself to the country; should be sent back to the bush-bush where people attack each other."[84]

Finally, as mentioned previously, announcements of certain forms of illegitimate positive action may also amount to a presumption of discrimination of this type. In order for this to be the case, the relevant announcement should be insufficiently likely to deter or mislead applicants from applying (as such speech would itself constitute direct discrimination—cf. *supra* §2.1.2.2), but it must nonetheless go further than is legally allowed. If, in those circumstances, an applicant from the group that was announced to receive preferential treatment is selected for the job, the announcement arguably could amount to a presumption of direct discrimination.

2.2.1.1. Transformative or revelatory speech indicating the occurrence of direct discrimination It is worth noting that this particular category of speech is also liable to change the prima facie nature of the presumed discrimination, as it may for instance show that an apparent (potential) indirect distinction was in fact *intended* and set up as a covert direct discrimination, due to its express discriminatory purpose. Although discriminatory intent is not required for there to be direct discrimination, the presence of such intent nonetheless conceptually leads to the qualification of (a presumption of) direct discrimination, despite other formal reasons being provided by the alleged perpetrator for his contested practice

83 Again, of course, such speech can also concern other grounds than race and religion: see Equal Treatment Commission opinion 2010-137 of 16 September 2010, in which a man was (allegedly) told: "One can simply see that you're gay, it's not excessive, but you can clearly see it nonetheless and some people here have great difficulty with that." Confronted with the claim that this had been said, and that it amounted to discrimination, the firm declared that the man had indeed been told that he came across as "being very gay," but that his rejection was nonetheless due to other reasons. Since the firm was unable to adequately substantiate the latter claim, however, the ETC found that the man's sexual orientation had played a role in rejecting him, and that the decision had therefore been directly discriminatory.

84 Correctional Tribunal of Dendermonde, 24 April 2005; Court of Appeals of Ghent, 25 April 2007. The labor case resulted—again, in appeal—in a ruling that the dismissal had been unlawful (Labor Court Ghent, 7 May 2007, www.progresslaw.net). See J. Vrielink, *Van haat gesproken? Een rechtsantropologisch onderzoek naar de bestrijding van rasgerelateerde uitingsdelicten in België* (Maklu 2010), 347 and 357.

or provision.[85] After all, in such cases there arguably turns out to be a direct causal link to the protected characteristic, with people as such being treated "less favourably *on the grounds*" involved (direct discrimination), rather than being "an *apparently neutral* provision, criterion or practice" with a disparate impact (indirect discrimination).

Often such a discriminatory intent will be evidenced by speech. As such, in cases in which speech can demonstrate that an ostensible indirect distinction was in fact intentionally "based on the grounds" of religion or race, a presumption of direct discrimination might be inferred from such speech, thereby transforming the initially supposed nature of the discrimination involved. This transformative or rather revelatory capacity of speech liable to create a presumption of direct discrimination is relevant in the light of the possibilities of negation and justification that a respondent has, more specifically excluding the possibility of an objective and reasonable justification (*supra* §1.2).

The aforementioned would imply, for instance, that if preceding or following the introduction of a general dress code, including a prohibition on head gear, one or more of the decision-makers would indicate by means of verbal or written speech that the prohibition was specifically introduced to exclude Islamic headscarves or to exclude Sikh turbans, such speech could arguably "transform" the initial presumption of indirect discrimination, based on the apparent nature of the provision or practice, into a presumption of direct discrimination.[86]

An interesting example of such "transformative speech" —albeit outside of the realm of employment and hiring, and concerning goods and services—occurred in Belgium in the summer of 2007. A local town council issued a demand for everyone in the pools and recreation domains in their district to wear classical bathing trunks (i.e. "Speedos"), officially for reasons of hygiene. However, a number of the officials responsible for the decision, the mayor and the alderman of sports for example, were quoted as saying that a main reason for introducing the rule was in fact to keep out "trouble makers," more specifically: youths of Moroccan origin. The officials explained that research had shown that said youths were, due to their culture and religion, highly reluctant or even unable to wear

85 M. J. Busstra, *The Implications of the Racial Equality Directive for Minority Protection Within the European Union* (Eleven International Publishing 2010), 226; M. Ambrus, M. J. Busstra and K. Henrard, "The Racial Equality Directive and Effective Protection Against Discrimination: Mismatches Between the Substantive Law and Its Application," 3 *Erasmus Law Review* 165 (2010), 171–172; D. Schiek, L. Waddington and M. Bell (eds), *Non-discrimination Law* (Hart Publishing 2007), 185–186.

86 See also the chapter by Titia Loenen in this volume (arguing that a "neutral" employer dress policy should be approached as direct discrimination if it was used to hide an intent to exclude headscarves or *burqas*). See also M. J. Busstra, *The Implications of the Racial Equality Directive for Minority Protection Within the European Union* (Eleven International Publishing 2010), 226.

the required bathing suits (wearing Bermudas instead).[87] If the officials had not been quoted in this sense, the case would have, at most, amounted to indirect discrimination, subject to the relevant general justification possibilities (*supra* §1). Arguably, however, the officials' speech amounted to a presumption of *direct* discrimination instead, on account of its prima facie revealing the measure's non-neutral and even discriminatory aims.[88]

2.2.2. Speech that is liable to facilitate discriminatory decision-making

Secondly, direct discrimination in the context of hiring might also be presumed on the basis of speech that is liable to facilitate discriminatory decision-making. This will mostly concern inquiries by prospective employers[89]—either on the job application, in a testing process or during the interview—regarding issues that are not (directly) related to the job for which an individual is applying. Discrimination law will often not be the only means by which such speech can be tackled; many countries have specific legislation or (self-) regulation concerning the questions a prospective employer can ask.[90] For the current purposes, however, such queries are relevant only to the extent that they amount to a presumption of direct discrimination. In order for this to be the case, an employer's questions

87 The alderman of sports was more specifically quoted as follows: "The Town Council decided to introduce that rule, because we know on the basis of research that youths of foreign origin do not feel comfortable wearing regular swimming trunks."

88 Strikingly, following the controversy, the CEOOR organized a meeting with the council, during which it was concluded that the measure was neither directly nor indirectly discriminatory. In a subsequent press release the CEOOR accepted the council's claim that the aim and intent of the measure were not discriminatory: "the new regulations for visitors of the swimming pool are intended for reasons of hygiene only and not to exclude certain groups of people." The mayor, the alderman and others involved having been quoted in the opposite sense was attributed to "unfortunate communication," "confusion" and "misunderstandings." The press release did not discuss the (potential) disparate impact of the measure (CEOOR, "Iedereen blijft welkom in Huizingen" [Everyone Remains Welcome in Huizingen], *Press release*, 26 June 2007).

89 The focus on inquiries by employers, or more generally decision-makers, implies that applicants themselves are of course free to provide any personal information they wish on a voluntary basis, without this, in principle, subsequently being able to lead to a presumption of discrimination (save in cases in which the decision-maker responded to this information in a manner that raises reasonable suspicion that he would act upon such information in a discriminatory way). Cf. H. Norton, "You Can't Ask (or Say) That: The First Amendment and Civil Rights Restrictions on Decisionmaker Speech," 11 *William & Mary Bill of Rights Journal* 727 (2003), 770.

90 The harm of such inquiries is not limited to the (possibility of) its resultant information being used for discriminatory purposes, but also consists in the extracted information often being "deeply private even if never used against the applicant": "[t]he individual is injured in part simply because someone else (moreover someone in a position of power) now possesses what would otherwise be closely held personal information" (ibid., 740).

must be directly related to an individual's protected characteristics.[91] Examples concerning religion most obviously include asking what religion someone practices, what holy days he or she observes, or finally—depending on the context of the question—whether an applicant is prepared to take off visible expressions of a religious conviction, such as the Islamic headscarf, the Jewish kippa or the Sikh turban.[92] Concerning race or ethnic origin one can think likewise of questions about those characteristics, such as asking about the ethnic background from which an applicant comes.

If such questions are followed by a negative decision in a recruitment procedure, they could generally lead to a presumption of direct discrimination, since it raises the reasonable suspicion that the questions led to or fueled a discriminatory decision.[93] The solicited pre-employment information about protected characteristics in that case suggests that those characteristics might have been used as a basis for making unlawful discriminatory selection decisions. The (incidental) limitation on speech by decision-makers in hiring procedures that the potential use of this speech implies would again not seem problematic, since the information gathered with such questions is valueless, as it may not be used to support choices in hiring, and must therefore be considered irrelevant, except for illegal purposes.

Moreover, to the extent that such questions are benignly posed by well-intentioned employers, the latter will still be able to demonstrate that the acquired information was not actually used as a basis for discriminatory decision-making, but that there were other, non-discriminatory, reasons for not hiring the applicant. Finally, if and when the decisions indeed were based on the solicited information, it will still be possible in certain cases for the queries to have been legitimately posed due to them being justified. That will be the case, first, if the characteristic that was inquired about—be it race, religion or another protected characteristic—constitutes an occupational requirement. Secondly, employers may legitimately

---

91 Concerning a presumption of *indirect* discrimination one could—regarding race and ethnicity—think of questions concerning citizenship, native tongue, familiarity with native culture, etc., while questions having indirectly to do with religion could concern the type of clubs or social organizations that a person belongs to, etc.

92 The latter type of query could amount to either a presumption of *direct* or *indirect* religious discrimination, depending on whether the decision-maker's question is aimed specifically at preventing the expression of religion or a particular religion (presumption of direct discrimination), or whether he is asking this for reasons unrelated to religion, for instance because there is a general prohibition of head gear in place on the work floor (presumption of indirect discrimination).

93 As mentioned (cf. *supra* footnote 51), these situations should be distinguished from cases in which such a query is followed by a clear and unequivocal announcement of a causal relationship between a particular answer by the applicant and his exclusion or disadvantaging (as in the example of the contractor in §2.1.1).

require—and as such inquire about—information about potential employees' or applicants' race or religion for positive action purposes.[94]

Conclusion: Direct discrimination, protected speech and line-drawing difficulties

In this chapter it was argued that certain categories of speech and communication are relevant for assessing whether direct discrimination in recruitment took place, either because they amount to direct discrimination themselves, or because they can reasonably be taken to establish a presumption of direct discrimination.

Regarding the former, three partially overlapping categories of speech were identified: speech that directly and unmediatedly excludes or disadvantages persons from opportunities on a discriminatory basis (1); speech that is (highly) likely to deter applicants from pursuing or continuing to pursue opportunities on a discriminatory basis (2); and speech that is (highly) likely to mislead applicants from pursuing or continuing to pursue opportunities on a discriminatory basis (3). As for speech that can serve to establish a presumption of direct discrimination, two main categories were identified and analyzed: types of speech that indicate that the disadvantaging or the exclusion of persons from important opportunities on a discriminatory basis (likely) took place (1), and speech that facilitates discriminatory decision-making (2).

The criteria that were provided for identifying these categories of speech leave significant room for interpretation. Due to the complex nature of human communicative interaction and the rights and interests involved in it, such line-drawing difficulties are not only unavoidable, but also necessary. The assessment of whether a particular instance of speech concerns one of these categories should not take place in the abstract by creating clear-cut criteria which disallow any flexibility. Rather, this should entail a case-by-case consideration that permits the examination of the specific context in which a communicative act occurs, on the basis of which it can be concluded what standards ought to be applied. On the one hand, the fact that, technically speaking, speech is involved in a discrimination case, does not necessarily result in heightened scrutiny or protection, since—as mentioned before—not all of such speech "seriously implicates the values and principles that lie behind freedom of speech."[95] On the other hand, however, one should carefully weigh the concrete interests and contextual factors at hand, since freedom of speech and other rights and interests could easily get restricted if

94 Regarding disability, moreover, it would also seem legitimate for employers to ask if candidates have disabilities so that reasonable adjustments can be made that enable them to attend interviews.

95 K. Greenawalt, *Speech, Crime, and the Uses of Language* (Oxford University Press 1989), 3.

the categories of speech that are regarded as amounting to discrimination or as establishing a presumption thereof become over-inclusive.

By way of conclusion, it may therefore be useful to highlight a number of central and cautionary points that may assist in finding the right balance. First, it is essential that virtually all actionable speech categories that were identified concern speech in the *context* of decision-making regarding recruitment and *speakers* as decision-makers. This implies that discrimination law—at least in prohibiting direct discrimination—should not limit alternative avenues for individuals to engage in political, religious or other expressions, outside their role as decision-makers and outside the process of decision-making. One should always determine whether, for instance, an employer is in fact speaking as a decision-maker, communicating about job opportunities, or whether he is speaking as a player in a societal or policy debate.[96]

Speech, for instance, by a company decision-maker that criticizes discrimination law should generally be regarded neither as discrimination nor as being able to establish a presumption thereof, as long as it is not done in a context or in a manner that would serve to deter potential employees from applying for future vacancies at the speaker's company. It is anyone's right to share their views on the morality or wisdom of discrimination laws, for instance, and to argue and call for their abolition.[97]

Furthermore, to the extent that slurs and discriminatory speech—or, more generally, hate speech—might amount to a presumption of direct discrimination or even to direct discrimination itself, it is important to keep the rationale for this in mind to avoid over-broad applications. This rationale does not (and may not) consist of the offense that such speech causes. Under the EU non-discrimination directives, the purpose of the prohibition of direct discrimination does not include alleviating this type of harm.[98] As such, the prohibition of direct discrimination does not imply a blanket prohibition against the use of racially or religiously discriminatory language in the workplace: it may not be used as alternative hate speech legislation. Discriminatory comments or slurs become relevant in the context of direct discrimination *only* if an employer takes an adverse action against a member of the racial group that was the target of the comment or slur, or if such

96 Cf. H. Norton, "You Can't Ask (or Say) That: The First Amendment and Civil Rights Restrictions on Decisionmaker Speech," 11 *William & Mary Bill of Rights Journal* 727 (2003), 750.

97 Cf. ibid., 774.

98 The hate speech legislation that the EU seeks to have its members enact—through the Council Framework Decision 2008/913/JHA of 28 November 2008 on combating certain forms and expressions of racism and xenophobia by means of criminal law—comes closer to serving this aim. However, the criteria that the Framework Decision encompasses regarding the speech that Member States must prohibit are quite strict, as a result of considerations of free speech being far more relevant when speech restrictions are intrinsic rather than incidental to legislative action.

speech is sufficiently exclusionary or deterring to itself constitute such an adverse action (cf. *supra*). As such, it is not (the content of) the speech as such that is being targeted, just what it could imply in the highly specific transactional context in which it is uttered. Someone making such statements outside the context of a hiring procedure is something else entirely than an employer or other decision-maker doing so when communicating with potential applicants about available opportunities.[99] Moreover, "[t]he decision maker can easily conduct an employment transaction without airing his political views,"[100] so that it is hard to regard the incidental speech restriction that this de facto results in as disproportionate.

Finally, *religious speech* by employers would seem to take up an even more exceptional place. Whereas racist speech (like sexist or homophobic speech) may not always be actionable under discrimination law,[101] it *is* generally regarded as undesirable and immoral. The same cannot be said of religious speech and expression, which, at least in the eyes of many, has a "societally recognized and constitutionally enunciated value."[102] Even though eliminating religious discrimination in employment is an important goal in European discrimination law, "that goal must be achieved in a manner that is cognizant of the explicit, affirmative value that religious speech and expression are generally and legally accepted to have for employers as well as employees."[103] Therefore, in the absence of additional indications that such speech aimed or served to deprive an applicant of employment opportunities on the basis of religious status or other characteristics, it should—even within the context of the workplace and hiring procedures—generally not be seen as amounting to a presumption of direct discrimination, let alone as constituting direct discrimination in itself.

---

99 H. Norton, "You Can't Ask (or Say) That: The First Amendment and Civil Rights Restrictions on Decisionmaker Speech," 11 *William & Mary Bill of Rights Journal* 727 (2003), 750.

100 Ibid., 750.

101 At least not under its prohibition of direct discrimination. The use of such speech can, however, sometimes give rise to a claim for harassment, if it is sufficiently severe or pervasive to be said to take "place with the purpose or effect of violating the dignity of a person," and when it moreover creates "an intimidating, hostile, degrading, humiliating or offensive environment." On this issue, in the context of the European Directives and concerning religion, see, for example, L. Vickers, "Is All Harassment Equal? The Case of Religious Harassment," 65 *Cambridge Law Journal* 579 (2006).

102 L. S. Underkuffler, "'Discrimination' on the Basis of Religion: An Examination of Attempted Value Neutrality in Employment," 30 *William & Mary Law Review* 581 (1989), 610.

103 Ibid.

Chapter 7

Religious-Ethos Employers and Other Expressive Employers under European and Belgian Employment Law

Yves Stox

Introduction

Since the adoption of the Employment Equality Directive, the status of religious-ethos employers and other expressive employers under European and Belgian employment law is enjoying renewed attention. The Employment Equality Directive includes a specific exception for religious-ethos employers, although its practical significance remains unclear. Because of the lack of case law of the European Court of Justice, the turbulent legislative drafting process of this provision remains the main source for discovering the significance of the ambiguous religious-ethos exception.

This chapter is organized as follows. The first section explores the notion "expressive employer," showing its various meanings. Not only employers with a religious or philosophical ethos seek to realize a specific identity, but various kinds of employers, like political pressure groups and commercial companies, claim to develop and maintain a particular identity.

The second and third sections focus on the Employment Equality Directive, its legislative history and its implementation under Belgian law. The political decision-making process within the Council shows how difficult it was for the Member States to reach a political agreement on the exception for religious-ethos employers. These extensive debates resulted in an ambiguously drafted compromise text, giving rise to several possible interpretations. The case law of the Belgian Constitutional Court, however, seems to downplay its practical significance.

The fourth section crosses the boundaries of discrimination law and looks at the case law of the European Court of Human Rights (ECtHR). In the absence of a difference of treatment based on a discrimination ground, the balancing of the conflicting fundamental rights of the employee and his expressive employer is not structured by the occupational requirement test. Recent cases of the ECtHR equally stress the importance of an *in concreto* analysis, focusing on the particular function of the employee concerned.

I. The notions "expressive employer" and "religious-ethos employer"

Every company invests in developing a brand and a corporate image, thereby creating and upholding an identity in order to distinguish itself and create a sense of uniqueness, both towards clients and employees. A heterogeneous group of employers goes beyond this general commercial goal-setting and intends to maintain, develop and disperse a particular philosophical, religious, moral, political, ecological, charitable or other (legitimate) set of thoughts or beliefs.[1] The main (but not necessarily exclusive) purpose of these "expressive employers" is indeed the desire to *express* a "philosophy of life" or "view of society." "Religious-ethos employers" then are expressive employers maintaining, developing and dispersing a particular religion or philosophy of life.

In view of the dense network of Roman Catholic educational and social service organizations in Belgium, most Belgian case law concerns employment within these religious-ethos organizations. Nevertheless, a wide range of employers, such as think tanks, pluralist associations,[2] political parties,[3] non-governmental organizations[4] and labor unions[5] also seek to maintain and strengthen their particular identity or ethos.

However, a mere vague link with a philosophy of life or view of society is not sufficient in order to qualify as an expressive employer.[6] Every employee is bound to execute loyally his employment contract, irrespective of the nature of his employer. Thus, even a purely commercial undertaking can rightfully expect its employees to respect the company's image and brand. An expressive employer

1 W. Rauws and H. Schyvens, "De bescherming van werknemersgrondrechten binnen de individuele arbeidsverhouding," in *De toepasselijkheid van de grondrechten in private verhoudingen* (K. Rimanque, ed., Kluwer 1982), 223.

2 P. Humblet, "Arbeidsovereenkomst en politiek mandaat: kan een werknemer twee heren dienen?" 52 *Rechtskundig Weekblad* 1356 (1988–1989), 1364.

3 H.-V. Tens, *Die Politischen Parteien als Tendenzbetriebe* (unpublished, Diss. Doktor der Rechte, Freie Universität Berlin – Rechtswissenschaftliche Fakultät 1972), 6–9.

4 At the time of the enactment of the Belgian Anti-discrimination Act of 2003, it was argued in Parliament that Greenpeace should be able to engage (only) confirmed environmentalists (*Doc. Parl.* Sénat 1999–2000, 2-12/15, 58).

5 Labor Court Hasselt 17 May 2004, *Chroniques de droit social* (2008), 140.

6 A gymnastics association linked with a political party, although set up to accommodate the party's members, should not be considered as a political organization (Council of State 25 March 1975, No. 16.943, *Van Craen*). An economic cooperative linked with a social movement qualifies as an expressive employer only to a limited extent. The dismissal of a blue-collar worker denouncing the cooperative ideal is thus unjust (Labor Court Ghent 2 December 1976, 41 *Rechtskundig Weekblad* (1977–1978), 1699). The opinion of P. Waquet, following case law of the French *Court de Cassation* (Cass. Fr. 22 January 1992, *Droit Social* 4 (1992), 334—concerning the employee of a Renault franchise holder who drove a Peugeot), was that, at least partly, certain commercial companies qualifying as expressive employers seems too far-stretched (P. Waquet, "Loyauté du Salarié dans les Entreprises de Tendance," 116 *Gazette du Palais* 1427 (1996), doctrine, 1427).

is distinct from other employers because he maintains an identity based on a philosophy of life or view of society, even when developing commercial activities to a certain extent. Indeed, commercial goals do not necessarily jeopardize an employer's expressive character when that identity is unambiguous.[7]

The question whether neutrality can constitute, together with pluralism, a particular company identity surpasses the scope of this chapter. It should be noted, however, that some Belgian Labor Courts have accepted the neutrality policy argument invoked by commercial companies in order to justify bans on religious symbols (in particular headscarves) from the working place.[8]

Belgian legislation does not expressly define or recognize the particular character of expressive employers, except for religious-ethos organizations and only since the Anti-discrimination Act of 2007 which implements—for the second time—the EU Employment Equality Directive. Belgian case law,[9] however, does recognize the impact of expressive employers' specific nature on the employment relationship, either by validating a contractual loyalty clause or by requiring the execution of the employment contract in good faith, without losing sight of the particular function of the employee concerned.[10]

The specific character of expressive employers is highlighted by the conflict between, on the one hand, the identical or similar fundamental rights of the expressive employer and, on the other hand, the (future) employee. The employer who seeks to defend an identity based on religion or belief can be confronted with an employee expressing conflicting opinions or practicing a conflicting lifestyle. An employee entering into the service of a religious-ethos company or other expressive employer will not forfeit his fundamental rights (for instance his freedom of religion, freedom of expression or right to respect for privacy). Because the expressive employer seeks to maintain, develop and disperse his identity based on similar fundamental rights,[11] the employee's fundamental rights are, however, subject to contractual restrictions, either explicitly, by means of, for

7 Cantonal Court 's-Hertogenbosch 6 June 2007, LJN: BA6522, 498705 (concerning a Catholic newspaper); Labor Court of Appeals Paris 25 May 1990, *Recueil Dalloz Sirey* (1990), 597 (concerning a Jewish kosher restaurant).

8 Labor Court of Appeals Brussels 15 January 2008, *Journal des tribunaux du travail* 1003 (2008), 140; Labor Court Antwerp 27 April 2010, A.R. 06/397639/A, http://www.juridat.be.

9 See, for instance, Labor Court of Appeals Antwerp, 28 August 1989, 52 *Rechtskundig Weekblad* (1989–1990), 1368 (concerning an employee of a Christian sick fund adhering to a socialist–liberal coalition of political parties); Labor Court Hasselt 17 May 2004, *Chroniques de droit social* (2008), 140 (concerning a socialist labor union employee adhering to a Christian labor union); Labor Court Brussels 10 October 1994, *Revue de droit social* (1994), 349 (concerning a transsexual employee of a Roman Catholic hospital).

10 Y. Stox, *Discriminatie en identiteit – Identiteitsgebonden werkgevers in het Belgisch en Europees arbeidsrecht* (Larcier 2010), 107–117.

11 *Id.* at 14.

instance, a loyalty clause in the employment contract, or implicitly.[12] An example of the balancing of conflicting rights can be found in the decision of the European Commission of Human Rights in the *Rommelfanger* case.[13] The Commission considered that the dismissal of an employee who expressed a pro-abortion standpoint in the press was necessary in order for the religious-ethos employer to maintain its credibility, and did not infringe the employee's freedom of expression:

> The Commission is satisfied that German law, as interpreted by the Federal Constitutional Court,[14] takes account of the necessity to secure an employee's freedom of expression against unreasonable demands of his employer, even if they should result from a valid employment contract. If, as in the present case, the employer is an organisation based on certain convictions and value judgements which it considers as essential for the performance of its functions in society, it is in fact in line with the requirements of the Convention to give appropriate scope also to the freedom of expression of the employer. An employer of this kind would not be able to effectively exercise this freedom without imposing certain duties of loyalty on its employees. As regards employers such as the Catholic foundation which employed the application in its hospital, the law in any event ensures that there is a reasonable relationship between the measures affecting freedom of expression and the nature of the employment as well as the importance of the issue for the employer. In this way it protects an employee against compulsion in matters of freedom of expression which would strike at the very substance of this freedom.[15]

The balancing of the conflicting fundamental rights of the employee and his "expressive employer" takes place either in the framework of the Employment Equality Directive as implemented by the Belgian Anti-discrimination Act (by means of the genuine and determining occupational requirement or proportionality tests) or via the techniques of "traditional" Belgian employment law (in particular, unfair dismissal or abuse of law).

The status of expressive or religious-ethos employer does not necessarily benefit the employer, but can operate as a double-edged sword. Following the reciprocal character of an employment contract, both the employee and the employer are bound to carry it out in good faith. Consequently, the employee can also invoke his employer's particular status.[16] French case law supports an employee seeking to exercise his freedom of religion over the employer's objections as a result of the latter's status as expressive employer. The dismissal of a worker because of religiously motivated absence by a Jewish kosher restaurant, serving meals

12 For further reading, see *Id.* at 30–33.

13 EComHR 6 September 1989, *Rommelfanger* v. *Germany*, App. No. 12242/86.

14 BVerfG 4 Juni 1985, *Loyalitätspflicht*, *BVerfGE* 70, 138.

15 EComHR 6 September 1989, *Rommelfanger* v. *Germany*, App. No. 12242/86.

16 Y. Stox, *Discriminatie en identiteit – Identiteitsgebonden werkgevers in het Belgisch en Europees arbeidsrecht* (Larcier 2010), 33.

in line with orthodox religious regulations, was unlawful. Precisely because of the employer's qualification as a religious-ethos employer, the employee was rightfully absent in order to observe Jewish religious rules on mourning.[17]

II. Religious-ethos employers under the Employment Equality Directive

The Employment Equality Directive in Article 4.2 provides for a specific exception for only one particular category of expressive employers, namely religious-ethos employers:

> Member States may maintain national legislation in force at the date of the adoption of this Directive or provide for future legislation incorporating national practices existing at the date of adoption of this Directive pursuant to which, in the case of occupational activities within churches and other public or private organisations the ethos of which is based on religion or belief, a difference of treatment based on a person's religion or belief shall not constitute discrimination where, by reason of the nature of these activities or of the context in which they are carried out, a person's religion or belief constitute a genuine, legitimate and justified occupational requirement, having regard to the organisation's ethos. This difference of treatment shall be implemented taking account of Member States' constitutional provisions and principles, as well as the general principles of Community law, and should not justify discrimination on another ground.
>
> Provided that its provisions are otherwise complied with, this Directive shall thus not prejudice the right of churches and other public or private organisations, the ethos of which is based on religion or belief, acting in conformity with national constitutions and laws, to require individuals working for them to act in good faith and with loyalty to the organisation's ethos.

Consideration 24 to the Employment Equality Directive explicitly states that in view of Declaration No 11 annexed to the Final Act of the Amsterdam Treaty—which recognizes that the Amsterdam Treaty respects and does not prejudice the status under national law of churches and religious associations or communities on the one hand and of philosophical and non-confessional organizations on the other hand[18]—Member States may maintain or lay down a specific occupational requirement test justifying a difference in treatment by religious-ethos employers.

---

17 Labor Court of Appeals Paris 25 May 1990, *Recueil Dalloz Sirey* (1990), 597. For further reading, see L.-L. Christians, "Le principe de non-discrimination religieuse en droit belge et comparé: entre obligation du législateur et obligation des contractants," *Antidiscriminatiewet en contracten – La Loi Anti-discrimination et les contrats* (S. Stijns and P. Wéry, eds, die Keure 2006), 192–194.

18 The text of the Declaration No 11 lies at the origin of Article I-52 of the Draft Constitution for Europe (G. Robbers, "State and Church in the European Union," in *State*

The Employment Equality Directive thus seems to make a direct link between the respect of the EU for the specificity of each Member State's system between state and faith communities[19] and the exception for religious-ethos employers. Moreover, it does not hold a unique position in EU labor law: the European Commission noted that it borrowed the provision from the European Works Council Directive,[20] the latter being highly influenced by German collective labor law as laid down in the *Betriebsverfassungsgesetz*.[21]

Other expressive employers, such as political parties, labor unions and non-governmental organizations, cannot invoke this exception and are bound to justify discrimination by means of the genuine and occupational requirement test of Article 4.1 of the Employment Equality Directive.

1. The political decision-making process of the religious-ethos exception[22]

The initial proposal of the European Commission for the Employment Equality Directive[23] states on genuine occupational qualifications in Article 4.2 that

> Member States may provide that, in the case of public or private organisations which pursue directly and essentially the aim of ideological guidance in the field of religion or belief with respect to education, information and the expression of

and Church in the European Union (G. Robbers, ed., Nomos 2005), 585–587) and Article 17 of the Treaty on the functioning of the European Union.

19 P. De Pooter, *De rechtspositie van erkende erediensten en levensbeschouwingen in Staat en maatschappij* (Larcier 2003), 120.

20 The Commission was referring to Article 8.3 of the Directive of 22 September 1994 (94/45/EEC) on the Establishment of a European Works Council or a procedure in Community-scale undertakings and Community-scale groups of undertakings for the purposes of informing and consulting employees, which meanwhile has been replaced by the Works Council Directive of 6 May 2009 (2009/38/EC), without affecting Article 8.3 itself; Outcome of proceeding of the Working Party on Social Questions on 11 January 2000, doc No. 5231/00 SOC 5 JAI 3, 31 January 2000, 13, fn. 20.

21 F. Dorssemont, "Het communautair inspraakrecht, een leerstuk in wording?" in *Herstructurering doorheen het (arbeids)recht* (J. Peeters and W. Rauws, eds, Intersentia 2006), 123–124.

22 Under the European Community Treaties, the Council is the chief legislation institution. The right of initiative is generally empowered to the Commission, which is entitled to amend its proposal at any time so long as the Council has not reached a decision. As a part of the Council's internal organization, the Committee of Permanent Representatives (Coreper) prepares the work of the Council—each Member State delegates to it a Permanent Representative. The Working Party (on Social Questions)—consisting of national civil servants and representatives of the Commission—operates under the auspices of the Coreper and hosts the first discussions of Commission proposals for legislation. The Working Party (on Social Questions) reports to the Coreper, which in turn refers the matters to the Council.

23 Proposal for a Council Directive establishing a general framework for equal treatment in employment and occupation, 25 November 1999, COM (1999) 565 final, 31 p.

> opinions, and for the particular occupational activities within those organisations which are directly and essentially related to that aim, a difference of treatment based on a relevant characteristic related to religion or belief shall not constitute discrimination where, by reason of the nature of these activities, the characteristic constitutes a genuine occupational qualification.

The Commission considered it evident "that in organisations which promote certain religious values, certain jobs or occupations need to be performed by employees who share the relevant religious opinion." Religious-ethos employers are thus allowed "to require occupational qualifications which are necessary for the fulfillment of the duties attached to the relevant post."[24]

Consequently, the Commission's proposal puts forward an instrumental approach. The exception for religious-ethos employers focuses on the job responsibilities of the individual employee, meaning that the discrimination can indeed only be justified if the employee concerned exercises a function that is directly and essentially linked to the ideological aim of his employer. It thus seems to exclude the influence of elements from the employee's private life on his employment. If the individual's capacity to do his job is not jeopardized by private acts, then the employer cannot withhold the job offer or initiate the dismissal, even if the employer's identity based on religion or belief opposes the employee's lifestyle or private life.[25]

During the discussions in the Working Party on Social Questions, Ireland proposed adding "or the context in which they are carried out."[26] This would result in a shift from the individual approach of the initial proposal ("the nature of the activities") to an organic position enabling employers to safeguard their identity based on religion or belief via their human resources policy. The final text of the Employment Equality Directive would incorporate this shifting away from the Commission's initial proposal, so that a genuine occupational requirement can more easily be invoked by a religious-ethos employer.

Gradually, the scope *ratione personae* of the exception broadened from public or private organizations, which pursue directly and essentially *the aim of ideological guidance in the field of religion or belief with respect to education, information and the expression of opinions*, to those which pursue directly and

24 Proposal for a Council Directive establishing a general framework for equal treatment in employment and occupation, 25 November 1999, COM (1999) 565 final, Explanatory memorandum, 10.

25 O. De Schutter, *Discriminations et marché du travail – Liberté et égalité dans les rapports d'emploi* (P.I.E.-Peter Lang 2001), 73. See also Cass. fr. (soc) 17 April 1991, *Painsecq c. Association Fraternité Saint Pie X, Droit Social* (1991), 489.

26 Outcome of proceeding of the Working Party on Social Questions on 11 January 2000, doc No. 5231/00 SOC 5 JAI 3, 31 January 2000, 13, fn. 20.

essentially *the aim of promoting certain values on the basis of religion or belief.*[27] Moreover, Germany proposed inserting an explicit reference to "churches and religious associations or communities."[28] The Employment Equality Directive would in the end refer to "*churches* and other public or private organisations the ethos of which is based on religion or belief" [author's emphasis].

Although the European Commission considered a religious-ethos exception as self-evident, France, the UK and Spain questioned the need for Article 4.2. In their opinion, the exception for religious-ethos employers potentially causes more problems than it solves. They argued that the provision was solely a repetition of Article 4.1 where, because of the particular occupational activities or the context in which they are carried out, a religious characteristic is a genuine and determining occupational requirement provided that the objective is legitimate and the requirement is proportionate.[29, 30]

The difficult political discussions which took place in the Working Party on Social Questions and the Permanent Representatives Committee is illustrated by the fact that on 12 October 2000, the derogation for religious-based employers was still one of the two main outstanding issues, and the Council was invited by the Permanent Representatives Committee to settle the issue with a view of reaching a political agreement on the text.[31] The Permanent Representatives Committee made a final examination of this issue on the basis of the Presidency compromise text on 12 October 2000.[32] While Germany, a major supporter of a specific derogation, gave its

27 Outcome of proceeding of the Working Party on Social Questions on 14 and 28 March 2000, doc No. 6941/00 SOC 102 JAI 25, 31 March 2000, 18.

28 Outcome of proceeding of Working Party on Social Questions on 14 and 28 March 2000, doc No. 6941/00 SOC 102 JAI 25, 31 March 2000, 18 and fn. 30.

29 Outcome of proceeding of Working Party on Social Questions on 14 and 28 March 2000, doc No. 6941/00 SOC 102 JAI 25, 31 March 2000, 18, fn. 30; Outcome of proceeding of the Working Party on Social Questions of 13 June 2000, doc No. 9423/00 SOC 226 JAI 69, 20 June 2000, 16, fn. 20.

30 Following the case law of the Belgian Constitutional Court, the actual consequences of the exception for religious-ethos employers is brought into question (see below).

31 Addendum to report from Permanent Representatives Committee to Employment and Social Policy Council – Political agreement, doc No. 12270/00 ADD 1 SOC 345 JAI 113, 12 October 2000, 1.

32 In order to reach an agreement, the Presidency proposed on 11 October 2010 the following compromise text: "Member States may provide, by means of legislation, that in the case of churches or other public or private organisations based on religion or belief, as regards the occupational activities within those organisations, a difference of treatment based on a person's religion or belief shall not constitute discrimination where, by reason of the nature of these activities or of the context in which they are carried out, a person's religion or convictions constitute a genuine, legitimate and necessary occupational requirement, having regard to the organisation's objectives. This difference of treatment shall be implemented taking account of Member States' constitutional provisions and principles, as well as the general principles of Community law, and should not justify discrimination on another ground" (Forwarding of a text from Coreper to Employment

agreement, other delegations expressed their reservations. The Belgian delegation "[regretted] that on top of the watering down of the text on other points, the professional requirement was now '*necessary*' and not—as before—'*determining*,' and the vagueness of the reference to the 'context' in which the activities are carried out."[33] The conclusion of the Chairman was remarkable: "the difficulties and reservations in various quarters showed that the proposed compromise text was well-balanced," so that the text would be submitted as it stood to the Council.[34]

The Commission presented an amended proposal on 12 October 2000[35] to cover social work undertaken by religious organizations, expanding the provision's scope to a much larger and more diverse group of employers than churches' counseling and catechesis organizations.[36] At the same time, the Commission sought to underline that the exception will not justify discrimination on any other grounds than religion or belief. This concern was already covered by the initial proposal,[37] but remained clearly an issue throughout the proceedings of the Working Party on Social Questions. In particular, the UK raised the issue of possible conflicts between different grounds of discrimination (e.g. gay teachers in religious schools).[38] Although the Commission significantly broadens the range of employers able to invoke the derogation, it clearly sticks to the more stringent

---

and Social Policy Council – Political agreement, doc No. 12269/00 SOC 344 JAI 112, 11 October 2000, 14).

33 Addendum to report from Permanent Representatives Committee to Employment and Social Policy Council – Political agreement, doc No. 12270/00 ADD 1 SOC 345 JAI 113, 12 October 2000, 2.

34 Addendum to report from Permanent Representatives Committee to Employment and Social Policy Council – Political agreement, doc No. 12270/00 ADD 1 SOC 345 JAI 113, 12 October 2000, 2.

35 Article 4.2 was amended as follows: "Notwithstanding section 1, the Member States may provide that in the case of public or private organisations based on religion or belief, and for the particular occupational activities within those organisations which are directly and essentially related to religion or belief, a difference in treatment based on a person's religion or belief shall not constitute discrimination where, by reason of the nature of these activities or the context in which they are carried out, a person's religion or belief constitute a genuine occupational requirement. This difference of treatment may not, however, give rise to any discrimination on the other grounds referred to in Article 13 of the EC Treaty" (Amendment 37 of the Amended proposal for a Council Directive establishing a general framework for equal treatment in employment and occupation, 12 October 2000, COM (2000) 652 final).

36 O. De Schutter, *Discriminations et marché du travail – Liberté et égalité dans les rapports d'emploi* (P.I.E.-Peter Lang 2001), 75–76.

37 Explanatory memorandum to the Proposal for a Council Directive establishing a general framework for equal treatment in employment and occupation, 25 November 1999, COM (1999) 565 final, 10.

38 Outcome of proceeding of Working Party on Social Questions on 13 June 2000, doc No. 9423/00 SOC 226 JAI 69, 20 June 2000, 16, fn. 20.

approach of its initial proposal by requiring that the particular occupational activity be directly and essentially related to religion or belief.

The proceedings of the Employment and Social Policy Council on 17 October 2000 resulted, however, in a text bearing considerably more resemblance to the compromise text of the Presidency than the amended proposal of the Commission. The exception for religious-ethos employers on which the Council reached final political agreement consists of two sections. The first section[39] is the direct result of the above-mentioned proposals and amendments, building up to a specific occupational requirement exception for religious-ethos employers. The second section[40] imposes a loyalty requirement on the employees of religious-ethos employers. Although not mentioned *expressis verbis* in the proceedings of the Working Party on Social Questions earlier on, this loyalty requirement is formulated as a self-evident executive summary, wrapping up the earlier discussions and specifying the Member States' constitutional provisions and principles considered to be really at stake.

2. The interpretation of the religious-ethos exception

The religious-ethos exception of the Employment Equality Directive (Article 4.2) exists in two layers. At first, the general occupational requirement exception (Article 4.1) is reshaped into a more flexible occupational requirement exception for religious-ethos employers, the latter only applicable to justify discrimination based on the employee's religion or belief. The enactment of the Employment Equality Directive shows that the second layer of the religious-ethos exception was only added at the final stage. It requires employees of religious-ethos employers to act in good faith and with loyalty to their employer's ethos, hereinafter referred

39 "Member States may maintain existing national legislation or provide for future legislation incorporating existing national practices pursuant to which, in the case of churches or other public or private organisations the ethos of which is based on religion or belief, as regards the occupational activities within those organisations, a difference of treatment based on a person's religion or belief shall not constitute discrimination where, by reason of the nature of these activities or of the context in which they are carried out, a person's religion or belief constitute a genuine, legitimate and justified occupational requirement, having regard to the organisation's ethos. This difference of treatment shall be implemented taking account of Member States' constitutional provisions and principles, as well as the general principles of Community law, and should not justify discrimination on another ground" (Outcome of proceedings of Employment and Social Policy Council on 17 October 2010 – Political agreement, doc No. 12494/00 SOC 365 JAI 125, 20 October 2000, 13–14).

40 "Provided that its provisions are otherwise complied with, this Directive shall thus not prejudice the right of churches and other public or private organisations, the ethos of which is based on religion or belief, acting in conformity with national constitutions and laws, to require individuals working for them to act in good faith and with loyalty to the organisation's ethos" (Outcome of proceedings of Employment and Social Policy Council on 17 October 2010 – Political agreement, doc No. 12494/00 SOC 365 JAI 125, 20 October 2000, 13–14).

to as the "loyalty requirement." The difficult and long political decision-making process and the unclear relation between the layers of the religious-ethos exception causes a dual ambiguity, with respect to a) the exception's standstill obligation, and b) the genuine occupational requirement, the latter being the most difficult issue. Because the European Court of Justice has not yet had the opportunity to adjudicate on the boundaries of the religious-ethos exception, little certainty is offered to religious-ethos employers and their employees. In any case, neither the general occupational requirement exception (Article 4.1) nor the religious-ethos exception (Article 4.2) results in a total exemption of religious-ethos employers.

a. The Member States' standstill obligation

According to Article 4.2, Member States may *maintain* national legislation in force on 27 November 2000 or provide for future legislation incorporating national practices *existing* at that time. Clearly, the Member States are not obliged to implement the exception for religious-ethos employers. The standstill character of this provision opposes the adoption of new legislation justifying discrimination based on religion or belief by religious-ethos employers, unless the legislation concerned codifies already-existing case law.[41]

The second section of Article 4.2, requiring employees to act in good faith and with loyalty to their employer's ethos, underlines religious-ethos employers' freedom of religion, expression and organization, despite the Member States' standstill obligation: "[The Employment Equality Directive] shall *thus* not prejudice the right of churches and other public or private organisations, the ethos of which is based on religion or belief, acting *in conformity with national constitutions and laws*, to require individuals working for them to act in good faith and with loyalty to the organisation's ethos" [author's emphasis]. The use of the word "thus" suggests that this loyalty requirement should be considered as merely explicating the first section which provides religious-ethos employers with a specific occupational requirement exception. In any case, the Employment Equality Directive cannot deprive a religious-ethos employer from exercising its freedom of religion, expression or organization. These fundamental rights should be balanced against the principle of equal treatment as formulated by the Employment Equality Directive.[42]

---

41 C. Bayart, "De opmars van het discriminatierecht in de arbeidsverhoudingen – Europees discriminatierecht van de tweede generatie en aandachtspunten voor de Belgische wetgever bij de implementatie in de Belgische rechtsorde," *Journal des tribunaux du travail* 309 (2003), 322, fn. 175; I. Sewandono, "De Rassenrichtlijn en de Algemene wet gelijke behandeling," 47 *Sociaal-economische wetgeving* 218 (2001), 223.

42 O. De Schutter, *Discriminations et marché du travail – Liberté et égalité dans les rapports d'emploi* (P.I.E.-Peter Lang 2001), 74. With respect to religious-ethos employers, see in particular the *Rommelfanger* case (EComHR, 6 September 1989 *Rommelfanger* v. *Germany*, App. No. 12242/86), the *Obst* case (ECtHR 23 September 2010, *Obst* v. *Germany*, App. No. 425/03) and the *Schüth* case (ECtHR 23 September 2010, *Schüth* v. *Germany*, App. No. 1620/03).

b. The expressive employer's employees subject to occupational requirements

A religious-ethos employer can justify discrimination based on the employee's religion or belief "by reason of the nature of [the occupational] activities or of the context in which they are carried out … having regard to the organisation's ethos." As discussed above, the initial proposal of the Commission referred only to the "nature" of the employee's activities, while the "context" was only added later on by the Council. The question arises what the actual impact of this insertion will be.[43]

One could consider the reference to the "context" of the employee's professional activities as a way to further redraw from the general principle of non-discrimination, certainly in comparison with the Commission's initial proposal. Thus, the Employment Equality Directive not only accommodates the Commission's instrumental perspective, focusing on the particular activities conferred to the employee concerned, but seems to accept also a collective approach, under which the individual employee is considered a member of a broader community. Understandably, the latter approach is generally supported by religious-ethos employers and other expressive employers.[44]

De Schutter argues that one can interpret Article 4.2 in such a fashion that a religious-ethos employer can justify the refusal to engage a job applicant or the dismissal of an employee based on the individual's religion or belief, solely on the basis of the employer's self-determined ethos. The religious-ethos employer would not be constrained by having to take into consideration the actual requirements of the function concerned. This interpretation is supported by the lack of an explicit proportionality test, contrary to Article 4.1 which requires that the employer's objective is legitimate and the imposed requirement proportionate.[45] Such an interpretation is furthermore in line with the second section of Article 4.2 requiring employees to act in good faith and with loyalty to their employer's ethos: "[The Employment Equality Directive] shall *thus* not prejudice the right of churches and other public or private organisations, the ethos of which is based on religion or belief, acting in conformity with national constitutions and laws, to *require individuals working for them to act in good faith and with loyalty to the organisation's ethos*" [author's emphasis]. The use of the word "thus" embodies the political compromise since it suggests that this loyalty requirement merely explicates the specific occupational requirement exception. By underlining the employees' membership of a broader community, the loyalty requirement seems to push back interpretations supporting that not every occupation within a religious-

43 O. De Schutter, *Discriminations et marché du travail – Liberté et égalité dans les rapports d'emploi* (P.I.E.-Peter Lang 2001), 75.

44 A. Overbeeke and G. Geudens "Wij zijn zo vrij u af te wijzen … Onderscheid in personeelsbeleid bij identiteitsgebonden onderwijsinstellingen," in *Vrijheid en Gelijkheid. De horizontale werking van het gelijkheidsbeginsel en de nieuwe antidiscriminatiewet* (J. Velaers and J. Vrielink, eds, Maklu 2003), 663.

45 O. De Schutter, *Discriminations et marché du travail – Liberté et égalité dans les rapports d'emploi* (P.I.E.-Peter Lang 2001), 75.

ethos employer is subject to the occupational requirement exception, "but only those which are specifically concerned with religion or belief."[46]

The notion "context" lies at the heart of the text's ambiguity. Does it refer to the religious-ethos employer's organization as a whole or is a more narrow interpretation required? "Context" is not defined in the preparatory works of the Employment Equality Directive, even though the general occupational requirement exception (Article 4.1) also refers to "the *nature* of the *particular* occupational activities concerned or of the *context* in which they are carried out" [author's emphasis]. However, since the Racial Equality Directive applies the same definition of occupational requirements, the preparatory works of the latter can be used for further guidance.[47] In its Explanatory Memorandum, the Commission refers as an example to the situation

> where the holder of a particular job provides persons of a particular ethnic group with personal services promoting their welfare and those services can most effectively be provided by a person of that ethnic group.[48]

This example suggests that, although discrimination on the grounds of religion or belief can be justified by invoking the context in which the professional activities are pursued, and not only the nature of the activities, one should take into consideration the concrete context in which the particular function is exercised.

Recent German case law has validated this approach, at least conceptually. The refusal by the Evangelical Lutheran church to engage a Muslim applicant for not meeting the membership requirement for a position as social worker in an immigrant integration project, was deemed discriminatory. The German Labor Court considered that in the case at hand, neither the nature of the particular function, nor the context in which the function is exercised make the employee's religious beliefs constitute a genuine, legitimate and justified occupational requirement.[49]

---

46 See U. O'Hare, "Enhancing European Equality Rights: A New Regional Framework," 8 *Maastricht Journal of European and Comparative Law* 144 (2001), 151, in support of an interpretation which seems more in line with the Commission's initial proposal (see above).

47 It should however be noted that, while in the framework of the Race Directive the racial or ethnic origin will only be accepted as an occupational requirement in highly exceptional cases, discrimination on the basis of grounds of religion or belief can be more easily justified under the Employment Equality Directive.

48 Explanatory Memorandum to the Proposal for a Council Directive implementing the principle of equal treatment between persons irrespective of racial or ethnic origin, 25 November 1999, COM (1999) 566 final, 8. See also the *Van der Heijden* case (EComHR 8 March 1985, *Van der Heijden* v. *the Netherlands,* App. No. 11002/84).

49 Arbeitsgericht Hamburg 4 December 2007, 20 Ca 105/07, http://www.landesrecht.hamburg.de. This decision was overturned in appeal because the applicant concerned did not hold the required qualifications (Landesarbeitsgericht Hamburg 29 October 2008, 3 Sa 15/08, http://landesrecht.hamburg.de) and an appeal against this reversal was rejected

The nature or the context of the *particular* professional activities exercised by the employee concerned must be taken into account in order to determine whether the characteristic related to a discrimination ground constitutes a genuine and determining occupational requirement. The loyalty requirement of Article 4.2 of the Employment Equality Directive should be interpreted accordingly. The discriminatory refusal of a religious-ethos employer to engage an applicant or the discriminatory decision to dismiss an employee can therefore not be solely justified based on an element of the individual's private life, even though the organization's ethos opposes that particular lifestyle.[50] The expressive employer's requirements should be linked to the particular function of the employee concerned.[51] Making a loyalty claim, which is not underpinned by the particular function, even if the loyalty to the ethos is stipulated explicitly by the employment contract, is as such not sufficient.[52]

However, although certain functions may seem neutral at first glance, they can require an increased loyalty duty of the employee. A striking example: the Dutch Equal Treatment Commission determined that the Salvation Army was allowed to require a Christian religious conviction as occupational requirement for a kitchen helper. The set of tasks trusted to that particular kitchen helper surpassed the mere preparation and serving of meals since the employee was also supposed to assist with scripture readings and to act as the children's dedicated point of contact.[53]

(Bundesarbeitsgericht, 19 August 2010,8 AZR 466/09, http://juris.bundesarbeitsgericht.de). This interpretation would bring the Employment Equality Directive in line with Article 1.2 of the ILO Discrimination (Employment and Occupation) Convention, No. 111, concluded in 1958: "Any distinction, exclusion or preference in respect of a *particular* job based on the inherent requirements thereof shall not be deemed to be discrimination" [author's emphasis].

50 See below concerning the *Obst* case (ECtHR 23 September 2010, *Obst* v. *Germany*, App. No. 425/03) and the *Schüth* case (ECtHR 23 September 2010, *Schüth* v. *Germany*, App. No. 1620/03).

51 See the *Painsecq* case of the French *Court de Cassation.* The *Association Fraternité Saint Pie X*, a traditional catholic church refuting the orientation of the Roman Catholic Church after the Second Vatican Council, dismissed a sexton who was outed as homosexual. The Court considered this dismissal as unjust. Since French employment law forbade the dismissal of an employee "*pour le seul motif tiré de ses mœurs ou des ses convictions religieuses*," the Court upheld that "*il peut être procédé à un licenciement dont la cause objective est fondée sur le comportement du salarié qui, comte tenu de la nature de ses fonctions et de la finalité propre de l'entreprise, a créé un trouble caractérisé au sein de cette dernière.*" (Cass. fr. (soc) 17 April 1991, *Painsecq c. Association Fraternité Saint Pie X, Droit Social* 6 (1991), 489).

52 See the *Rommelfanger* case (EComHR 6 September 1989, *Rommelfanger* v. *Germany*, App. No. 12242/86).

53 Equal Treatment Commission 23 December 1996, decision 96/118, http://www.cgb.nl.

III. The transposition and interpretation of the religious-ethos exception in Belgium

Similar to the political decision-making process of the Employment Equality Directive, its implementation in Belgium (both in 2003 and 2007)[54] further stresses the political compromise behind the specific exception for religious-ethos employers. Although the complex phrasing of the exception highlights the unique character of this group of employers, recent case law of the Belgian Constitutional Court nuances the practical impact of the specific exception for religious-ethos companies from a Belgian (employment) law perspective, and this in view of the justification of (direct) discrimination by a "genuine and determining occupational requirement."

1. Religious-ethos employers and other expressive employers under the Anti-discrimination Act of 2003

The question of whether or not the religious-ethos exception of the Employment Equality Directive should be implemented in Belgian discrimination law provoked a passionate debate, both in Parliament and amongst the general public. If an exception was to be established, two options seemed to be available: either limiting the scope of the anti-discrimination provisions by excluding the internal organization of religious communities or associations, a real exemption,[55] or by transposing the religious-ethos exception of the Employment Equality Directive.[56] In the end, a political compromise was found by inserting the general statement that the Anti-discrimination Act would not prejudice the protection and application of the fundamental rights as determined by the Constitution and international human rights treaties, thus leaving it up to the courts to strike a balance between the principle of non-discrimination and the fundamental right at stake.[57]

---

54 The Employment Equality Directive has been implemented in Belgium by the Act of 25 February 2003 combating discrimination and modifying the Act of 15 February 1993 installing a Centre for equal opportunities and against racism (*Moniteur Belge* 17 March 2003, 1st edition, err., *Moniteur Belge* 13 May 2003) for the first time. Following the judgment by the Belgian Constitutional Court of 6 October 2004 annulling partially the Anti-discrimination Act of 2003, rendering it virtually powerless (Constitutional Court 6 October 2004, No. 157/2004), a new act has been adopted by the Belgian Parliament implementing the Equality Directive for a second time, i.e. the Act of 10 May 2007 combating certain forms of discrimination (*Moniteur Belge* 30 May 2007, 2nd edition).

55 This proposal clearly found its inspiration in the Dutch Equal Treatment Act, which does applies to neither legal relations within religious communities or other associations of a spiritual nature, nor to the clergy (Article 3 Equal Treatment Act).

56 For an overview of the different proposals and the debate in Parliament, see Y. Stox, *Discriminatie en identiteit – Identiteitsgebonden werkgevers in het Belgisch en Europees arbeidsrecht* (Larcier 2010), 61–65.

57 *Doc. Parl.* Sénat 2001–2002, No. 2-12/15, 118.

Even though no specific provision was inserted with respect to expressive employers and in particular religious-ethos employers, based on the preparatory works[58] a justification would still be possible by way of a genuine and determining occupational requirement, as provided for under Article 4.1 of the Employment Equality Directive.[59, 60]

2. Religious-ethos employers and other expressive employers under the Anti-discrimination Act of 2007

The Anti-discrimination Act of 2007 prohibits discrimination on grounds of age, sexual orientation, marital status, birth, wealth, religious beliefs or philosophy of life, political opinion, language, current or future health conditions, a disability, a physical or genetic characteristic, or social origin.[61] Following the judgment by the Belgian Constitutional Court of 2 April 2009,[62] labor union membership ("*opinion syndicale*") has been added as a protected ground.[63] The Anti-discrimination Act does not only include additional protected grounds compared to the Employment Equality Directive, but its scope is also much broader.[64] The relationship between

58 Amendement No. 5 du gouvernement, *Doc. Parl.* Chamber 2001–2002, No. 50 1578/003, 4.

59 P. De Pooter, "De doorwerking van het gelijkheidsbeginsel in de religieuze gemeenschappen en levensbeschouwelijke groepen," in *Vrijheid en Gelijkheid. De horizontale werking van het gelijkheidsbeginsel en de nieuwe antidiscriminatiewet* (J. Velaers and J. Vrielink, eds, Maklu 2003), 495; J. Velaers, "De horizontale werking van het discriminatieverbod in de antidiscriminatiewet. Enkele constitutionele beschouwingen," in *Vrijheid en Gelijkheid. De horizontale werking van het gelijkheidsbeginsel en de nieuwe antidiscriminatiewet* (J. Velaers and J. Vrielink, eds, Maklu 2003), 308–309; J. Vrielink, "De Belgische antidiscriminatiewet. Een kritische bespreking," in *Vrijheid en Gelijkheid. De horizontale werking van het gelijkheidsbeginsel en de nieuwe antidiscriminatiewet* (J. Velaers and J. Vrielink, eds, Maklu 2003), 218.

60 It is worth noticing that, as discussed above, at the time of the enactment of the Employment Equality Directive, the necessity and actual usefulness of Article 4.2 was already questioned.

61 The grounds of gender and racial or ethnic origin are covered by the Belgian Act combating discrimination between women and men (*Moniteur Belge* 30 May 2007, 2nd edition) and the Belgian Act amending the act of 30 July 1981 sanctioning acts of racism or xenophobia (*Moniteur Belge* 30 May 2007, 2nd edition).

62 Constitutional Court 2 April 2009, No. 64/2009, B.8.15-8.17.

63 Article 107 and Article 108 of the Act of 30 December 2009 containing various provisions (1), *Moniteur Belge* 31 December 2009.

For further reading, see J. Vrielink & D. De Prins, "Die Wiederkehr des Gleichen. Het Grondwettelijk Hof en de (federale) discriminatiewetgeving," 63 *Tijdschrift voor Bestuurswetenschappen & Publiekrecht* 579 (2009), 579–614.

64 Besides the areas of employment and occupation, it covers amongst others social protection and access to and supply of goods and services which are available to the public (Article 5 Anti-discrimination Act). With respect to the competencies of the

the recognized religions and their ministers, whose wages and pensions are paid by the State, does not qualify as an employment relationship[65] and falls outside the scope of the Belgian anti-discrimination legislation.[66]

As a rule, as regards employment and occupation, discrimination based on the protected grounds of the European Equality Directive should be justified by means of the genuine and determining occupational requirement test (Article 8 of the Anti-discrimination Act) and the religious-ethos exception (Article 13 of the Anti-discrimination Act), while discrimination based on one of the other protected grounds can be justified by means of the regular proportionality test (Article 7 of the Anti-discrimination Act).[67]

In contrast to the long discussions—weighty declarations included—between "believers" and "non-believers" during the adoption of the Anti-discrimination Act of 2003, the parliamentary debate concerning the religious-ethos exception during the adoption of the Anti-discrimination Act of 2007 was rather limited. Parliament adopted the religious-ethos exception as suggested in the Government's pre-draft, the wording being copied faithfully from the Employment Equality Directive:[68]

> In the case of occupational activities within public or private organisations, the ethos of which is based on religion or belief, a direct difference of treatment based on religion or belief, does not constitute discrimination where, by reason

---

Belgian federated entities, i.e. Communities and Regions, the federal Anti-discrimination Act is not applicable. The Communities and the Regions have adapted their own legislation implementing the Employment Equality Directive. In general, this legislation is based on the blueprint of the Employment Equality Directive and the Belgian Anti-discrimination Act. Its field of application with respect to the areas of employment and occupation is limited to the personnel of the Communities and Regions, the field of education and employment seeking.

65 The relationship between church ministers and the authorities of the recognized religions is solely controlled by the internal regulations of the particular religion (R. Torfs, "State and Church in Belgium," in *State and Church in the European Union* (G. Robbers, ed., Nomos 2005), 26).

66 Constitutional Court 12 February 2009, No. 17/2009, B.102.8. See also the European Parliament resolution on Petition 395/2001 on discrimination towards priests in the UK, submitted by the Reverend Raymond Owen (2002/2209(INI)), *Official Journal* 22 January 2004, C 13 E/56.

67 Projet de loi tendant à lutter contre certaines formes de discrimination du 26 Octobre 2006, Exposé des motifs, *Doc. Parl.* Chamber 2006–2007, No. 51 2722/001, 51. For an in-depth analysis, see S. Sottiaux, "De rechtvaardigingsgronden in het federale discriminatierecht," in *De nieuwe federale antidiscriminatiewetten – Les nouvelles lois luttant contra la discrimination* (C. Bayart, S. Sottiaux and S. Van Drooghenbroeck, eds, die Keure 2008), 227–256.

68 Projet de loi tendant à lutter contre certaines formes de discrimination du 26 Octobre 2006, Exposé des motifs, *Doc. Parl.* Chamber 2006-2007, No. 51 2722/001, 55; Rapport fait au nom de la commission de la justice par M. Eric Libert, *Doc. Parl.* Chamber 2006-2007, No. 2720/009, 112.

> of the nature of these activities or of the context in which they are carried out, the religion or belief constitutes a genuine, legitimate and justified occupational requirement, having regard to the organisation's ethos. Based on this provision, no other direct difference of treatment based on another protected criterion can be justified, unless this justification takes place in application of another provision of this title.[69]
>
> Provided that its provisions are otherwise complied with, this Act shall not prejudice the right of public or private organisations, the ethos of which is based on religion or belief, to require individuals working for them to act in good faith and with loyalty to the organisation's ethos.[70]

The ambiguity of the EU religious-ethos exception has thus been taken over in the Belgian legislation: Article 13 of the Anti-discrimination Act not only reproduces the occupational requirement exception for religious-ethos employers (the first section of Article 4.2 of the Employment Equality Directive), but also the loyalty requirement (the second section of Article 4.2 of the Employment Equality Directive).

This is so even though, under the first pre-draft as proposed by the Belgian Government to Parliament, the scope of the exception was widened to employers whose ethos is based on political opinion.[71] Although not criticized by the Belgian Council of State,[72] the Government limited the exception to religious-

69 This second section was added following the advisory opinion of the Council of State (Avis du Conseil d'Etat, No. 40.689/AV, No. 40.690/AV, No. 40.691/AV, *Doc. Parl.* Chamber 2006–2007, No. 2722/001, 124), so that a discrimination on another ground than religion or belief can nevertheless be justified by a religious-ethos employer via another justification method, such as a genuine and determining occupational requirement (Article 8 of the Anti-discrimination Act).

70 The official French language text of Article 13 of the Anti-discrimination Act reads as follows: "*Dans le cas des activités professionnelles des organisation publiques et privées, dont le fondement repose sur la conviction religieuse ou philosophique, une distinction directe fondée sur la conviction religieuse ou philosophique ne constitue pas une discrimination lorsque, en raison de la nature des activités ou du contexte dan lequel celles-ci sont exercées, la conviction religieuse ou philosophique constitue une exigence professionnelle essentielle, légitime et justifiée au regard due fondement de l'organisation.*

Sur base de cette disposition, aucune autre distinction directe fondée sur un autre critère protégé ne peut être justifié, à moins qu'elle ne le soit en application d'une autre disposition du présent titre.

Pourvue que ses dispositions soient par ailleurs respectées, la présente loi ne porte pas préjudice au droit des organisations publiques ou privées dont le fondement repose sur la conviction religieuse ou philosophique de requérir de personnes travaillant pour elle une attitude de bonne foi et de loyauté envers l'éthique de l'organisation."

71 Article 13 Avant-projet 1 de loi tendant à lutter certaines formes de discrimination, *Doc. Parl.* Chamber 2006–2007, No. 51 2722/001, 80.

72 Avis du Conseil d'Etat, No. 40.689/AV, No. 40.690/AV, No.40.691/AV, *Doc. Parl.* Chamber 2006–2007, No. 2722/001, 124.

ethos employers in its second pre-draft.[73] In line with the Employment Equality Directive, the Anti-discrimination Act of 2007 states consequently that a religious-ethos employer can invoke the derogation only when justifying direct discrimination based on religion or belief. When seeking to justify discrimination based on another protected ground, the religious-ethos employer should invoke the genuine and determining occupational requirement exception (Article 8 of the Anti-discrimination Act); the latter being the sole justification instrument for other expressive employers, irrespective of the ground of the difference of treatment.

The preparatory works of the Anti-discrimination Act of 2007 demonstrate, however, that the right to require an employee to act in good faith and with loyalty to his employer's ethos is not limited to religious-ethos employers only. The Government was of the opinion that the loyalty requirement can also be extended to other expressive employers such as political parties and affiliated lobby groups, even though the text of the Anti-discrimination Act itself does not substantiate this viewpoint.[74]

3. Downplaying the significance of the religious-ethos exception: The case law of the Belgian Constitutional Court

When assessing the actual impact of the religious-ethos exception, a twofold question arises. The first part is whether the Anti-discrimination Act of 2007 contains a de facto innovation vis-à-vis the Anti-discrimination Act of 2003, the latter not transposing the religious-ethos exception. The second is whether the religious-ethos employers (who wish to differentiate on the basis of belief or religion) find an advantage compared to other expressive employers who have to rely on the genuine and determining occupational requirement exception.

The Belgian Constitutional Court was called to decide whether an unconstitutional discrimination exists between religious-ethos employers on the one hand and other expressive employers on the other hand. The Constitutional Court's decision seems to limit the practical impact of the explicit religious-ethos exception (Article 13 of the Anti-discrimination Act).

Non-religious expressive employers can justify discrimination based on their philosophy of life or view of society only by invoking a genuine and determining

73 Article 13 Avant-projet 2 de loi tendant à lutter certaines formes de discrimination, *Doc. Parl.* Chamber 2006-2007, No. 51 2722/001, 135.

74 In its *Exposé des motifs* to the members of Parliament, when discussing the justification of direct discrimination on the ground of political opinion via the proportionality test (as provided for by Article 7 of the Anti-discrimination Act), the Government confirmed that the Anti-discrimination Act will not prejudice the right of organizations, the ethos of which is based on a political ideology, to require individuals working for them to act in good faith and with loyalty to the organization's ethos (Projet de loi tendant à lutter contre certaines formes de discrimination du 26 Octobre 2006, Exposé des motifs, *Doc. Parl.* Chamber 2006–2007, No. 2722/001, 47).

occupational requirement (Article 8 of the Anti-discrimination Act).[75] It has been said that the failure to transpose the religious-ethos exception in the Member State's legislation "means that religious groups are unable to impose religious or loyalty requirements on other employees" and that by imposing the genuine and determining occupational requirements test, "where the requirements of proportionality and necessity are stricter … it may be that some degree of religious freedom is denied to religious groups …"[76] This would mean that a political party or a labor union would not have the same freedom to differentiate (based on, for instance, the employee's political viewpoints or his labor union alliance)[77] and that such an employer is also prevented from imposing similar loyalty requirements as a religious-ethos employer. In the cases before the Constitutional Court, the plaintiffs—the leaders of a right-wing political party[78] and two labor unions[79]—argued indeed that political parties and labor unions can only justify discrimination based on their relevant opinion by means of the genuine and determining occupational requirement exception, thus being prevented from imposing the same requirements on their staff as religious-ethos employers. Their complaints were waived by the Constitutional Court.

The Constitutional Court underlined, by referring to the preparatory works of the Anti-discrimination Act of 2007,[80] that the religious-ethos exception should be considered essentially as a *specific confirmation* of the general justification method by means of a genuine and determining occupational requirement.[81] Consequently, the Constitutional Court holds that the Anti-discrimination Act does not create a different treatment between religious-ethos employers and other expressive

75 "*Il découle du système général de justification « ouvert » que les organisations publiques ou privées dont le fondement est constitué par une conviction autre que religieuse ou philosophique, qui ne bénéficient pas de l'article 13 attaqué, peuvent pratiquer à l'égard de leurs travailleurs … des distinctions sur la base de l'un des motifs mentionnés dans la loi pour autant que ces distinctions soient objectivement justifiées par un but légitime et que les moyens de réaliser ce but soient appropriés et nécessaires. En ce qui concerne les relations de travail, … ces organisations peuvent en principe justifier une distinction directe fondée sur l'âge, l'orientation sexuelle, la conviction religieuse ou philosophique ou un handicap par des exigences professionnelles essentielles et déterminantes (article 8)*" (Constitutional Court 2 April 2009, No. 64/2009, B.11.3).

76 L. Vickers, *Religious Freedom, Religious Discrimination and the Workplace* (Hart Publishing 2008), 215.

77 The reader should bear in mind that both political opinion and labor union membership (*opinion syndicale*) are a protected ground under the Belgian Anti-discrimination Act (see above).

78 Constitutional Court 11 March 2009, No. 39/2009.

79 Constitutional Court 2 April 2009, No. 64/2009.

80 Rapport fait au nom de la commission de la justice par M. Eric Libert, *Doc. Parl.* Chamber 2006–2007, No. 2720/009, 112.

81 Constitutional Court 11 March 2009, No. 39/2009, B.38.

employers.[82] The Constitutional Court indeed gives no weight to the lack of an explicit proportionality requirement in the religious-ethos exception, while under the genuine and determining occupational requirement test the proportionate character of the occupational requirement must be verified. Identical discrimination justification principles apply to all expressive employers, irrespective of the set of thoughts they maintain or seek to disperse.[83]

The judgments of the Belgian Constitutional Court, however, do not imply that expressive employers can no longer call for their employees' loyalty to the philosophy of life or view of society they seek to disperse as an organization. Both religious-ethos employers and non-religious expressive employers can still justify the refusal to hire a job candidate who holds conflicting religious or political viewpoints, if considered an occupational requirement in the case at hand. Indeed, the identity of the expressive employer will still come into play when balancing the clashing fundamental rights of the employee and the expressive employer via the proportionality test, either structured as the religious-ethos exception or the genuine and determining occupational requirement test (for non-religious expressive employers).[84] The Belgian labor courts have not yet, however, had the opportunity to adjudicate on the expressive employers' boundaries under the Belgian Anti-discrimination Act.

Up to now, we have focused on the consequences of the transposition of the first layer of the religious-ethos exception in Belgian employment relationships (the first section of Article 4.2 of the Employment Equality Directive).[85] The Belgian Constitutional court has, however, also assessed (rather indirectly) the impact of its second layer, i.e. the loyalty requirement (the second section of Article 4.2 of the Employment Equality Directive).[86] This provision underpinning the religious-ethos employer's right to require of its employees to act in good faith and with

82 "*En conséquence, la différence de traitement critiquée par les parties requérantes entre, d'une part, les organisations qui sont fondées sur une conviction religieuse ou philosophique et, d'autre part, les organisations dont le fondement est constitué par une autre conviction n'existe pas.*" Constitutional Court 2 April 2009, No. 64/2009, B.11.4; see also Constitutional Court 11 March 2009, No. 39/2009, B.38.

83 As discussed above, the initial proposal of the Belgian Anti-discrimination Act widened the application of Article 4.2 of the Employment Equality Directive to political-ethos employers.

84 See S. Sottiaux. "De rechtvaardigingsgronden in het federale discriminatierecht," in *De nieuwe federale antidiscriminatiewetten – Les nouvelles lois luttant contra la discrimination* (C. Bayart, S. Sottiaux and S. Van Drooghenbroeck, eds, die Keure 2008), 243–244; J. H. Gerards, "Proportionaliteit en gelijke behandeling," in *Het proportionaliteitsbeginsel in het publiekrecht* (A. Nieuwenhuis, B. Schueler and C. Zoethout, eds, Kluwer 2005), 105–106.

85 Transposed in Belgium by the first section of Article 13 of the Anti-discrimination Act.

86 Transposed in Belgium by the third section of Article 13 of the Anti-discrimination Act.

loyalty to its ethos, as interpreted by the Belgian Constitutional Court, *confirms* the general obligation for both employer and employee to execute the employment contract in good faith.[87]

The claim of two labor unions (arguing that they qualify as religious-ethos associations) that the Anti-discrimination Act installs an unconstitutional discrimination because the requirement to act in good faith and with loyalty cannot be invoked towards their members, but only vis-à-vis their employees, was not accepted by the Constitutional Court because the Anti-discrimination Act's general grounds of justification can be applied.[88] Since the impossibility of imposing a loyalty requirement on the associations' members can be absorbed by the general discrimination justification grounds, the Constitutional Court seems to consider the requirement "to act in good faith and with loyalty" as an element of the regular proportionality test (Article 7 of the Anti-discrimination Act) or the genuine and determining occupational requirement test (Article 8 of the Anti-discrimination Act), depending on the discrimination ground.[89]

Following the jurisprudence of the Belgian Constitutional Court, the religious-ethos exception of the Anti-discrimination Act of 2007 cannot be invoked to grant any more opportunities to religious-ethos employers then other expressive

87 For further reading on the execution of the employment contract in good faith under Belgian law, see W. van Eeckhoutte, "De goede trouw in het arbeidsovereenkomstenrecht: een aanzet tot herbronning en reïntegratie," 27 *Tijdschrift voor privaatrecht* 971 (1990), 971–1092.

88 "*En ce que les parties requérantes critiquent ensuite le fait que l'article 13 empêcherait les organisations visées d'exiger de la part de leurs membres et de leurs mandataires une attitude de bonne foi et de loyauté, il convient de constater que les organisations publiques ou privées dont le fondement est constitué par la conviction religieuse ou philosophique peuvent, sous le contrôle du juge, également invoquer les motifs généraux de justification contenus dans la loi attaquée*" (Constitutional Court 2 April 2009, No. 64/2009, B.11.5).

89 Y. Stox, *Discriminatie en identiteit – Identiteitsgebonden werkgevers in het Belgisch en Europees arbeidsrecht* (Larcier 2010), 90. Contrary to the Belgian Constitutional Court, the Supreme Court of the Netherlands (*Hoge Raad*)—which cannot exercise constitutional review—does not gloss over Article 4.2 of the Employment Equality Directive so easily. The Dutch Supreme Court, when evaluating the Equal Treatment Act in view of the Employment Equality Directive, focuses on the specific character of religious-ethos employers. It considers that the religious-ethos exception of Article 4.2 of the Employment Equality Directive enlarges the opportunities of religious-ethos employers in comparison with other expressive employers who can only invoke the occupational requirement test of Article 4.1 of the Employment Equality Directive. The entitlement of religious-ethos employers to require employees to act in good faith and with loyalty would mean that, taking into consideration all the facts and circumstances of every case (function, organization and context), the employer's requirements may concern the employee's private life and should not be restricted to behavior in the workplace (Evaluatie Algemene wet gelijke behandeling, Advies Raad van State en nader rapport, Tweede Kamer, Kamerstukken II 2009/2010, 28481, No. 7, 10.)

employers, who also seek to justify discrimination based on their organization's philosophy of life or view of society. Since a non-religious expressive employer can bring into play his identity and justify a differentiation by way of the genuine and determining occupational requirement exception in a similar way as a religious-ethos employer by way of the religious-ethos exception, the Anti-discrimination Act of 2007 seems not to provide more powerful discrimination justification tools to religious-ethos employers compared to the Anti-discrimination Act of 2003.[90] Thus, while a Roman Catholic hospital can dismiss a physician or nurse for publicly denouncing the Roman Catholic Church's teachings on, for instance, abortion or euthanasia—since such an act can be considered as a breach of the employment contract's execution in good faith[91]—a staff member's dismissal for being homosexual will fail to pass the determining occupational requirement test.[92] The same goes for an employee of a political party's think thank who is required to refrain from publicly denouncing the political views of his employer. Since Belgian labor courts have not yet adjudicated explicitly on the impact of the religious-ethos exception and the enclosed loyalty requirement, religious-ethos employers and their employees still face uncertainty on the outcome of more ambiguous facts and circumstances.

IV. Beyond the boundaries of the Employment Equality Directive: The European Court of Human Rights and religious-ethos employers

Recent case law of the ECtHR concerning expressive employers—the *Obst*[93] and *Schüth*[94] cases—offers some guidelines for balancing conflicting fundamental rights, which may also prove its usefulness if the balancing is shaped as a discrimination justification test. Furthermore, both cases help to determine the boundaries of the loyalty requirement which may be invoked if the employer's ethos opposes an element of the employee's private life. These two cases form a

---

90 Should the Constitutional Court have wished to open the religious-ethos exception to non-religious expressive employers, instead of downplaying it, the Court would have agreed with the plaintiffs, which it did not, and would have ruled this gap in the Anti-discrimination Act to be unconstitutional (similar to the Belgian Constitutional Court's judgment of 2 April 2009 adding labor union membership as a protected ground).

91 See the *Rommelfanger* case (EComHR 6 September 1989, *Rommelfanger* v. *Germany*, App. No. 12242/86).

92 See the *Painsecq* case of the French *Court de Cassation* (Cass. fr. (soc) 17 April 1991, *Painsecq c. Association Fraternité Saint Pie X*, *Droit Social* 6 (1991), 489).

93 ECtHR 23 September 2010, *Schüth* v. *Germany*, App. No. 1620/03.

94 ECtHR 23 September 2010, *Obst* v. *Germany*, App. No. 425/03. See also the chapters by Lucy Vickers and Saïla Ouald Chaib in this volume discussing these cases.

welcome update following the *Van der Heijden*[95] and *Rommelfanger*[96] cases of the European Commission of Human Rights, dating back to the 1980s.

1. The balancing of conflicting fundamental rights requires an in concreto *analysis*

The European Commission of Human Rights considered in the *Rommelfanger* case that the dismissal by a Roman Catholic hospital of a physician for having expressed a pro-abortion standpoint in the press was necessary in order for the religious-ethos employer to keep its credibility and did not infringe the employee's freedom of expression.[97] In the *Van der Heijden* case, the European Commission of Human Rights also reached a decision in favor of the dismissing expressive employer in the case of a foundation promoting the integration of immigrants. Because of the employee's combined status as regional director and board member of the foundation on the one hand and district chairman of a political party holding a hostile attitude to alien workers on the other hand, the European Commission of Human Rights indeed considered that the termination of the employment relationship was an authorized infringement of the employee's freedom of expression and his freedom of association and assembly.

The *Obst* and *Schüth* cases show a number of striking similarities: both judgments of 23 September 2010 concern Church employees who were dismissed (without notice period or indemnity in lieu of notice) after their extra-marital affairs came to their employer's attention. In both cases the ECtHR applies the reasoning developed by the European Commission of Human Rights in the *Rommelfanger* case. The Court stresses the collective dimension of the freedom of religion which safeguards the autonomy of the religious-ethos employers.[98] Thus, the Court underpins the duty of loyalty of the employee in order to maintain the religious-ethos employer's credibility,[99] which brings into play the conflict between the fundamental rights of the employee and his employer, i.e. the freedom of expression (in the *Rommelfanger* case) or the right to respect for privacy (in the *Obst* and *Schüth* cases) of the employee vs. the freedom of religion (in the light of the freedom of assembly) of the religious-ethos employer. Subsequently,

95 EComHR 8 March 1985, *Van der Heijden* v. *the Netherlands*, App. No. 11002/84.

96 EComHR 6 September 1989, *Rommelfanger* v. *Germany*, App. No. 12242/86.

97 Contrary to Mr Rommelfanger, neither Mr Obst nor Mr Schüth sought the attention of the media or tried to contest in public the opinions expressed by their religious-ethos employer (ECtHR 23 September 2010, *Schüth* v. *Germany*, App. No. 1620/03, par. 67; ECtHR 23 September 2010, *Obst* v. *Germany*, App. No. 425/03, par. 51).

98 EComHR, 6 September 1989, *Rommelfanger* v. *Germany*, App. No. 12242/86; ECtHR 23 September 2010, *Schüth* v. *Germany*, App. No. 1620/03, par. 58; ECtHR 23 September 2010, *Obst* v. *Germany*, App. No. 425/03, par. 44.

99 ECtHR 23 September 2010, *Schüth* v. *Germany*, App. No. 1620/03, par. 63; ECtHR 23 September 2010, *Obst* v. *Germany*, App. No. 425/03, par. 48.

the Court proceeds with a quality assessment of the balancing of these conflicting fundamental rights by the (German) labor courts,[100] while considering the margin of appreciation conferred to the State[101] and taking into consideration all facts and circumstances of the case at hand.[102] Whereas the Court decided on a violation of the right to respect for privacy in the *Schüth* case, it concluded that there had been no violation of the employee's right to respect for privacy in the *Obst* case.[103] Despite the striking similarities of the facts (at least at first sight), by using identical reasoning the Court came to the opposite conclusion.

The key differentiator between the cases is the function of the employees, which explains the different outcomes: Mr Obst was engaged as director of public relations for Europe by the Mormon Church, while Mr Schüth had been the organist and choirmaster of a Roman Catholic parish. The Court examined the nature of the particular *function* exercised by Mr Obst and Mr Schüth in the *context* of the religious-ethos employer concerned.[104]

In the *Obst* case, the Court accepted the dismissal taking into consideration the *important position*[105] of Mr Obst as director of public relations for Europe, and found an increased duty of loyalty as stipulated by his employment contract

---

100 G. de Beco, "Le droit au respect de la vie privée dans les relations de travail au sein de sociétés religieuses – L'approche procédurale de la Cour européenne de droits de l'homme," 86 *Revue trimestrielle des droits de l'homme* 375 (2011), 386–387.

101 ECtHR 23 September 2010, *Schüth* v. *Germany*, App. No. 1620/03, par. 55–56; ECtHR 23 September 2010, *Obst* v. *Germany*, App. No. 425/03, par. 41–42.

102 G. de Beco, "Le droit au respect de la vie privée dans les relations de travail au sein de sociétés religieuses – L'approche procédurale de la Cour européenne de droits de l'homme," *Revue trimestrielle des droits de l'homme* 86 (2011), 389.

103 In the *Obst* and *Schüth* cases, the German labor courts reached their verdicts in favor of the religious-ethos employers based on the case law of the German Federal Constitutional Court of 4 June 1985 (BVerfG 4 June 1985, *Loyalitätspflicht*, *BVerfGE* 70, 138), which was confirmed by the European Commission of Human Rights in the *Rommelfanger* case.

104 "Une *décision de licenciement fondée sur un manquement à une* [*obligation de loyauté*] *ne peut pas* être *soumise, au nom du droit d'autonomie de l'employeur, uniquement à un contrôle judiciaire restreinte, effectué par le juge de travail* étatique *compétent, sans que soit prise en compte* la nature du poste *de l'intéressé et sans qu'il soit procédé à une mise en balance effective des intérêts en jeu à l'aune du principe de proportionnalité*" [author's emphasis] (ECtHR 23 September 2010, *Schüth* v. *Germany*, App. No. 1620/03, par. 63). G. de Beco seems to focus less on the difference between the functions exercised by Mr Obst and Mr Schüth. He highlights that the different outcome of the *Obst* and *Schüth* cases is mainly, or even solely, caused by the succinct reasoning of the German Federal Constitutional Court in the case *Schüth* (G. de Beco, "Le droit au respect de la vie privée dans les relations de travail au sein de sociétés religieuses – L'approche procédurale de la Cour européenne de droits de l'homme," 86 *Revue trimestrielle des droits de l'homme* 375 (2011), 389).

105 ECtHR 23 September 2010, *Obst* v. *Germany*, App. No. 425/03, par. 51.

justified.[106] Self-evidently, the leading function of a public relations manager responsible for the whole of Europe involves an important element of external visibility. In the *Schüth* case however, the balancing exercise by the Court resulted in the exact opposite outcome. The Court observed that the German labor court of appeal had confined itself to stating that although Mr Schüth did not exercise a function in counseling, catechesis or management, his function as organist and choirmaster was so closely linked to the Church's preaching mission that he could no longer be employed without taking away the parish's credibility.[107] The Court underlines that the labor court should, however, have taken the nature of the employee's function into consideration.[108] Although Mr Schüth also consented to an explicit duty of loyalty, this obligation did not attain the same degree as in the case of Mr Obst.[109] Thus, Mr Schüth's right to respect for privacy was held to be violated.

Furthermore, the fact that Mr Schüth had only limited opportunities for finding another full-time job as organist and choirmaster was also of particular importance.[110] It seems that in the *Obst* case, however, the Court did not question the future job opportunities for a public relations manager. Finding a job may indeed be less easy for an organist and choirmaster.

Bringing the employee's job opportunities into the proportionality check may seem to cause a disparity between the Court's findings with respect to the right to respect for privacy on the one hand and the freedom of religion on the other hand. The freedom of religion of the individual seeking to challenge the working schedule in place with his employer because of his religious obligations is guaranteed by his freedom to resign. By entering into an employment relationship, the individual has freely consented to an interference with his freedom of religion, an interference which can be brought to an end by the resignation of the employee.[111] This "freedom to resign" doctrine is applied in order to put aside employees' claims for religious accommodation which do not seem reasonable.[112]

The "freedom to resign" doctrine can be used in order to support the *in concreto* analysis. Because of their essential position, an increased loyalty requirement can be imposed on clergymen. Thus, in case a conflict emerges

106 ECtHR 23 September 2010, *Obst* v. *Germany*, App. No. 425/03, par. 50.

107 ECtHR 23 September 2010, *Schüth* v. *Germany*, App. No. 1620/03, par. 66. For an overview of earlier national case law, see L.-L. Christians, "Le principe de non-discrimination religieuse en droit belge et comparé: entre obligation du législateur et obligation des contractants," in *Antidiscriminatiewet en contracten – La Loi Anti-discrimination et les contrats* (S. Stijns and P. Wéry, eds, die Keure 2006), 175, fn. 74.

108 ECtHR 23 September 2010, *Schüth* v. *Germany*, App. No. 1620/03, par. 69.

109 ECtHR 23 September 2010, *Schüth* v. *Germany*, App. No. 1620/03, par. 71.

110 ECtHR 23 September 2010, *Schüth* v. *Germany*, App. No. 1620/03, par. 73.

111 See the chapter by Saïla Ouald Chaib in this volume.

112 See, for instance, EComHR 12 March 1981, *X* v. *UK*, App. No. 8160/78; EComHR 3 December 1996, *Konttinen* v. *Finland*, App. No. 24949/94; EComHR 9 April 1997, *Stedman* v. *UK*, App. No. 29107/95.

between the ecclesiastical hierarchy and a clergyman who no longer agrees with the hierarchy, the individual has to choose between submitting to ecclesiastical discipline or giving up his office.[113] This case law should not be applied in the case of lay individuals entering into a "regular" employment relationship with a religious-ethos employer since the Court in the *Rommelfanger*, *Obst* and *Schüth* cases imposes a positive obligation to weigh the employee's interests against those of his employer, despite an explicit loyalty requirement being stipulated in the employment contract.

2. Returning to the Employment Equality Directive

The *Obst* and *Schüth* cases, together with the *Rommelfanger* and *Van der Heijden* cases, substantiate that national labor courts, in order to honor the State's positive obligation under the European Convention on Human Rights,[114] should always take into account the nature or the context of the particular professional activities of the employee concerned when applying the religious-ethos exception or the genuine and determining occupational requirement exception. The particular character of the function, as exercised by the employee concerned, should indeed be the main point of attention in the judge's decision-making process. Thus, not only professions directly or essentially linked to the employer's ethos[115] (which are, for instance, engaged in the religious-ethos employer's core activities such as counseling or catechesis), but also functions implying a management position (such as, for instance, in the *Van der Heijden* case) or an increased external visibility (such as, for instance, in the *Obst* case) imply an increased duty of loyalty of the employee pursuing such a representative function with respect to the employer's identity or ethos. This can be approved since such employees have a more significant effect on an employer's credibility, thus jeopardizing the latter's goal to maintain and disperse his ethos.

The assessment should be based on the actual facts and circumstances, which obliges courts to actually examine the arguments of the employer.[116] This

113 EComHR 8 March 1976, *X* v. *Denmark*, App. No. 7374/76; EComHR 8 March 1985, *Knudsen* v. *Norway* E.C.R.M., App. No. 11045/84; EComHR 8 September 1988, *Karlsson* v. *Sweden*, App. No. 12356/86.

114 ECtHR 23 September 2010, *Schüth* v. *Germany*, App. No. 1620/03, par. 55; ECtHR 23 September 2010, *Obst* v. *Germany*, App. No. 425/03, par. 41. See also G. de Beco, "Le droit au respect de la vie privée dans les relations de travail au sein de sociétés religieuses – L'approche procédurale de la Cour européenne de droits de l'homme," 86 *Revue trimestrielle des droits de l'homme* 375 (2011), 382–384.

115 See above concerning the initial proposition of the Commission for the religious-ethos exception.

116 A delicate balancing act is needed in order to satisfy the Court's case law requiring States to restrain from appreciating the legitimacy of the concerned religious beliefs (constant case law since ECtHR 26 September 1996, *Manoussakis and Others* v. *Greece*, App. No. 18748/91, par. 47).

in concreto analysis remains a difficult exercise, which is inevitably subject to changing public opinions and can differ from country to country (hence the margin of appreciation). Transposing without hesitation the outcome of the *Rommelfanger* case (dating from the 1980s) may therefore not be correct. Nevertheless, even if the loyalty obligation of a physician with a Roman Catholic hospital may have been trimmed down meanwhile, contesting the employer's ethos in public would still be reprimanded.

Furthermore, the *Obst* and *Schüth* cases require, as is also shown by the *Rommelfanger* case, that it should be examined on a case-by-case basis whether the loyalty requirement can be imposed in line with the Employment Equality Directive. Solely claiming a loyalty requirement, even if such a requirement is stipulated explicitly by the employment contract, is indeed not sufficient. The expressive employer's loyalty claim should be justified in view of the particular function of the employee concerned.

Concluding remarks

The conflicting fundamental rights of the employee and the expressive employer can be balanced either via the justifications and exceptions provided for by the Employment Equality Directive, or via the techniques of "traditional" Belgian employment law (in particular, unfair dismissal and abuse of law). In the absence of case law of the European Court of Justice, the preparatory works of the Employment Equality Directive are the principle source for grasping the meaning of the specific exception for religious-ethos employers.

The assessment of the legislative drafting process demonstrates that several interpretations of the religious-ethos exception are possible, leaving open whether religious-ethos employers have gained a benefit over other expressive employers. The 2009 case law of the Belgian Constitutional Court downplays the significance of the specific religious-ethos exception, thus leveling out the privileges of religious-ethos employers. Nevertheless, both religious-ethos employers and non-religious expressive employers can still develop a human resources policy supporting the organization's philosophy of life or view of society.

The case law of the ECtHR underscores that the particular nature of each function, as exercised by the employee concerned, should be the central element of the judge's decision-making process. This *in concreto* analysis supports an individual approach which focuses on the nature of the *particular* function and the context in which that function is exercised. Pursuing a function which implies a leading position or an increased external visibility results in an increased duty of loyalty of the employee concerned to his employer's identity or ethos. This means that the enforceability of contractual stipulations seeking to impose an increased loyalty should be examined on a case-by-case basis.

PART II
Identity, Neutrality, Secularism: Case Studies and Comparative Perspectives

Section I
Country Studies: Turkey, France and Belgium

Chapter 8

Religion in the Public and Private Turkish Workplace: The Approach of the Turkish Judiciary

Mine Yıldırım

Introduction

Throughout the last three decades in Turkey, the headscarf has become the icon of a conflict between various groups in society. On the one hand, there are the strict secularists who perceive the headscarf and all that it symbolizes as a threat to the secular republican principles and, on the other hand, there are those who advocate more relaxed rules for Muslim manifestations in the public sphere. In this highly polarized context the Turkish judiciary has played a paramount role in defining the scope of the prohibition on certain dress for public servants and the extent of sanctions imposed.

This chapter focuses on the approach taken by the Turkish judiciary to religious symbols in the public and private workplace, with a particular emphasis on the Muslim headscarf. The chapter begins with a brief overview of the meanings and significance attached to religious dress and symbols, specifically the Islamic headscarf. Turkish secularism, which is the overarching principle that forms the basis of the prohibition of religious symbols in public workplaces, is outlined in section two with reference to the jurisprudence of the Turkish Constitutional Court (TCC). Then, rules concerning the appearance of public servants in Turkey are briefly reviewed. I will examine the approach of the Turkish judiciary in the application of these rules with a view to understanding which interests are and are not taken into account in the reasoning of Administrative Courts,[1] by looking into certain key cases. Section three turns to the private sector. Due to the lack of case law related to religious symbols in the private sector, this part will touch upon the possible reasons and suggests how the prohibition in the public sector is de facto affecting the private sector.

---

1 Administrative courts deal with cases which are brought against administrative organs because of the implementation of administrative legislation. The administrative decisions and judgments of courts can be appealed to the Turkish Council of State, which is the last instance for reviewing decisions and judgments given by administrative courts.

It is argued that the approach of the Turkish judiciary has been overly restrictive and is, to a great extent, based on a perceived threat against Turkish secularism. Thus, in section four I propose some elements for an alternative approach by the Turkish judiciary. This includes the search for a harmonized interpretation of the principle of secularism and freedom of religion or belief, the problematization of the understanding of religious symbols used by public servants,[2] the headscarf in particular, and the rethinking of the principles of neutrality and secularism.

1. Religious symbols as manifestations of religion

Religious symbols[3] in the Turkish workplace can vary from small posters of Quranic verses in Arabic, to prayer beads, Islamic headscarves, crosses or the holy books of particular religions. The use and social and legal significance of these symbols vary greatly. Prayer beads are carried freely by many male public servants, and these objects do not appear to have been the subject of any legal disputes. Similarly, the cross has apparently not been subject of legal proceeding. This is not because it is considered insignificant, but rather because the few Christian public servants generally refrain from wearing the cross at their workplace, thus demonstrating a form of self-censorship.[4]

The Islamic headscarf, in contrast, has been the subject of numerous regulations as well as legal disputes because of a certain meaning attributed to it, namely that of a political symbol. Yet the headscarf does not have one particular meaning, and its significance is highly personal and contextual. It may be just a cultural way of

---

2 The term "problematization," though not a legal term, is used in order to emphasize the need to take a step that goes deeper than taking a critical approach or re-evaluating. "Problematization" requires "the development of a given into a question" and the need to "step back from a way of acting or reacting, to present it to oneself as an object of thought or question it as to its meaning, its conditions, and its goals." Thus, a problematizing mode of critique may have a transformative aim and outcome; see M. Foucault, "Polemics, Politics, and Problematization," in *The Foucault Reader* (P. Rabinow, ed., Pantheon 1984), 388–389.

3 Human rights law refers to both religious symbols and practices as manifestations of religion or belief. It does not seem possible to differentiate the two in a clear-cut manner since a religious symbol may also be considered a practice, or vice versa. The Human Rights Committee in its General Comment No. 22 on Article 18 of the ICCPR refers to observance and practice, and lists, among others, ceremonial acts, the wearing of distinctive clothing or head coverings. Therefore it may be assumed that practices would include wearing religious symbols. U.N. Doc. HRI/GEN/1/Rev.1 at 35 (1994), General Comment No.22 of the Human Rights Committee on Article 18, para. 4. Here, by referring to the Islamic headscarf as a religious symbol I follow the common usage of the term in Turkey.

4 This observation is based on interviews conducted by the author for a report on the Protestant community in Turkey. The Association of Protestant Churches (Turkey), *"A Threat" or Under Threat – Legal and Social Problems of Protestants in Turkey*, Report (Anadolu Ofset 2010), available at www.protestankiliseler.org.

dressing up, a religious symbol that has or does not have a strong proselytizing effect, a political symbol or—in the eyes of some—even a symbol of dominion of men over women. In the Turkish context, Cindoğlu observes two basic approaches in this respect.[5] First, covering, per se, indicates an objection to the secular modernization and Westernization project of the modern Turkish Republic, where veiling is seen as an obstacle to women's liberation and is viewed as a symbol of women's oppression on the basis of religion.[6] The second view points to the possibilities of constructing *modernity* differently from, and alternatively to, the Western understanding.[7] The latter view challenges the dominion of Western modernism and the idea of progress based on the contrast between religion and secularism, private and public, particularism and universalism.[8] In this last view, first, by maintaining their *mahrem*—meaning privacy, including secrecy: a woman's sphere from which strangers are banned—in the public sphere, the presence of women is facilitated.[9] Thus they can be part of public life without compromising their beliefs. Second, the headscarf may be an indicator of objection to the image of compliant and oppressed Muslim woman.[10]

2. The domestic legal framework applicable to the public sector

2.1. Turkish secularism as a constitutional principle

Since the understanding and function of the principle of secularism plays an important role in informing and determining the assessment of cases that will be considered in this chapter, a brief overview of the position of Turkish secularism in the Turkish Constitution as well as the corresponding jurisprudence developed by the TCC seems appropriate.[11]

In the 1982 Turkish Constitution,[12] secularism (*laiklik*) is deemed one of the attributes of the Republic (Article 2). The secular feature of the Republic is

---

5 D. Cindoğlu, *Başörtüsü Yasağı ve Ayrımcılık: Uzman Meslek Sahibi Başörtülü Kadınlar* [The Headscarf Ban and Discrimination: Specialized Professional Women Who Wear the Headscarf], (TESEV Publications 2010), 31–32.

6 *Id.*

7 *Id.*

8 N. Göle, *Modern Mahrem* [The Forbidden Modern], (Metis Publications 1991), 15.

9 *Id.*

10 *Id.*

11 According to Article 148 of the Turkish Constitution, the Constitutional Court examines the constitutionality, in respect of both form and substance, of laws, decrees having the force of law, and the Rules of Procedure of the Turkish Grand National Assembly. Constitutional amendments are examined and verified only with regard to their form. The judgments of the Constitutional Court are final.

12 1982 Turkish Constitution, available at www.anayasa.gen.tr/1982constitution.htm. I use the term Turkish secularism to emphasize its autonomous meaning and application.

unchangeable and no proposal may be made to change it (Article 4). One of the State's fundamental responsibilities is to protect the Republic that is virtually identified by secularism (Article 5). The Preamble of the Constitution clearly stipulates that no activity that is contrary to Atatürk's nationalism, principles, reforms and civilization that are based on secularism can find protection (Preamble para. 5). Sovereignty rests in the people, and the Constitution thus excludes any divine source of authority (Article 6). An explicit provision rejecting a religious foundation for the state is found in Article 24/5, which provides that the state's fundamental social, economic, political and legal order cannot be based on religious tenets. Reform laws,[13] most of which are directly or indirectly linked to secularism, are under constitutional protection and cannot be understood as contradictory to the Constitution (Article 174). Political parties also have to abide by the principle of secularism or risk closure (Article 68). Secularism also finds its reflection in the restriction of fundamental rights. These cannot be used in order to establish a state order, or any part of this order, based on religion (Article 14/1).

In contrast—but arguably because of the strong protection of Turkish secularism—when it comes to state–religion relations, a reciprocal non-interference principle or a strict separation of state and religion affairs is not envisioned in Turkey.[14] This is particularly evident in the substantial restriction on the autonomy of religious communities as well as the state monopoly on certain religious services, such as those provided by the Presidency of Religious Affairs (*Diyanet*) and religious education provided by the Ministry of Education and the universities. According to the 1982 Constitution, religious education is placed under the supervision and control of the State. Article 24 (3), introducing compulsory Religious Culture and Ethics Knowledge lessons in primary and middle education, is the most significant change that the said Constitution brings in terms of regulating

13 Reform Laws include revolutionary laws adopted in the early years of the Turkish Republic. These are: Tevhid-i Tedrisat Kanunu [Law on the Unification of the Educational System] Act No. 430 of 3 March 1340 (1924); Şapka Kanunu [Law on Wearing Hats] Act No. 671 of 25 November 1341 (1925); Tekke ve Zaviyelerin Kapatılmasına İlişkin Kanun [Closure of Dervish Monasteries and Tombs, the Abolition of the Office of Keeper of Tombs and the Abolition and Prohibition of Certain Titles] Act No. 677 of 30 November 1341 (1925); Article 110 of Medeni Kanun [Civil Code] No. 743 of 17 February 1926; Yeni Türk Harflerinin Kabulü ve Tatbiki Hakkında Kanun [Law on the Adoption and Application of the Turkish Alphabet] Act No. 1353 of 1 November 1928; Efendi, Bey, Paşa gibi Lakap ve Ünvanların Kaldırılmasına Dair Kanun, [Law on the Abolition of Titles and Appellations such as Efendi, Bey or Pasa] Act No 2590 of 26 November 1934; Bazı Kisvelerin Giyilemeyeceğine Dair Kanun Act [Law on the Prohibition of the Wearing of Certain Garments] No. 2596 of 3 December 1934.

14 B. Tanör and N. Yüzbaşıoğlu, *1982 Anayasasına Göre Türk Anayasa Hukuku* [Turkish Constitutional Law According to the 1982 Constitution], (YKY Publications 2005), 89.

religion. The National Security Council (NSC),[15] acknowledging that religion is a unifying factor in society, advised the drafters of the Constitution that compulsory religious education under state control was appropriate, but it needed to be in the form of religious culture.[16] Unsurprisingly, the compulsory nature of this education is viewed by many as a feature irreconcilable with the secular nature of the state.[17]

The TCC has expressed the view that the principle of secularism has a privileged position in the Constitution in relation to other constitutional rules and principles.[18] It is the essence of the establishment and philosophy of the Republic, as well as the paramount consideration.[19] The TCC mandates itself with what Dinçkol refers to as an "active" approach toward the protection of the principle of secularism and views it as the "heart" of the system.[20]

Turkish secularism is generally criticized for not reflecting a complete separation of state and religion in contrast to the way secularism is generally conceptualized in Europe.[21] Indeed, the TCC recognizes this difference and explains the Turkish position by pointing out that the circumstances and the conditions of each religious constellation necessitate a difference in the overall understanding of secularism in different countries.[22] It is explained that the difference lies in the conditions of Christianity and Islam and in particular the respective existence and lack of a hierarchical clergy structure. This particular situation in Islam makes it impossible to grant independence in internal affairs for those involved in places of worship and religious affairs.[23] In the light of another feature of Islam, i.e. that it

15 According to Article 187 of the Constitution, the NSC comprises the Chief of Staff, select members of the Council of Ministers and the President of the Republic (who is also the Commander-in-chief). The NSC develops the national security policy.

16 *Cumhuriyet* newspaper, 27 June 1987.

17 B. Dinçkol, *1982 Anayasası* Çerçevesinde *ve Anayasa Mahkemesi Kararlarında Laiklik* [Secularism Within the Framework of the 1982 Constitution and the Judgments of the Constitutional Court], (Kazancı Kitap 1992), 64. See the case of *Hasan and Eylem Zengin* v. *Turkey* on the compulsory nature and content of the Religious Culture and Ethics classes and the inadequate exemption possibilities in Turkey. ECtHR 9 January 2008, *Hasan and Eylem Zengin* v. *Turkey* ECHR 1448/04, par. 58–76.

18 Turkish Constitutional Court, 7 March 1989, E/1989/1 and K/1989/12, Anayasa Mahkemesi Kararları Dergisi [Journal of Judgments of the Constitutional Court] (AMKD) No. 12 (1991), 133–165.

19 B. Tanör and N. Yüzbaşıoğlu, *supra* note 14, 92.

20 B. Dinçkol, *supra* note 17, 178 and 212.

21 I. Gözaydın, *Diyanet, Türkiye Cumhuriyeti'nda Dinin Tanzimi* [The Presidency of Religious Affairs: The Regulation of Religion in the Republic of Turkey], (Iletişim 2009), 246–272. This line of criticism overlooks the many variations of state–religion relations found in European countries. The main point, however, is to emphasize the inadequacy of the protection of the collective dimension of the right to freedom of religion or belief in Turkey.

22 Turkish Constitutional Court 21 October 1971, E/1970/53 and K/1971/76, AMKD No. 10, 52–79.

23 *Id.*, at 61–62.

regulates not only religious belief in the conscience of individuals but also social relations, state affairs and law, it is argued that an unlimited freedom of religion and independent religious associative freedom is dangerous for Turkey.[24] Dinçkol rightly notes that the TCC understands the principle of secularism to mean first, that religion cannot in any way interfere in state affairs, and secondly, taking into account historical realities, that the state will reflect an interventionist, restrictive, supervisory and even controlling approach toward religious manifestation.[25]

It is important to note that secularism is not understood as an abstract concept but as a notion that is embodied in the systems of state, law and education.[26] This implies that religion cannot be involved in these key areas that are envisioned as strictly secular, and that there is a particular effort to protect secularism within and through these systems. The importance of these key spheres also explains the sweeping measures that were put in place in order to exclude or drive out religious influences from what was viewed as the sphere of the state.[27] It may also explain the rules concerning dress codes for public servants and the strict application of these rules and key constitutional principles in related cases by the Turkish judiciary.

2. 2. Civil servants and dress code

As a constitutional rule, all Turkish citizens have the right to enter the public service. No criteria other than the qualifications for the office concerned may be taken into consideration for recruitment into public service.[28] Public servants sign a "certificate of oath" when they start their office whereby they express

---

24 *Id.*, at 66.

25 B. Dinçkol, *supra* note 17, 182.

26 Turkish Constitutional Court 25 October 1983, E2/1983 and K2/1983, AMKD, No. 20, 364.

27 Some key structural changes include: the abolishment of the monarchy by TBMM'nin Hukuku Hakimiyet ve Hükümraninin Mümessili Hakikisi Olduğuna Dair Heyeti Umumiye Kararı [Decision on the Turkish Grand National Assembly being the Real Representative of Legal Sovereignty and Rule] No. 308, (1929), and the abolishment of the *khalifat,* Hilafetin İlgasına Dair Kanun [Law on the Abolishment of the Khalifat] by the Act No. 431 of 3 March 1924, Tevhid-i Tedrisat Kanunu [Law on the Unification of the Educational System] Act No. 430 of 3 March 1340 (1924); imposed changes on the manner in which people were to dress through Şapka Kanunu [Law on Wearing Hats] Act No. 671 of 25 November 1341 (1925) and Bazı Kisvelerin Giyilemeyeceğine Dair Kanun Act [Law on the Prohibition of the Wearing of Certain Garments] No. 2596 of 3 December 1934; significant restrictions on manifestations of religion through Tekke ve Zaviyelerin Kapatılmasına İlişkin Kanun [Closure of Dervish Monasteries and Tombs, the Abolition of the Office of Keeper of Tombs and the Abolition and Prohibition of Certain Titles] Act No. 677 of 30 November 1341 (1925); exclusion of application of personal law based on religious affiliation through Article 110 of Medeni Kanun [Civil Code] No. 743 of 17 February 1926.

28 Article 70 of the Turkish Constitution.

their allegiance to, among others, the Turkish Constitution, Atatürk's Reforms and Principles and the national, democratic, secular state of law.[29] The general provisions of the Law on Public Servants naturally have implications for religious practice, and there could be situations where manifestations of religion or belief may interfere with work requirements.[30] Public servants working in the schools connected to the Ministry of Education are subject to a regulation requiring one's head to be uncovered.[31]

There was little regulation of clothing of public servants until the 1980 military intervention.[32] The Framework Regulation of October 1982 (the Regulation of October 1982) was based on a law and decrees from 1925 and 1934.[33] It has been suggested that the military regime "remembered" the 1925 Decree that was almost completely forgotten and used it as a legal basis for the new regulation.[34] The Decree in question did not regulate the details of the clothing of public servants, but only made references to "contemporary clothing," that "the head would be uncovered" and the "hat" would be used as headgear. Given that these rules were not in any way connected with disciplinary sanctions, the legality of the relevant regulations restricting fundamental rights has been questioned on the basis that they were actually not based on a related law.[35]

---

29 Devlet Memurları Kanunu [Law on Public Servants] No. 657, 14 July 1965; Resmi Gazete [Official Gazette] (R.G.), 23 July 1965, No. 12056, Article 6.

30 *Id.,* Article 6.

31 Milli Eğitim Bakanlığına ve Diğer Bakanlıklara Bağlı Okullardaki Memurların ve Öğrencilerin Kılık Kıyafetine İlişkin Yönetmelik [Regulation on Attire and Clothing for Officials and Students in Schools Under the Ministry of Education and Other Ministries], No. 8/3349, December 1981, R.G. No. 17537, 7 December 1981.

32 On the other hand, state interest in how public servants dress is not a completely new affair. Until 1951, in the secret efficiency reports on public servants, follow-up and evaluation on clothing remained a common practice. Gemalmaz notes that the Regulation on Public Servants Efficiency Reports, urging the supervisor to inspect employees under his/her supervision, gave supervisors the opportunity to consider any piece of clothing as a "political symbol" and thus to act according to the wishes of those in political power. S. Gemalmaz, *Türk Kıyafet Hukuku ve Türban* [The Turkish Law on Dree and the Turban] (Legal Publications 2005), 141–144. This practice was reinstated in 1986 with the Regulation on Public Servants Efficiency Reports. See Regulation on Public Servants Efficiency Reports No. 86/1985, 08.09.1986, R.G. No. 19255, 18.10.1986.

33 Kamu Kurum ve Kuruluşlarında Çalışan Personelin Kılık ve Kıyafetine Dair Yönetmelik [Regulation Pertaining to the Attire of Personnel Employed at Public Institutions] (October 1982 Regulation), R.G. 25.10.1982, 17849. The October 1982 Regulation is based on a Ministerial Decree, Bilimum Devlet Memurlarının Kıyafetleri ile İlgili Kararname [Decree on the Clothing of Various Public Servants] 25/01/1925, No. 2431, and Bazı Kisvelerin Giyilemeyeceğine Dair Kanunun Tatbik Suretini Gösterir Nizamname [the Regulation on the Implementation of the Law on the Impermissibility to Wear Certain Garments], R.G. 06/02/1935 No. 2/1958.

34 S. Gemalmaz, *supra* note 32 at 128.

35 *Id.*, 128.

The purpose of the Regulation of October 1982 is to ensure that public servants have uniformity in terms of clothing and wear modest and contemporary clothes that are in line with the reforms and principles of Atatürk.[36] The Regulation of October 1982 regulates many aspects of appearance, inter alia the length and form of hair, moustache, beard, shirts, ties, how much a shirt or blouse can reveal, how loose or tight trousers can be, heels of shoes, nails, make-up, etc.[37] Both male and female personnel have to work bare-headed.[38] The Regulation of October 1982 is applicable to public servants of all categories and levels as well as contract and temporary workers, excluding personnel that have their own clothing regulations such as the military and police forces.[39] Contract workers include personnel such as cleaning, catering and delivery workers. As expressly stated in Article 1 of the Regulation, the purpose is to create unity in the way public servants dress. According to Gemalmaz, the Regulation of October 1982 strives to create a "civil uniform" for public servants and was motivated by a desire to prohibit any piece of clothing to which those in political power could attribute a political meaning.[40] In addition, it is explicitly stated that clothing must be contemporary and in line with the reforms and principles of Atatürk.[41] It is not possible to find a definition in any positive law document of what these terms mean or imply for clothing. This was later determined by jurisprudence.

As far as sanctions are concerned, according to the Regulation of October 1982, those who act contrary to it are subject to the Law on Public Servants No. 657.[42] Thus, the first-degree supervisor of a person who acts contrary to this Regulation may give a warning and, in the case of repetition of the same action, various degrees of sanctions, such as reprobation, short-term suspension, long-term suspension, temporarily laying off and other penalties, may be imposed.[43] It is important to note that Law No. 657 did not originally contain any disciplinary measures connected to clothing. Through an amendment that was changed in 1982, actions contrary to the "determined provisions" related to clothing became subject to disciplinary measures.[44]

---

36 Article 16 of the October 1982 Regulation.

37 Article 5 of the October 1982 Regulation.

38 Article 5 of the October 1982 Regulation.

39 Article 2 of the October 1982 Regulation.

40 S. Gemalmaz, *supra* note 32 at 129.

41 Article 1 of the October 1982 Regulation.

42 Devlet Memurları Kanunu [Law on Public Servants] No. 657, 14.07.1965, R.G., 23.07.1965, No. 12056.

43 Article 125 of the Law on Public Servants.

44 657 Sayılı Kanun'da Değişiklik Yapan 2670 Sayılı Kanun [Law No. 2670 Amending Law No. 657] (Article 125/A), 12/05/1982, R.G. No. 17696, 16/05/1982. Additional Article 19 to Law No. 657 explicitly states that public servants have to abide by the legal, regulatory and statutory rules concerning clothing.

2.3. The approach of the administrative courts

The Turkish judiciary has a strong tendency to protect the state and sanction severely what it perceives as a threat to the state.[45] In accordance with its self-assumed role to protect the regime, the Turkish judiciary has interpreted secularism functionally so as to exclude not only the headscarf, but also in general "persons with certain religious affiliations" (*dinci*)[46] from the public workplace. This was done by attributing manifestations of religion, in particular the headscarf, a meaning or significance which is ideologically incompatible with secularism, and also by the imposition of heavy sanctions upon persons who use these symbols. The timing of the cases examined below coincides with the period generally referred to as the post-28 February period, following the 1997 National Security Council Memorandum calling for the strict implementation of codes on clothing and the prevention of infiltration of reactionary groups into the educational system and bureaucracy.[47] The perception of threat embodied in the Memorandum and the subsequent process form the immediate context of the bans and judicial practice of concern in this chapter.[48]

---

45 M. Sancar and E. Ü. Atılgan, *Adalet Biraz Es Geçiliyor* [Justice is Somewhat Overlooked], (TESEV Publications 2009), 124–150.

46 An exact English translation for the word *dinci* is hard to find. More than the literal meaning, which could be read as 'religious', it refers to a practicing Muslim who is considered backward, anti-modern and a supporter of an Islamic order.

47 National Security Memorandum on the Measures that Need to be Taken Against Actions Contrary to the Regime and Reactionary Movements. Articles 13 and 9 of the National Security Council Decision No. 406, 28 February 1997. The role played by the military in the making of this memorandum is considered a soft intervention or, as popularly named, a "postmodern coup" by the military into the political system. Through this intervention, the Prime Minister Necmettin Erbakan was removed from his position, without dissolving the parliament. The memorandum started a process called the 28 February Process where measures were taken to protect secularism. Other measures included eight years' compulsory primary education, closure of Islamic sects and closure of illegal Quran courses. Generally on this period see Ali Bayramoğlu, *28 Şubat: Bir Müdahalenin Güncesi* [February 28: The Diary of an Intervention], (İletişim Publications 2007), and for the text of the Memorandum and its implications see N. Günay, "Implementing the 'February 28' Recommendations: A Scorecard," Research Notes No. 10, Washington Institute for Near East Policy, May 2001, 14. For an overview of the February 28 period and the absence of a space for negotiation and mediation between society and state on unavoidable disagreements related to such public policies see A. A. An-Naim, *Islam and the Secular State: Negotiating the Future of Shari'a*, (Harvard University Press 2008), 206–215.

48 A report by AK-DER claims that during 1998–2002 approximately 5,000 public servants were dismissed and another 10,000 were forced to resign. A Report by AK-DER, İstatistiki *Verilere Göre Türkiye'de Kadınların Genel Konumu ve Başörtüsü Yasağının Cinsiyet Endekslerine Etkileri* [A Statistical Analysis of the Situation of Women in Turkey and the Effect of the Headscarf Ban on Gender Index] (AK-DER 2008), 7.

The Turkish judiciary's perspective is illustrated in the case of *Züheyla Zeybel* which led to the judgment setting the precedent for deeming the wearing of a headscarf in a public workplace as disruptive towards the order of an institution for ideological or political purposes and as warranting dismissal from work.[49] Actions contrary to the provisions in the Regulation of October 1982 are subject to certain disciplinary measures, but dismissal from a job is not a prescribed measure for such dress code breaches. On the other hand, according to Article 125 E/a of the Law on Public Servants, a person who disrupts the peaceful order of an institution for ideological or political reasons can be dismissed from his/her job.[50] Ms Zeybel worked as a telephone operator at Istanbul University with the status of supporting services employee, and was thus subject to the October 1982 Regulation. The fact that she insisted on wearing the headscarf and thereby acted contrary to clothing rules and disrupted the order of the institution with ideological or political purposes constituted the basis for her dismissal.[51] By equating the wearing of the headscarf with an ideological act requiring dismissal from work, the judiciary transformed the action of wearing the headscarf to a different category. Thus, the effect and strength of the prohibition and its sanction was aggravated.

The Council of State, General Council of Chambers of Administrative Cases, decided that Ms Zeybel's dismissal was legitimate. Thus, it became lawful to regard the wearing of a headscarf as an *action* that would disrupt the order of a workplace with an ideological or political purpose and dismiss the person from their job. The reasoning of the Council of State does not provide any details as to how the connection is established between wearing the headscarf and that of ideological or political actions disrupting the order in a workplace. It is clear, however, that a physical/actual disruption of order in the workplace was not required.

The rules concerning dress were, de facto,[52] extended to include manifestations of religion or belief such as religious symbols, practices or religious affiliation *outside* the public workplace in several judgments with reference to broader principles

49 See the case of Züheyla Zeybel, 25.01.2001, E2000/1244, K2001/474, Council of State, General Council of Chambers of Administrative Cases.

50 Article 125 E/a of the Law No. 657 on Public Servants. As explained in the previous section, the Law on Public Servants lays out the sanctions regime for public servants including for the Regulation of October 1982.

51 Decision by the High Disciplinary Council of the Presidency of the Higher Education Council, Decision No. 98/44, 29 July 1998, based on Articles 5/g and 11/a of the Regulation of Discipline for Administrators, Teaching Personnel and Civil Servants Working in Higher Education Institutions. The provisions in question set forth the dismissal of personnel based on actions contrary to clothing rules and disrupting the order of institutions with ideological or political purposes, respectively. In effect, repeating Article 125 e/a of the Law on Public Servants.

52 For more examples of similar cases and administrative actions see a report by the Lawyers Association: T. Hüsnü, "The Scope and the Consequences of the Ban on the Headscarf in Turkey," Lawyers Association Report 3 (Warsaw, OSCE Human Dimension Implementation Meeting, 2–13 October 2006), available at www.osce.org/odihr/21430.

found in the Turkish Constitution and other laws. This was demonstrated in a case dealing with the removal from office of the Principal of a Preschool before starting her new office.[53] After being appointed as the Principal for Gölbaşi Preschool, Ms Altindag went to report to her place of work and, as she entered the premises, without a headscarf, she showed her teacher's ID card—previously obtained from the Ministry of Education—on which she was shown with a headscarf.[54] She was refused entry into the premises because of the photo on her ID card and—since it was not possible to determine her ID through other means at the time—she was not able to start her job. The situation was reported to the authorities and an investigation was started. As a result of the investigation Ms Altindag was given a disciplinary punishment as well as an administrative punishment which resulted in her removal from the position of a preschool principal and reappointment as a preschool teacher.[55] The disciplinary punishment was based on her not complying with workplace rules and orders. The administrative measure, however, was based on broader considerations that will be examined below.

The judgment of the Council of State demonstrates that the headscarf, even though it was worn outside the workplace, is viewed by the judiciary as a religious manifestation that undermines certain qualities that are expected from teachers:[56] inter alia, "being a good example" and the secular character of the public education. It was specifically noted that Ms Altindag did not wear the headscarf at her workplace. The reason for the investigation was her presentation of an ID card with a photo on which she appeared wearing a headscarf. Yet, as is evident in the reasoning, the decision was clearly based on her actions outside the workplace.[57] Ms Altindag was said to have acted in contradiction to the *essential principles* found in the Constitution and relevant legislation. The Council of State emphasized that the system of contemporary education and teaching prescribed in Article 130 of the Turkish Constitution could not be a system ignoring the principle of secularism. This meant that students will not be subject to—what the Council of State saw to be—"non-scientific influences." The judgment was based on the Basic Law on National Education, where the essential purpose of Turkish National Education is specified as, inter alia, raising all Turkish individuals to adhere to Atatürk's reforms, principles and nationalism as stated in the Constitution, to be

53 Case of Aytaç Altındağ, Council of State 8th Chamber, 26 October 2005 E2004/4051, K2005/3366.

54 The teacher identification card with her photo wearing a headscarf was given to her by the Ministry of Education at a time when it was not required for public servants to uncover their heads on the photo used for identification, however at the time of presenting it at her new place of work, that was no longer the case.

55 This was in accordance with Article 125 /C (a-ı) of the Law No. 657.

56 The decision talks generally about teachers, but the qualities are also applicable for principals. Her transfer to a teaching position does not imply that she was allowed to wear the headscarf coming and going to school as a teacher.

57 Case of Aytaç Altındağ, Council of State 8th Chamber, 26 October 2005 E2004/4051, K2005/3366.

respectful of human rights and to know their responsibility towards the Turkish Republic.[58] It was argued that in addition to the knowledge and behavior of teachers, their appearance also creates an effect on students. She was expected to be a good example in her school environment *and* the outside environment, which is a reflection of the education and teaching. Regarding the particular case of Ms Altındağ, the Council of State was of the opinion that:

> while the applicant states that she provides service with her head uncovered in school, she also made statements that sometimes she wears the headscarf while coming to school and going from school … taking also into account that she will be an administrator in an educational institution where those who are educated are very young of age … the applicant who must be a *good example* in the environment where she is and in the external environment which is, in a way, the reflection of education and teaching, has clearly acted in contradiction to the essential principles stated in the provisions and laws mentioned above *while coming to and going from school.*[59]

The same broad approach is further demonstrated by the judgment of an administrative court upholding the decision of the Ministry of Education for the transfer of an educational administrator, Mr Mustafa Ünsal, based on manifestations of religion or belief such as his religious affiliations or practices outside the workplace:

> his relations with the segment who are known as *dinci* [religious, for religion, not modern] outside of his office, that he never misses Friday prayers even if within office hours, that his wife wears the "turban" that is accepted as a symbol and dressing veiled and she has relations only with the segment [of society] that dresses like her, that he does not attend any [official] meetings with his wife, including National Holidays and Republic Day Ball … In spite of his success in his education and teaching activities … while there is no concrete example, it is spoken about widely in the small province thus qualifying as a violation of principle of neutrality that is one of the most important qualities required in an administrator.[60]

The overly broad approach by the judiciary raises questions about the predictability and clarity of the application of relevant laws. In the assessment of the compatibility of one's actions with the dress code and the principle of

58 Milli Eğitim Temel Yasası [Basic Law on National Education], 14 June 1973 No. 1739, R.G. 24.06.1973, No. 14574, Article 2.

59 Own translation and emphasis. Case of Aytaç Altındağ, Council of State 8th Chamber, 26 October 2005 E2004/4051, K2005/3366.

60 Own translation and emphasis. Case of Mustafa Ünsal, Council of State 5th Chamber, E1999/4212, K1999/4325.

secularism, dress outside the public workplace, "sincerity" in abiding by the relevant regulations,[61] manifestations of religion, belief outside the workplace and affiliations with certain groups and religious world-view may also be taken into account. It is not possible to find a detailed set of reasons as to exactly how the nexus between, on the one hand, manifestations of religion, such as religious garb and practice outside the workplace and, on the other hand, the threat to secularism is drawn. The assumed connection seems to be based on general perceptions and presuppositions rather than on the nature of concrete acts by individuals which (could) pose an immediate and material threat to the secular nature of the public service they are delivering.

It is also important to note that among all the detailed rules and instructions found in the Regulation of October 1982, the headscarf seems to be singled out as the only element where the rules are enforced. Provisions of the same Regulation dealing with the length of hair, moustache, etc. are not enforced. Hence, in practice, a certain component of an ostensibly neutral code is implemented, which in effect results in a discriminatory application of law only affecting women wearing the headscarf. The specific application and its timing strengthens the idea that the headscarf is primarily viewed as a political symbol threatening Turkish secularism. It has been suggested that the question of political legitimacy lies at the heart of the ban and the manner in which it is justified.[62]

It is striking that in the cases considered above, the Turkish judiciary does not include the right to freedom of religion or belief aspect in its assessment. The right to freedom of religion or belief is protected in the Turkish Constitution,[63] as well as through Turkey's international human rights commitments.[64] The interest in protecting the secular system may ultimately be based on the legitimate aims of protecting public order and the rights of freedoms of others. However, the balancing of competing interests are absent in the reasoning. Neither is the proportionality of

61 The wearing of a wig over the headscarf by a teacher was considered as a sign that the applicant was not really sincere in abiding by the applicable dress code. Case of Kevser Sönmez, Sakarya Second Administrative Court, 26 December 2001, E2001/14, K2001/2854.

62 Ö. Denli, "The Head Cover Controversy in Contemporary Turkey," in *Facilitating Freedom of Religion or Belief: A Deskbook*, (T. Lindholm, W. C. Durham, Jr. and B. G. Tahzib-Lie, eds, Martinus Nijhoff Publishers 2004), 504.

63 Article 24 of the Turkish Constitution.

64 According to Article 90 of the Constitution, "in the case of a conflict between international agreements in the area of fundamental rights and freedoms duly put into effect and the domestic laws due to differences in provisions on the same matter, the provisions of international agreements prevail." No appeal to the Constitutional Court can be made with regard to these agreements, on the grounds that they are unconstitutional. Thus, constitutionally, the Turkish judiciary is under the obligation to give precedence to international jurisprudence in this field, and in order to do that it must first include international jurisprudence in its assessment.

the restriction weighed.[65] The effect of the prohibition, intensified due to extensive interpretations, on the applicants, in relation to the right to freedom of religion or belief and the right to work, are not considered in evaluating the proportionality of the measure. The notion of reasonable accommodation for religious dress/headscarf is not even touched upon. Interestingly, the relationship of religious symbols and state neutrality or impartiality and the possible problems in this respect find limited reflection in the jurisprudence. While it may be argued that the gender dimension is present implicitly through the reference to Atatürk's reforms there is no direct reference to any symbolic meaning attributed to the headscarf in relation to undermining gender equality.

Therefore one can reasonably argue that the protection of secularism as the paramount interest functions as a trump card or a hierarchically superior interest against which other competing interests cannot even be regarded as legitimate interests that require balancing. Religious symbols and/or practices are not assessed as legally protected manifestations of religion or belief, but as indicators of certain affiliations that are viewed as threats to secularism. Thus, the legal dispute is constructed as a clash between manifestations of religion or belief and secularism.

An approach amounting, in effect, to a general ban on religious dress in and—at times—outside of public workplaces is difficult to reconcile with the core values of a pluralistic and democratic society.

3. Private sector

There is no direct and explicit prohibition or regulation related to religious symbols in the private workplace in Turkey. Dress code rules are determined explicitly or implicitly by private companies through company culture and image, professional chambers and the legislation that affects the intersection of public and private. Private education and legal sectors stand out in this regard as private school teachers are subject to Ministry of Education rules concerning teachers, and lawyers are subject to court rules which prohibit the display of religious symbols in court.[66]

---

65 In contrast, proportionality is a principle employed in the practice of administrative courts. See Y. Oğurlu, "A Comparative Study on the Principle of Proportionality in Turkish Administrative Law," in *Kamu Hukuku Arşivi Ilhan Akın'a Armağan*, March 2003 (1).

66 Teachers working in private schools are subject to dress codes applicable to personnel of National Education. See Article 58, Milli Eğitim Bakanlığı Özel Eğitim Kurumları Çerçeve Yönetmeliği [Ministry of National Education Framework Regulation on Private Schools] 22 July 2005, R.G. 22.07.2005 No. 25883.

All lawyers are subject to the Law on Practice of Law: Avukatlık Kanunu [Law on Practice of Law] No.1136 R.G. 7 April 1969, No.13168. According to Article 49 lawyers must abide by the dress code determined by the Union of Turkish Bar Association (UTBA). In the Rules of Profession (9 January 1971) issued by the UTBA, Article 20 requires lawyers and interns to perform their duties without any headgear. It is reported that the Istanbul Bar Association has actively sought to apply disciplinary measures against women

The potential duties of private employers and protection in the private employment relationship ensuing from Turkey's international as well as domestic obligations to protect manifestations of religion or belief seems in need of inquiry and clarification. Labor law protects against religious discrimination.[67] But anti-discrimination legislation in Turkey is weak and existing legal remedies are rarely accessible for various reasons.[68] The possibility of effectively benefiting from the available legal protection against religious discrimination is significantly diminished by the lack of information among employees, the difficulty of proving that the discrimination was based on religion and the general powerlessness felt by those affected, e.g. religious minorities and women, in the light of the power dynamics involved in the available complaint procedures.[69]

It is difficult to provide a meaningful comparison of the approach of the Turkish judiciary to religious symbols and practices in the public and private workplace due to the lack of relevant cases related to the latter setting.[70] However, the results of a study on professional women wearing the headscarf, and a complaint on discrimination on the basis of religion discussed below, demonstrate some of the complexities surrounding manifestations of religion in the private workplace. Thus, it is possible

---

wearing the headscarf outside the courtroom and in the courthouse as well. According to a news report, the Istanbul Bar Association placed notices asking to be informed about women wearing the headscarf in court houses in order to start disciplinary investigation. See X., "Ve Baro Başörtülü Avukat Arıyor" (And the Bar is Watching for Lawyers Who Wear the Headscarf) *Zaman Newspaper* 28 June 2008, available at www.haber5.com/archive_details?id=321180.

67 Other prohibited grounds are language, race, gender, political opinion, philosophical beliefs, religion and denomination and similar grounds: Article 5 of Labor Law, 22.05.2033 İş Kanunu [Labor Law] No. 4857, R.G. 0/06/2003 No. 25134. For an analysis of protection against discrimination based on religion in Turkish Labor Law see N. Sural, "Islamic Outfits in the Workplace in Turkey, a Muslim Majority Country," *Comparative Labour Law and Policy Journal*, Spring (2009), 569–596. For an overview of the application of the European Convention of Human Rights in the context of the private workplace see L. Vickers, *Religious Freedom, Religious Discrimination and the Workplace*, (Hart Publishing 2008), Chapter 4.

68 At the time of writing, a comprehensive draft law on the elimination of discrimination, including the establishment of a Committee on Equality and the Elimination of Discrimination with the capacity to receive complaints, is pending at the Turkish Grand National Assembly. See draft (in Turkish) at www.icisleri.gov.tr/default.icisleri_2.aspx?id=5692.

69 A recent report sheds light on how protection against discrimination in work life is not a reality in the lives of, for instance, Protestants in Turkey. The report serves to provide an insight into the experience of minority and vulnerable groups. See The Association of Protestant Churches (Turkey), *'A Threat' or Under Threat – Legal and Social Problems of Protestants in Turkey*, Report (Anadolu Ofset 2010), available at www.protestankiliseler.org.

70 The Ministry of Labor also confirms that women do not complain of dismissal or discrimination based on their religion as a result of wearing the headscarf but concludes that there are no complaints because there is no discrimination. Interview by the author with researcher Özge Genç (TESEV) for D. Cindoğlu study September 2010.

to gain some insight into the situation in the private sector and, in particular, note how the public sector prohibition on headscarves is affecting the private sector. In Turkey only 6.5% of women have higher or university education.[71] About 16% of university graduates wear the headscarf.[72] Women only make up 24.9% of the population in employment in Turkey.[73] A recent study on the difficulties faced by professional women wearing the headscarf in the private workplace thus concentrates on a sample of women from the segment of the 16% of the 6.5%.[74] According to the study, women experience discrimination in employment, promotions and dismissals based on the fact that they are wearing the headscarf.[75] The research points to a spillover effect of the prohibition in the public sphere to the private sector.[76] This is a result not only of the attitudes of the employers, but also the structure of work connections between public workplaces and private workplaces. In particular, lawyers, pharmacists, teachers, journalists, those working in television, engineers and accountants must have contacts with institutional clients, professional chambers and public institutions, as well as pass many professional exams in order to receive necessary licenses for working in their respective professions.[77] The prohibition of wearing a headscarf while taking exams organized by state institutions, the arbitrary application of the rules by professional chambers to interns or professional women wearing the headscarf and the general prejudice against the latter create conditions that are conducive to discrimination against these women.[78]

As regards religious symbols/practices or religious persons in the private workplace in general, a complaint concerning the dismissal of the janitor of an apartment building by the management helps to demonstrate some attitudes in society and the challenges involved in cases involving discrimination based on religion. The contract of a janitor, Mr Naci Sekiner, stated that:

---

71 D. Cindoğlu, *Başörtüsü Yasağı ve Ayrımcılık: Uzman Meslek Sahibi Başörtülü Kadınlar* [The Headscarf Ban and Discrimination: Specialized Professional Women Who Wear the Headscarf], (TESEV Publications 2010), 14.

72 About 70% of the women in Turkey wear the headscarf. See A. Çarkoğlu, “Women’s Choices of Head Cover in Turkey: An Empirical Assessment,” in 29 (3) *Comparative Studies of South Asia, Africa and the Middle East* 2009.

73 This ratio is the lowest in OECD countries. See the Report by the General Directorate on the Status of Women (of the Prime Minister’s Office), Türkiye’de Kadının Durumu [The Situation of Women in Turkey], (Ankara 2008), available at www.ksgm.gov.tr/Pdf/trde_kadinin_durumu_2011_subat.pdf.

74 D. Cindoğlu, *Başörtüsü Yasağı ve Ayrımcılık: Uzman Meslek Sahibi Başörtülü Kadınlar* [The Headscarf Ban and Discrimination: Specialized Professional Women Who Wear the Headscarf], (TESEV Publications 2010), 14.

75 *Id.*

76 *Id.*, 68.

77 *Id.*, 68–81.

78 N. Akbulut, Örtülemeyen *Sorun Başörtüsü, Temel Boyutlarıyla Türkiye’de Başörtüsü Yasağı Sorunu* [The Headscarf – An Issue That Cannot be Covered: The Basic Dimensions of the Issue of the Turkish Headscarf Ban], (AK-DER Publications 2008), 15.

> He, his wife, and children cannot walk around in *takke* [skullcap], *shalvar*, *takunya* [clogs] and slippers that are in bad shape. His wife and daughters cannot wear the "turban,"[79] which has become a political symbol. They cannot practice their religious worship in front of everyone and cannot use these as excuse for not fulfilling their duties.[80]

When dealing with the application, the prosecutor focused on the complaint that Mr Sekiner was dismissed after several visits from his relatives who were wearing the headscarf. Figen Tüzün, the apartment building administrator, acknowledged that there was a provision in the work contract regarding clothing. She stressed, however, that the reason for the dismissal was not the said provision but the fact that there were complaints that the janitor had not fulfilled his duties.

Consequently, since it was not possible to prove that the applicant was dismissed on grounds of his religious affiliation the charges were dropped. The prosecutor did not evaluate the provisions in the contract in terms of their possible implications for discrimination on religious grounds. Despite a specific reference to the right to freedom of religion or belief in the complaint, the prosecutor's assessment did not take into account this important element in relation to the contract provisions. If the contract clauses prohibiting religious manifestations such as religious clothing or performing *namaz* in the workplace were addressed by the prosecutor, according to Sural in the light of the high courts' decisions that reflect their approaches to secularism, we may expect that "having a politically and religiously neutral workplace" will most likely be accepted as a legitimate aim by the courts.[81] The *Sekiner* complaint demonstrates the prejudice against religious manifestations in some parts of the private sector, as reflected in the contract clauses that draw a stereotypical picture of a religious person and explicitly restrict manifestations of religion, religious symbols and practices. In addition, it reveals some of the difficulties in proving discrimination and the inefficiency of legal remedies as evident in the approach of the prosecutor in refraining from including freedom to manifest one's religion or belief in his assessment.

The apparent lack of case law concerning religious symbols or practices in the private sector is by no means an indication that this sector is relatively less affected

79 The term "turban," instead of headscarf, is used by some parts of the society in Turkey with the purpose of drawing a distinction between the Anatolian traditional headscarf that they consider authentic and what they consider the politically motivated headscarf, the "turban." Thus the use of the term in the contract reflects a certain political view on the part of the apartment building administration.

80 Complaint of Naci Sekiner, Izmir Prosecutur's Office, Decision 2010/3391. The pieces of clothing described in the contract reflect a stereotype of a religious person or someone who is not "modern." The quote from the contract is my own translation.

81 N. Sural, "Islamic Outfits in the Workplace in Turkey, a Muslim Majority Country," *Comparative Labour Law and Policy Journal*, Spring (2009), 569–596.

by de facto restrictions.[82] The underlying complexities that result in restrictive practices in the public sector seem also to be present—to a certain extent—in the private sector. Whether or not and to what extent manifestations of religion or belief are allowed or accommodated appears to be determined solely by the employers. The extent of the obligations of employers in terms of non-discrimination based on religion and the right to freedom of religion or belief are not clear.

Ultimately, the accommodation of manifestations of religion or belief in a private workplace may be determined by the particular employer and general attitudes towards manifestations of religion or belief in society. There seems to exist a certain prejudice in some parts of the private sector towards religious symbols and practices.[83] On the other hand, some private companies, even if these do not explicitly situate themselves as faith-based companies, might facilitate or even encourage certain religious manifestations. Thus, women who do not wear the headscarf or individuals who do not perform *namaz* or keep the Ramadan fast may experience problems in employment relations in certain companies.[84] An explanation of the underlying problem causing both situations might be the idea that the coexistence of religious and modern lifestyles and of different religious identities is incompatible. Legal provisions or public policies that aim to ensure or foster religious diversity in the workplace would need to address this perception of incompatibility.

82 Experiences seem to vary from accommodation of the *namaz* (Islamic prayer) in private workplaces to explicit statements by companies against any accommodation of the *namaz*. For instance, a company owner openly announces that it is prohibited to perform *namaz* at his workplace and thus perhaps precludes the employment of those practicing *namaz* in the first place. Since this statement does not appear to be prosecuted so far, one is led to conclude that a clear obligation on the part of the employer to allow manifestations of religion or belief does not exist. X., "Merinos'ta Namaz Kılmak" Yasak (It is Prohibited to Perform the *Namaz* at Merinos), *Dogru Haber* 8 December 2011, available at www.dogruhabergazetesi.com.

83 A Report AK-DER, İstatistiki *Verilere Göre Türkiye'de Kadınların Genel Konumu ve Başörtüsü Yasağının Cinsiyet Endekslerine Etkileri* [A Statistical Analysis of the Situation of Women in Turkey and the Effect of the Headscarf Ban on Gender Index] (AK-DER 2008), 6.

84 A research study reveals a significant degree of "neighborhood pressure" on girls and women to wear the headscarf and loose-fitting clothes in Anatolia. The research does not provide examples of women being discriminated against in the private sector for not wearing the headscarf. But based on the many examples of exclusion, degrading treatment and pressure on girls and women not wearing the headscarf, it would not be far-fetched to suppose that women not wearing the headscarf would be discriminated against in employment in the private sector. B. Toprak, *Türkiye'de Farklı Olmak, Din ve Muhafazakarlık Ekseninde* Ötekileştirilenler [Being Different in Turkey: Those Who Are Made "The Other" on the Religion and Conservatism Axis], (Boğaziçi University Publication, 2008), 80–100, report available at www.osiaf.org.tr/images/basin/pdf/turkiyede_farkli_olmak.pdf.

4. Proposal for an alternative approach

Considering that the Turkish jurisprudence views certain religious manifestations as incompatible with the secular nature of the state, I propose an alternative approach, which would entail applying the principle of harmonization of legal norms, problematizing the current understanding of manifestations of religion by the Turkish judiciary and rethinking secularism. In this part, I do not suggest a solution that is easy or complete. Instead, I aim to bring forward a few initial steps that might open the way for change.

First, I suggest the harmonized interpretation approach that is based on the general principle of harmonization in law indicating that when several norms apply to the same issue, to the extent possible, they give rise to compatible obligations. In the case of Turkey and the specific focus of this chapter, this principle requires that when dealing with cases on manifestations of religion or belief in workplaces, all norms, international, constitutional and legislative, must be taken into account and interpreted in harmony. Fair trial obligations also require that all applicable rules that may have a bearing on the judgment be taken into consideration. In the Turkish legal system there is no legal rule that would prevent the Turkish judiciary from taking this approach. The supremacy given to Turkey's international obligations in the Constitution[85] would be an important factor facilitating the process. The high courts would need to be the actors of change as the lower courts will follow their legal interpretation.

Additionally, the harmonizing principle would be conducive for norms influencing each other's interpretation. I argue that the inclusion of the right to freedom of religion or belief will be key in affecting and potentially softening the current strict and narrow interpretation of the principle of secularism.[86] While it is not possible to estimate the effect of this inclusion, it will certainly require balancing of competing interests. For an optimum outcome, it would be important to refrain from weighing secularism and freedom of religion or belief against each other. A rigorous assessment of the necessity of restrictions on the right to manifest one's religion or belief would need to be employed. If the scope of protection for manifestations of freedom of religion or belief is insufficient, however, this balancing may not be as effective as is hoped.

Second, as the case law considered above reveals, the meaning attributed to the headscarf, namely that of a political symbol, is seen in contradiction to Turkish

85 Article 90 of the Constitution.

86 Interestingly, Judge A. Sajo, in a concurring opinion about a Turkish case concerning Article 9 of the ECHR, observes that the relevant Turkish high court ignored the right to manifest one's religion in its assessment. He notes that the States must interpret their laws by taking into account the ECHR. Concurring Opinion of Judge A. Sajo, ECtHR, 23 February 2010, *Ahmet Arslan and others* v. *Turkey*, Application No.41134/98. The case deals with the conviction of the applicant on grounds of his religious garments worn in the public sphere. In this case the ECtHR found a violation of Article 9.

secularism. This perception is a defining element in the judgments. The current understanding of religious manifestations in general and the headscarf in the legislation in particular, as reflected in dress regulations of public servants as well as the overly restrictive application of the judiciary, needs to be problematized. The neutrality of the Turkish approach needs to be questioned as it depends on and reflects a certain understanding of Islam and Muslim women. This particular stance excludes the need for the possibility of change of this assumed "knowledge" by individual experiences or different meanings. In the changing paradigm, where Islamic manifestations of religion increasingly appear in the public sphere, the supposedly neutral references to, inter alia, neutrality, secularism, modernity and equality, do not seem neutral themselves. New and individual viewpoints need to be taken into account in order to challenge the existing knowledge, significance and meaning attached to it.

The reality check of the approach taken by the Turkish judiciary is problematic in the light of the social facts and possible consequences of the approach for particular persons and groups. For example, in a country where a significant portion of women wear the headscarf, how can one include women in public workplaces if the symbol of the headscarf is found categorically incompatible with secularism or state neutrality? Likewise, the effectiveness of efforts for the inclusion of women in work life and fostering equality of sexes in public life would inevitably be diminished by the current implementation of the ban. This restrictive approach continues the exclusion of those who wear the headscarf. The notion that the headscarf is categorically incompatible with the equality of sexes functions as an obstacle that will not allow Turkish women wearing the headscarves to be part of the Western idea of equality. Muslim women need to be part of the making of the idea of equality by entering this sphere, with their headscarves if they so choose. Thus, the result may be what Göle calls "hybrid" equality and not what has been envisaged under some Western conceptions.[87]

The problematization of the current understanding of the headscarf in the public sector may potentially influence the legal reasoning that is applied in relevant cases. The absence of the assumption that the headscarf is incompatible with Turkish secularism would moderate the perception that the wearing of it by public servants or wives of public servants is a manifestation categorically threatening secularism in Turkey. Thus, the judiciary may refrain from an effort to actively exclude the headscarf. This will allow for individual cases to be treated based on individual merits with a view to establishing whether there are factors, other than the headscarf, that pose a threat to secularism.

Finally, the demands by religious/practicing Muslims for the accommodation of religious practices in the public workplace constitute challenges to existing and conventional understandings of secularism and neutrality in Turkey. While these demands are not problem-free, they certainly call for an approach that takes into account different views on the meaning and significance of manifestations

87 N. Göle, *Modern Mahrem* [The Forbidden Modern], (Metis Publications 1991).

of religion and invites rethinking secularism and the neutrality of the state. Secularism or neutrality should not function as exit options for avoiding issues that seem complicated.[88] Rethinking what neutrality looks like when it concerns public servants' dress and how it should be reflected through them may be a way out of the dilemma created by the perceived incompatibility of manifestations of religion, such as symbols and practices or affiliations, and the neutrality requirement for public servants. The so-called "real neutrality"[89] that views wearing visible religious attire worn in public schools as incompatible with the neutrality of the state does not appear as a viable solution in a pluralistic society. On the other hand, the Dutch model of "open neutrality," which views the wearing of religious attire not necessarily as an indication of lack of neutral attitude and focuses on the general capacity of teachers in the public schools, may be one that Turkey ought to consider.[90] The new definition of neutrality may be guided by a desire to achieve a workable solution that allows the existence and participation of all members of religious or non-religious convictions. Therefore, a shift of focus from appearance to neutrality of processes seems necessary. In order to secure neutrality in terms of effect this shift must be balanced by a strong commitment on the part of the state to impartiality towards all religions in its state–religion relationship. An open and accommodating approach to manifestations of all religions would be a *sine qua non* of this new approach.

A new kind of civil servant training that focuses on neutral attitudes, as well as a new kind of citizen who is not easily offended or affected by coming into contact with religious symbols, might be necessary. The civil servant, regardless of his/her religious convictions must be able to deliver service in an impartial and non-discriminatory manner. Service receivers, on the other hand, do not have the right not to come into contact with civil servants who, by their appearance, convey their religious or non-religious convictions. While it can be argued that persons have a right not to come into contact with religious manifestations while receiving a public service, one has to accept that this would mean the exclusion of a significant portion of the population from public service. Also, it can be argued that there is no "neutral" appearance, per se, i.e. a person without a religious symbol also conveys a certain message.

---

88 Lauder and Augsberg argue that this kind of avoidance results in indifference and undermines law's function of conflict resolution. K.H. Lauder and I. Augsberg, "The Myth of the Neutral State: The Relationship Between State and Religion in the Face of New Challenges," 8 (2) *German Law Journal* 2007, 144.

89 H. Werdmölder, "Headscarves at Public Schools: The Issue of Open Neutrality Reconsidered," in *Religious Pluralism and Human Rights in Europe: Where to Draw the Line?* (M.L.P. Loenen and J.E. Goldschidt, eds, Intersentia 2007).

90 Approach of the Dutch Equal Treatment Commission as relayed in H. Werdmölder, *Id.*; see also the chapter by Titia Loenen in this volume discussing the opinions issued by the Dutch Equal Treatment Commission.

Conclusion

There has been an intentional effort to exclude manifestations of religion or belief, in particular the headscarf, from the public workplace in Turkey, and the Turkish judiciary has played a significant role in the demarcation of the scope of applicable laws. The relevant judgments demonstrate the perception of a clash between, on the one hand, secularism, and, on the other hand, manifestation of religion or belief, through the use of headscarf or other actions in and outside the public workplace. This construction excludes any serious consideration of the right to and the expression of freedom of religion or belief in the workplace. Current norms and their application reflect a perception of incompatibility of practicing religion and the secular nature of state that needs to be conveyed by civil servants. In order to ensure the representation of a pluralistic society in public service, a harmonized interpretation of various applicable national and international laws, a problematization of the understanding of manifestations of religion, in particular the headscarf, and a rethinking of the principle of secularism may be some ways forward.

Chapter 9

The Practice of Religion in the French Public and Private Workplace: In Search of an Elusive Balance

Rim-Sarah Alouane

Introduction

France recognizes and guarantees freedom of opinion and religion in constitutional Article 10 of the Declaration of Human and Civic Rights of 1789, which states that "[n]o one may be disturbed on account of his opinions, even religious ones, as long as the manifestation of such opinions does not interfere with the established Law and Order."[1] But this recognition is also limited: this freedom is guaranteed as long as "the expression of such opinions does not cause a breach of the peace as established by law." Freedom of religion in France must coexist with the principle of neutrality and of *laïcité*, resulting from the Law on Separation of the Churches and State of 9 December 1905[2] and proclaimed in the first Article of the French Constitution of 4 October 1958. Moreover, France is also signatory to the European Convention of Human Rights and Fundamental Freedoms (ECHR), which recognizes and protects freedom of conscience and religion in its Article 9.

It has been said that this *laïcité* sets France apart from "countries that combine protection of religious pluralism and a state religion, but also from those which embrace separation of Church and State with an asserted sense of accommodation."[3] Religion is a private matter that has to be exercised in the private sphere, but freedom of religion also covers the right to manifest one's religion or belief, for instance through specific practices. This includes the wearing of signs inherent

1 Official translation by the Constitutional Council, see www.conseil-constitutionnel.fr/conseil-constitutionnel/root/bank_mm/anglais/cst2.pdf.

2 Due to their respective histories, the Law on Separation of the Churches and State does not apply in the *région* Alsace and the *département* Moselle, which are both governed instead by the *Concordat* of 1801. As a result, the State officially recognized the Roman Catholic Church, the Lutheran Church, the Calvinist Church and the Jewish religion, and all of them benefit from state funding. This is also the case in French Guiana, where the Catholic religion is still subsidized by the *département*.

3 D. Custos, "Secularism in French Public Schools: Back to War? The French Statute of 15 March 2004," 54 *American Journal of Comparative Law* 337 (2006), 337–399.

to the exercise of religion within the public space and in the workplace, which is where potential conflicts with other fundamental rights can occur.

This chapter examines, through a review of the relevant case law and legal scholarship related to religion in the workplace, to what extent freedom of religion is guaranteed in the French workplace. After analyzing the distinction between the public and private sectors in the French context (I), the situation in the public sector (II) and in the private sector (III) will be assessed.

I. Distinction between the public and private sectors in the French context

The distinction between the public and private sectors seems crucial in the French context. The workplace is defined very broadly by the French Labor Code as the place where employees will normally carry out their work duties, which can also include a place of residence. The French *Cour de cassation* adopted a functional definition of the workplace in a ruling of 1985.[4] The French judges, the *Haute Autorité de Lutte contre les Discriminations et pour l'Egalité* (HALDE, the former French Equality Body that operated until May 2011),[5] and now the *Défenseur des droits* will not only have to preserve the interests of the employer, but also try to be attentive to the requests of individuals, who expect protection of their rights and freedoms. In the religious field, French judges and the HALDE have always sought to find an appropriate balance between the rights of employers and employees. But first of all, a distinction is made between public and private sector.

According to the classic definition, public service consists of all activities provided by a public authority or by a private entity under the control of the public authority (e.g. the Administration or the State) in order to satisfy a mission of

4 Cour de cassation, Labor Division, 19 June 1985, No. 84-60.914. *Bulletin V*, No. 352, 254 (1985).

5 The *Haute Autorité de Lutte contre les Discriminations et pour l'Egalité* was a French independent statutory authority created by law on 30 December 2004, whose goal was to promote equality and to fight and judge direct or indirect discrimination. On 29 March 2011, the French Parliament adopted the organic law on the *Défenseur des Droits* (Defender of the Rights) that created the *Défenseur des droits* and dissolved the HALDE, the *Défenseur des Enfants* (Defender of Children), the *Commission Nationale de Déontologie et de Sécurité* (National Commission of Ethics and Security) and the *Médiateur de la République* (Ombudsman of the Republic) effective 1 May 2011. This new institution will be in charge of all of the activities of the HALDE. The *Défenseur des Droits* is chaired by Dominique Baudis and is composed of three colleges, and one of them, co-chaired by Maryvonne Lyazid, is in charge of the fight against discrimination and for the promotion of equality. This will not affect the substantial analysis and the content of this chapter since the recommendations of the HALDE are still in force and up to date. Moreover, the *Défenseur des Droits* is expected to work in the same way as the HALDE and take over all pending cases.

public interest.[6] The French public service is governed by the so-called "Laws of Rolland," named after the professor who drafted them. There are three legal principles which every public service must follow and respect: the principle of continuity (the functioning of the public service has to be constant, regular and without interruption), the principle of mutability (the public service has to be adapted to its time and to the variations of the notion of public interest) and the principle of equality[7] (which follows the principle of neutrality and *laïcité*). The principle of continuity and the principle of neutrality are of particular interest and importance for the topic of religious practice in the French public workplace.

The principle of neutrality is related to the principle of equality as, under the French understanding of equality, an authority or a person in charge of a public service must treat the users of the public service in an identical way. In the public sector, the rules are a priori very clear and framed: civil servants, but also those occasionally assisting in providing a public service (e.g. parents volunteering to accompany teachers and pupils for a school trip),[8] are subjected to the principle of *laïcité*, which means that they must be neutral and not display any signs of belonging to a specific religion.

Furthermore, civil servants' duty of neutrality also implies a duty of reservation.[9] In practice, this principle of neutrality has been difficult to reconcile with the freedom of

6 The definition of the public service in France is still controversial and changing. But this global definition will not affect our analysis. For the most thorough study of the definition of the public service in France, see G-J. Guglielmi, G. Koubi and G. Dumont, *Droit du Service Public* (Monchrestien 2007). See also D. Truchet, "Renoncer à l'expression 'service public'," 11 *Actualité Juridique de Droit Administratif* 553 (2008); G. Marcou, "Maintenir l'expression et la notion de 'service public'," 16 *Actualité Juridique de Droit Administratif* 833 (2008).

7 This principle was elevated to the rank of principles with a constitutional value by the decision of the Constitutional Council, No. 86-217 DC-18 September 1986—*Loi relative à la liberté de communication* [Act on freedom of communication], and the *Conseil d'Etat* considers it as a General Principal of the Law since its ruling: Conseil d'Etat, Section, 10 May 1984, *Denoyez et Chorques* (*Recueil Lebon,* 274). General Principles of the Law "are the totality of unwritten rules which the judge draws from the spirit of legislation and which he applies with the same validity as the written law." See R. Drago, "The General Principles of the Law in the jurisprudence of the French Conseil d'Etat," 11 *American University Law Review* 126 (1962), 133.

8 Regarding the collaborators of the public service, the HALDE adopted the opposite position to the scholars and the administrative judges. In a recommendation in 2007 on the exclusion of mothers of pupils from participation in school activities/trips because of the wearing of the Islamic headscarf, the HALDE considered that the principle of religious neutrality does not interfere with the wearing of the headscarf by volunteers that participate in a public service, and that such an exclusion is a form of discrimination concerning access to the public service: Recommendation No. 2007-17, 14 May 2007, available at www.halde.fr.

9 C. Fourrier, "La liberté d'opinion du fonctionnaire: essai de droit public comparé: France, Grande-Bretagne, Etats-Unis, U.R.S.S, Allemagne, Suisse, Belgique," (R. Pichon and R. Durand-Auzias, eds, Librairie générale de droit et de jurisprudence 1957).

religion. Also, an equilibrium between these two had to be found, taking into account the ruling of the European Court of Human Rights (ECtHR), which requires a "fair balance … between the individual's fundamental right to freedom of expression and the legitimate interest of a democratic State in ensuring that its civil service properly furthered the purposes enumerated in Article 10 (2) [of the Convention]."[10]

The issue seems resolved in the public sector: civil servants are automatically subjected to the principle of religious neutrality and, consequently, to the principle of *laïcité*, as are the users of public services:

> The users of the public service have the right to express their religious beliefs within the limits of respect for the neutrality of the public service … A civil servant has a duty of strict neutrality … For a civil servant to manifest his/her religious beliefs in the exercise of his/her duties are a breach of his/her obligations.[11]

The private sector, on the other hand, refers to all of the activities that are not public services and in which the State does not intervene. The judges, as well as the HALDE, use accommodation cautiously, in order to find the right balance between the rights of the employee and the employer.

The conflict between the freedom of religion and *laïcité* is at the heart of very controversial and passionate disputes, and more and more cases are being brought before the French courts claiming discrimination or dismissal based on religion. In the public sector, even though problems do arise now and then, the rules are pretty clear. But the situation remains problematic in the private sector, where the principle of *laïcité* is not applicable, and where the principle of freedom of religion is the rule.[12] There is clearly no ban on religious signs in the private workplace. But limits can be established if an action related to the practice of a religion interferes with the normal functioning of the business, limits that are also mentioned in the second paragraph of Article 9 of the ECHR.

II. Religion in the public sector: Searching for a balance between freedom of religion and the principle of religious neutrality

The role of the judge has drastically evolved towards recognizing and strengthening the protection of civil servants' freedom of conscience (A). However, courts

10 ECtHR 2 September 1996, *Vogt* v. *Germany*, App. No. 17851/91, par 53.

11 Circulaire relative à la Charte de la laïcité dans les services publics [Circular on the Charter of *laïcité* in public services], 12 April 2007. Own translation ("*Les usagers du service public ont le droit d'exprimer leurs convictions religieuses dans la limite du respect de la neutralité du service public … Tout agent public à un devoir de stricte neutralité … Le fait pour un agent de manifester ses convictions religieuses dans l'exercice de ses fonctions constitue un manquement à ses obligations.*").

12 Article L-1121 of the Labor Code.

are still aiming for legal solutions to the questions regarding the expression of religious beliefs in a public service (B).

A. The prohibition of discrimination based on religion in the recruitment and the revocation of the civil servant: The adjustments made by the case law to protect civil servants' freedom of conscience

The freedom of religion of French civil servants is guaranteed by a number of legal provisions, such as Article 5 of the Preamble to the Constitution of 1946,[13] but also Article I of the Law Of The Separation of Church and State of 9 December 1905, and Article 6 of the *Statut Général des Fonctionnaires* (the General Civil Servants' Statute) of 1983, which states that "no distinction, whether direct or indirect, can be made between civil servants because of their political, union, philosophical or religious opinions."[14] This protection starts at the stage of recruitment and continues throughout the career of the public servant until their retirement. The case law shows that civil servants enjoy freedom of religion as do other individuals, and the duty of neutrality incumbent upon all public officials cannot justify a violation of these freedoms.

The prohibition of discrimination based on religion at the stage of recruitment of a civil servant has not always been recognized, and the position of case law has evolved in favor of protecting this freedom.

The initial position was quite restrictive, as was shown in the famous ruling of the French *Conseil d'Etat* in *Abbé Bouteyre*.[15] The facts are the following: a clergyman wanted to pass the *agrégation*[16] of philosophy to teach in a secondary school. The Minister of Education rejected his candidacy on the grounds that his ecclesiastical status would be in conflict with the principle of religious neutrality inherent to the position of civil servant, and the Ministry of Education forbade him to take the examination. The *Conseil d'Etat* justified this decision and held that the Ministry had looked out for the interest of the service and not committed an error of law: the ecclesiastical status of the applicant was deemed incompatible with the rank of teacher of public secondary education, considering that an outward

13 Official translation provided by the Constitutional Council: "Each person has the duty to work and the right to employment. No person may suffer prejudice in his work or employment by virtue of his origins, opinions or beliefs." Available at www.conseil-constitutionnel.fr/conseil-constitutionnel/root/bank_mm/anglais/cst3.pdf.

14 Loi portant droits et obligations des fonctionnaires [Act on Rights and Obligations of Civil Servants] No. 83-634 July 13, 1983. Own translation ("*Aucune distinction, directe ou indirecte, ne peut* être *faite entre les fonctionnaires en raison de leurs opinions politiques, syndicales, philosophiques ou religieuses.*").

15 Conseil d'Etat, Section, 10 May 1912, *Abbé Bouteyre*, No. 46027 *Recueil Lebon* 553.

16 The *agrégation* in France is a competitive examination to enter the civil service.

manifestation of opinion could be expected which would not be compatible with the principle of religious neutrality which governed public school teaching.

It was not until 1970, in the case of *Spagnol*[17] in the Paris Administrative Court, that priests were finally allowed to teach in public secondary schools. The facts in that case were similar to the *Abbé Bouteyre* affair, only here the priest wanted to pass the *agrégation* of Italian to teach in a public secondary school. Again, the Ministry of Education had refused his candidacy for the same motives as in the 1912 *Abbé Bouteyre* case. The *Conseil d'Etat* annulled the decision of the Ministry considering that the status of a priest, by itself, could not be grounds for the refusal to admit a candidate for a competitive examination. Two years after, in 1972,[18] the *Conseil d'Etat* followed the line of the Administrative Court in an opinion given to the Ministry of Education, which asked if a tenured professor of a secondary school on temporary leave who decided to join the clergy could keep his job in a public school without violating the principle of religious neutrality. The judges of the *Conseil d'Etat* declared: "A tenured teacher of secondary school cannot be legally dismissed from his post on the grounds that he embraced the ecclesiastical status."[19] This decision of the *Conseil d'Etat* meant a major turnaround, as it overruled the *Abbé Bouteyre* ruling.

This evolution of the position of the *Conseil d'Etat* had a major consequence: administrations could no longer reject an application for a competitive civil servant examination based on the clerical status of the candidate. This complies with the principle of religious neutrality. The *Conseil d'Etat* had tried to find a compromise in order to protect/balance two fundamental principles: the principle of neutrality of the public service and the freedom of conscience. The *Conseil d'Etat* decided that the principle of neutrality was not violated and a limitation to the freedom of conscience was unconstitutional and disproportionate. According to the *Conseil d'Etat*, as long as the religious affiliation or status of a person does not interfere with or threaten the normal functioning of a public service, and as long as the person does not proselytize while performing his/her duties, the freedom of conscience has to prevail and be protected.

The *Conseil d'Etat* recognized freedom of religion as a fundamental freedom. For example, the administrative judges of the *Conseil d'Etat* will declare void any decisions adopted by an administration which might contain elements of discrimination based on the religion of civil servants. Established case law deems illegal all forms of discrimination against servants with non-religious status based on beliefs that they show outside of their service: *Demoiselle Weis (*1938)[20] concerned a student-teacher in a primary school whose tenure was rejected by the administration

17 Administrative Court of Paris, 7 July 1970, *Spagnol*, *Recueil Lebon*, 851.

18 Conseil d'Etat, opinion No. 309-354, 21 September 1972.

19 Own translation ("*Un professeur titulaire de l'enseignement du second degré ne peut légalement* être écarté *de ses fonctions par le motif qu'il aurait embrassé l'état ecclésiastique.*").

20 Conseil d'Etat, 28 April 1938, *Demoiselle Weiss*, *Recueil Lebon*, 379.

because of religious beliefs expressed outside of her work in school. In its 1939 *Demoiselle Beis* judgment,[21] the *Conseil d'Etat* also annulled an administrative decision to reject the application for a competitive entrance examination submitted by a person solely on the grounds that she studied in a denominational school. Finally, in *Demoiselle Jamet* (1950), the administrative decision firing a teacher who belonged to a religious group outside of her workplace and her service was also annulled.[22] Thus, as long as religious opinions are expressed outside of the service, the *Conseil d'Etat* considers these expressions as a matter of private life.[23] For the *Conseil d'Etat,* a civil servant is a citizen and possesses all the rights that every citizen has, including freedom of conscience and religion.[24]

A civil servant is also subjected to the rules of public law, including strict observance of the principle of *laïcité* and religious neutrality in the workplace. In its 1992 *Kherouaa* decision,[25] the *Conseil d'Etat* reaffirmed and reiterated the fact that the principle of neutrality of public services prohibits any kind of distinction or discrimination between users based on their religious affiliation. Likewise, the principle of religious neutrality applies to civil servants who are not allowed to express any religious views while carrying out their duties.

B. Accommodating religious signs, observance of rituals and religious holidays: A double-edged sword?

Generally, French judges tend to adopt a very strict position toward the wearing of religious signs, while showing some flexibility with regard to other practices, such as observance of rituals and religious holidays.

The notion of religious sign remains controversial, fuzzy and poorly developed under French law. The Act of 15 March 2004 on the wearing of religious symbols in public schools does not really contain a precise definition of the religious symbol. The circular letter of 18 May 2004 on the implementation of the Act of 2004,[26] does try to provide a definition of a religious symbol as "one which, when

21 Conseil d'Etat, 25 July 1939, *Demoiselle Beis*, *Recueil Lebon*, 524. See also Conseil d'Etat, 8 December 1948, *Demoiselle Pasteau*, *Recueil Lebon*, 464.

22 Conseil d'Etat, 3 May 1950, *Demoiselle Jamet*, *Recueil Lebon*, 247.

23 See, in contrast, the situation in Turkey in the chapter by Mine Yıldırım in this volume.

24 The *Conseil d'Etat* also deemed illegal all the questions relating to religious practices asked by a jury to a candidate for a competitive examination: Conseil d'Etat, 10 April 2009, No. 311888, *Abdeljalel B.*

25 Conseil d'Etat, 2 November 1992, *Kherouaa*, *Recueil Lebon*, 389.

26 Circulaire de 18 mai 2004 relative à la mise en œuvre de la loi No. 2004-228 du 15 mars 2004, encadrant en application du principe de laïcité, le port de signes ou de tenues manifestant une appartenance religieuse dans les écoles, collèges et lycées publics [Circular letter of 18 May 2004 on the implementation of Law No. 2004-228 of 15 March 2004, on the principle of *laïcité*, the wearing of symbols or clothing denoting religious affiliation in schools, secondary schools and public high schools].

worn, is immediately identified by its religious affiliation, such as the Islamic veil, whatever the name given to it, the *kippa* or a cross."[27] This definition is, however, too vague, allowing one to include among religious symbols any clothing (a headscarf, a robe, a *kippa*, a turban, …) or objects (e.g. a piece of jewelry such as a cross, the Star of David, …) aimed at demonstrating one's belief or faith. But the demarcations between religion, fashion or art are difficult to draw. A person wearing jewelry depicting a religious symbol is not necessarily a believer. A woman wearing a kerchief is not necessarily Muslim, Jewish or Amish. When the issue of banning the wearing of religious signs arises, it often faces complex and confusing problems of qualification.

According to the *Conseil d'Etat*, civil servants, regardless their function, are not allowed to express their allegiances during their activities. That is clear from the *Mademoiselle Marteaux* ruling (2000),[28] where it was stated that "the principle of *laïcité* is an obstacle to … the right to manifest their [civil servants'] religious beliefs." This ruling concerned the demand for the cancellation of a revocation order given by a chief education officer to a school supervisor who wore a *hijab*. The administrative courts reiterated this position. Another example was the 27 November 2003 ruling of the Lyon Administrative Court of Appeal in the case *Ben Abdallah*. Here also a civil servant working as an inspector wore an Islamic headscarf during her work hours. After a warning, her superior dismissed her, and the claimant went to court. The Administrative Court confirmed the dismissal holding that not only had she committed an act of negligence, but her way of dressing had not been "honorable."[29] The Administrative Court also stated that this principle applies to all the civil servants, whenever they should be in contact directly or indirectly with the users of the public service.[30]

In April 2009, this principle was repeated in the noteworthy case of *Sabrina Trojet* v. *Université Paul Sabatier*, which involved the dismissal of a doctoral microbiology researcher who worked at the Paul Sabatier University in Toulouse—a position which made her a temporary civil servant, subject to the rules of public law and public service—for wearing the *hijab*.[31] Even though she

---

27 Own translation ("*Les signes … dont le port conduit à se faire immédiatement reconnaître par son appartenance religieuse tels que le voile islamique, quel que soit le nom qu'on lui donne, la kippa ou une croix.*").

28 Conseil d'Etat, 3 May 2000, *Mademoiselle Marteaux*, *Recueil Lebon* 169.

29 In full, the relevant consideration reads: "*Les faits qui ont motivé la sanction contestée d'exclusion temporaire des fonctions, tels qu'ils ressortent de l'instruction, et qui ont consisté à porter un signe ostensible d'appartenance à une religion et à refuser, de façon réitérée, d'obéir aux ordres d'avoir à l'enlever, sont contraires à l'honneur professionnel.*"

30 I. Gallala, "The Islamic Headscarf: An Example of Surmountable Conflict between Shari'a and the Fundamental Principles of Europe," 12 *European Law Journal* (2006), 593–612.

31 Administrative Court of Toulouse, 17 April 2009 (summary judgment), *Sabrina Trojet* v. *Université Paul Sabatier*, No. 0901424, unpublished decision; see M. Inizan, "Une doctorante licenciée pour port du voile islamique," *Rue 89*, 17 April 2009, www.rue89.com.

was not in direct contact with the public—she was not teaching—and she was mainly doing laboratory research for her PhD thesis,[32] the University asked her not to wear a headscarf. The claimant decided to wear her headscarf "the Sicilian way" (i.e. tied under her neck) and her lawyer claimed that, worn this way, it had no religious connotation. Nevertheless, she was dismissed by the President of the University for failure to respect the principles of religious neutrality and *laïcité*. The doctoral student contested her dismissal and filed a suit (through a summary judgment) against this decision with the Toulouse Administrative Court.[33] The University argued that the dismissal was justified because she was required to respect the duty of confidentiality and the obligation of neutrality as a state official. The doctoral student tried to argue that wearing a headscarf "the Sicilian way" did not necessarily mean that it was a religious symbol or that she was a Muslim, but instead that it was the President of the University who had violated the principle of neutrality by assuming that the doctoral student was a Muslim on the basis of a personal interpretation of her dress. The Administrative Court, however, upheld the qualification as a religious sign and confirmed the decision of the University President to dismiss the young woman for violation of the principle of neutrality.

In a ruling of the Administrative Court of Appeal of Versailles in 2006, a childcare provider, employed by a commune—and therefore considered a public servant—who mainly worked at her own home, was dismissed for wearing an Islamic headscarf. The judge confirmed the dismissal and ruled that the claimant had disregarded the principle of religious neutrality by wearing the headscarf during her activity, despite the fact that she worked predominantly in the private sphere of her own home, and that the parents never complained about her way of dressing.[34] The judge considered, however, that there were also some occasions where she took part in exterior activities.[35]

While the courts have taken a highly restrictive approach regarding the wearing of a religious symbol and the observance of a ritual, they seem more flexible regarding religious holidays.

---

32 Administrative Court of Toulouse, 17 April 2009 (summary judgment), *Sabrina Trojet* v. *Université Paul Sabatier*, No. 0901424 ("*Elle soutient en outre qu'elle n'exerce aucune mission d'enseignement et doit se concentrer uniquement à la rédaction de sa thèse et son action ne se rattache pas à une mission de service public.*").

33 See the motion to quash against the decision of the President of the University available at www.islamlaicite.org/IMG/pdf/refere_Annulation_ta.

34 Administrative Court of Appeal of Versailles, 2nd chamber, No. 04VE03227, 26 February 2006, *Madame Rachida X.*

35 Administrative Court of Appeal of Versailles, 26 February 2006, *Madame Rachida X.* ("*que si la requérante fait* état *de ce que son activité professionnelle se déroule à son domicile, elle ne conteste pas participer, en tout* état *de cause, ainsi que son statut le lui impose, aux multiples activités organisées au sein de la crèche familiale ainsi qu'aux diverses sorties extérieures proposées aux enfants et à leurs assistantes maternelles ... dans ces circonstances, Mme ... a commis une faute grave.*").

Despite the principle of *laïcité*, numerous Christian holidays are celebrated and are considered French public holidays.[36] One might argue that the observance of these holidays tends to favor Christian civil servants, who won't encounter obstacles to observing their rituals, since they are legally authorized to be off work on those days. Thus, in order to treat everybody equally, civil servants who practice another religion than Christianity may be permitted to be absent from work on their religious holidays. This possibility rests on a circular letter dated 23 September 1967[37] from the Ministry of the *Fonction Publique*[38] that lists religions and the dates of their celebrations, and is updated every year. This circular letter, effective for the public sector, only explains that department heads "may award public servants who wish to participate in the religious ceremony at the occasion of the principal holidays of their confession the necessary authorizations to be absent."[39] Religious celebrations listed for the year 2011 are:

- Catholic and Protestant celebrations;
- Orthodox celebrations (Theophany, Good Friday and Ascension of Jesus);
- Armenian celebrations (Christmas, St Vartan day, Genocide Victims Memorial Day);[40]
- Muslim celebrations (*Eid Al-Fir*, *Eid Al-Adha*, *Mawlid an-Nabi*);
- Jewish celebrations (*Shavuot*, *Rosh Hashanah*, *Yom Kippur*);
- Buddhist celebrations (Buddha's birthday).

The circular letter also specifies the date on which the celebrations begin, so that the department head can accurately provide the authorization of absence for religious motive. Moreover, the head of a department can refuse to allow the leave of absence, but he cannot refuse to *examine* a request. Since the list of religions mentioned is not exhaustive, the department head can examine an authorization of absence for a religion that is not mentioned in the list.[41] However, the circular letter also fixes a limit on the authorization of absence for a religious celebration:

36 The Christian celebrations considered as public holidays in France and mentioned in Article L. 3133-1 of the Labor Code are: Easter Monday, Ascension of Jesus, Pentecost, Assumption of Mary, All Saints' Day and Christmas.

37 *Circulaire* FP No. 901—23 September 1967.

38 The complete name is *Ministre du Budget, des Comptes publics, de la Fonction publique et de la Réforme de l'État.*

39 *Circulaire* FP No. 901—23 September 1967. Own translation ("*Les chefs de service peuvent accorder aux agents qui désirent participer aux cérémonies célébrées à l'occasion des principales* fêtes *propres à leur confession, les autorisations d'absence necessaries.*").

40 This holiday is considered as a religious holiday in the circular letter, whereas it is not in Armenia.

41 That is what the judge decided in a ruling of the Administrative Court of Appeal of Paris in 22 March 2001, No. 99PA02621, *Christian X.*

the *sine qua non* condition is that absences are "compatible with the normal functioning of the public service."[42]

In contrast to the situation regarding religious dress, the approach to the observance of religious celebrations and rituals seems more accommodating. Indeed, the obligation of neutrality does not prohibit the public authority from finding a way to allow civil servants to practice their religious rituals. For example, a civil servant is allowed to leave work or can modify his schedule to observe ritual prayers. But here again, this possibility is strongly framed and controlled since the principle of continuity of the public service[43] and its normal functioning will always have to be protected as a priority, which was confirmed by the *Conseil d'Etat* in the 2004 summary judgment *Ahmed X.*[44] The case concerned a janitor of subsidized low rent public flats, who asked his superior for a leave of absence to go to the mosque for an hour every Friday. His demand was rejected based on the ground that the service required his presence at the time of the prayer and could be disrupted by his absence at that time. The *Conseil d'Etat* confirmed the superior's decision, considering that the presence of the janitor was required at very specific moments, and his absence could interfere with the proper functioning of the service. Hence, in practice a refusal of a request of absence will have to be justified specifically in the light of the needs of the functioning of the public service.

If the public sector is still in search of its balance, we shall see that the private sector is in a quite similar position.

III. Religious freedom in the private sector: In search of a balance between the employee's freedom of religion and the interests of the company

In the private sector workplace, the difficulty lies in reconciling two potentially conflicting principles: on the one hand, the freedom of religion of the employee and, on the other hand, the interests of the company.[45] There is an obligation incumbent upon the employer to allow employees to practice their religion during their work hours (A). However, this obligation has no legislative foundation and its interpretation has not been without difficulties (B).

42 *Circulaire* FP No. 901—23 September 1967. Translation ("*dans la mesure où cette absence est compatible avec le fonctionnement normal du service.*").

43 Conseil d'Etat, 12 February 1997, *Mademoiselle Henry*, *Recueil Lebon*, 891.

44 Conseil d'Etat, 16 February 2004, No. 264314, *Monsieur Ahmed X.* See G. Guglielmi and G. Koubi, "Service public et autorisation d'absence pour prière," 15 *Actualité Juridique de Droit Administratif* 822 (2004).

45 The freedom of enterprise is constitutionally guaranteed since a decision of the Constitutional council, 16 January 1982, 81-132 DC, *Loi de Nationalisation* (Act on Nationalization of Private Companies). See L. Favoreu and L. Philip, *Les Grandes Décisions du Conseil Constitutionnel* (Dalloz 2009), 401–438.

A. Recognition of the prohibition of religious discrimination: the case law adjustments made to protect the employee's freedom of conscience

In contrast with the public sector, private companies are not subject to the principle of religious neutrality and *laïcité*, and hence the employee is in principle allowed to freely express his or her religious beliefs. This was noted in a recommendation of the HALDE of 3 March 2008,[46] following a question by a retailing firm that wanted to add a clause in their policies to prohibit the wearing of any religious or political sign. The HALDE noted that

> [t]he principle in the private sector is the freedom of belief and freedom of religion that includes the freedom to manifest one's religion. The company cannot be set up in a neutral or *laïque* manner, in the absence of a legislative provision that would restrict such a fundamental freedom.[47]

The HALDE confirmed this position in two later recommendations. The first, on 6 April 2009, announced that "[f]reedom of religion and belief applies in the private sector."[48] But this freedom is not without limit, and the HALDE qualified its previous statement explaining that freedom of religion in the workplace can be exercised short of any "abuse of freedom of expression, proselytizing or acts of pressure towards other employees."[49] The second, of 28 March 2011, reiterated that:

> While freedom of religion and belief is absolute, the freedom to manifest one's religion may be limited in strictly defined circumstances in order to be reconciled with another freedom or principle of equal value.[50]

---

46 Recommendation of the HALDE *relative à l'intégration dans le règlement intérieur d'une entreprise de la grande distribution d'une clause visant à interdire à tous les salariés le port d'un signe religieux ou politique*, No. 2008-32 of 3 March 2008, available at www.halde.fr.

47 Recommendation of the HALDE No. 2008-32 of 3 March 2008. Own translation ("*Le principe dans l'entreprise privée est celui de la liberté de convictions et de la liberté religieuse, qui comprend celle de manifester sa religion. L'entreprise ne saurait* être érigée *en lieu neutre ou laïque en l'absence d'une disposition législative venant restreindre une telle liberté fondamentale.*").

48 Recommendation of the HALDE *relative aux règles fixées par la loi et la jurisprudence pour l'expression religieuse dans l'entreprise*, No. 2009-117 of 6 April 2009, available at www.halde.fr.

49 *Id.*

50 Recommendation of the HALDE No. 2011-67 *sur le fait religieux* of 28 March 2011. Own translation ("*Si la liberté de religion et de croyance est absolue, en revanche la liberté de manifester sa religion peut* être *limitée dans des circonstances strictement encadrées, afin de pouvoir se concilier avec d'autres principes ou libertés d'égale valeur.*").

But how can employers ensure a proper balance between these conflicting rights and freedoms? How can they guarantee freedom of religion in the organization of the company? What are the risks? Should the legislator create a law to establish the rules regarding the wearing of religious signs and the observance of religious rituals—possibly prohibiting them in the private sector as well? Considerate discretion is already given to employers who will have to find the right balance between the interests of business and the obligation to respect and protect freedom of religion through various accommodations, which might lead to legal conflicts (cf. Part B).

The principle of the neutrality of the employer remains the rule in labor law. This starts at the stage of recruitment. Indeed, it is illegal for the employer to ask any questions regarding religion during an interview:

> No one shall be excluded from a recruitment procedure or access to an internship or a training period in a company, no employee may be sanctioned, dismissed or subjected to discrimination, direct or indirect, particularly in terms of pay, training, redeployment, assignment, qualification, classification, professional promotion, transfer or renewal of a contract because of ... religious beliefs.[51]

Article 225-1 of the Penal Code prohibits any dismissal based on religion, and Article 255-2 adds that such an offense could be punished by three years' imprisonment and a fine of 45,000 euros. The *Cour de cassation* (Criminal Division) judged in 1986[52] that the Penal Code "prohibits not only a dismissal based on racist grounds ... but also a refusal of recruitment."[53]

Therefore, prohibition of discrimination (direct and indirect) is a tool to protect freedom of conscience and freedom of religion in the workplace. As a result, an employer is not allowed to require any kind of information concerning employees' or job applicants' religious beliefs or practices: the *Cour de cassation* deemed illegal the dismissal of an employee on the ground that he had hidden that he was a

51 Article 1132-1 of the Labor Code. Own translation ("*Aucune personne ne peut* être écartée *d'une procédure de recrutement ou de l'accès à un stage ou à une période de formation en entreprise, aucun salarié ne peut* être *sanctionné, licencié ou faire l'objet d›une mesure discriminatoire, directe ou indirecte ..., notamment en matière de rémunération ... de mesures d'intéressement ou de distribution d'actions, de formation, de reclassement, d'affectation, de qualification, de classification, de promotion professionnelle, de mutation ou de renouvellement de contrat en raison de ... ses convictions religieuses.*"). One might note that the Act No. 2008-496 of 27 May 2008 *Portant diverses dispositions d'adaptation au droit communautaire dans le domaine de la lutte contre les discriminations*, implements Employment Equality Directive 2007/78 and added the article 1132-1 in the Labor Code.

52 Cour de cassation, Criminal Division, 14 October 1986, No. 85-96369, *Bulletin des arrêts de la Cour de Cassation: Chambre criminelle*, 733.

53 Own translation ("*[Les provisions du Code pénal] prohibent toute discrimination fondée sur des considérations raciales ... à l'occasion du licenciement ... mais* également *lors de son embauche.*").

priest when he was recruited even though his ecclesiastical status would not affect either his job performance or the interests of the company.[54] However, the difficulty in such cases is to provide evidence of discrimination (whatever its nature). The French Anti-discrimination Act of 16 November 2001 (*Loi sur la lutte contre les discriminations*) specifies the regime of the burden of the proof, categorizing two types of situation. In one, an employee alleges that he is a victim of discrimination. In that case, the claimant will have to file a civil, rather than criminal, suit,[55] and be required to provide proof that he was subjected to discriminatory treatment.[56] In the other type of situation the employer who seeks to justify differential treatment of an employee will have to provide proof that the treatment was motivated by objective circumstances.[57]

B. The interests of the company versus the protection of employees' freedom of religion

Manifestations of an employee's religion can be restricted, and this possibility of restriction is spelled out even in those texts that assert and protect freedom of conscience and religion, including Article 9 par. 2 of the ECHR and Article 1132-1 of the French Labor Code. All those restrictions on religious freedom which can be justified by the need for good organization and normal functioning of the company are considered legal. However, it seems that the existing legal interpretation of the place of religion in the workplace and the inherent obligations to the employee are ambiguous. The notion of the interests of the company is a decisive factor in validating refusals of recruitment or dismissals based on religious grounds and in examining various forms of religious adjustments made by the employer.

As we mentioned above, private sector employees are not subject to the principle of neutrality and of *laïcité*. As long as the employee does not proselytize in the workplace or disturb the normal functioning of the company, a private sector employee has the right to express his/her religious opinions. But this practice can be limited or strictly curbed for security reasons and for the sake of the interests of the company. This can be illustrated by the following three cases.

The first case involved a woman who worked in a clothes store and was instructed to represent the brand and to advise customers. She started to show her faith through her way of dressing.[58] Her employer obliged her to change her

54 Cour de cassation, Labor Division, 17 October 1973.

55 Indeed, if it were a criminal action, the burden of proof would be heavier on the employee, since the presumption of innocence is a strong constitutionally guaranteed protection.

56 Article L.1134-1 Labor Code.

57 Cour de cassation, Labor Division, 3 April 2002, No. 00-42583; Cour de cassation, Labor Division, 15 October 2008, No. 07-40064.

58 S. Farnocchia, "Liberté religieuse et intérêts de l'entreprise," 171 *Recueil Dalloz-jurisprudence* 546 (1998).

"provocative" way of dressing in order to comply with the brand image of the company that represents "the young Reunion modern, liberated woman, who feels good about herself, who assumes her femininity in her speech but also in her clothes."[59] In other words, according to the employer, the claimant's way of dressing was not in conformity with the policy of the company.[60] The litigant refused to comply, citing her freedom of religion, and was dismissed. The *Conseil des Prud'Hommes* (the French Employment tribunal) declared the dismissal unlawful on the grounds that it was based on a violation of the freedom of religion of the employee and on the violation of the (former) Article L. 122-45[61] of the Labor code which states that employees cannot be dismissed because of their religious beliefs.[62] However, the employer appealed the decision and the Court of Appeal of Saint Denis[63] reversed the judgment of the *Conseil des Prud'Hommes*, confirming the dismissal. The case presented the classic issue of searching for a balance between, on the one hand, the freedom of religion of the employee and, on the other hand, the interests of the company.

The Court of Appeal made its decision in two steps. First, the Court made a clear distinction between the freedom of religion and the "external expressions" of this religion,[64] which are two different things: whereas the first one has to be protected, the second one might be limited. Further, the Court looked at the proportionality between the advantages and the inconveniences of the wearing of religious signs. In the particular case at hand, the judge decided that freedom of religion was not an absolute principle in the workplace, and that the wearing of religious signs might cause serious damage to the corporate image. As a consequence, the employer had the right to limit the employee's expression of religion, and the interests of the company were deemed superior in this situation. This does not mean that religious signs are banned in the private workplace per se, but that in individual cases a right and pragmatic balance between freedom of religion and freedom of enterprise must be sought. This position confirmed the ruling that the *Cour de cassation* made in 1986[65] concerning the refusal of an employee to undergo a compulsory

59 Own translation of the letter of dismissal sent to the claimant: ("*C'est pourquoi notre communication est basée sur un personage représentant les caractéristiques de notre cible principale: la jeune femme réunionnaise moderne, libérée, bien dans sa peau, qui assume sans complexes sa féminité tant dans son discours que dans sa tenue.*") See S. Farnocchia, *Id.* at 546.

60 There was talk of "*un type de vêtement la recouvrant de la tête aux pieds, dont le style est en totale opposition avec l'image de la marque du magasin.*"

61 This article was abrogated on 1 May 2008 and replaced by Article 1132-1.

62 Own translation ("*Aucun salarié personne ne peut* être ... *licencié ... en raison de ... de ses convictions religieuses.*").

63 Administrative Court of Appeal of Saint-Denis de la Réunion, 9 September 1997.

64 S. Farnocchia, "Liberté religieuse et intérêts de l'entreprise," 171 *Recueil Dalloz-jurisprudence* 546 (1998).

65 Cour de cassation, Labor Division, 29 May 1986, No. 83-45409, *Droit Social* 788 (1986).

medical examination for religious reasons. The Court ruled that this behavior was a "real and serious cause"[66] to justify a dismissal and declared it legal, because the interests of the company might be strongly affected by such behavior. But the decision of the Court of Appeal of Saint Denis can be criticized. Indeed, here again is the question of the interpretation of the facts: who can say that this employee did not feel young, modern and good about herself? Also, there was no actual proof that the religious dress caused damage to the employer's brand.

The second case concerns a Muslim employee who worked in a supermarket in Mayotte[67] and was transferred from the fruit and vegetables department to the butchery. After two years of regular contact with pork meat, he asked his employer to transfer him to another service, arguing that "this situation was not compatible with his Muslim faith."[68] The employer refused a transfer, and the employee was dismissed. The employee went to court to get unemployment benefits claiming dismissal "without a real and serious cause." After reiterating the fact that freedom of religion had to be protected by the employer, the judges of the *Cour de cassation* explained that:

> the employer commits no fault by asking the employee to execute the task for which he was hired.[69]

The Court explained that the contract did not contain a special clause that would mention any religious accommodations:

> the employer must respect the religious beliefs of his employee, which are not relevant under the work contract except in the case of a specific clause.[70]

---

66 *Loi portant réforme du droit du licenciement* [Reform Act on Dismissal Law] of 13 July 1973 does not give a clear definition of that notion; the judge did not try to fill in this legal gap, and consequently issued a very broad and flexible interpretation of it. Hence, the classic, though still questionable, definition given during the debates at the National Assembly before the adoption of the law still remains in force. The "real" cause is "an objective cause," independent of "the good or bad mood of the employer." The cause has to "exist" and has to be "exact." The "serious cause" is "a cause of a certain degree of gravity, which makes impossible, without damage to the company, the continuation of work." For a close study, see J. Pelissier, A. Supiot and A. Jeammaud, *Droit du Travail*, (Dalloz 2008), 582–595.

67 Mayotte is an overseas *département* of France established on 31 March 2011. Some 95% of its population is Muslim, and even if the French Civil Code is applied to the population, a special statute that uses Islamic Law exists, and the Mahorais people can choose between both. More information available at www.outre-mer.gouv.fr/?presentation-mayotte.html.

68 Cour de cassation, Labor Division, 24 March 1998.

69 Own translation ("*L'employeur ne commet aucune faute en demandant au salarié d'exécuter la tâche pour laquelle il a été embauché.*").

70 Own translation ("*L'employeur est tenu de respecter les convictions religieuses de son salarié, celles-ci, sauf clause expresse, n'entrent pas dans le cadre du contrat de travail.*").

Hence, in absence of such a clause, the contract remained neutral and the employer only tried to preserve the interests of his company. Thus, according to the Court, the employer has no obligation to modify or accommodate the activity (i.e. separate pork from other meats or transfer him to another department) and the employee had to execute his task in the absence of a specific clause in the contract.[71]

A third case that can be mentioned concerns the dismissal of an employee of a private day nursery because of her Islamic headscarf. On 13 December 2010, the *Conseil des Prud'Hommes* of Mantes La Jolie upheld for the first time the dismissal of an employee of a private day nursery. The decision was based on a new by-law adopted by the private day nursery which provided for an obligation to respect the principle of religious neutrality[72] and went against the recommendations of the HALDE, given in a non-binding deliberation nine months before.[73] But we can wonder how the employee is supposed to stay neutral during recruitment and at the same time bring up religious needs to obtain adjustments. This vicious circle has no real legislative or case law solution.

The notion of religious accommodation to observe religious holidays or festivities has no legal foundation in the private sector—e.g. the circular letter of 1967 only applies in the public sector—and therefore remains fragile. However, to protect the employee's freedom of conscience, the employer could make adjustments to allow their employees to observe their rituals. For example, regarding the question of diet in the workplace, employers have often dealt with special needs based on religion, such as the ban on eating pork meat and the prohibition of eating fish on Fridays or during periods of fasting, and they have to take specific needs into account in the organization of the company.[74]

---

71 The *Cour de cassation* broke the ruling of the Court of Appeal of Mamoudzou (Mayotte) of 6 June 1995, whose decision ruled in favor of the claimant. Indeed, the Court of Appeal explained that in light of the specificity of Mayotte and the importance of Islam there, the employer had to warn the employee about the presence of pork meat, or to assign him to another section of the supermarket. The Court of Appeal ruled that the employer failed to protect the employee's freedom of religion and condemned the employer. Indeed, we can deduce that if the employer had taken the initiative to accommodate the employee, the latter would never have stopped work and the normal functioning of the activity would never have been affected.

72 Conseil des Prud'Hommes of Mantes La Jolie, 13 December 2010, No. 2010/856, *Mme A. c. Association Babyloup*: "*Dans l'exercice de son travail, celui-ci doit respecter et garder la neutralité d'opinion politique et confessionnelle en regard du public accueilli.*" In 2001, the president of the Association BabyLoup reaffirmed that the application of the principle of neutrality applies in the day-care nursery in a letter addressed to Mrs A.

73 Recommendation of the HALDE: *licenciement pour faute grave fondé sur le refus de la salariée d'ôter son voile*, No. 2010-82, 1 March 2010.

74 J. C. Sciberras, "Travail et religion dans l'entreprise: une cohabitation sous tension" 1 *Droit Social* 72–75 (2010): "*Il est fréquent que* la religion impose des *contraintes alimentaires ... là encore, il est fréquent de devoir en tenir compte. Pour les entreprises du bâtiment et des travaux publics, c'est même assez classique pendant le ramadan que*

In 2008 the HALDE considered the case of a jobseeker who had applied for a position as a coordinator in an association that organized educational school trips to the seaside and required staff to share meals with the children.[75] The employer had questioned the jobseeker on his diet based on religious obligations and the jobseeker had declared that he only ate *halal* meat. After the association did not recruit him, the jobseeker argued that his application was rejected because of his religious beliefs and turned to the HALDE. First, the HALDE declared unlawful any questions related to the personnel opinions (political, religious, etc.) during the recruitment process, citing Article 1132-1 of the Labor Code. But the HALDE goes further and states that the obligation imposed by the employer on the employee to follow the same diet and eat the same things as the children can create a "specific disadvantage for persons who want to follow a diet because of their religious beliefs or their medical conditions."[76] The HALDE took a different approach than the *Cour de cassation*, namely that accommodations could be made to protect the employee's freedom of conscience and religion, and that the organization of the association had to be modified in order to meet the employee's needs. Hence, the HALDE considered the refusal to recruit the person discriminatory and advised the association to create an objective procedure of recruitment based on the qualifications of applicants.

Regarding the observance of rituals, the motivation to guarantee the normal functioning of the company plays a big part. This is perhaps because religious rituals like weekly prayers might negatively affect work processes. Here, the *Cour de cassation* has decided that if an employee leaves work to pray, the law considers it a breach of the work contract that can justify a dismissal. The same goes for the observance of religious holidays. The *Cour de cassation* confirmed the dismissal of an employee who did not come to work on the day of the Muslim celebration of the *Eid Al-Adha* not only because she did not ask for an authorization of absence, but also because her absence prevented delivery of a significant shipment,[77] and her behavior was a "real and serious cause of dismissal."

Conclusion

To conclude, the principles of neutrality and *laïcité* in the public sector are deeply rooted and continue to be reinforced through the development of case

---

d'alléger la charge de travail des salariés qui l'observent, ne serait-ce que pour des raisons de sécurité du travail."

75 Recommendation of the HALDE No. 2008-10, 14 January 2008 *refus d'embauche en raison des convictions religieuses du candidat.*

76 Own translation ("*[Cette règle a pour effet] d'entraîner un désavantage particulier pour des personnes désireuses de suivre un régime alimentaire, en raison de leurs convictions religieuses ou de leur* état *de santé.*").

77 Cour de cassation, Labor Division, 16 December 1981, No. 79-41300, Dame X.

law regarding the wearing of distinctive religious symbols by public servants. In practice, however, adherence to these principles coexists with willingness to protect public employees' freedom of religious expression. In particular, some accommodations have been foreseen for the observance of religious holidays and religious rituals by civil servants (Circular letter FP No. 901, 23 September 1967). Still, the principles of continuity of public service and of the obligation to maintain its normal functioning will always prevail over the exercise of religious rights, and accommodation will be refused by the department in cases of perceived threats to the continuity of public service or its normal functioning.

In the private sector, we can note the tendency to introduce a touch of *laïcité* in the case law governing relations between the employer and the employee regarding the expression of religion in the company. Even though the principle of freedom to exercise a religion is the rule, and if Article 1132-1 of the Labor Code prohibits any kind of discrimination, we can nevertheless observe a trend of *laïcisation* of the private sector and a willingness of employers to apply the rules of neutrality and *laïcité* in their companies.[78]

The case law fluctuations are mainly due to legal gaps that the legislator refuses to close and the courts' search for a balance between various interests, such as the expression of freedom of religion and the normal functioning of the company. Trying to find proper balances between the two principles, the judge proceeds case by case. For instance, it seems that the fact of public contact is important for assessing the proportionality of a dismissal based on the wearing of a headscarf.[79]

The HALDE on its part has tried to find compromises between the protection of employees' religious rights and company interests. Witnessing this growing tendency of employers to try to include a clause of *laïcité* in their by-laws,[80] the HALDE had to reiterate the principle of religious expression in the private sector, while defining the limits of its application,[81] and "the appreciation of the situation has to be done *in concreto*."[82] The HALDE also recommended that the situation has to be analyzed "case-by-case" by the employer, and encouraged the employer and the employee to find a consensus, or at least an alternative way to resolve the

78 See the recommendation of the HALDE of 3 March 2008 *relative à l'intégration dans le règlement intérieur d'une entreprise de la grande distribution d'une clause visant à interdire à tous les salariés le port d'un signe religieux ou politique*.

79 For example, the judge of the Court of Appeal of Paris (Court of Appeal of Paris, 16 March 2001, *Madame Charmi* v. *SA Hamon*) confirmed the dismissal of an employee of a grocery store who refused to take off her *hijab* (See C. Puigelier, "Bien fondé d'un licenciement reposant sur le refus d'une salariée d'abadonner le port ostentatoire du foulard islamique," 31 *Semaine Juridique Entreprise* 1339 (2001), 1339–1342).

80 Recommendation of the HALDE *relative à l'intégration dans le règlement intérieur d'une entreprise de la grande distribution d'une clause visant à interdire à tous les salariés le port d'un signe religieux ou politique*, No. 2008-32 of 3 March 2008.

81 Recommendation of the HALDE No. 2011-67 *sur le fait religieux* of 28 March 2011, 9.

82 *Id.* at 9.

conflict. The HALDE was frequently criticized for its stance on this issue, and it remains to be seen how the successor, the *Défenseur des Droits*, will fill the role with regard to the prohibition of religious discrimination and the place of religion in the workplace.

Chapter 10

Jewish Women in the Belgian Workplace: An Anthropological Perspective

Efrat Tzadik*

Introduction

This research introduces an anthropological perspective to the debate on religious identity and the workplace. In particular, it examines the relationship between Jewish identity and practices and the workplace in Belgium, with a focus on gender issues. Thanks to in-depth interviews with a number of Jewish women in Brussels about their daily experiences in the workplace, and extensive field work in this community, valuable and generally difficult-to-access data regarding Jewish women's workplace participation, perceptions and experiences has been collected and analyzed. There is a complex relationship between Jewish identity, practices and the perception of the respondents as it relates to the workplace and their own position.

Perceived hostility towards Israel and the Jewry is a recurrent issue amongst the respondents. As Judaism is often connected to the Israeli state and the current political climate, individual Jewish women are sometimes confronted with unpleasant or negative comments or experiences in the workplace. Besides forming a strong deterrent for many of the respondents to participate in the mainstream workforce, this also puts a lot of pressure on those women working for non-Jewish organizations.

To a certain extent, Jewish practices are adapted, modified and negotiated by the working Jewish women in order to meet the demands of dominant norms in the modern Belgian workplace. In addition, the "coping mechanisms" that are applied by the respondents are frequently gender specific and family motivated.

1. Methodology and research questions

In order to gain insight in the dynamics between work and religious identity in the case of Jewish women in Brussels, both interviews and anthropological fieldwork were carried out in the community. This chapter is drawn from doctoral research

* I wish to thank in particular Katayoun Alidadi for her insightful comments and suggestions for improvement of this chapter.

that looks at identity and the notion of belonging for Jewish women in Belgium and, more specifically, in Brussels. An initial respondent pool was established through personal contacts, after which a "snowball" technique was used to broaden the scope of the research pool. All women participating in the research were very accepting and wanted to be interviewed. Some liked the idea of talking about subjects they do not often get the occasion to reflect on.

The field research was conducted over a period of three years in the Jewish and Israeli communities in Brussels by way of participatory observation.[1] This intensive field work[2] led to productive and dynamic interviews, as it allowed trust to be gained and the comfort levels of the respondents to be increased, encouraging them to increased openness.

Personal interviews using open-ended questions allowed for the collection of workplace data and life stories from 29 Israeli and Jewish women by the researcher, herself a Jewish and Israeli woman. Oakly suggests that an effective way to obtain information from the field is when the interviewer is also willing to share information.[3] Grossman and Chester support this assumption, stating that unveiling people's traits is best achieved when the relationship between the interviewer and the interviewee is non-hierarchical and when the interviewer is prepared to invest his or her personal identity in the actual relationship.[4]

Skevington has pointed out that women are more aware of emotions. There are occasions when people feel the need to access their emotions when they experience various social situations.[5] Furthermore, Edwards illustrates the point of researching sensitive and delicate subjects, such as interpersonal relations.[6]

1 A full immersion in the field is crucial. Participatory observation enables the researcher to learn a lot about the respondents' behaviors and attitudes through daily interaction with them. There is an understanding of nuances and unspoken language. Fieldwork also allows the researcher to establish a good relationship with the respondents before the interviews and therefore creates an atmosphere of trust. In addition, as respondents' behavior may not always be congruent with their replies given during the interviews, this problem may be attenuated by complementary field work in which actions can be observed and tested against the answers during interviews. For further discussion see W. Foddy, *Constructing Questions for Interviews and Questionnaires: Theory and Practice In Social Research* (Cambridge University Press 1993).

2 In order to have a full grasp of the field, the researcher participated in many events such as private and public parties, lectures and trips. The researcher also met with people from the Jewish community on a daily basis and spent time discussing relevant issues with them.

3 A. Oakly, "Interviewing Women: a Contradiction in Terms," in *Doing Feminist Research* (H. Roberts, ed., Routledge & Kegan Paul 1981), 30–61.

4 H. Y. Grossman and N. L. Chester, *The Experience and the Meaning of Work in Women's Lives* (Lawrence Erlbaum Associates Publishers 1990).

5 S. Skevington, "A Place for Emotions in Social Identity Theory," in *The Social Identity of Women* (S. Skevington and D. Baker, eds, Sage Publications 1989).

6 R. Edwards, "An Education in Interviewing – Placing the Researcher and the Research," in *Researching Sensitive Topics* (C. M. Renzetti and R. M. Lee. London, eds,

Therefore, the interview questions were related to the situation of Jewish women in the Belgian Diaspora and their family situation in general, as well as their work aspirations. For the group of women employed outside the house, interviews inquired into the ways in which the women seek to reconcile Jewish religious and cultural practices in the workplace in particular. Through these questions, we sought to gain insight into the dynamic relationship between Jewish identity and intensity of religious practice, on the one hand, and the employment choices, perceptions and experiences on the other hand. We also inquired into the influence of being part of a religious minority on daily interactions in the workplace, for instance with colleagues.

Before delving into the findings of this anthropological research, some background with regard to the Jewish community in Belgium will be useful in framing the larger picture in which the respondents make their workplace decisions.

2. Background: The Jewish community in Belgium

In order to understand the complexity of the current relationship between the Jewish community of Belgium and the Belgian workplace, a look at the history of the Jewish population in Belgium is necessary.

While the origins of the Jewish community in Belgium date back several centuries, this concerns a largely new community in the sense that it had to be rebuilt after the Second World War. The first Jewish arrivals in Belgium started with the Roman conquests. During the thirteenth century Jews suffered from hostility, which included being blamed for causing the "Black Death" plague. Most Jews died during the plague, and those who survived were eventually killed by the local population.[7] During the sixteenth century, following the Spanish and Portuguese expulsions, Jewish settlers returned to Antwerp and started trading in diamonds, after which they became a strong economic force. During the seventeenth century, Ashkenazi Jews[8] arrived when Austria governed what is now Belgian territory.

After Belgium declared its independence in 1831, relations with Judaism were established and Judaism was recognized as a religion by the state.[9] The Jewish community concentrated its presence in the two cities of Brussels and Antwerp, with a smaller presence in the rest of the country. During the Second World War, Belgian Jews were sent to concentration camps, with few returning.

The Jewish community in Belgium currently consists of approximately 35,000 people; this number is estimated according to different sources. The Jewish

Sage Publications 1993), 181–196.

7 A. Oreck, "The Virtual Jewish History Tour – Belgium. Jewish Virtual Library; the American-Israeli Cooperative Enterprise," in *Jewish Virtual Library*, available at dev.jewishvirtuallibrary.org.

8 Ashkenazi Jews are Jews coming from different countries in Eastern Europe.

9 A. Oreck, *supra*, note 7.

community in Brussels is predominantly made up of second and third generation holocaust survivors. This creates a very strong ethos of survival but also a sense of insecurity, strikingly noted by one of the respondents:

> We are looking to stay together because it is in our history … We are different due to what we and our ancestors experienced in our history. We are not secure. (Mina)

This research indicates that within this community, a distinction can be made between "Belgian Jews" and "Israeli Jews," who often reside in Belgium only temporarily. The Jewish community in Brussels is partially made up of Israeli citizens, mainly expatriates.[10] Most Israelis came to Brussels because of the job of one of the partners, in most cases the husband's. Others came to Brussels to study, and then stayed. Most working Israelis in Brussels are employed in Jewish or Israeli institutions with a special working status. A small number have a Belgian work permit through marriage, and even fewer hold a second European passport and work permit.

The relationship between the Jewish and the expatriate Jewish community is somewhat ambivalent in Belgium. Expatriates do not always feel welcomed by the local Jewish community.[11]

3. Jewish women in the Brussels workplace

The pool of respondents interviewed for this research consists of 29 participants, all women from the Jewish community in Brussels. All respondents positioned themselves as belonging to the middle to upper class, and are between the ages of 29 and 49. Many are married and all of them are mothers of relatively young children. 25 of the women hold university degrees ranging from law, psychology and education to geography, translation and so on. Belgian Jews obtained their degrees mainly in Belgium, while Israeli women obtained their degrees mainly in Israel. Three of the four women who do not hold higher education degrees can be considered as orthodox practitioners. One woman, Ada, is a convert who did not complete her education as she longed early on to form a family. The respondents come from various Jewish religious groups, relating to their intensity of practice

10 Israeli Jews settled in different places in the world. According to the Israeli Ministry of Migration, there are approximately 750,000 people holding an Israeli passport abroad—as quoted by N. Guttman and G. Beckerman, "Israelis Debate Giving Expats a vote they don't seem to want …," *Forward* (Jewish daily online newspaper) 17 February 2010, available at www.forward.com.

11 Similar feelings are expressed around the world. See, for example, D. Brent, *Identity and Integration Among Israeli Migrants in Canada* (MA Diss., University of British Columbia (Canada) 2009).

and beliefs. From very orthodox women to "atheist Jews," in general the women can be divided into three groups. The first group consists of "Belgian Jews" who are part of the local Jewish community and speak French, and in many cases Dutch as well. These women grew up in Belgium and were exposed to the general culture in the society, often attending a Belgian university. The second group is made up of a number of women who are (expatriate) Israelis who can be qualified as an ethnic group.[12] In contrast, these women often do not speak French or Dutch. The third group consists of Jewish women who came to Belgium from other countries such as France and Canada.

Significantly, 13 of the women are not employed outside the house. Of the 16 women who are employed, nine work in fields unrelated to their studies. A significant segment works in their family businesses (e.g. real estate, shops, movie industry, etc.) and reported facing barriers in their search for suitable employment.

Based on the composition and work situations of the respondents, a further division into four groups was made, and the perceptions and experiences of these women are thus presented per group. The first group consists of women who are not participating in the Belgian employment market. The second group is made up of women who are self-employed or work in or for their family businesses. The third group consists of women who work in Jewish or Israeli institutions. The second and third groups are presented together since they show significant similarities. The fourth group consists of women who work in public institutions such as public schools, the European Commission or the private sector. This last group is the smallest, with only six women.

The women are referred to by their fictive names in the interest of safeguarding their privacy. In order to allow these women to "speak for themselves" direct quotes from interviews are used.

3.1. Group 1: Women not participating in the workforce

A relatively large number of women are not working outside the house. Various reasons can be identified for this. A first category of reasons are the legal or structural obstacles. A second set of reasons relates to personal choice or circumstantial situations. In addition, there are sometimes certain obstacles such as language. This group mainly concerns Israelis or other expatriates who in many cases did work when they lived in Israel. For instance, Dorit, 41 years old and a mother of three, worked as a psychologist in Israel but has no permit to work as a psychologist in Belgium. Coming to Brussels with no knowledge of the language and with no work permit left her in a position where she was financially dependent on her husband's income. It is important to note, however, that there are women

12 "An ethnic group defined through the dynamic interaction between ethnic identity and identification preserving borderlines and moving within them" (L. Lev Ari, *The American Dream – For Men Only? Gender, Immigration and the Assimilation of Israelis in the United States* (LFB Scholarly Publishing LLC 2008), 104).

who are happy with this situation. It can be said that women who work have more authority than women who do not. And, in the modern world, women with a career tend to hold more modern values of individualism. Some women expressed this, like Neomie, 42 years old and formerly a lawyer in Israel:

> When you don't work, you are depending on your husband, financially. At the beginning, I wasn't comfortable "wasting" his money. It was a strange situation where I felt a little dependent on him.

Very few of the women have found a job in an English-speaking company. One such woman is 38-year-old Limor who works for a communication company. Limor, whose working language is English, does not speak French.

A number of women also choose to be(come) housewives. The fact that they do not work outside the house, or work part-time, facilitates the management of the household, in particular during days when children are off school due to holidays and the Jewish calendar. Some women do not necessarily want to climb the work hierarchy.[13] Instead, they prefer to invest fully in their children. Migrating to another country can, sometimes, be "a way out" for women in societies which present them with a double bind: namely between, on the one hand, the responsibility for taking care of the children and, on the other hand, being a successful career woman. Living abroad, they do not struggle with making this decision.

Rona, a 40-year-old woman who worked in a big communications company back in Israel, explains:

> In Israel I worked a lot, I was non-stop at work. I didn't have a life. I just worked. Coming to Belgium put things in a better perspective; as I didn't need to work I stayed home with the children. I like it. Now, when we'll go back to Israel I will never go back to such a demanding job.

3.1.1. Gender aspect and the mother role

The domestic sphere plays a significant role in the lives of most of the respondents, whatever the intensity of their religious adherence and practices. Being a Jewish mother and working in non-Jewish settings raises some particular gender-related issues. When the children attend a Jewish school, the women have to take the different holiday schedule into account. The children will be off on Jewish holidays—whether the family celebrates those or not—and a working mother has to find either a child-care solution or take time off work. This dualism results in mothers—as opposed to fathers—having to negotiate more days off with their employers.

13 L. Bailey, "Bridging Home and Work in the Transition to Motherhood – a Discursive Study," 7 *The European Journal of Women's Studies* 53 (2000), 53–70.

For instance, Limor is an Israeli woman who is married to a Belgian Jewish man. She holds a Belgian work permit and works at an international communications company. She compares the situation she faces now to what she was used to in Israel:

> In Israel you don't choose. When it is a holiday, it is a holiday. The country shuts down.

In contrast, in Belgium she has to make conscious choices about Jewish holidays. She has decided for instance not to take time off on Shavuot (a Jewish holiday that takes place seven weeks after Passover) but only on the three important holidays:

> There are three holidays that are important to me: *Rosh Hashanah*, *Kippur*, and Passover. These are the days that I'm off work. All the rest ... It gets more intense as the children grow up. If at the beginning I said "never mind, I'll take a babysitter." Now, I take a day off during these three holidays.

This is an example of a "coping mechanism" that Limor has adopted, namely to make conscious decisions about the extent to which she holds on to Jewish traditions in a Belgian context, working under a largely Christian-inspired schedule. Indeed, in response to a number of obstacles or difficulties noted above, the respondents have adopted a variety of such "coping mechanisms." Their aim is generally to try to hold on to religious or cultural practices they feel are important to them, but this also implies that these women have to deviate and—to a certain extent—depart from their traditional practices in order to reconcile their personal life with their professional one. Where the woman is very traditional or orthodox it is easier not to have to find ways to reconcile the two aspects of life, and to stay at home and take care of her children, even though it benefits the family to have a certain level of financial and economic stability.

Certain gender-specific community pressures can also play a role in the decision of women not to work. In the Jewish and Israeli cultures, women play an essential role in preserving the continuity of cultural patterns, family norms and values.[14] Migrant women tend to surround themselves in the domestic sphere. Freedman, who conducted her research on Turkish immigrant women in Germany, states that Turkish women do not integrate fully in local society.[15] They rather tend to stay within their own community and do not integrate in any real sense. They might feel rootless after a while, and feel that they do not belong anywhere. Khater shows that the Lebanese migrant society in the US places the family as a central aspect of their authentic identity.[16] Women who do work face a lot of pressure from their

---

14 L. Lev Ari, *supra*, note 12.

15 J. Freedman, *Gender and Insecurity: Migrant Woman in Europe* (Ashgate 2003).

16 A. F. Khater, "Queen of the House? Making immigrants Lebanese Families in the Mahjar," in *Family History in the Middle East Household, Property and Gender* (D. Beshara, ed., State University of N.Y. Press 2003).

cultural group. These findings are supported by research by Lev Ari concerning Israelis in the US and by Scrinzi on female immigrants in Italy, where it was shown that women with no specific training often entered the domestic sphere.[17] Gerson, analyzing the process of "turning to the domestic sphere," demonstrated that 60% of the women she interviewed did not envision themselves as being in the domestic sphere, but moved into it gradually.[18]

In Israeli society, there is an increase in the number of women in the workplace. However, employed women still invest 66% to 100% more time in the domestic sphere than men.[19] There is a common expectation in Israeli society that women should take care of the children and domestic chores. In contrast, men are far less likely to do housework. This gender segregation continues when migrating, so it is expected that the woman gives up her career or skips a day at work to take care of a sick child.[20] In particular, Israeli mothers who choose to work face a lot of "unspoken" pressure from other women from the same cultural circuit to be "a good mother," and social expectations are still for the mothers to take care of the children and to provide, in the words of Cheal,[21] "intensive parenting." This might offer some explanation as to the high number of non-working expatriate women. Nevertheless, some Belgian Jewish women also chose not to work:

> I don't need to work. I worked hard in the past and now, I don't need any more. I go to the gym, I see friends. (Simon)

3.2. Groups 2 and 3: Self-employed women, women working for their family businesses or working in Jewish or Israeli institutions

A number of women work in their family businesses. These range from real estate to the movie industry, and others. Some women work for their parents, like Mina, a 38-year-old woman who works in construction. Others work with their husbands, like Danielle, a 36-year-old woman who has two adult children, and Ada, a 47-year-old woman who has one child. Both Danielle and Ada consider themselves "intensive parents." Some women do not officially work in the business and do not earn any money of their own but still help out with some of the work.

---

17 F. Scrinzi, "The Globalization of Domestic Work: Women Migrants and Neo Domesticity," in *Gender and Insecurity: Migrant Women in Europe* (J. Freedman, ed., Ashgate 2003).

18 K. Gerson, "What do Women want from Men?—Men Influence on Women's Work and Family choices," in *Changing Men: New Directions in Research on Men and Masculinity* (M. S. Kimmel, ed., Sage Publications 1987), 115–129.

19 U. Rebhun and L. L. Ari, *American Israelis: Migration, Transnationalism, and Diasporic Identity* (Brill Academic Publishers 2010).

20 M. Eichler, *Family Shifts. Family Policies and Gender Equality* (Oxford University Press 1997).

21 D. Cheal, *Sociology of Family Life* (Palgrave 2002).

The fact of working in a family business does not necessarily mean that a woman is more in touch with her Jewish identity. In certain cases, it is the opposite. Galit, who currently works in her father's company, recalls about her parents:

> My father hides his Judaism. My parents are anti-community. They didn't want to be part of it. My mother [an Israeli] never spoke Hebrew to us or to the grandchildren … they wanted to assimilate.

Galit, who was raised in Belgium and can be considered a "Belgian Jew," has an Israeli mother. However, she notes that her mother spoke French rather than Hebrew to her children, and she never stressed their Israeli identity.

For some Jewish women, working in Jewish or Israeli organizations offers a number of advantages. For instance, neither negotiation nor specific accommodation is needed when it comes to observing the Sabbath.[22] This makes it a good midway option for many women who want to work but who are deterred by the prospect of confrontations and compromises in the mainstream work setting. Orthodox women prefer to work in Jewish or Israeli institutions which do not challenge their Judaism. In these workplaces, they have more freedom to express their religious identity.

While women who work in non-Jewish settings frequently feel they have to represent their group, surprisingly even women like Rina who work in a Jewish workplace feel they have to explain their religion and culture on an everyday basis. Rina works in a Jewish school which employs a large number of non-Jewish persons, and she feels that even if she does not agree with the position of the Israeli government, she has to defend it. She calls herself a "representative of the Israeli state:"

> I feel as if I am the representative of Judaism, I also feel like the ambassador of Israel, especially if something happens in Israel.

Ruth works as a religion teacher in a public school, for the "Consistoire Central Israélite de Belgique/Centraal Israëlitisch Consistorie van België,"[23] and the great Rabbi of Brussels. She explains:

> Working for a Jewish institution, I don't need to explain that I need days off for my holidays. The school received a list of all the Jewish holidays so they know in advance.

---

22 The Jewish Sabbath starts on Friday night, an hour before sunset. In the winter, the days of Sabbath start very early in Belgium. When working in a non-Jewish workplace, it is very difficult for practicing women to leave their workplace early. Woman should light the Sabbath candles at a specific time. During the Belgian winter it could be as early as four o'clock in the afternoon.

23 The official representative of the Jewish community of Belgium.

Depending on the business they are in, and the contacts they have with the non-Jewish community, women in these categories share some of the experiences of the women in the previous group. For self-employed women the situation is easier as they need no permission from anyone to set their schedule and meet the constraints of religious holidays. For instance, Elie, an independent psychologist, says:

> I take days off when I want. I book my schedule so I don't have the problem of asking for days off.

Jewish women who work in non-Jewish institutions must negotiate their days off. It is therefore easier for a Jewish woman to work in a Jewish or Israeli institution or to be self-employed.

3.3. Group 4: Women working in public institutions, such as public schools or the European Commission, or in the private sector

Six of the 29 women fall under this category. Surprisingly, only one of the women works in a private company. There could be various explanations for this: in general, working women, as explained above, prefer working where it is easier to negotiate religious needs even if they are not orthodox practitioners of their religion. When a Jewish woman is looking for a job she has to have enough flexibility to manage the additional school holidays of her children. The Brussels setting does explain the appeal of the European institutions for work opportunities. For women who hold less strict interpretations of Jewish traditions and practices, work in public institutions is considered a good option, even though according to the participants it is not always easy. As Penina wrote in an article for *Wizo*[24] magazine of April 2010:

> For those who observe the *Shabat* it is difficult to explain to their employer that in the winter they have to leave early and that it is not flexible ... and this without talking about the enormous amount of holidays that falls on different days during the year.

Working in Belgium, whether in a private or public setting, in any case raises several obstacles that need to be overcome. In many cases these obstacles are strongly related to working in a Belgian workplace, but there are some that are related to working with non-Jews as well. These obstacles include perceived lack of knowledge or disinterest in Judaism and Jewish people.

Eleven respondents state that they feel that public knowledge of Judaism is "very basic," and in many cases they had to explain certain aspects of Judaism to

---

24 *Wizo* is an international organization for Jewish women which has a branch in Belgium. They use their magazine to discuss relevant subjects to the community of women in Belgium.

their colleagues. Overall, there is a very strong feeling that non-Jews just do not know very much about Judaism or base opinions on incorrect information, making it more difficult for the women to build relationships in the workplace. Galit, 40 years old, who works at her father's business, says:

> There is nothing to do but they [non-Jews] don't understand us as other Jews do.

Ada, who works with her husband occasionally, related this to inadequate reporting in the media:

> People don't know much. They judge with what they hear, read and see in the press.

A number of respondents clearly find this frustrating. According to Chaya, 32 years old, who works in a Jewish institution related to the European Commission:

> The biggest thing is ignorance. They really, really don't know … there is also "I don't want to know." There is Anti-Semitism, "it's the Jew's fault" … the most is "I don't know who you are; I don't know why you're doing things."

Chaya does engage in conversations with her colleagues. She thinks that the way Jews act from day to day, including food restrictions or behavioral codes, should be explained to other cultural groups. Sigal, a 49-year-old businesswoman, reports that there is also a lack of curiosity:

> I find that they are not curious. If I wasn't Jewish, I would be more curious. I try to explain things to them. I sent them an email with an explanation about the high holidays, as I was away from the office. I wished them a "happy new year," they laugh that it is in September … They haven't grasped it.

Mina, a 38-year-old woman who works for her father, on the other hand, does find her colleagues to be curious about Jewish customs and traditions:

> They want to know what we celebrate. What does it represent? Why are we different?

3.3.1 Judaism and the (politics of the) state of Israel are often confused[25]

Related to the perceived lack of knowledge about Judaism is the widespread confusion women find among their colleagues about, on the one hand, Judaism and, on the other hand, the news and politics with regard to the state of Israel. Some note that their Belgian colleagues connect Judaism immediately with Israel and sometimes blame the Jewish women for what is happening in Israel. Ilanit, a 51-year-old woman who works in a multinational company in Brussels, says:

> Many people don't know the difference between being Jewish and being Israeli. It shocks me. They criticize Israel but by doing this, criticize the Jews. They don't understand that Judaism is a religion.

Mina, another respondent, similarly says:

> They don't distinguish between being a Jew and an Israeli. I have explained that I have a nationality and a religion. Sometimes they just don't know or weren't in contact with many Jews. They think we are much more than what we are.

3.3.2. Strangers and community

In the context where members of two contrasting (minority and majority) communities and cultures meet and communicate on a daily basis, issues of minority identity frequently come to the surface. It is as if the contrasting Belgian context makes the Jewish identity of these women come out much more prominently than is the case, for instance, for the women working in Jewish organizations. For some respondents this creates a sense of "us versus them" which is further strengthened by the existence of a strong internal community sense within the Jewish community in Brussels. Limor, a 38-year-old Israeli woman, who works at a communications company, feels like she is a "stranger" at work:

> They know I'm a stranger. I feel like it as well. Everyone at work knows I am an Israeli. This is not something I hide.

Sigal, a 49-year-old businesswoman, would agree with this feeling, linking it to the internal sense of community that exists among the Jews in Brussels:

> They are surprised that you have so many contacts, that you can call someone for advice even if you don't know him personally … they don't understand how it works. It worries them. I think this is the main reason for racism. They

25 The fact that non-Jews relate the Jews to Israel enforces the idea that a place is linked to identity, as put forward by K. Dovey, "An Ecology of Place and Placemaking," in *Place and Placemaking* (K. Dovey, P. Downton and G. Missingham, eds, Paper 85 Proceedings RMIT 1985), 93–109.

> are afraid of "groups." For every small thing they think of how you got this information. For us, to know someone who knows someone is enough to call.

The fact that Sigal feels strongly that non-Jewish people look at her as part of a larger group is described in the literature on social identity. Sociologists currently see identities as "dynamic, positional, hybrid and constructed within relations of power."[26] Social identity creates a strong sense of commitment.[27] Where people derive their self-image from group membership they will compare the group to which they belong favorably with other relevant groups. This process contributes to a positive social identity.[28]

On the other hand, some women see themselves as being part of a minority in general. Eva is a doctor in Brussels, working in a private clinic but associated with a big hospital. Her clients are Israelis, Belgian Jews and Belgians. She is not related to the Judaism tradition and refers to herself a "historical Jew." Eva sees herself as related to the history of the Jewish people rather than to traditional Judaism. She expresses it by stating that at the hospital where she works, there are good relations amongst the individuals belonging to various minorities:

> We, people who come from different minority groups in the hospital, have very nice contact; it is something like between minorities.

3.3.3 Hostility and harassment in the workplace

Some of the women have been confronted with what they perceive as racist remarks in the workplace. Naama, who is a psychologist in a public hospital, says:

> Where I work now I don't have any problems but in another job a person told me to go back from where I came from.

Eva, who is now a self-employed doctor, recalls that during her specialization period at one of the Brussels hospitals, she had to put up with negative comments like "you, the Jews" from a senior colleague. After a long time of remaining silent about this treatment, she decided to complain, which put an end to it.

3.3.4 Evading the topic of Israel

Most participants say they prefer to avoid discussions or arguments about Israel. Since the issues are complicated and some women do not feel they have enough knowledge or they do not want to get into conflicts in the workplace, they avoid

---

26 H. Easthope, "Fixed Identities in a Mobile World? The Relationship between Mobility, Place and Identity," 16 *Identities: Global studies in Culture and Power* 61 (2009), 61–82.

27 B. Doosje, N. Ellemers and R. Spears, *Social Identity* (Blackwell Publishers 2000).

28 *Id.* at p. 26.

the topic. History explains why women tend to avoid arguments and any tense situations. Danielle, 36 years old, says:

> I leave these arguments to my husband … I don't think I know enough.

Those women who do answer feel they are put in a position where they have to explain and defend Israel despite the fact that they do not fully agree with its policy. Sigal, a 49-year-old businesswoman, says she tries to explain things if the issue of Israel comes up, but most of the time she feels "it's too complicated." For others, holding back seems impossible and even presents the risk of escalating conflicts with colleagues. Penina, who works in the European Parliament, says:

> I try to avoid the subject of Israel with non-Jews. They don't understand the meaning. Once I said something very moderate and one of my colleagues, a Moroccan woman, said "these are our brothers and we have to defend them." I said: "What are you talking about? Do you really understand what's going on there?" I changed the subject immediately.

3.3.5 Hiding their Jewish identity in the workplace

Some women contrast their own experiences with that of their family, for instance mentioning that their fathers hide their Judaism in the workplace. Sophie, who works in a non-Jewish institution, says:

> My father always hides his identity. He never says that he is Jewish or that we went to Israel on holiday. Thanks to my husband, I never hide my Judaism. I have the experience of my father who had to hide all the time. I think things are clearer when you don't need to hide.

However, sometimes encounters with non-Jewish colleagues strengthen the women's feeling of belonging and Jewish identity. Ana, who worked as a teacher, says:

> My first identity? Israeli! It's because we live here [in Belgium]. It's because you always feel that you need, in certain situations, to hide it. It's because other people see you as such.

3.3.6 Timing and negotiation

Jewish practices and rules in some cases conflict with the dominant, mainstream rules and norms. There are a number of religious and cultural practices that in particular collide with Belgian workplace norms. First, Jewish holidays and the Sabbath do not always fit in with the work schedule. Second, adhering to a kosher diet is rendered difficult in the work setting, especially when cafeteria food presents few options. Third, very common Belgian gestures, such as kissing or shaking hands, present particular difficulties for Jewish women.

Since official days of rest in Belgium do not correspond with Jewish holidays,[29] most of the women who participated in this research take important Jewish holidays such as *Kippur* as a day off from work. When they work in non-Jewish workplaces, they have to ask for permission, and it is a question of negotiation between the woman and her employer. As noted, when children are attending Jewish schools (where there are both Christian and Jewish holidays) their need to take time off is even more pressing. One of the solutions women use is to take these days as part of their yearly vacation days. For those women who work in the European Parliament, it seems to be easier. According to Penina:

> There are rules that there is no "religion of the EU." We have the Catholic holidays but if a person from another religion wants to take a day off on his holidays, they have to give it [to you].

Even in this context, some negotiation is required. Penina continues that even though there is this rule, her boss asked her to take a day off for *Yom Kippur* on another day:

> He asks me to take it [day off for *Yom Kippur*] on another day. I told him no. I can't change the day of the holiday. He had to agree.

In certain circumstances, women need not negotiate the days off, for instance when they work in a non-Jewish institution, such as a school, but are connected to a Jewish institution such as the "Consistoire Central Israélite de Belgique." In that case, the holidays are fixed and known in advance. Ruth, an orthodox Jew who works as a Jewish teacher in a non-Jewish school, says:

> I'm working as a Jewish teacher so there is no problem. The inspector of Judaism has already sent my dates. There are difficult days like the evening of *Succot* [according to Jewish law, the holiday starts the evening before with sunset]. I thought the whole morning when I had to cook. I organize. I don't ask for another day off.

Other women also choose to limit their need to ask for extra days off by planning ahead of time for Jewish holidays. Ruth, for instance, invites many people to her Sabbath meals, for which she needs a very long time for preparations. She notes that as Jewish law does not allow cooking on the Sabbath, it demands a lot of planning in advance to have everything according to schedule.

---

29 The ten Belgian official public holidays are New Year's Day, Easter Monday, Labor Day, Ascension, Pentecost Monday, National holiday, Assumption of Mary, All Saints, Armistice Day, Christmas. On other days, employers are not obliged to give their employees a day off.

3.3.7 Socializing over food and handshakes

Both Israeli and Jewish women respondents claim that they have very good relationships at their working place, but only a few of the participants say that they have good friends at the workplace with whom they also socialize outside of working hours.

It is noteworthy that several respondents say that their wish to eat kosher keeps them from socializing with their colleagues. Jewish women interpret kosher restrictions differently. Some women will, for instance, eat from any local butcher, but will not have pork and will not mix milk and meat. When they feel comfortable enough to eat in non-kosher restaurants, they find practical solutions, so they can better socialize with colleagues. According to Penina:

> When I eat I choose according to what there is. For vegetarians, it is more difficult than my *Kashrus* (Kosher rules). I find it great to explain everything regarding food restrictions.

Sophie similarly explains that during Passover, a holiday when it is forbidden by the Jewish law to eat bread or any flour products, she just eats salads, and that way avoids any questions about her diet as nobody notices it. For Ruth, adherence to a kosher diet functions more like a pretext not to socialize with Belgian colleagues:

> My school organizes dinners three times a year. You don't know how happy I am to say "no," I prefer to have something with meaning. I don't feel like sitting and eating with them.

Several religious women mentioned that they do not feel comfortable shaking hands with men, although this is a very common gesture amongst Belgians. They find themselves in embarrassing situations where a man presents his hand. This can happen whenever a woman is in a work situation where she encounters non-Jewish men. Merav, a 27-year-old orthodox woman who works in a Jewish institution but has contacts with non-Jews, says:

> If someone tries to shake my hand, I have learned to put my hands crossed on my chest and bend a little. When people see that you respect them, they respect that.

In contrast to Merav, Ruth says that she prefers not to put the person who comes to shake her hand in an embarrassing position and shakes his hand despite certain interpretations of the Jewish law prohibiting this action.

3.3.8 Remaining in the domestic sphere

Considering a number of obstacles noted above that are difficult—or impossible—to overcome for some, especially more orthodox, women, not working outside the home and investing completely in the domestic sphere can be considered the "ultimate coping mechanism."

Concluding remarks

The intercultural exchange that some Jewish women experience in the Belgian workplace provides these women a place where they have to question the way they see Judaism. Questions asked by non-Jewish colleagues place the women in a position where they have to explain and justify to themselves and to others their Jewish identity and practices. The women who are most willing to step outside their comfort zone in this way and participate in the Belgian workplace are most confronted with issues of identity affirmation. In talking about these issues and in order to explain aspects of their religion and culture to their colleagues they, in some cases, have to learn about themselves. The exchange regarding Jewish life provides a constant reminder of their particular (group) identity, and encounters with the "others" reinforce their separate and distinct identity. The way Jewish women think the "others" look at them makes these women investigate the way they look at their own identity.

There is a difference between, on the one hand, orthodox women who stick firmly to their identity and practices, such as refusing to shake hands with unknown men, and have firmer stances on how they see other people and, on the other hand, women with somewhat "hybrid identities" who are comfortable with interpreting and experiencing their Judaism in a much more flexible way. These last women, for instance, eat kosher meat but will socialize with colleagues and join them in non-kosher restaurants, eating dairy products, vegetables or fish.

The research also demonstrates the relevance of the gender factor in seeking accommodation from generally applicable workplace rules or practices. In particular, Jewish women with children enrolled in Jewish schools are confronted with the Jewish calendar in a very tangible way as they are in the primary caretaker role. Certain gestures, such as shaking hands, are problematic for women in particular. On the other hand, the dress issue did not come up frequently in the interviews while it could be expected that it is an issue for Jewish men wearing a *kippa* (a small hat some Jewish men wear).

This research illustrates how experiencing new cultures gives rise to a number of "coping mechanisms" for Jewish women and by extension for the Jewish community as a whole. While exploring whether and how these workplace "coping mechanisms" create new ways of practicing Judaism in Diaspora settings is beyond the scope of this chapter, the findings do support the idea that decisions and practices of working Jewish women to a significant extent also affect the wider family life within the Jewish community.

These experiences of a sample of women in the Jewish community of Brussels invite the reader into a wider consideration of the situation of the Jewish community in Belgium. It indicates that conducting research on Jewish men in the Belgium workplace and on other ethnic and religious groups who arrived more recently would provide similarly rich results.

Overall, women who are employed experience good relationships in their workplace. Still, there are ways forward which would deter women less from entering the workplace or would affect the current need for adopting "coping mechanisms." Field research can help identify ways to improve the workplace setting. For instance, one of the recurring themes in this research is the fact that respondents note a lack of knowledge within the general society regarding Judaism. In the light of the findings of the research, we believe that increasing knowledge and awareness of the predominant religions and related practices will lead to greater tolerance and comfort in the workplace. Therefore, we could suggest investigating this further and looking into ways of improving general knowledge of at least the most common minority religions in Belgium, potentially through the public educational system.

Section II
Comparative Perspectives in the Public and Private Workplace

Chapter 11

Muslim Women Made Redundant: Unintended Signals in Belgian and Dutch Case Law on Religious Dress in Private Sector Employment and Unemployment

Katayoun Alidadi[*]

Introduction

Europe's judges are facing the challenges of increasing cultural and religious diversity, not least with regard to the workplace, an important gateway to the effective integration and social mobility of minorities. When it comes to Muslim women and their dress, the challenges have received wide public attention in a number of European countries. Considerable attention has been directed at the *hijab* or Islamic headscarf in the public school context,[1] where there is a strong subtext of state neutrality concerns as well as potential pressure exerted by religious symbols on children and families.[2] In the employment area, the religious dress of public school teachers and other civil servants has somewhat overshadowed debates surrounding the situation in the private sector.

---

[*] This work was supported by the RELIGARE project, which received funding under the European Commission's Seventh Framework Programme (Socio-economic Sciences and Humanities) under grant agreement number 44635. An earlier version of this chapter was presented at the International Symposium "Religious Diversity and the European Workplace," held on 13 January 2011 at the Catholic University of Leuven. I wish to thank the symposium participants for their questions and observations, and in particular Marie-Claire Foblets and Veit Bader for the many helpful comments and suggestions for improvement.

1 D. McGoldrick, *Human Rights and Religion: The Islamic Headscarf Debate in Europe* (Hart Publishing 2006); more recently much attention has been paid to face-covering veils (*burqas* and *niqabs*) in the public services and the public sphere, *infra*.

2 L. Vickers, *Religious Freedom, Religious Discrimination and the Workplace* (Hart Publishing 2008), 163; for an example, see the British Sabina Begum case: R (on the application of *Begum (Sabina))* v. *Denbigh High School Governors* [2006] UKHL 15 (protecting other Muslim pupils from family and societal pressure to wear the more conservative *jilbab* considered an important goal).

The focus of this chapter is on case law regarding private sector employment and the unemployment of Muslim women, in particular with regard to the topic of dress accommodation (or lack thereof). This angle is chosen since it can provide insights into the dynamic of labor relations and illustrate the tensions in the (at least theoretical) absence of *state* neutrality concerns, while at the same time reveal dominant standards in the organization of labor and working life that form particular barriers to the participation of Muslim women.

Indeed, employers, policy-makers and courts are more and more being confronted with conflicts between private employers and religious employees wishing to sport "non-conformist" dress and head coverings in the workplace. For instance, conflicts between workers and European employers seeking "neutral" looking staff have at times escalated and found their way into courts. The responses have a profound effect on Muslim women's lives and prospects. Modesty in dress is regarded by many Muslim women as a significant and even determining aspect of their personal identity and integrity, but the importance of employment should also not be understated: it is often much more than a simple means of subsistence, touching on self-worth, self-confidence and identity as well. The fact that these cases will not go away is confirmed by the fact they often involve young Muslim women seeking to wear a headscarf while pursuing a job position or internship. And while case law perhaps only reveals a small sliver or the very tip of the iceberg, articulated and publicized judicial decisions, in particular when they receive media attention, have the potential to send out powerful signals and incentives.

The question is whether, and to what extent, a choice is forced between, on the one hand, faith and religious identity and, on the other hand, employment, financial security and career prospects. For many Muslim women, who are especially prone to becoming victims of multiple or intersectional discrimination,[3] the search for employment appears layered with encounters of various forms of disadvantage and obstacles.[4] With already problematic labor market participation

3 European Union Agency for Fundamental Rights (FRA), *EU MIDIS Data in Focus Report 5: Multiple Discrimination,* February 2011, available on the FRA website; D. Schiek, "Just a piece of Cloth? German Courts and Employees with Headscarves," 33 *Industrial Law Journal* 63 (2004), 73. Unequal treatment on the basis of religious dress is predominantly framed as discrimination on the basis of religion and rarely on the basis of gender, or indirect intersectional discrimination, for an exception see H. Skjeie, "Headscarves in Schools: European Comparisons," in *Religious Pluralism and Human Rights in Europe: Where to Draw the Line?* (M. L. P. Loenen and J. E. Goldschmidt, eds, Intersentia 2007), 129–145 (the Norwegian Ombud held that prohibiting a Muslim employee from wearing a headscarf at work amounted to indirect discrimination on the basis of sex, thus illustrating a very different underlying conception of the meaning of the headscarf).

4 I. Glorieux, S. Koelet and I. Laurijssen, *Gekleurd door het leven. Getuigenissen van jonge Turkse en Marokkaanse vrouwen over hun schooljaren en eerste ervaringen op de arbeidsmarkt* [Coloured through life. Testimonies of young Turkish and Moroccan women on their school years and first experiences on the labor market] (Garant Uitgevers 2011).

and unemployment rates,[5] the accommodations with regard to religious dress could be of significant importance.

Taking on a European and comparative perspective, this chapter starts by discussing the legal frameworks in place under Article 9 of the European Convention on Human Rights (ECHR) (Part I) and the protection against discrimination on the basis of religion under the EU Employment Equality Directive (Part II). The European Court of Human Rights (ECtHR) has emphasized the "margin of appreciation" of states when it comes to controversial issues such as religious manifestation and religious pluralism where no consensus can be found amongst the Council of Europe states.[6] In addition, the "freedom to resign doctrine" has prevented adequate consideration for employees' religious interests.[7]

The 2000 Employment Equality Directive has provided EU Member States with a largely unified language, but interpretations under already differing national anti-discrimination legislation vary considerably. The European Court of Justice (ECJ) has not yet had an opportunity to decide on the scope and extent of protection against religious discrimination in the workplace, but this should only be a matter of time.[8]

---

5 For data on labor participation and unemployment in Belgium, see See Federale Overheidsdienst Werkgelegenheid, Arbeid en Sociaal Overleg, *De Immigratie in België: aantallen, stromen en arbeidsmarkt* [Immigation in Belgium: Numbers, origins and labor market] (2009), 46–48, Table 13 (data on the basis of religion is not collected in Belgium, so available data on the basis of nationality has to be utilized). In 2007, Moroccan women made up 28.5% of the total Moroccan workforce in Belgium (Turkish women made up 29.5% and Algerian women 24.3% of the respective total workforce) compared to autochthonous Belgian women who made up 45.6% of the total autochthonous Belgian workforce. For the Netherlands, see the website of the Centraal Bureau voor de Statistiek (CBS), www.cbs.nl, and Dutch Temporary Commission Research Integration Policy, *Bruggen Bouwen* (*Building Bridges*) (Sdu Publishers 's-Gravenhage 2004), 246.

6 ECtHR 10 November 2005, *Leyla Sahin* v. *Turkey*, App. No. 44774/98, par. 109 ("where questions concerning the relationship between states and religions are concerned, on which the opinion in democratic society may reasonably differ widely, the role of national decision-making body must be given special importance.").

7 For example, in a number of cases where an employee's work schedule conflicted with the observance of religious holidays or Sabbath, no interference was found with the right to manifest religious beliefs under Art 9.2 of the ECHR, e.g. EComHR, 3 December 1996, *Konttinen* v. *Finland*, App. No. 2494/94; see S. Knights, "Approaches to Diversity in the Domestic Courts: Article 9 of the European Convention on Human Rights," in *Legal Practice and Cultural Diversity* (R. Grillo et al., eds, Ashgate 2009), 290–93 (noting how this "clear line of authority" from Strasbourg has caused domestic courts to take on a restrictive approach); also see the chapter by Saïla Ouald Chaib in this volume.

8 The CEOOR unsuccessfully attempted to have the Antwerp Labor Tribunal in the 2010 case discussed *infra* request a preliminary ruling from the ECJ regarding the Employment Equality Directive—namely whether an absolute ban on the wearing of religious symbols in the workplace would amount to direct or unjustifiable indirect discrimination on basis of religion; see also the chapter by Titia Loenen in this volume on the dilemmas the ECJ will face in this regard.

Thus, since the current lack of guidance from the ECtHR and the ECJ means decisions on the proper limits or accommodations of employees' religiously inspired dress are left up to national states, Part III focuses on Belgian and Dutch case law with regard to Muslim women's dress in the mainstream private sector workplace. Religion and religious dress can play a role in every stage of the employment relationship, such as in access to the labor market, during the selection and hiring process, throughout an existing work relationship and in the context of a termination or dismissal. In addition, issues of religious dress also come up in the unemployment benefits context. Therefore, the national cases discussed include employment rights and conflicts (employer–employee conflicts) as well as unemployment compensation cases (conflicts between ex-employees and the state unemployment agency).[9] The choice of Belgium and the Netherlands, two relatively closely related Western legal systems, in this context is justifiable.[10] Besides sharing a geographical border, the Dutch language[11] and EU membership, both countries have comparable social security systems[12] and alarmingly high unemployment rates for ethnic minorities.[13] However, there are marked differences as well, for instance with regard to the acceptance of the Islamic headscarf in the private workplace.[14] There have been different dynamics

9 The unemployment rate for Muslim women is disproportionately high, even compared to men of the same social group: Federale Overheidsdienst Werkgelegenheid, Arbeid en Sociaal Overleg, *De Immigratie in België: aantallen, stromen en arbeidsmarkt*, 2009 report, 41, Table 15 (in 2007, the unemployment rate for Moroccan women in Belgium was 45.5% as opposed to 38.3% for the entire Moroccan workforce, compared to an 11.2% unemployment rate for autochthonous Belgian women and a 9.4% unemployment rate for the entire autochthonous Belgian workforce).

10 This is not to say other European countries would not present interesting case studies—for example the German situation, see A. Seifert, "Federal Labor Court strengthens religious freedom at the workplace," 6 *German Law Journal* 559 (2003), 4 (pointing to polarizing debates on the headscarf in the private sector employment in Germany). On the French situation, see Rim-Sarah Alouane in this volume.

11 At least in the Flemish part of Belgium, Dutch is the official language.

12 Even though there are some significant differences in the respective systems; see D. Pieters and P. Schoukens, *Triptiek Sociale Zekerheid. De beginselen van socialezekerheidsrecht en hun toepassing in België en Nederland* (Acco 2006).

13 See *supra*, note 5.

14 This was recently illustrated head-on by the dismissal of a Muslim saleswoman from a Belgian branch of Hema, a Dutch department store chain. This case, which received wide national coverage in Belgium, was all the more remarkable since Hema is known to accommodate its Muslim sales staff in the Netherlands—providing headscarves in company colors: see P. Lesaffer, "Hema ontslaat winkelbediende voor hoofddoek," *De Standaard*, 8 March 2011; X., "Hema 'schikt zich naar gewoonten van het land'" [Hema is 'conforming itself to the customs of the country'], *De Standaard*, 8 March 2011 and Y. Delepeleire, "Hema voor rechter na ontslag voor hoofddoek" [HEMA before the court after dismissal because of headscarf], *De Standaard* 6 March 2012. The case is discussed in the Introduction to this volume. See also K. Alidadi, "From Front-Office to Back-Office: Religious Dress Crossing

when it comes to accommodating cultural, religious and ethnic minorities in the respective countries,[15] and the Equality Bodies—the Belgian Centre for Equal Opportunities and Opposition to Racism (CEOOR) and the Dutch Equal Treatment Commission (ETC)—have different functions and competencies, playing different roles in the development of equality norms.[16] This mix of basic commonalities and particularities would seem to allow for useful comparative lessons.

The title of this chapter alludes to a problem with the case law regarding religious accommodations at the intersection of the employment and unemployment areas. In a worst-case scenario, when a woman is fired because of her headscarf (or other religious dress) or if she resigns "voluntarily" following a denial of accommodation, she could in turn be excluded from unemployment benefits if she is considered to be "voluntarily unemployed." The question of how judicial decisions with regard to dress accommodations in the employment context compare with decisions in the unemployment context has important policy implications. While the importance of freedom of religion in each context needs to be emphasized, it is argued that mandating (more) accommodation from the unemployment services rather than from private employers unintentionally sends out the wrong signals. Great caution—and ideally some harmonization—is thus warranted to prevent the undesired effect of keeping Muslim women out of the workplace and pushing them into the unemployment statistics.

I. The European Court of Human Rights: Surrender of the clashing headscarves issue to national states

Freedom of thought, religion and conscience has been called one of the "foundations of a democratic society" and one of the "most vital elements that go to make up the identity of believers and their conception of life" by the ECtHR.[17] But in diverse democratic societies restrictions on the freedom to manifest one's

---

the Public–Private Divide in the Workplace," in *Religion in Public Spaces: A European Perspective* (S. Ferrari and S. Pastorelli, eds, Ashgate 2012 forthcoming).

15 For the Netherlands, see B. P. Vermeulen, "On Freedom, Equality and Citizenship. Changing Fundamentals of Dutch Minority Policy and Law (Immigration, Integration, Education and Religion)," in *Cultural Diversity and the Law. State Reponses from Around the World* (M.-Cl. Foblets, J.-Fr. Gaudreault-DesBiens and A. D. Renteln, eds, Bruylant 2010), 47–143.

16 Equality bodies in Europe come in all sorts of shapes and forms, see G. Moon, "Chapter Eight: Enforcement bodies," in *Cases, Materials and Text on National, Supranational and International Non-Discrimination Law* (D. Schiek, L. Waddington and M. Bell, eds, Hart Publishing 2007), 871 *et seq*. EU law only mandates setting up an equality body under the Racial Equality and Gender Directives, there is no duty to set up a body for the enforcement of equality on the basis of religion, but most Member States have done so.

17 ECtHR 25 May 1993, *Kokkinakis* v. *Greece*, App. No. 14307/88, par. 31.

religion or belief may be necessary to reconcile the interests of various groups and to guarantee respect for everyone's beliefs.[18]

The freedom of religion[19] has two aspects, the *forum internum* and the *forum externum*. The *forum internum*, which is enshrined in Article 9.1 of the ECHR, refers to the right to have inner thoughts and beliefs, and as this is absolute, the state cannot intervene with it. The *forum externum*, on the other hand, refers to expressions[20] or manifestations of inner religious convictions in public and private spheres. The latter is subject to limitations "prescribed by law" and "necessary [i.e. proportionate to the legitimate pursued aims] in a democratic society in the interest of public safety, for the protection of public order, health or morals, or for the protection of the rights and freedoms of others."[21] In the employment relations context, the "rights of others" includes the right of employers, colleagues and customers who value the negative aspect of religious freedom, i.e. the right to be free from religion and to work or have services delivered in a "neutral" or non-religious setting.[22] The fundamental human right to freedom of religion has horizontal effect, meaning that it applies in the relationship between private parties such as between employers and employees.[23]

The issue of religious dress in private sector employment has not directly come before the ECtHR.[24] A number of relevant decisions, however, indicate that

---

18 ECtHR 25 May 1993, *Kokkinakis* v. *Greece*, App. No. 14307/88, par. 31 and ECtHR 10 November 2005, *Leyla Sahin* v. *Turkey*, App. No. 44774/98, par. 106.

19 Which has its roots in religious convictions rather than being an invention of the Enlightenment, see M. De Blois, "Two Cities in Conflict," in *Religious Pluralism and Human Rights in Europe: Where to Draw the Line?*," (M. L. P. Loenen and J. E. Goldschmidt, eds, Intersentia 2007), 170–171.

20 In the light of the general protection for freedom of expression in Article 10 of the ECHR, Article 9 ECHR can be considered *lex specialis*; M. Evans, "From Cartoons to Crucifixes: Current Controversies Concerning the Freedom of Religion and the Freedom of Expression before the European Court of Human Rights," 26 *Journal of Law and Religion* 345, 368 (noting that religious manifestations as forms of expression require additional protection to be meaningful).

21 Article 9.2 of the ECHR; E. Bribosia, I. Chopin and I. Rorive, *Rapport de synthèse relatif aux signes d'appartenance religieuse dans quinze pays de l'Union européenne* (Migration Policy Group, 2004), 24, available at www.cestim.it (noting that while secularism is not included in this list it de facto sweeps in).

22 L. Vickers, *Religious Freedom, Religious Discrimination and the Workplace* (Hart Publishing 2008), 102.

23 J. Krzeminska-Vamvaka, "Horizontal effect of fundamental rights and freedoms – much ado about nothing? German, Polish and EU theories compared after Viking Line," (Jean Monnet Working Paper 2009), available at centers.law.nyu.edu. However, only state parties to the Convention can be brought before the ECtHR.

24 For example, ECtHR 15 February 2001, *Dahlab* v. *Switzerland*, App. No. 42393/98, concerned a Swiss public school teacher, ECtHR 24 January 2006, *Kurtulmus* v. *Turkey*, App. No. 65500/01 and ECtHR 5 April 2007, *Kavakçi* v. *Turkey*, App. no. 71907/01 concerned, respectively, a university professor and a parliamentarian in Turkey.

the ECtHR is unlikely to afford strong protection under Article 9 of the ECHR, possibly in conjunction with Article 14, to the right to manifest religious beliefs through a dress code in the private sector workplace.

A. Dress and the headscarf in the ECtHR's case law

While dress can be an element of freedom of expression, it has received limited weight under the proportionality test and is thus capable of being trumped by other rights.[25] Dress has also been explicitly recognized as a way of manifesting religious beliefs.[26] In past cases involving religious dress, the "rights of others" considerations were found to be strengthened by the particular circumstances and the employee position has received limited attention.[27]

The ECtHR has been criticized for endorsing the notion that the headscarf is a symbol of women's inferiority and "hard to square with the principle of gender equality."[28] This sweeping generalization about the meaning of the headscarf is rightfully contested.[29] There are complex and multidimensional reasons why Muslim women choose to wear or not to wear the headscarf.[30] Available research shows that the headscarf is worn for various reasons, and for some young educated Muslim women in the West it can be a source of empowerment to be able to show that they hold on to their Islamic identity.[31]

---

25 E.g. EComHR 22 October 1998, *Kara* v. *UK*, App. No. 36528/97 (the case of a cross-dressing man was found manifestly ill-founded as it was not considered disproportionate to interfere with expressional rights to protect the right of the employer to carry out a particular image).

26 ECtHR 10 November 2005, *Leyla Sahin* v. *Turkey*, App. No. 44774/98; ECtHR 23 February 2010, *Ahmet Arslan et al.* v. *Turkey*, App. No. 41135/98.

27 E.g. ECtHR 15 February 2001, *Dahlab* v. *Switzerland*, App. No. 42393/98 (noting the influence of a veiled teacher over the emotional and intellectual development of young children).

28 E.g. ECtHR 15 February 2001, *Dahlab* v. *Switzerland*, App. No. 42393/98; ECtHR 10 November 2005, *Leyla Sahin* v. *Turkey*, App. No. 44774/98, par. 111.

29 E.g. I. Rorive, "Religious Symbols in The Public Space: In search of a European Answer," 30 *Cordozo Law Review* 6, 2669, 2680 and 2683; T. Loenen, "Botsing tussen de vrijheid van godsdienst en gelijke behandeling ongeacht geslacht of seksuele oriëntatie" in *Rechtsstaat en religie* (A. Nieuwenhuis and C. Zoethout, eds, Wolf Legal Publishers 2009).

30 C. Joppke, *Veil. Mirror of Identity* (Polity Press 2009), 3–5 (noting at 5 that "it has become commonplace to stress the modernity of the headscarf … as a self-chosen sign of female emancipation … but [adding that] it is a highly truncated kind of modernity").

31 C. Killian, "The Other Side of the Veil: North African Women in France Respond to the Headscarf Affair," 17 *Gender & Society* 567 (2003), 567–590; F. El Guindi, *Veil: Modesty, Privacy And Resistance* (Berg 1999) (for the position that contemporary veiling tends to be about resistance).

Two important ECtHR decisions with regard to the headscarf in particular, both involving a public educational setting, can be mentioned. In *Dahlab* v. *Switzerland*,[32] a primary school teacher was fired from a public school in Switzerland for wearing an Islamic headscarf, and the landmark case of *Sahin* v. *Turkey*[33] concerned a ban on headscarves for university students at Turkish state universities. The Court has not yet ruled a headscarf issue in favor of the applicant.[34] Nor has it generally ruled favorably in other cases equivalent to requests for reasonable accommodation for reasons of religion based on Article 9 of the ECHR.[35]

However, in a recent decision, *Ahmet Arslan* v. *Turkey*,[36] it was held that the *criminal* conviction of 127 members of the religious order known as *Aczimendi tarikatÿ* for wearing their distinctive religious clothing, reminiscent of the Prophet Mohammad's dress, while touring the streets of Ankara following a religious ceremony and during a judicial proceeding violated Article 9 of the ECHR. The religious order members had been convicted under Turkish law for a breach of the law on the wearing of headgear and the wearing of religious garments in public other than for religious ceremonies. According to the ECtHR, the Turkish ruling was not based on legitimate aims of protection of public safety and protection of the rights and freedoms of others but solely upon a reference to legal provisions. While this case may point to limits in regulating dress practices, the criminal law and public sphere contexts of this case seem to set it apart from a contractual labor relations situation.

Since there are so many different and varying veiling (and non-veiling) practices amongst Muslim women, the question often comes up whether the *headscarf* is a religious *obligation* under Islamic doctrine. The relevance of the answer has been disputed as the freedom to interpret one's own doctrine is a core part of religious freedom.[37] The ECtHR has stated that Article 9 of the ECHR "excludes any discretion on the part of the state to determine whether religious beliefs …

32 ECtHR 15 February 2001, *Dahlab* v. *Switzerland*, App. No. 42393/98.

33 ECtHR 10 November 2005, *Leyla Sahin* v. *Turkey*, App. No. 44774/98.

34 See also ECtHR 4 December 2008, *Dogru* v. *France*, App. No. 27058/05, and ECtHR 4 December 2008 *Kevanci* v. *France*, App. No. 31645/04 (no infringement of the right to religion found in the case of 12-year-old Muslim girls expelled in 1999 from French elementary school for covering their head during physical education class).

35 S. Knights, "Approaches to Diversity in the Domestic Courts: Article 9 of the European Convention on Human Rights," in *Legal Practice and Cultural Diversity* (R. Grillo et al., eds, Ashgate 2009), 290–93; E. Bribosia, J. Ringelheim and I. Rorive, "Aménager la Diversité: Le Droit de L'Egalité face à la Pluralité Religieuse," 19 *Revue Trimestrielle Des Droits De l'Homme* 320 (2009), 349; see, however, ECtHR 7 December 2010, *Jakóbski* v. *Poland*, App. No. 18429/06, where Article 9 was held violated because the prison had refused to provide "simple meat-free meals" to a Buddhist prisoner. Also discussed by Kristin Henrard and Saïla Ouald Chaib in this volume.

36 ECtHR 23 February 2010, *Ahmet Arslan et al.* v. *Turkey*, App. No. 41135/98.

37 ECtHR 13 December 2001, *Metropolitan Church of Bessarabia and Others* v. *Moldova*, App. No. 45701/99.

are legitimate."[38] The assumption is that bona fide "religious" practices fall under Article 9.1 of the ECHR.[39] Thus, the ECtHR gives deference to the subjective understanding of the person concerned,[40] without however unquestioningly accepting an applicant's characterization of an act as a manifestation.[41] The practical importance of this generous stance seems limited when, under Article 9.2 of the ECHR, wide restrictions are possible on the manifestation of a religious belief or practice.

B. Freedom to resign defeats interference or violation of freedom of religion

There remains a question as to what extent Convention rights apply in the workplace. The ECtHR has not taken a consistent view on this.[42] The Convention does not cover access to employment, and the freedom to leave one's job or to choose a different profession has been considered as adequate protection for an employee's freedom of religion under the case law of the former European Commission on Human Rights (EComHR). The "choice principle" or the "free to resign" doctrine[43] has been a cornerstone of the interpretation of Article 9 in the area of employment.[44] The Strasbourg institutions have held that there is no interference with the manifestation of religion when an employee enters into a work relationship voluntarily by contract or accepts a position, thereby consenting to certain limits on his or her exercise of religion within that context. These cases have involved requested time off to attend religious holidays or weekly days of rest. In particular, the decision in *Ahmad* v. *United Kingdom* (1982)[45] is illustrative: a schoolteacher of the Muslim faith employed by a local authority requested time

---

38 ECtHR 26 October 2000, *Hasan and Chaush* v. *Bulgaria* (2000), App. No. 30985/96, par. 78.

39 P. Cumper, "The Accommodation of 'Uncontroversial' Religious Practices," in *Religious Pluralism and Human Rights in Europe: Where to Draw the Line?* (M. L. P. Loenen and J. E. Goldschmidt, eds, Intersentia 2007), 208.

40 E.g. ECtHR 5 October 2006, *Moscow Branch of the Salvation Army* v. *Russ.*, App. No. 72881/01.

41 ECtHR 13 April 2006, *Kosteski* v. *The former Yugoslav Republic of Macedonia*, App. No. 55170/00.

42 L. Vickers, *Religious Freedom, Religious Discrimination and the Workplace* (Hart Publishing 2008), 96.

43 P. Cumper, "The Accommodation of 'Uncontroversial' Religious Practices," in *Religious Pluralism and Human Rights in Europe: Where to Draw the Line?* (M. L. P. Loenen and J. E. Goldschmidt, eds, Intersentia 2007), 208—noting that this "free to resign and find another job approach" was not the approach the ECtHR took in an employment dispute involving sexual orientation in ECtHR 27 September 1999, *Smith and Grady* v. *United Kingdom* (1999), 29 EHRR 493 (under Article 8 of the ECHR).

44 L. Vickers, *Religious Freedom, Religious Discrimination and the Workplace* (Hart Publishing 2008), 87–88.

45 EComHR 1982, *Ahmad* v. *United Kingdom* (1982) 4 EHRR 126.

off from work to attend the local mosque on Fridays for the purposes of worship. Emphasizing that the right to exercise freedom of religion may be limited by contractual obligations, including those of employment, the EComHR held that the employee was "free to resign if and when he found that his teaching obligations conflicted with his religious duties."[46] Similarly, in *Stedman* (1997)[47] it was held that the Christian employee was "free to resign" if her job obligations stood in the way of observing the Sunday Sabbath.[48]

This jurisprudence has been criticized for its formalism.[49] After all, the protection of religion is rendered largely meaningless in contexts where in fact there might not be a *real* choice for the religious adherent to move on to another job of similar worth without considerable hardship. Also, even though *Stedman* involved a Christian employee, this approach tends to disadvantage employees who adhere to minority religions since their religious beliefs and practices are most likely not taken into account in the state labor law system or workplace organization. For instance, the predominant European working week with Sundays off is based on the Christian calendar which tends to disadvantage Muslim, Sikh and Jewish minorities with different days of rest. Similarly, it seems that it is mainly minorities' religious dress that collides with "neutral" dress policies.[50]

Considering the ECtHR's case law it seems highly unlikely that Article 9 of the ECHR would become a basis for introducing reasonable accommodations for religious dress in the private workplace.[51] The anti-discrimination framework

46 *Id.*, at 135; P. Cumper, "The Accommodation of 'Uncontroversial' Religious Practices," in *Religious Pluralism and Human Rights in Europe: Where to Draw the Line?* (M. L. P. Loenen and J. E. Goldschmidt, eds, Intersentia 2007), at 208 critiques this "choice principle."

47 EComHR 1997, *Stedman* v. *UK* (1997) 23 EHRR CD 168 (application manifestly ill-founded).

48 See also EComHR 3 December 1996, *Konttinen* v. *Finland*, App. No. 2494/94 (the claim of a Seventh-day Adventist employee dismissed for refusing to work on the Sabbath was held manifestly ill-founded: "In these particular circumstances the Commission finds that the applicant was not dismissed because of his religious convictions but for having refused to respect his working hours … having found his working hours to conflict with his religious convictions, the applicant was free to relinquish his post. The Commission regards this as *the ultimate guarantee of his right to freedom of religion*." (author's emphasis)).

49 L. Vickers, *Religious Freedom, Religious Discrimination and the Workplace* (Hart Publishing 2008), 87; see the British case of *Copsey* v. *WWB Devon Clays Ltd* [2005] EWCA Civ 932, where all three judges of the Court of Appeals criticized the decisions in *Ahmed* v. *UK*, *Konttinen* v. *Finland* and *Stedman* v. *UK*, finding them to be logically unsatisfactory, excessively harsh and limiting of the right to religious freedom.

50 There are exceptions though and requests for accommodations have also been presented by Christian employees as well. For two workplace crucifix cases: Court of Appeals Amsterdam 15 June 2010, BM7410, 200.054.861/01 SKG and *Eweida* v. *British Airways plc*, 12 February 2010 (UK Court of Appeals).

51 See *Copsey* v. *WWB Devon Clays Ltd* [2005] EWCA Civ 932, where the British Court of Appeals held that the requirement for a shop worker to work on a Sunday did

would seem more promising for that. However, Vickers has argued that support can be found in other areas of ECtHR jurisprudence for the notion that dismissals or other work-related detriments can amount to interference with Convention rights.[52] Recently, the ECtHR rejected the "free to resign" argument advanced by the Russian Government in the context of paid parental leave for military personnel, but here the Court pointed to the "unique nature of the armed forces and, consequently, the difficulty in directly transferring essentially military qualifications and experience to civilian life."[53] It remains to be seen whether the doctrine will be discarded in certain other (work) contexts as well.

While the qualified right to manifest religion seems to be of limited use to Muslim women wanting to don a headscarf in the workplace—both because of the "freedom to resign" doctrine and the minimal weight given in the proportionality equation to a woman's wish to wear a headscarf—it may be of considerable indirect use in determining the proper parameters for the protection against religious discrimination. Under the Employment Equality Directive, religious interests must be protected in the employment setting, and this must be interpreted to comply with the principles under the ECHR.[54]

---

not infringe on Article 9 of the ECHR while emphasizing that different decisions might be made regarding unlawful discrimination under employment legislation (that had not entered into force in the UK in the relevant time frame); it could be that ECtHR 7 December 2010, *Jacóbski* v. *Poland*, App. No. 18429/06, opens up perspectives, but to what extent the ECtHR will pursue this course is yet to be seen.

52 L. Vickers, *Religious Freedom, Religious Discrimination and the Workplace* (Hart Publishing 2008), 87.

53 ECtHR 7 October 2010, *Konstantin Markin* v. *Russia*, App. No. 30078/06, par. 58: the "freedom to resign" argument presented by the Government was rejected as it was considered that: "Servicemen are thereby forced to make a difficult choice between nursing their new-born children and pursuing their military career … The Court reiterates in this respect *the unique nature of the armed forces* and, consequently, the difficulty in directly transferring essentially military qualifications and experience to civilian life. It is therefore clear that, if they choose to resign from military service to be able to take care of their new-born children, servicemen would encounter difficulties in obtaining civilian posts in their areas of specialization which would reflect the seniority and status that they had achieved in the armed forces" (author's emphasis). See also Chapter 2 in this volume by S. Ouald Chaib.

54 See Article 6(2) of the EU Treaty and Recital 1 of the Employment Equality Directive; see L. Vickers, *Religious Freedom, Religious Discrimination and the Workplace* (Hart Publishing 2008), 119.

II. Employment Equality Directive: Convergence of terminology, divergence of understanding

The principle of non-discrimination on the ground of religion or belief in employment is included in the Employment Equality Directive of 2000,[55] which forms the common framework for assessing religious dress conflicts in both private and public sector[56] workplaces in the EU Member States. This Directive has been implemented, albeit certainly not uniformly,[57] in national legislation in all EU Member States.

The Directive prohibits direct and indirect discrimination as well as harassment and instruction to discriminate on the basis of religion or belief, as well as disability, age and sexual orientation.[58] "Direct discrimination" occurs when one person is treated less favorably than another on the basis of one of the protected characteristics, while "indirect discrimination" means "an apparently neutral provision, criterion or practice" which places persons because of such a protected characteristic at a particular disadvantage compared with other persons.[59] Differences in treatment directly based on religion or belief cannot be justified unless the conditions for a "genuine occupational requirement" are met, and provided that "the objective is legitimate and the requirement is proportionate."[60] When the link to religion or belief under a difference of treatment is indirect, however, there is an open justification regime, i.e. the measure can be justified by

---

55 The Racial Equality Directive could be relevant in the context of the headscarf, as a ban on the headscarf could be argued to amount to indirect discrimination on the basis of ethnic origin as it may particularly adversely affect an ethnic group. On the German situation: M. Mahlmann, "Religious Tolerance, Pluralist Society and the Neutrality of the State: The Federal Constitutional Court's Decision in the Headscarf Case," 4 *German Law Journal* 1099 (2003), 1113.

56 See Article 3 Council Directive 2000/78/EC of 27 November 2000 Establishing a General Framework for Equal Treatment in Employment and Occupation, *OJ* 303 L 02/12/2000, 16–22 (hereafter "Employment Equality Directive"). It is not discussed whether formal bans that are in place for certain public sector employment are compatible with the Directive, "art 2.5. This Directive shall be without prejudice to measures laid down by national law which, in a democratic society, are necessary for public security, for the maintenance of public order and the prevention of criminal offences, for the protection of health and for the protection of the rights and freedoms of others."

57 For more on the implementation see L. Vickers, *Religion and Belief in Employment—The EU Law*, European Network of Legal Experts in the non-discrimination field, (European Commission 2007).

58 Article 1 of the Employment Equality Directive.

59 Article 2.2 (a) and (b) of the Employment Equality Directive.

60 Article 4.1 of the Employment Equality Directive: a difference in treatment based on religion or belief may be justifiable under the Directive; Article 4.2 refers to the particular regime for so-called religious ethos companies.

showing that there is a legitimate goal and the means of achieving this goal are appropriate and necessary.[61]

A. Religious dress: Direct discrimination versus indirect discrimination

Workplace dress code conflicts can arise in a multitude of ways. It could be that a company has a dress code policy—perhaps prescribing a uniform—that is challenged by a job applicant or an employee because it contradicts some form of religious dress. It could also be that no such code is in place, and an applicant is rejected (or an employee is dismissed) for ostentatiously wearing a religious dress or head covering, with the employer possibly coming up with post facto arguments related to, for instance, safety concerns or image.

Considering the different justification regimes, a central question is whether the rejection of an applicant or the dismissal of an employee because of wearing religious dress or symbols should be considered as *direct* religious discrimination or rather as *indirect* discrimination on the ground of religion.[62] According to the Dutch Equal Treatment Commission (ETC), the Dutch Equality Body that issues non-binding opinions in concrete disputes and requests for opinions, there is a direct discrimination[63] on the basis of religion when the employer directly refers to the headscarf.[64] However, when the prohibition is based on a broader dress code it concerns an indirect discrimination, which can be justified.[65]

A similar distinction is proposed by Bribosia et al.: in the potential case of a department store prohibiting the wearing of head covering by all personnel, it is probably the indirect discrimination regime (with the possibility of justification) that is applicable. After all, there is a seemingly neutral provision that applies to all staff but results in a particular disadvantage for adherents of certain religions such as Islam (women), Orthodox Jewish religion (men) and Sikhism (both men and women). It would be up to the employer to show a legitimate pursued aim and the fact that the measure (the dress code) is reasonable and necessary (proportionate).

---

61 Article 2.2 (b) (i) of the Employment Equality Directive.

62 E. Bribosia, I. Chopin and I. Rorive, *Rapport de synthèse relatif aux signes d'appartenance religieuse dans quinze pays de l'Union européenne* (Migration Policy Group, 2004), 13.

63 The Dutch Equal Treatment Act speaks in terms of "distinction" ("onderscheid") and does not use the term "discrimination," while in the case law of the European Court of Justice the two terms are used interchangeably, as is done in this chapter. R. Holtmaat, "Discriminatie of onderscheid: het kleine verschil met grote gevolgen of het grote verschil met kleine gevolgen?" in *Gelijke behandeling, principes en praktijken. Evaluatieonderzoek Algemene Wet Gelijke Behandeling* (M. L. M. Hertogh and P. J. J. Zoontjens, eds, Wolf Legal Publishers 2006), 3–113.

64 Equal Treatment Commission opinion (hereafter ETC) 1995-31 (cleaning staff); ETC 1999-103 (intern in a school); ETC 1999-18 (intern in a school); ETC 1997-14.

65 ETC 2001-53 (clerk); ETC 1996-85 (packaging); ETC 1996-16 (doctor's assistant); ETC 2002-125; ETC 2002-123.

Such a legitimate aim could certainly be health and safety, but the issue is more controversial when it is the desire to create a religion-free space or to hold on to a "neutral" image without any particular specific need thereto (e.g. a book store selling a wide variety of books). In contrast, when there is no such dress code policy and an applicant is refused a position (or an employee is dismissed) because of wearing a headscarf, turban or *kippa*, that person would be a victim of direct discrimination according to Bribosia et al.[66] However, even in the latter scenario courts have found a pre-existing "practice," or "unwritten company dress code."[67]

For justification under either form of discrimination, the court is called upon to assess whether the restriction on an individual's religious freedom, e.g. through a company dress code, is proportionate to this aim. This proportionality exercise in search for a proper balance between conflicting rights will thus determine the scope of the protection for religious "non-conformist dress," and consequently the look of tomorrow's workforce. The proportionality tool's "multi-purposeness" is at the same time its biggest limitation. On the one hand, the proportionality concept is poly-interpretable in that it allows for the taking into account of various factors that could be seen as relevant in particular contexts (and are thus not established a priori). This does not mean that "anything goes" and that *any* kind of argument can be taken into account: clearly certain arguments can be considered unreasonable or simply not to the point. Nonetheless, on the other hand, the resulting factual and cultural specificity of the balancing method does not promote the development of clear precedent and legal certainty in the non-discrimination area on a national level, let alone on a European scale.

This is also where the link with European human rights protection comes in. In the assessment of the proportionality of exceptions to the non-discrimination principle, limitations that have been accepted in the scope of the duty to respect the freedom of religion can be considered.[68] The role the ECJ will play in the enforcement and harmonization of the Employment Equality Directive is not entirely clear. While the ECJ to a large extent follows the jurisprudence of the ECtHR in interpreting human rights,[69] and for that reason a ruling by the ECJ might seem unlikely to hold a ban on headscarves or other religious dress in the workplace to be contrary to EU law, it must be noted that the role of the ECJ as a supranational court differs from that of the ECtHR. The fact that EU Directives are

---

66 *Supra*, note 32.

67 As was held by the Antwerp Labor Tribunal on 27 April 2010, discussed *infra*. The unwritten rule was considered "confirmed by the behavior of the ex-employee who for years did not wear a headscarf on the job" and whose dismissal after expressing the wish to start wearing a headscarf (thus because of a disregard of an instruction to dress neutrally) was considered justified.

68 L. Vickers, *Religion and Belief in Employment—The EU Law*, European Network of Legal Experts in the non-discrimination field, (European Commission 2007), 39.

69 See, for example, ECJ 22 October 2002, *Roquette Frères*, C-94/00, 29.

binding as to the result achieved[70] justifies a much more guided case law from the ECJ in the area of religious employment discrimination. Arguments based on the free movement of workers in the private sector, an important objective of the EU, could strengthen the case for clarity of guidance and require a level of uniformity across Member States.[71] But even if the issue is addressed through the angle of religious freedom, it is not excluded that the human rights protection offered under the EU Charter of Fundamental Rights exceeds that under the ECHR.[72]

B. Reasonable accommodations for religion or belief in Europe?

Under the Employment Equality Directive, the right to reasonable accommodations in the workplace only applies for disabled people, and thus not on the basis of religion or belief.[73] As a consequence, unlike the US and Canada where the issue of religious dress in the workplace can be viewed under a reasonable accommodation framework and jargon,[74] the shared European parlance speaks in terms of (direct and indirect) discrimination. The concepts "reasonable accommodation" and "indirect discrimination" are clearly related. In fact, there may be a good argument that the right to reasonable accommodation could in some cases be derived from the prohibition of indirect discrimination based on religion or belief.[75] It has even been argued that the latter goes beyond the duty to reasonably accommodate

70 Article 288, par. 3 of the Treaty on the Functioning of the European Union ("A directive shall be binding, as to the result to be achieved, upon each Member State to which it is addressed, but shall leave to the national authorities the choice of form and methods.").

71 See consideration 11 of the Employment Equality Directive; art 45 (ex-39) of the Treaty on the Functioning of the EU (not applicable on employment in the public service) and Article 15.2 of the EU Charter of Fundamental Rights of the European Union.

72 Article 10.1 of the EU Charter of Fundamental Rights of the European Union (2010/C 83/02), binding since the entry into force of the Lisbon Treaty, is textually identical to Article 9.1 of the ECHR. A provision similar to Article 9.2 of the ECHR is missing. See also K. Lenaerts and P. Van Nuffel, *Europees Recht* (Intersentia 2011), 550 *et seq.*

73 Article 5 of the Employment Equality Directive.

74 *Webb* v. *City of Philadelphia*, 562 F.3d 256 (3rd Cir. 2009), 7. As noted by the court, the crucial issue in these types of religious discrimination cases often boils down to whether an employer "can show reasonable accommodation would work an undue hardship" on it. See, for example, S. Gregory, "Abercrombie Faces a Muslim-Headscarf Lawsuit," *Time Magazine*, 23 September 2009, where there is talk of discrimination and lack of reasonable accommodation on the basis of religion where a similar case in Europe would be seen under the discrimination framework.

75 E. Bribosia, J. Ringelheim and I. Rorive, "Aménager la Diversité: Le Droit de L'Egalité face à la Pluralité Religieuse," *Revue Trimestrielle Des Droits De l'Homme* (78/2009), 361–62. The authors refer to certain jurisdictions that have in fact included a duty to reasonably accommodate for reasons of religion (including the Flemish Decree on Equal Participation).

employee requests.[76] In addition, the freedom of religion, possible in conjunction with the prohibition of discrimination, can also provide a basis for such duty.[77] Still, the lack of a clear legal basis for religious accommodation in Europe has important consequences for Muslim women in the workplace. First, the "reasonableness rhetoric"—which is currently not available in Europe—can be expected to resonate better in a conciliation mode of resolution than in the conflict-based discrimination framework. Indeed, a US employer can be approached for failing to reasonably *accommodate*[78] an employee, while the European employer is responsible for *discriminating* against an employee on the basis of his or her religion.[79] Second, as indirect discrimination is an abstract concept—developed through the case law of the ECJ in the area of gender equality—it obtains its practical meaning only in concrete contexts.[80] Much will thus depend on particular judicial decisions whether the "full potential scope of the protection"—i.e. whether it includes a de facto duty to reasonably accommodate requests based on religion or belief—is realized in a particular jurisdiction. This is not to say that the duty to reasonably accommodate requires no case-by-case interpretation—the ample US case law on this issue makes this clear.[81] But the two examples of Belgium and the Netherlands illustrate that the prohibition of indirect religious discrimination can lead to very different outcomes in similar fact situations. This divergent case law as to the accommodation of religious dress in the workplace has a number

76 M. De Vos, "De bouwstenen van het discriminatierecht in de arbeidsverhoudingen," in *De Wet Bestrijding Discriminatie in de praktijk* (M. De Vos and E. Brems, eds, Intersentia 2004), 81.

77 Although the *Thlimmenos* judgment of the ECtHR is often referred to in this context, this seems to concern an isolated decision. See, however, ECJ 27 October 1976, *Prais* v. *Council*, 130/75, consid. 19 (the claim of the Jewish woman who was unable to participate in an EU employment test because it was scheduled on a Jewish holiday was rejected, but the ECJ stated that "if informed of the difficulty in good time" the Council "would have been obliged to take reasonable steps to avoid fixing for a test a date which would make it impossible for a person of a particular religious persuasion to undergo the test").

78 Even though this failure amounts to religious *discrimination* in violation of Title VII, 42 U.S.C. § 2000e-2(a), the term accommodation does not by association acquire a pejorative connotation.

79 This pejorative connotation of the term "discrimination" is a reason why the Dutch Equal Treatment Act avoids the term and uses "distinction" ("*onderscheid*") instead. However, the European Commission has sent "reasoned opinions" to the Netherlands to correctly transpose amongst others the terminology used in the equality directives into its national law, which has been committed but not happened yet. As an *ultimum remedium*, the Commission could refer the matter to the ECJ.

80 This is not to say that under a duty of reasonable accommodation the limits of reasonableness and undue hardship are set in advance and are not fact-specific, as the developments in the US demonstrate; see the chapter by Gabrielle Caceres in this volume.

81 See, for example, the chapter by Gabrielle Caceres in this volume, noting the US Supreme Court's restrictive *de minimis* standard developed in *Trans World Airlines, Inc.* v. *Hardison*, 432 U.S. 63, 97 S. Ct. 2264, 53 L. Ed. 2d 113 (1977).

of consequences, such as the inhibiting of the freedom of movement of Muslim women within the EU.

Also, the EU 2020 strategy,[82] the long term strategy of the EU in the context of a prolonged economic and financial crisis, sets a number of targets with the aim of establishing a strong and sustainable economy with ample employment opportunity. One of the goals under the strategy is to create a high-employment economy. In particular, by 2020, the employment rate of the population aged 20–64 should increase from the current 69% to at least 75%. It speaks for itself that this goal is hard to achieve without focusing on issues such as integration and workplace discrimination[83] faced by the immigrant and religious minority workforce.

In the absence of guidance from the ECtHR and the ECJ, the issue of religious dress in the private workplace thus remains—for the time being at least—in the hands of the national states and judiciary. In certain EU Member States, including France and certain German Länder, the approach to religious symbols in (segments of) the public sector is clear, with a formal ban. In the private sector, contractual freedom and managerial freedom of business owners and companies—including religious-ethos companies—in addressing this issue play through.[84] Thus, in the absence of legislation in this area, the general and broader principles of religious freedom and non-discrimination on the basis of religion or belief are the essential guidelines whenever religious dress practices clash with private company dress codes. The challenge faced by national courts—called upon to interpret and apply general human rights principles and protection against religious discrimination—is to find a "subtle balance" between the religious interests of the individual employee and other conflicting values, freedoms and rights.[85] An array of issues

82 European Commission, *Communication from the Commission, Europe 2020. A strategy for smart, sustainable and inclusive growth*, COM(2010) 2020, Brussels, 3 March 2010. This replaces the Lisbon Strategy that covered the period 2000–2010; Member States are to translate the EU 2020 strategy into national targets.

83 It is noteworthy that the word "discrimination" appears only once in the Commission document, under Flagship Initiative: "European Platform against Poverty" (fifth poverty target). On the other hand, high employment is considered as an important reason to prohibit discrimination, see consideration 11 of the Employment Equality Directive.

84 The public–private sector divide seems to play an equivocal role. Restrictions on the religious dress of civil servants are now more commonplace in various European countries, and some authors argue that a ban on religious symbols is justified given that civil servants are representing the state and must remain neutral. However, it could also be argued that public sector staff should reflect the diversity of the community, and that bans effectively limit the freedom of veiled women to pursue chosen careers, especially in health and education where the state is virtually a monopoly employer. See L. Vickers, *Religious Freedom, Religious Discrimination and the Workplace* (Hart Publishing 2008), 160.

85 Point made by Lord Denning in *Ahmad* v. *ILEA* (1978) 1 All ER 574 at 578, namely that a subtle balance must be struck between protecting the rights of the religious employee without placing an undue burden on the employers or additional responsibilities on co-workers.

must be balanced to determine the proportionality of restrictions, an exercise which calls for an *in concreto* assessment of the case.

Needless to say, this assessment is embedded within particular legal cultures, including various models of Church–State relationships and political/societal ambivalences towards religion, religious diversity and integration. It may be that considering the background, a uniform response is not warranted or desirable in countries so diversified in respect to historic contexts, religious composition, integration patterns and policies. However, in the area of employment, the issue of the wearing of religious signs in the European Union has been called "particularly heterogeneous and confused."[86]

III. Religious dress in the private workplace: Balancing rights, freedoms and interests in tension in Belgium and the Netherlands

The question whether female Muslim employees are allowed to wear an Islamic headscarf or other religiously motivated dress on the job has come up frequently before the ETC and the Dutch courts.[87] Although ETC opinions are not legally binding, there is a high degree of compliance by parties[88] and the opinions are generally followed by courts.[89] The Belgian national equality body,[90] the Centre

86 E. Bribosia, I. Chopin and I. Rorive, *Rapport de synthèse relatif aux signes d'appartenance religieuse dans quinze pays de l'Union européenne* (Migration Policy Group, 2004), 24.

87 Or other aspects of the Muslim mandate to dress modestly (e.g. not showing calves in teacher's summer uniform (Belgium, *infra*) or elbows in hospital outfit (the Netherlands, *infra*)).

88 J. Goldschmidt, "Implementation of Equality Law. A Task for Specialists or for Human Rights Experts? Experiences and Developments in the Supervision of Equality Law in the Netherlands," 13 *MJ* 323 (2006), 325–27 (between 2001 and the first half of 2004 the compliance with opinions of the ETC went up from 60% to 84%; the compliance rates are attributed, among other things, to the way in which ETC hearings are handled).

89 In Hoge Raad 13 November 1987, *St. Bavo* v. *Gielen, Nederlandse Jurisprudentie* 1986/698, the Dutch Hoge Raad held that considerable weight must be given to a ruling and the recommendations of the Commission for Equal Treatment of Men and Women (one of the predecessors of the ETC) and sound reasons must be given to depart from these. The government did not follow the advice of the ETC to strengthen the authority of the opinions by amending the Equal Treatment Act to specify that courts must state the grounds for departing from its opinion; see ETC, *Het verschil gemaakt. Evaluatie AWGB en werkzaamheden CGB 1999–2004*, 95, available on the ETC website (between 2000 and 2004, 43 cases that the ETC had decided on came before courts: in 81% the opinion was given weight while in 61% the opinion was followed. Only in five cases did the court depart from the opinion without stating any grounds).

90 Equality bodies, set up in the EU since the 1970s, have a wide range of possible structures and functions. Their general goal is to make anti-discrimination laws more effective, but how they work towards that purpose differs from state to state. There are

for Equal Opportunities and Opposition to Racism (CEOOR), does not have quasi-judicial competencies, but mainly provides legal assistance to individual victims and claimants.[91] While the ETC has accumulated a considerable body of quasi-case law in this area, the CEOOR has focused its advocacy and resources on a limited number of legal cases under the Belgian Anti-discrimination Acts,[92] and Belgian courts have not always sided with its arguments.

A. Religious dress and the headscarf in the employment context in the Netherlands

As a result of the different equality enforcement setup, there is clearly more (quasi-) jurisprudence in the Netherlands on the situation of Muslim women in the workplace.[93] The Dutch courts and the ETC have on a number of occasions addressed the wearing of headscarves in public places, schools and places of employment.[94]

The prevailing tendency is towards accommodating religious symbols and dress in the workplace. The ETC examines the difference in treatment

---

single-issue equality bodies that focus on one issue, e.g. race or gender. Both the ETC and the CEOOR are multiple-issue equality bodies. There are only EU requirements to establish equality bodies for race and gender under Article 13 Racial Equality Directive (2000/43/EC), Article 8a of the Gender Employment Directive (2004/113/EC), Article 12 of the Gender Goods and Services Directive (2004/113/EC) and Article 20 (2) of the Recast Gender Employment Directive. See G. Moon, "Chapter Eight: Enforcement Bodies," in *Cases, Materials and Text on National, Supranational and International Non-Discrimination Law* (D. Schiek, L. Waddington and M. Bell, eds, Hart Publishing 2007), 871–955.

91 The ETC does not assist victims in pursuing their cases in court as this would conflict with the core task of considering complaints of unequal treatment in its quasi-judicial role; assistance is provided by local anti-discrimination agencies.

92 Wet van 10 mei 2007 ter bestrijding van bepaalde vormen van discriminatie, *Belgian Official Journal* 30 May 2007 (hereafter "Belgian Anti-discrimination Act"). The precursor was the Anti-Discrimination Act of 25 February 2003 (Wet ter bestrijding van discriminatie en tot wijziging van de wet van 15 februari 1993 tot oprichting van een Centrum voor gelijkheid van kansen en voor racismebestrijding), *Belgian Official Journal* 17 March 2003.

93 Although some decisions have been controversial: Rita Verdonck, the then Dutch Minister of Integration, called for the abolishment of the ETC in November 2006 following an issued opinion that a school cannot require a female Muslim teacher to shake hands with men. A 2007 bill proposed in the Dutch Parliament to this effect did not pass. X., "VVD, PVV: Hef Commissie Gelijke Behandeling op," 15 February 2007, Elsevier.nl.

94 For a list of ETC opinions involving the headscarf in various settings, see the site of Stichting Ontsluiert, a Dutch organization that aims to improve the participation and emancipation of veiled women in the Netherlands through dialogue with the government, employers and other stakeholders, http://www.ontsluiert.nl. To illustrate the ETC's stance, I will limit myself to a number of opinions, in particular those that can be considered "precedent opinions," i.e. illustrative for the approach taken.

under company dress codes or decisions in a methodical way for its objective and reasonable justification and its proportionality with the restriction on an employee's religious freedom. Protection against religious discrimination under the Dutch Equal Treatment Act includes protection for manifestations through religiously mandated dress.[95] Not surprising for an institution set up to promote diversity and enforce equality legislation, the ETC leaves considerable room for religious expressions by (mainly) minorities in the workplace. Headscarf bans are only accepted on narrow grounds, such as security considerations or inconsistency with an official government uniform.

Back in 1986, a lower Amsterdam court[96] held that, in the light of the "cosmopolitan" character of the city, employing a Sikh hotel worker who wore a turban and had grown a beard would not harm the hotel's goodwill even if that goodwill was based on the hotel's "Old Dutch" image. The hotel was not allowed to terminate the employment contract because the employee's change in physical appearance was not considered to amount to the required change in circumstances. A decade later, the ETC similarly held that a hotel was not allowed to dismiss a Sikh employee because of the wearing of a turban, beard and *kirpan*.[97]

The ETC considered its very first case involving an employer-imposed ban on wearing headscarves on the job in 1995.[98] A Muslim woman was prohibited from wearing a headscarf while doing cleaning work in different locations. The ETC held that the right to freedom of religion includes the right to manifest one's beliefs, referring to Parliamentary documents related to the Dutch Equal Treatment Act, and found that the employer had discriminated on the basis of religion.[99] Thus, early on the ETC found that the Dutch non-discrimination act protects the *forum externum*.[100]

In 2001, the ETC considered a case where a Muslim female trainee who applied to a bailiff's office was refused a position after she unambiguously insisted during the interview on wearing a headscarf on the job.[101] According to established ETC jurisprudence, it is not required that the protected ground, here religious manifestation through dress, be the *only* or determining reason for the different treatment in question. It suffices that the protected criterion plays at least *a role* in the decision or different treatment.[102] Based on the circumstances of the

95 *Infra*, ETC 1995-31, 7 August 1995.

96 Kantonrechter Amsterdam 24 January 1986, *Die Port van Cleve B.V.* v. *J. Singh, Rechtspraak Rassendiscriminatie* 1995, 171–173.

97 ETC 1997-24, 25 March 1997.

98 ETC 1995-31, 7 August 1995.

99 *Infra*.

100 In contrast, Antwerp Labor Tribunal 27 April 2010, case nr. AR/06/397639/A, *infra*.

101 ETC nr. 2001-79, 6 August 2001.

102 Discrimination based purely on the wearing of a headscarf is extremely difficult to prove. For example, a rejection following a job interview could be attributed to more

interview, the ETC did not accept the employer's assertion that the wearing of a headscarf and the applicant's expressed religious beliefs *in no way* played a role in the decision to reject the traineeship application. The ETC continued to consider whether there is a case of direct or indirect difference in treatment based on the protected criterion of religion, which depends on the total set of circumstances in a particular case. When the wearing of a headscarf, which is the manifestation of a religious conviction, is a reason behind the difference in treatment, then there is direct reference to a form of expression of an applicant's religious conviction, which makes it impermissible discrimination (*verboden onderscheid*). But when the wearing of the headscarf is not as such a reason for making a distinction, there still could be an indirect difference in treatment which is prohibited unless there is an objective justification. In the case of the rejected trainee, the difference in treatment was direct in nature because the employer was considered to have based its negative decision on the wearing of the headscarf as a religious symbol.

A 2006 call center case, on the other hand, involved an indirect difference in treatment. A Muslim woman with a headscarf was refused a job with a call center,[103] as the company was of the opinion that the sound transmission over the headset would be of lesser quality when worn over a headscarf, thus lowering the quality of the communication between phone operator and customers. The ETC did not consider the indirect difference in treatment to be justified as there was an alternative available that would satisfy both employer and employee, namely allowing the headset to be worn *under* the headscarf.[104] In this case, the understanding of the notion of indirect discrimination comes very close to the related concept of reasonable accommodation for reasons of religion and belief, as there was a reasonable (obvious and cost-free) compromise that should have been considered to allow both parties' interests to be met. This approach requires some initiative and creativity from the employer, taking into account the employee's interests, and differs from an approach accepted by Belgian courts whereby any duty on the employer to take affirmative steps when a request is made is rejected.

A reasonable effort on behalf of the employer was also recognized by the 's-Hertogenbosch court[105] in 2009 in a non-headscarf Muslim religious dress conflict in a hospital. The case involved the length of arm sleeves to be worn

---

general ethnic discrimination rather than the headscarf specifically, even though this may seem to be the case to the job applicant.

103 ETC 2006-215, 27 October 2006; for cases of indirect distinction that were not justified, see ETC 1996-85, 17 October 1996.

104 According to the ETC, special circumstances can justify an employer instituting a strict uniform policy. The ETC ruled that the Amsterdam police could institute a uniform without allowing a headscarf for positions that require contact with the general public. However, in determining to which functions this strict policy should apply, a careful balance must be made. ETC 2008-123, 23 October 2008.

105 Civil Court 's-Hertogenbosch 13 July 2009, *Jeroen Bosch Ziekenhuis* v. *X.*, case nr. 620353 (LJN: BJ2840).

under a hospital uniform. The procedure was initiated by the hospital requesting dissolution of the employment contract of a female Muslim nurse who had been an employee for seven years. The question was framed as follows: to what extent can a hospital dress policy restrict the right of a Muslim nurse to dress according to her faith? The nurse had sought to cover her arms, including her underarms, as she considered it a religious mandate under her Islamic faith to cover arms as much as possible. She was working in the dialysis department where short sleeves were required under hospital directives for hygiene reasons, namely to prevent infections. The Healthcare inspection confirmed this to be a professional standard.

Several alternatives (such as wearing a gown during patient contacts) had proven unsatisfactory for both parties and the nurse objected to being transferred to another department where long sleeves could be worn. The court sided with the hospital that the policy pursued legitimate aims, namely to limit risks of infection as much as possible.[106] The restriction on the freedom of religion was also considered necessary, proportionate and justified, especially since several alternatives or accommodations were tried out beforehand.[107] This case would most probably have been decided the same if there had been an explicit legal duty to accommodate for religious practices under Dutch law. In the US, when an employer faces undue hardship in accommodating an employee but has another job opening, an "accommodation by transfer" is often appropriate. In the *Shelton* case,[108] a nurse who for religious reasons refused to assist in abortions in the labor and delivery unit was offered a transfer to another hospital unit. The hospital was found to have met its duty to reasonably accommodate the nurse even though she preferred to stay in the same unit and trade shifts with colleagues. Thus it could be argued that under the Dutch interpretation of the anti-discrimination framework, adopting an explicit reasonable accommodation duty would have limited practical consequences.[109]

In a twist to the traditional workplace headscarf scenario, the ETC in 2005 considered a case where an elite Muslim school rejected the application of a Muslim teacher of Arabic (Samira Haddad) because she *refused to wear* a headscarf. This went against the school dress code that prescribed headscarves for female Muslim teachers but not for non-Muslim teachers.[110] The ETC found this treatment to be discriminatory. The ETC requires a policy to be uniformly

106 Civil Court 's-Hertogenbosch 13 July 2009, *Jeroen Bosch Ziekenhuis* v. *X.*, case nr. 620353 (LJN: BJ2840); the court did not require that scientific evidence be provided that wearing three-quarter sleeves entailed more risk than short sleeves.

107 However, the employee was awarded damages (about €8,500) because the way the hospital had handled the conflict had inflicted psychological damage.

108 *Shelton* v. *Univ. of Med. & Dentistry of N.J.*, 223 F.3d 220, 226 (3d Cir. 2000).

109 See also L. Waddington, "Reasonable Accommodation: Time to Extend the Duty to Accommodate Beyond Disability?" 36 *Nederlands Tijdschrift Mensenrechten/NJCM-Bulletin* 186 (2011), 186–198 (arguing against the adoption of an explicit duty of reasonable accommodation for religion).

110 ETC 2005-222, 15 November 2005.

applied to all its staff or students. Therefore, had the Muslim school required all teachers—Muslim and non-Muslim—to wear a headscarf, its policy would have been accepted as the school would be acting according to its religious convictions. This requirement could be criticized in the light of the existence of inherently distinctive notions within religious beliefs, e.g. the religious conviction that only Muslim women need to wear an Islamic headscarf. This context of religious-ethos employers is a domain where the ETC seems to be struggling with its commitment to offer "a space for pluriformity and individualism as an element of the right to equal treatment."[111]

It must be said that the ETC accepts non-public Dutch schools to place dress restrictions on pupils and teachers as long as the policy is necessary in the light of the school's religious identity and is applied consistently. Previously, the ETC had approved the policy of a Catholic school prohibiting pupils from wearing a headscarf or other non-Catholic symbols because it ran counter to their religious convictions,[112] but it more recently held that a Catholic school for continued education cannot prohibit students from wearing headscarves. It formally distinguished the latter situation in that the policy was not grounded on the religious ethos of the school but rather on the motivation that "caps and hats are not allowed either."[113]

B. Religious dress in the employment context in Belgium: Ambiguous message

While the situation in Belgium is not clear-cut when it comes to private workplaces,[114] the approach is much more restrictive than in the Netherlands in the

111 ETC, *Het verschil gemaakt. Evaluatie AWGB en werkzaamheden CGB 1999–2004*, 17, available on the ETC website.

112 ETC 2003-112; ETC 2007-61 (protestant-catholic elementary school).

113 ETC 2011-2, 7 January 2011.

114 The city of Antwerp in 2007 banned the wearing of headscarves and all other religious or political symbols by all front-office city staff. Women employed with the city nurseries are allowed to cover their hair with bandanas. In the public sector, a number of Belgian cities have banned the wearing of headscarves and all other religious or political symbols by municipal employees directly engaged in dealing with the public, amongst which being the city of Antwerp which prohibited headscarves for municipal employees directly engaged in dealing with the public amidst public protest in 2007: D. Hermans, "Scheldestad bant hoofddoek. 150 moslima's protesteren tevergeefs tegen verbod" [Antwerp bans headscarves. 150 Muslim woman protest to no avail], *Het Nieuwsblad*, 16 January 2007 (it was subsequently reported that of the seven personnel members working at the city counter, three decided to take their headscarves off and other positions were sought for the others). The Brussels regional government and a few other Flemish cities issued a similar ban for their employees. At the federal level there are no specific directives on wearing religious symbols, with the notable exception of judges, police officers and other uniformed officials. See US Department Of State, *International Religious Freedom Report Belgium*, 2007, available at www.state.gov/g/drl/rls/irf/2007/90166.htm. Also,

sense that the argued commercial interests of employers[115] generally trump those of the employee to dress in accordance with her religious beliefs and practices. The balancing between the interests of employee and employer is not always explicit in the judicial decision, but the basic assessment on the relative values of conflicting interests seems to form the backdrop of the judgment. Unlike in the Netherlands where effective "pluriformity" is emphasized, an exclusive and excluding interpretation of the neutrality principle has found its way into private sector settings, with courts accepting that "neutral workplaces" seek to *guarantee* tolerance for diversity and minority stand views.

B.1. Company neutrality policy justifies headscarf ban

The judgment of the Antwerp Labor Tribunal of 27 April 2010 can serve as an example.[116] The employer, G4S Security Systems, a large multinational company that offers reception and security services, operating, among other places, in Antwerp, dismissed a female Muslim employee who had been working as an outsourced receptionist in different locations for three years. As a valued staff member, she was on good grounds up until the day she informed her superiors she wanted to start wearing a headscarf on the job. Before that day she had worn the headscarf outside of work hours, taking it off when starting her shift, which had not raised any problems. She was informed that a headscarf would not be tolerated since it violated the "strict neutrality" the company strived for "both internally within the company and externally towards customers." During a period of absence due to illness, the conflict escalated and the competent company council (*ondernemingsraad*, which consists of representatives of the employees as well as of the employer) adopted a new uniform policy, explicitly banning all staff from wearing "visible symbols of their political, philosophical or religious convictions and/or any ritual connected thereto" in the workplace. Mediation attempts by the

---

the Charleroi city council on 30 March 2010 adopted a regulation prohibiting religious, political and philosophical symbols worn by teachers in the municipal schools following a dispute with municipal math teacher Nural Topal. The Belgian Council of State ruled in favor of the city: Council of State 21 December 2010, nr. 210.000, A. 196.031/g-117.

115 It can be noted that it can be in the employer's (long term) interest to allow headscarves as well.

116 Antwerp Labor Tribunal 27 April 2010, case nr. AR/06/397639/A; K. Alidadi, "Werkgever mag hoofddoek verbieden op basis van ongeschreven regels [Employer can ban headscarves based on unwritten rules], *Juristenkrant* nr. 210, 26 May 2010, 1–2; commenting on the decision. On 23 December 2011, the Antwerp Labor Court of Appeals rejected the appeal made by the employee and the CEOOR based on the fact that it found the employer had not abused its right to dismiss the employee who refused to work without a headscarf, see Antwerp Labor Court of Appeals 23 December 2011, case nr. AR/2010/AA/453 and 2010/AA/467. The decision left several questions unanswered (such as whether a private company's neutrality policy can be considered a legitimate goal) and the CEOOR has decided to bring the case, which it considers a bad precedent, before the Cour de Cassation.

CEOOR and the liberal labor union were unsuccessful as the parties held on tight to their stances. The Muslim woman was eventually fired, with a three-month severance payment. The new uniform policy for receptionists entered into effect the next day.

The woman, supported by the CEOOR which considered this an important test case, took the case to court.[117] On the merits, the Antwerp Labor Tribunal, for the purposes of deciding the claims of direct and indirect religious discrimination, considered the meaning of the term "religion or belief" under the Belgian Anti-discrimination Act. The Employment Equality Directive does not define these terms and most Member States have not done so in their national legislation. So the Tribunal held it can be debated whether "religion or belief" refers only to the *forum internum* or also entails manifestations of religion or belief by wearing religious dress and symbols—the latter being the position of the ETC. The CEOOR argued that an absolute ban imposed by a private employer on manifesting any religious convictions in the workplace amounted to a direct distinction that could not be justified.[118] The employer, on the other hand, argued that wearing a headscarf did not fall under the freedom of religion as it was not proven that it was obligatory under Islamic precepts. The Tribunal held that the freedom to wear a headscarf, even if a disputed precept of Islam, falls under the freedom of religion protected under Article 9 of the ECRM as the employee—who has the right to form her own opinion—genuinely considered it her religious duty. However, the Tribunal reiterated that under Article 9 of the ECHR manifestations of religion are subject to restrictions.

According to the Tribunal, under the Belgian Anti-discrimination Act, the "wearing out" of religious symbols does *not* fall within the protected criterion "religion or belief." After all, it was reasoned, accepting that different treatments based on religious manifestations could amount to direct discrimination would negate the possibility of restrictions.[119] Therefore, since the employee was not fired because she was an adherent of Islam—the employer had known for years she was of the Islamic faith and had no problem with it—but because she had explicitly refused to abide by an "instruction to dress neutrally," there was no direct discrimination on the basis of "religion or belief." The direct discrimination claim failed also as such a claim requires showing that "comparable employees" were treated differently. Here, the policy applied (formally) to all employees.

117 The summary proceedings had been unsuccessful, as the claim was dismissed by the Tribunal and confirmed by the Labor Court of Appeals because of procedural reasons (lack of standing), i.e. no risk of repetition of the alleged discrimination (Antwerp Labor Court of Appeals 14 January 2008, *Sociaalrechtelijke kronieken* 2009, nr. 2, 93–97).

118 The CEOOR requested a preliminary ruling from the ECJ, but the Tribunal did not follow that request, arguing the case did not involve "an absolute ban" on manifestations. The Labor Court of Appeals similarly refused to refer questions to the ECJ.

119 In case of direct discrimination, "genuine occupational requirements" constitutes the main justification.

Even though it was shown that other receptionists were in fact not wearing the uniform on the job *after* the uniform code was instituted, those employees were not considered "comparable": believers (the employee) and non-believers (the other receptionists) could not be compared when it comes to treatment for wearing religious symbols, according to the Tribunal. Also, a difference was noted that the other receptionists' failure to abide by the uniform rule was one-time only and they were reprimanded, while the employee had expressed her principled position on various occasions.

Perhaps unsurprisingly, the indirect discrimination claim failed as well. The ban of visible convictional symbols was considered proportionate with the legitimate aim of creating "a neutral and discreet image towards customers" and to "guarantee a peaceful and tolerant co-existence within the company," which according to the Tribunal can only be done through showcasing neutrality. The Tribunal considered that G4S is a "multicultural enterprise" that hires people of all faiths and 11% of its employees are Muslims. The Tribunal rejected the assertion of the CEOOR and the employee that the neutrality policy gives in to the discriminatory preferences of customers[120] who stand unfavorably against Muslim women with headscarves. On the contrary, it noted that the "neutrality aims to respect everyone's identity and convictions."

In addition, the Antwerp Tribunal did not accept that the restrictive dress code policy was merely adopted by the company council (*ondernemingsraad*) to respond to this particular incident notwithstanding several red flags, but it found that an "unwritten rule" was already in place (and this on the disputable basis of the company diversity policy and requirement for employees to be tolerant and not discriminate amongst co-workers) and in fact confirmed by the employee's previously abiding conduct.

This judgment could be contrasted with the Dutch situation where, as said, protection against religious discrimination includes protection for manifestations though religiously mandated dress.[121] Under the Antwerp Tribunal's interpretation, the Anti-discrimination Act's protective scope is considerably pushed back, becoming irrelevant for many fundamental religious practice aspects such as wearing religious dress.[122] Employer decisions, even if they are directly based

120 ECJ 10 July 2008, *Belgian Centre for Equal Opportunities* v. *Feryn*, Case C-54/07 (request for preliminary ruling submitted by Labor Court of Appeals Brussels), holding that giving in to discriminatory preferences of customers can amount to direct discrimination on basis of race or ethnic origin.

121 *Supra*: ETC 1995-31, 7 August 1995; see also *infra*, Civil Court 's-Gravenhage, 20 August 2007, *X.* v. *het college van burgemeester en wethouders van X.*, case nr. AWB 06-4333 (LJN: BC3697) (the term "religion" under the Dutch Equal Treatment act needs to be understood broadly).

122 One can assert that this interpretation considerably limits the protection under the anti-discrimination law by excluding manifestations of religious beliefs from direct discrimination, especially since justification (e.g. commercial interests) under the indirect discrimination scheme can readily be accepted; see K. Alidadi, "Werkgever mag hoofddoek

on religious dress (in which case it would involve direct discrimination in the Netherlands), must thus be evaluated as an indirect discrimination with the broader possibility of justification. Further, there is no reference to anything resembling a duty of reasonable accommodation under the Anti-discrimination Act or consideration for the religious interest of the employee in the workplace. The underlying position seems to be that religion is "a thing of the mind" and does not belong in the workplace, plain and simple, in contrast to the appreciation of "pluriformity" as an element of equal treatment under the opinions of the ETC and Dutch courts.

B.2. Headscarves, books and shoes

This was not the first decision where a Belgian employer's attempts to outlaw religious symbols from a private workplace was validated. On 15 January 2008, the Labor Court of Appeals of Brussels[123] held that "the freedom to express one's religion is not absolute and can be limited when the religious practice is of a nature to disturb the order." A well-known large bookstore chain, Club., had discharged a long-term female employee who upon her first day after returning from an extensive six-year leave wanted to wear a headscarf while shelving and selling books. The Brussels Court of Appeals found the bookstore's workplace neutrality policy prohibiting non-neutral clothing, including headscarves, for "front office personnel" to be based on objective criteria related to the company's "open, available, sober, family-oriented, and neutral" image. And since the policy applied to all personnel, it was not discriminatory as far as the Court of Appeals was concerned. What's more, the employee was chastised for her "clear and open violation of this written company policy" by wearing a headscarf even following an earlier "warning" on the phone that it would not be tolerated. This was considered to be "an aggravating factor" adding to the "grave fault" because the employee in violation of the company policy had failed to get in touch with the employer ten days before the return date to make the practical arrangements. This behavior of the "insubordinate" employee caused a breakdown of trust and thus justified the immediate termination of the employment contract without notice or severance payment, according to the Court of Appeals. The Muslim employee had, after her dismissal, stated she would have welcomed another position which did not involve customer contacts but the company did not look into that option. The Court stated explicitly that the company had no duty to do so.

Again this is in contrast to the Dutch cases, where the efforts of employers to look for alternative solutions are evaluated. Thus, even though the legal frameworks are comparable in the Netherlands and no explicit duty of reasonable accommodation exists under the Dutch Equal Treatment Act either, the situation "on the ground"

---

verbieden op basis van ongeschreven regels [Employer can ban headscarves based on unwritten rules], *Juristenkrant* nr. 210, 26 May 2010, 2.

123 Labor Court of Appeals (4th ch.) nr. 48.695, 15 January 2008, *Journal des tribunaux du travail* 2008, nr. 1003, 140.

seems considerably different. The Belgian judge explicitly states that as there is no duty of reasonable accommodation on the basis of religious beliefs or practices, there was no need for the employer to consider or offer a transfer to a "back office position" within the company. Under the US reasonable accommodation framework, even if it were to be accepted that allowing the employee to wear a headscarf while working in a general bookstore would amount to "undue hardship," a lateral transfer option should be considered if certain conditions are met, e.g. if there are openings available that meet the employee's profile.[124] In contrast, the Belgian judicial approach, by refusing to "burden" the employer, effectively channels the religious employee to the unemployment agency.

In the private sector, Belgian judges are not wary of "neutrality arguments." In comparison, in the rare[125] occasions that "religious neutrality" arguments were raised, they have not been readily accepted by the ETC. Even in the case of a court clerk, the ETC regarded the neutrality argument as insufficient justification to prohibit the wearing of a headscarf.[126] Even though the goal of independence and impartiality of the judiciary is itself a legitimate goal, the means of achieving that goal were disproportionate considering the role of the court clerk.[127]

But there have been Belgian cases more sympathetic to the religious practicing employee. In an older case that was decided before the first anti-Discrimination Act of 2003 entered into force, the Labor Tribunal Charleroi (1992)[128] found to be abusive the immediate discharge for "grave reasons" of a shoe saleswoman who for religious reasons wore "long and wide robes and skirts," which according to the employer did not fit in with the "commercial lifestyle of the city." The Tribunal considered that parties had not determined in advance any particular style of clothing that salespersons were to wear on the job, so that the woman was free to

124 EEOC Guidelines on Discrimination because of Religion, 29 C.F.R. §1605.2(d)(iii); *Rivera* v. *Choice Courier*, 2004 WL 1444852 (SDNY June 25, 2004) (employer's failure to consider transferring employee to a position with less stringent dress code so that he could wear a patch stating "Jesus is Lord" may have violated Title VII).

125 R. Van Den Boer, "Een open doekje voor de Commissie Gelijke Behandeling?" in *Gelijkheid en (andere) Grondrechten* (R. Holtmaat, ed., Kluwer, Deventer 2004), 158–59; see also ETC advice of 12 August 2004 to Meldpunt Discriminatie Amsterdam, 14.

126 ETC 2001-53 of 22 June 2001; this was a controversial decision. Dutch minister Korthals declared that it would not follow this (non-binding) opinion and the judiciary should refrain from expressing religious, political or other opinions. See M. Kuijer, "Vrouwe Justitia: blinddoek of hoofddoek? Noot onder Commissie gelijke behandeling 22 juni 2001, oordeel 2001-53," 26 *NJCM-Bulletin* 890 (2003), 890–902.

127 The neutrality argument has also failed in other settings: ETC 1996-59: the bank could not rely on its "religious neutrality" to stop one of its associates who was a Jehovah's Witness from proselytizing in the area where the bank was situated and most of its clientele lived. The ETC held that the bank does not make clear what neutrality stands for, and suggests that neutrality could also be achieved through a pluriform composition of its staff.

128 Labor Tribunal Charleroi, 26 October 1992, *Sociaalrechtelijke kronieken/Chroniques de droit social* 1993, 84–85.

follow her personal taste and wear clothes that were comfortable for carrying out her work. The employer was found to have fired her out of a mere subjective fear that her appearance would hurt his business even though there were no indications of actual financial loss, and no customer had ever complained.

Still, this does not take away from the fact that Belgian and Dutch case law is quite distinct when it comes to accommodating the religious dress of Muslim women in the private workplace. For this reason it could be argued that introducing an explicit duty of reasonable accommodation for reasons of religion in Europe would signify a general "leveling up" of protection in certain jurisdictions, and a more effective convergence in the interpretation of the shared legal framework across Member States. After all, while neither Belgium nor the Netherlands have currently adopted such explicit legal duty for employers in their legislation,[129] it can be argued that the ETC and Dutch courts are utilizing the potential of the concept of indirect discrimination to guarantee a similar level of protection for Muslim women wishing to adhere to their religious dress practices in the workplace as under a reasonable accommodation framework. This is not the case in Belgium, where an explicit adoption of reasonable accommodations could lead to more effective protection for religious manifestations in the workplace. A recent empirical study on the de facto practices of religious and cultural accommodations in Belgian companies concluded that the current case-by-case and employer discretionary method of dealing with claims for religious and cultural accommodations leads to legal insecurity, unequal treatment and arbitrariness.[130] The study also reveals that labor unions do not always have an incentive to support religious claims (which sometimes contradict other union goals),[131] in particular if there was no group of employees behind the request.

---

129 It should be noted that the Flemish Decree of 8 May 2002 concerning the Proportional Participation in the Labor Market, *Belgian Official Journal*, 6 April 6, 2007, implementing the Employment Equality Directive, has not limited the duty of reasonable accommodation for reasons of disability but was left open for all grounds including religion or belief. This decree applies amongst others to the Flemish government and educational institutions. However, there is no case law on the application of the reasonable accommodation provision. E. Bribosia, J. Ringelheim and I. Rorive, Aménager la Diversité: Le Droit de L'Egalité face à la Pluralité Religieuse," 19 *Revue Trimestrielle Des Droits De l'Homme* 320 (2009), at 366 (noting that this happened because of an oversight).

130 Institute For European Studies (VUB) and Metices-Germe (ULB), *Culturele Diversiteit op de werkvloer. Praktijken van redelijke aanpassing in België (study conducted in assignment of the Centre for Equal Opportunities and Opposition to Racism)*, September 2010, available on the site of the CEOOR, wwww.diversite.be.

131 For instance, the request of Muslim employees to skip lunch break during Ramadan and go home earlier is not supported by the labor union, as the right to reasonable breaks has been fought for a long time and is considered too important to compromise. *Id.* (*Culturele Diversiteit op de werkvloer*), 114. Under the EEOC Guidelines workers "use of lunch time in exchange for early departure" is mentioned as a type of reasonable accommodation by way of flexible scheduling. 29 C.F.R. §1605.2 (d) (1) (ii). However, the divergent interests of individual religious employees and labor unions is not unique

Still, introducing a legal duty of reasonable accommodation for religious observance and practice in Belgium remains highly contested.[132]

C. Religious dress in the unemployment context in the Netherlands and in Belgium

The issue of religious dress is also important in the unemployment context. The issues that arise in this context are partially spillovers from the lack of accommodation awarded by private employers in the workplace. For instance, when a Muslim woman is unsuccessful in obtaining a position or is fired because of her headscarf, she will turn to the state unemployment agency for unemployment compensation. To be entitled to that compensation, a number of conditions must generally be met: e.g. one has to be *in*voluntarily unemployed and available for the labor market. In case of a dispute, courts are called upon to decide whether the state agency must (continue to) support the applicant under the given circumstances.

When a woman's religiously mandated but "unconventional" dress considerably lowers the success rate for finding a job, how does and how should that affect her entitlement to unemployment benefits? Can an applicant be cut off from unemployment compensation or other assistance where an otherwise acceptable job was rejected or certain far-reaching reservations based on religious motives were formulated because of dress incompatibility? The incentives sent out by the combined—but not necessarily harmonized—jurisprudence in the employment and unemployment contexts have significant policy implications.

C.1. Burqas, job hunts and unemployment benefits in the Netherlands

In the Netherlands, certain public benefits require beneficiaries to make assisted efforts to integrate themselves in the job market. The issue has arisen with regard to the headscarf but also with regard to face-covering veils like the *burqa*. A number

---

in Belgium, as in the US labor unions are a major force in blocking legislation aimed at strengthening the reasonable accommodation duty under Title VII of the Civil Rights Act (Workplace Religious Freedom Act) beyond the *de minimis* standard because of fears that in some cases to accommodate employees' Sabbaths will mean overriding seniority systems (T. Berg, "Religious Liberty in America at the End of the Century," 16 *Journal of Law & Religion* 187 (2001), 214).

132 See the final report of the Belgian *Rondetafels van de Interculturaliteit* presented to the Federal Minister of Work and Equal Opportunities Milquet on 8 November 2010, which speaks of an irreconcilable difference of opinion within the reporting committee on workplace reasonable accommodations for religious practices, and therefore only recommends that "one should consider more in-depth the potential advantages and disadvantages of the extension of the concept of reasonable accommodation" (report available at www.interculturalite.be). See also K. Alidadi, "Studie over redelijke aanpassingen voor religie op Belgische werkvloer," [Study on reasonable accommodations for religious reasons in the Belgian workplace] *Juristenkrant* nr. 221, 4 January 2011, 6–7 (discussing the CEOOR's debatable stance against the introduction of a legally binding reasonable accommodation duty and instead choosing to rely solely on social dialogue procedures).

of *burqa*-clad Muslim women have fought to keep public assistance, refusing to compromise on far-reaching interpretations of religious precepts, thereby testing the limits of the Dutch policy of tolerance and inclusion.

In a 2007 case before the 's-Gravenhage Civil Court,[133] a Muslim woman had seen her public benefits reduced because her headscarf and traditional wide clothing—consisting of a *djellaba* (long overcoat with hood), large headscarf, small headscarf and wide clothing underneath—hampered a successful search for employment. The woman was asked to alter her appearance to increase her job chances, but had replied that her religious convictions stood in the way of changing her dress. She also objected to working in one space together with men. She was excluded from benefits because these reservations inhibited the acceptance of a generally suitable job position, and she had made too little effort to find employment.

The woman argued that the request to alter her dress violated the Dutch Equal Treatment Act and Articles 9 and 14 of the ECHR. The Civil Court first clarified that the term "religion" as mentioned under the Dutch Equal Treatment Act needs to be understood broadly in accordance with the concept of freedom of religion which is guaranteed by the Dutch Constitution and international human rights conventions, and includes not only the declaring of a religious conviction but also acting in accordance therewith. The interference at hand did not amount to direct discrimination as the request was not directed against the religious clothing itself but the supposed repercussions on the woman's employment search. Rather, the case involved indirect discrimination for which the justification would have to be assessed. The Civil Court found work safety to be a legitimate goal. The woman, considering her low schooling, would likely have to work with machines and wearing her traditional wide clothing would be dangerous in certain positions that require machine operation. However, the Civil Court did not find that the adjustment of the clothing to the extent requested was necessary because "more proportionate means" would be available. Thus, the Civil Court held that limiting the woman's benefits was unjustified.

Another 2007 case, this time before the Amsterdam Civil Court,[134] involved the temporary exclusion from assistance benefits of a Muslim woman who insisted on wearing a *burqa*. It was argued that the plaintiff was at fault for the failing of various job integration attempts. For instance, the woman was unable to meet the safety demands of a call center as those required that during check-in and during work hours the picture on the employee card could be matched up to the employee's face. Also, a position at another call center which allowed her to work from home was refused because the work entailed selling lottery tickets. Further, she was refused for another work experience because her appearance made

133 Civil Court 's-Gravenhage, 20 August 2007, *X.* v. *het college van burgemeester en wethouders van X.*, case nr. AWB 06-4333 (LJN: BC3697).

134 Civil Court Amsterdam, 24 May 2007, *X. v. het college van burgemeester en wethouders van de gemeente Diemen*, case nr. AWB 07/1635 WWB (LJN: BA6917).

communication with co-workers difficult, if not impossible. And a home work position was refused based on a number of practical problems.

The main arguments before the Amsterdam Civil Court centered around the lottery selling job. The Civil Court considered it general knowledge that Muslims are not allowed to gamble and thus it cannot be expected that the plaintiff who is of the Muslim faith *enable* gambling by selling tickets. The court found that it would be disproportionate to ask the plaintiff to take off her *burqa* to help the job mediation go more smoothly, as it was held that not *all possible alternatives* were pursued before asking the plaintiff to take off part of a piece of clothing that for her is the direct expression of her faith. Thus, even under these given circumstances, the Amsterdam Civil Court held that the woman's benefits should not have been limited.

Thus, it seems that while most European jurisdictions are struggling with the *headscarf* in the workplace and certain European localities and countries have banned or are considering banning face-covering veils in the public space,[135] the debate with regard to religious dress in the workplace includes face-covering veils in the Netherlands.[136] This is a highly contentious issue: even if the *burqa* bans in France and Belgium have been condemned, women who seek to wear *burqas* on the job in Europe have been publicly criticized by the Muslim community as "counterproductive" and for "breed[ing] considerable distrust of young Muslim women who are courageous enough to wear headscarves when starting new jobs."[137]

---

135 For a discussion, see M. Evans, "From Cartoons to Crucifixes: Current Controversies Concerning the Freedom of Religion and the Freedom of Expression before the European Court of Human Rights," 26 *Journal of Law & Religion* 345, 364–368 (noting that *burqa* bans will inevitably come before the ECtHR). France and Belgium in 2011 became the first European countries to institute a public *burqa* ban, see J. Vrielink and E. Brems, "Belgium bans 'burqa,'" *Open Democracy* 21 July 2011, available at www.opendemocracy.net. In Germany, the state of Hesse adopted a Decree prohibiting civil servants from wearing full-face veils on the job, but allowing headscarves. This was triggered by an announcement by a civil servant returning to work fully veiled. See A. Reimann, "Veiled Debate Arrives in Germany. State Prohibits Burqas at Work for Public Employees," *Spiegel Online International*, 3 February 2011, available at www.spiegel.de.

136 See also the case of *Azmi* v. *Kirklees Metropolitan Borough Council*, UK Employment Appeal Tribunal, 30 March 2007, Appeal No. UKEAT/0009/07/MAA (involving the wearing of a *niqab* by a teaching assistant) in the UK, another country with multiculturalist policies (which have, however, come under pressure).

137 See A. Reimann, "Veiled Debate Arrives in Germany. State Prohibits Burqas at Work for Public Employees," *Spiegel Online International*, 3 February 2011, available at www.spiegel.de (Nurhan Soykan, the secretary general of the Central Council of Muslims in Germany). Even in Muslim states, women under *burqas* or equivalent covering have trouble getting jobs, especially those requiring interaction with the public. In Dubai, banks do not allow women to wear a *niqab* during work and generally "no one takes women with *niqab* in the retail sector." See D. Hussein, "Women the World over Find Veil Limits Job," *Reuters*, 22 August 2007.

The question is how tenable a situation is where in one EU country *burqas* are banned in the public sphere while in the neighboring country courts remain hopeful that further attempts to integrate women with *burqas* in the labor market could be successful.[138] It is debatable whether in the current societal context it remains warranted to believe that women who insist on "masking" their identity can reasonably be expected to be integrated in the mainstream workplace. There are principled and practical considerations that would lead to the opposite conclusion. Objections to *burqas* and *niqabs* are not merely a subterfuge for discrimination. Judicial and policy decisions should distinguish between situations where women are being oppressed and where there are legitimate interests in not having to compromise religious identity in the workplace by adopting dominant standard dress practices. But even when a woman adopts the practice of her own free will, it is not unreasonable for her decision to have repercussions, in particular if she wishes to take advantage of government assistance.[139]

The ETC has taken a different approach to banning face-covering veils than with regard to the headscarf. In an opinion related to the school context, arguments that such full-body veils impose hindrances to communication and safety were accepted.[140] The British *Azmi* case[141] can be mentioned here as well. In that case, the UK Employment Appeal Tribunal found the dismissal of an assistant teacher who insisted on wearing a *niqab* not to be discriminatory as it was shown that not being able to see the teacher's expression disadvantaged the learning opportunities of already disadvantaged ethnic minority pupils.

C.2. Repercussions of workplace dress accommodation on the state unemployment system in Belgium

In a 2004 case, a female Muslim jobseeker refused a potential position in a sewing factory, where for safety reasons she was not allowed to wear her headscarf in the workplace. The Labor Court of Appeals of Antwerp on 3 June 2004[142] held she could do so without losing her right to unemployment benefits. Also, by insisting on wearing her headscarf on the job, the woman was not making

---

138 It must, however, be noted that in the Netherlands there are also proposals to ban *burqas*: B. Waterfield, "Netherlands to ban the burka," *The Telegraph*, 15 September 2011, available at www.telegraph.co.uk (noting that a burqa ban proposal was introduced in the Dutch Parliament by Geert Wilders back in 2005).

139 For a discussion of full-face covered women in a courtroom setting see N. Bakht, "Objections, Your Honour! Accommodating *Niqab*-Wearing Women in the Courtrooms," in *Legal Practice and Cultural Diversity* (R. Grillo et al., eds., Ashgate 2009), 123–124 (amongst others, defending the rights of female lawyers to appear in court in a *niqab*).

140 ETC 2003-40 (application dated 10 February 2003).

141 UK Employment Appeal Tribunal, *Azmi* v. *Kirklees Metropolitan Borough Council*, 30 March 2007, Appeal No. UKEAT/0009/07/MAA.

142 Antwerp Labor Court of Appeals (4th chamber) 3 June 2004, *Nieuw Juridisch Weekblad* 2004, 882; E. Van Hoorde, "Weigering hoofddoek af te leggen is geen werkweigering," *Juristenkrant*, 23 June 2004, 1 and 7.

herself unavailable for the general labor market as the court considered that "there are enough other positions in which she would be allowed to wear a religious headscarf."[143]

A job that is once suitable can become unsuitable when conditions change. In 2002, the Labor Court of Appeals of Brussels[144] considered the case of a young Muslim teaching trainee who had resigned in the middle of her six-month stage contract and was applying for unemployment benefits. A few months into her contract she was required to wear a "summer uniform" including Bermuda shorts that revealed her calves, which she felt would violate her Islamic duty of modesty in dress. This summer uniform was instituted despite earlier oral assurances from the employer that the "winter uniform" would be in place until the end of her contract, and the employer was not willing to make any adjustments for her. Her request for unemployment benefits was denied by the National Employment Office which argued that she had voluntarily abandoned a suitable position without a legitimate cause. The Labor Court of Appeals, however, ruled in her favor, holding that she had a legitimate reason for resigning as the position had become incompatible with her religious beliefs and thus "unsuited" for her. An older case of the Labor Tribunal of Hasselt in 1995[145] held similarly that a Muslim woman wearing a headscarf had legitimate reasons to resign from her job picking mushrooms when she was prohibited from wearing her veil.

These Belgian decisions finding in favor of continued unemployment benefits for employees experiencing the limits of tolerance in the labor market must be considered in the light of available data that reveals a bleak picture on the employment situation for women from predominantly Muslim countries of origin (Moroccan, Algerian, Turkish) living in Belgium.[146] These decisions should also be juxtaposed and compared with decisions discussed above where employers are liberated of the slightest efforts to make adjustments for Muslim women.

It can be questioned whether the Belgian case law which, on the one hand, rejects any legal duty of reasonable efforts on employers to help Muslim women reconcile work and dress but, on the other hand, instructs to generously hand out unemployment benefits to the same Muslim women, is sending out the right

143 The truth in this statement made in an unemployment case on the labor market condition might be threatened in case the "neutral workplace" becomes something of an industry standard in Belgium, confirmed by workplace jurisprudence to that effect. If it will no longer be correct to say that enough options for employment remain for veiled Muslim women, unemployment benefits would be stripped as well.

144 Brussels Labor Court of Appeals (7th Chamber) 17 October 2002, *Journal du droits des jeunes 2002*, nr. 220, 77 (available at www.jdj.be).

145 Labor Tribunal Hasselt, 1 March 1995, *Sociaalrechtelijke kronieken/Chroniques de droit social* 1996, 409; *Tijdschrijft voor Vreemdelingenrecht* 1997, 432; *Sociale Kroniek* 1996, 409, note M. Palumbo and C. Radermecker, "Le voile islamique, ou 'l'éternel' conflit entre un impératif religieux et une norme étatique."

146 Belgian National Employment Office (RVA), Migration reports 2007–2009, *supra* note 5.

signals. The unemployment agency is told to accommodate the casualties of the workplace in the social benefits area while attempts of private employers to create "neutral" workplaces by excluding all religious expressions through dress are endorsed. It is not hard to understand that this sends out the wrong message to vulnerable women from within largely socio-economically disadvantaged groups.

In a recent qualitative study on the first experiences of Muslim women in the Belgian labor market, some of the interviewed women said they considered the unemployment benefits they were receiving—without actively looking for jobs—as an "opportunity" (*kans*) the government was giving them to stay at home.[147] The women admitted that if they were not receiving unemployment benefits, they would have to work, and they were convinced they would find something.[148] The study also showed that once women "fall in the unemployment trap" it is hard for them to come out, as lower paying jobs are not always financially attractive enough.[149] According to the authors, this is one of the (many) reasons why women who during their school years had a dream of "becoming someone" in the end fail to break through the traditional pattern of school, early marriage, lots of kids and unemployment.[150]

Conclusion

One aspect of the pluralist society is the diverse religious affiliations of its members, which presents both political and legal challenges. Policy should seek to design rules to diminish rather than confirm current society's prejudices and intolerances. In the labor relations context, we need to acknowledge that the dominant standards in European societies are not neutral, and in a variety of ways can have de facto exclusionary effects on religious minority groups. In many ways this goes beyond the issue of discrimination and social integration, which has moved up the European policy agenda.

The judicial cases discussed above form but the tip of the iceberg, indicating the reality for Muslim women for whom their (chosen) religious dress can serve as a constitutive barrier to access and advancement in Europe's workplaces. It is unfortunate that outward religious allegiance must stand in the way of equal

147 I. Glorieux, S. Koelet and I. Laurijssen, *Gekleurd door het leven. Getuigenissen van jonge Turkse en Marokkaanse vrouwen over hun schooljaren en eerste ervaringen op de arbeidsmarkt* [Coloured through life. Testimonies of Young Turkish and Moroccan women on their school years and first experiences on the labor market] (Garant Uitgevers 2011).

148 *Id.* at 92 ("even if it were as a cleaning lady," Emine, one of the respondents in the study added).

149 *Id.* at 94.

150 *Id.* at 108.

opportunities for young trainees as well as equal treatment of previously highly valued employees who were dismissed once they sought to wear a headscarf.[151]

National courts across Europe are dealing differently with the growing visibility of religious pluralism and especially Islam in the workplace. Even though the Employment Equality Directive has arguably introduced a convergence in terminology and framework, it has not produced uniformity as far as the level of protection in the workplace for religious manifestations by employees. The different results achieved in Belgium and the Netherlands in comparative headscarf–employment conflict scenarios illustrate that the shared discrimination framework does not necessarily ensure harmonization of protection throughout the EU. Where in the Netherlands the concept of indirect discrimination has allowed the ETC and Dutch Courts to insist on a level of accommodation for religious dress as though there had been an explicit legal duty to accommodate, Belgian case law is far from doing the same. In contrast to the Netherlands where arguments based on neutrality are rarely accepted when advanced by private sector employers, Belgian courts have readily taken sides with employers who stand behind an exclusive interpretation of this mystifying concept in eradicating any "pluriformity," ironically sometimes in the name of "tolerance" towards diversity.

The policy to accommodate or not to accommodate for religion or belief in the workplace will have repercussions on the unemployment system. Freeing employers of any effort to make adjustments for Muslim women or offer alternatives will not make the issue go away. The case instead will merely shift to the unemployment turf. In both Belgium and the Netherlands, there is a *discrepancy* between decisions on accommodation in the workplace and in the unemployment context. The contradiction between the responses in employment and unemployment cases when it comes to taking into account "non-conformist" religious dress practices is most striking and arguably more problematic in Belgium. "Accommodation" in the unemployment context appears to want to make up for the tight confines of religious tolerance in the mainstream workplace. As a result, unintended signals that tend to keep many Muslim women from participation in the mainstream labor market and push already disadvantaged socio-economic groups into further unemployment, dependence and isolation, are being sent out by the uncoordinated Belgian jurisprudence.

This message has not failed to reach Muslim women, as recent sociological research shows. Unemployment benefits are meant to function as a "safety net" but can also work as a disincentive to employment participation. And the tension between the two areas of case law is already under pressure. A movement towards "neutral workplaces" accompanied by stigmatization of the headscarf in the mainstream workplace could perpetuate de facto exclusion in the labor market.

It is clear that it is time to turn the tide. A Europe with religion-hostile workplaces will fail to fully integrate into society a growing Muslim constituency that is here to

151 ECtHR 15 February 2001, *Dahlab* v. *Switzerland*, App. No. 42393/98; Antwerp Labor Tribunal 27 April 2010, case nr. AR/06/397639/A, *infra*.

stay. Undeniably, the fact that the headscarf is quickly becoming a prevalent sight in the streets of Europe will—to some extent—incentivize commercial interests.[152] Some employers might consider it advantageous to hire veiled saleswomen to be in contact with clientele, some of whom are women and girls with headscarves who would feel more comfortable in a store that accepts an openly Muslim employee. However, other employers will—making a different assessment of the toleration level of their customer base—fear financial loss or damage to their image if they allow employees to show their religious commitments publicly in the workplace.

Adopting a legal duty of reasonable accommodation for religious practices would mean a "leveling-up" and harmonization of protection of religious interests of employees in the workplace across Europe. While for some jurisdictions such as in the Netherlands this would to a large extent signify the formalization of the existing judicial practice under the anti-discrimination framework, even a relatively light duty—i.e. similar to the *de minimis* standard in the US[153]— can be meaningful in the Belgian legal context and holds potential to make a difference for some Muslim women. For instance, lateral transfers of employees will often cost little and could even save the company money in recruiting and training new staff, while preventing the employee from falling into an "unemployment trap."[154]

The case law of the ECtHR provides too little support for this development in the area of labor law. The question is how the ECJ will decide on the thorny question of how religious workplace dress under the Equality Directives should be approached. In deciding how much leeway to give to national states, the EC—unlike the ECtHR—cannot deny the economic and other impediments of highly divergent national interpretations of EU equality norms.

Socio-economic participation and other issues related to the workplace, including how to guarantee access, participation and progress of immigrants and religious minorities in the European workplace, hold great risk and potential for the integration debate. Which are the right incentives to send out to the various stakeholders if in the end the aim is to effectively include Muslim women in the labor force and offer chances towards social mobility in society? Both principled and more pragmatic considerations are to be taken into account. The acceptance of religious dress practices can be seen as one (low-cost) element of tolerance and acceptance of not only the Islamic but various religious communities in Europe. After all, "protecting religious interests in society helps to prevent alienation of minorities. Thus it is not full scale civil war that is prevented, but more generalized

152 On the Internet one can find sales sites for shawls to *hijab* bonnets catering to a Muslim clientele interested in fashion, with youtube videos showing how to correctly tie a *hijab* in various styles, or tie a Sikh turban crisply and without creases.

153 *Trans World Airlines, Inc.* v. *Hardison*, 432 U.S. 63, 97 S. Ct. 2264, 53 L. Ed. 2d 113 (1977).

154 This is not to say that *de minimis* is the most desirable standard for reasonable accommodations in the light of the need to provide effective employment opportunities to minorities.

social unrest within societies. Social exclusion from … participation in … economic life of the country, will lead to conflict and unrest, even if this is not demonstrated in violence."[155]

155 L. Vickers, *Religious Freedom, Religious Discrimination and the Workplace* (Hart Publishing 2008), 33.

Chapter 12

Reasonable Accommodation as a Tool to Manage Religious Diversity in the Workplace: What about the "Transposability" of an American Concept into the French Secular Context?

Gabrielle Caceres*

Introduction

Religious diversity generates new challenges with regards to diversity management. In fact, different religious groups within society have asked that their religious specificities be recognized and respected. These demands for recognition touch upon different aspects of social life but mainly the employment domain, which occupies a large part in individuals' everyday lives. Today, numerous issues arise when religious identities are taken into account in the workplace, such as those related to wearing religious signs or clothing, observing religious days of rest or religious festivals, dietary requirements and the organization of prayer times. The reactions to these issues vary, sometimes considerably, from one country to the other, which can be explained because of different historical experiences with immigration, varying Church–State regimes and perceptions regarding religion. For instance, from its origins the US has seen the migration of a vast number of people from different backgrounds. It is therefore understandable that this country has addressed the issue of religious diversity and possible responses to it early on in its history. In contrast, France is strongly influenced by a secular tradition of Republican integration of the citizen, and therefore seems to be much more reluctant to embrace religious pluralism.

* This chapter, written under the supervision of Profs. Emmanuelle Bribosia and Isabelle Rorive, is part of the research project *Outsiders in Europe: The Foreigner and the "Other" in the Process of Changing Rules and Identities*. This is a collective research project combining diverse disciplinary fields (anthropology, law, social psychology, social and political sciences) carried out by the trans-disciplinary Centre "Migrations, Asylum and Multiculturalism" (MAM) of the Free University of Brussels, ULB (2006–2011, ARC project), and financially supported by the French Community of Belgium.

One way of taking into account different religious identities in the professional context is the technique of reasonable accommodation, a legal concept which was first developed in the US within the framework of religious diversity management and the right to equality.[1] Faced with the social reality that some people were disadvantaged on the grounds of certain characteristics—such as age, disability, religious beliefs—the idea emerged that perhaps the environment should be adapted to the needs of individuals so as to provide each and every person equal access to employment, services, education or other activities.[2] Therefore, reasonable accommodation aims at relaxing generally applicable rules in order to guarantee a more substantive equality in which the specificities of everyone are taken into account.

With respect to religious diversity management in the workplace, religious reasonable accommodation offers the possibility of obtaining the adjustment of certain rules, practices or policies that are applicable to all employees but the effects of which lead to a disadvantage on the basis of religion.[3] Hence, there is a close link between the concept of reasonable accommodation and the concept of indirect discrimination. The adjustment of practices which do not take the religious beliefs of certain employees into account takes away the restriction of employee's religious freedom by allowing for different but still "reasonable" treatment. Thus, there exist two justifications for granting reasonable accommodations on the basis of religion in the employment context: on the one hand, the right to freedom of religion and, on the other hand, the principle of non-discrimination on the grounds of religion.

As said, the US was the first to consider adapting the rules in the employment context to the religious needs of workers. For this reason it is impossible to ignore developments in this pioneer country in this area, even though the Canadian experience in the matter is more often referred to in Europe.[4] In order to better understand the logic underlying reasonable accommodation, it is crucial to examine the issue starting from its first manifestations (I). This analysis will then lead to an assessment of whether this way of dealing with religious diversity can be "transplanted" to Europe. France is the European country which in terms of comparison is most interesting because it lies at the opposite end of the spectrum from the US. Ingrained in its very history, France advocates a "militant secularism,"[5] and seems to close itself off from any recognition of religious

1 E. Bribosia, I. Rorive and J. Ringelheim, "L'Aménagement Raisonnable pour Motif Religieux: Un Concept Issu d'Amérique du Nord en Voie d'Intégration en Belgique et en Europe?" in *Actuele Topics Discriminatierecht—Actualités du Droit de la Lutte Contre la Discrimination* (C. Bayart, S. Sottiaux and S. Van Drooghenbroeck, eds, La Charte/Die Keure 2009), 2.

2 E. Bribosia, I. Rorive and J. Ringelheim, *supra* note 1, at 2.

3 J. Woehrling, "Neutralité de l'Etat et Accommodements: Convergence ou Divergence?" 28 *Options politiques* 20 (2007), 20.

4 See, for example, *Institutional Accommodation and the Citizen: Legal and Political Interaction in a Pluralist Society*, Trends in social cohesion No. 21 (Council of Europe Publishing 2009).

5 C. Haguenau-Moizard, *Etats et Religions en Europe* (P.U.G. 2000), 59.

specificities.[6] However, like many other Western societies, this country is just as affected as any other country by questions relating to religious pluralism. Therefore, it seems especially interesting to examine whether the concept of reasonable accommodation could be introduced in France (II).

Thanks to this comparison between the Atlantic neighbors one can address the issue of a potential transplant of reasonable accommodation to France as a technique of religious pluralism management in the employment context. While this concept—albeit somewhat contested—has been applied for several decades in the United States, it is instead far from clear whether France would welcome the introduction of reasonable accommodation, both because of the "*laïcité*" ideology and because of the fact that the mechanism of reasonable accommodation is possibly not the best way, at the practical and theoretical level, to address the French situation. Hence, it becomes necessary at the end of this chapter to analyze the feasibility, opportunity and even the admissibility of this Northern American technique in a typically French environment.

I. Reasonable accommodations in the US

Chronologically, the US was the first on the Northern American continent to adopt the technique of reasonable accommodation. The question arose in the context of individual rights demands. The federal legislation on civil rights adopted in the 1960s provided the first basis for a duty of reasonable accommodation, justified by equality and non-discrimination principles on the ground of religion (A). The demands by American citizens to freely exercise their religious beliefs and to avoid encroachments provided the second basis for such a duty in the 1960s, this time based on religious freedom (B).

A. The prohibition of discrimination on the grounds of religion

The equality of citizens before the law is enshrined in the American Constitution. Besides this very general principle, Americans had to fight to obtain the prohibition of discrimination on several grounds, including religion. This struggle continued until the right to reasonable accommodation in the employment context was established legislatively, based directly on the right to non-discrimination.

1. The civil rights movement

In the 1960s, Americans demanded that their highest authorities fully implement the promises contained in the Constitution's Fourteenth Amendment and its principle of equal protection of the laws. Pursuant to the Equal Protection Clause, some advocated a prohibition of discrimination on the grounds of a number of

6 In France, the identity of the republican citizen, free from any community belonging, is so firmly rooted that the State denies the existence of minorities.

criteria, mainly to fight against racial segregation. As a result of the civil rights struggle, Congress adopted the 1964 Civil Rights Act, the main purpose of which was to prohibit racial discrimination.[7] Whereas the initial bill was primarily designed to protect the rights of African Americans it was quickly amended in order to protect the rights of everyone. Therefore, not only does the Act protect from discrimination on the grounds of race, color and national origin but also on the basis of sex and religion. Title VII of the Civil Rights Act specifically addresses the employment context by stating that discrimination on the five listed grounds will not be tolerated at the level of hiring, firing, employment conditions, compensation, training, etc.

However, merely prohibiting discrimination based on religion was not considered sufficient to effectively implement the equality principle.[8] In consequence, proposals were made to amend the Civil Rights Act with the aim of including the right to reasonable accommodation.[9] In 1966 and 1967, the Equal Employment Opportunity Commission (EEOC) published guidelines concerning the application of Title VII of the Civil Rights Act.[10] In these guidelines the EEOC established that an employer's refusal to "reasonably accommodate the religious practices of its employee" is a violation of the anti-discrimination legislation, "unless the employer can prove that to do so would create a serious inconvenience to the conduct of the business."[11] Thus the EEOC tried to extend the definition of prohibited discrimination contained in the 1964 Civil Rights Act to include the absence of reasonable accommodation of religious practices.[12] However, this attempt was not followed by many courts, since the judges found that a federal agency did not have the powers to extend the terms of anti-discrimination

7 *Public Law* 88-352, 78 Stat. 241, 2 July 1964.

8 Discrimination for the purposes of the Civil Rights Act entails that an employer cannot discriminate against his employees on the basis of race, color, national origin, sex or religion (for example, he cannot create disparities in pay between Christian and Jewish employees), but an employer is not obliged to adopt a non-discriminatory rule applicable in the company which disadvantages employees on the basis of race, color, national origin, sex or religion (for example, he is not bound to allow an employee to take the day off on Saturdays to observe the Sabbath).

9 State Personnel Manual, "Title VII of the Civil Rights Act of 1964 as Amended by the Equal Employment Opportunity Act of 1972, effective March 24, 1972," available at www.osp.state.nc.us.

10 The EEOC is an independent federal agency responsible for the enforcement of Title VII of the Civil Rights Act, and therefore for the enforcement of laws against workplace discrimination. See www.eeoc.gov.

11 *EEOC Guidelines on Discrimination Because of Religion*, 29 C.F.R. §1605.1 (b) (effective 10 July 1967).

12 R. L. Corrada, "Toward an Integrated Disparate Treatment and Accommodation Framework for Title VII Religion Cases," 77 *University of Cincinnati Law Review* 1411 (2008–2009), 1428.

legislation in this way.[13] The *Dewey* decision is a perfect example of this position.[14] In that case, an employee of the Reynolds Company complained about the weekly day of rest on Sunday which conflicted with his religious obligation to observe the Sabbath on another day. The Michigan Civil Rights Commission rejected the complaint and the case moved on to the EEOC, which brought it before a federal District Court. The District Court decided in favor of the employee Dewey.[15] However, the federal Court of Appeals reversed that judgment, holding that it could not impose a duty of reasonable accommodation on an employer on the basis of an EEOC guideline, when the Civil Rights Act only prohibits discrimination. This decision was then affirmed by the US Supreme Court.[16]

However, *Dewey* led to an amendment of the Civil Rights Act in 1972, thanks to an initiative by Senator Randolph, a Seventh Day Baptist who observed the Sabbath on Saturday himself. Pursuant to that amendment an employer has a duty to reasonably accommodate the religious observances and practices of his employees—or prospective employees—in the employment organization, unless it would create an "undue hardship" to the business.[17]

Thus, the duty of reasonable accommodation finds a first basis in anti-discrimination legislation. This first basis is limited to the employment domain and therefore responds to the specific problem of recognizing religious identities in the workplace. In this respect, reasonable accommodation can achieve an adjustment of both private and public workplaces to the religious practices of employees. Moreover, even though the legislator at first imposed such a duty only for religious reasons, the duty of accommodation was extended to people with disabilities in the 1990 Americans with Disabilities Act (ADA).[18]

2. *The concept of religious accommodation under the Civil Rights Act*

The Civil Rights Act imposes a duty of reasonable accommodation and allows devotees of even the most minoritarian religions not to be restricted in their deep beliefs and thus to have their religious identity recognized in a domain where curtailment is particularly felt. The terms used by the legislator have nevertheless led to some difficulties of interpretation. In fact, lower courts have for a long time

---

13 J. M. Oleske, "Federalism, Free Exercise, and Title VII: Reconsidering Reasonable Accommodation," 6 *Universlty of Pennsylvania Journal of Constitutional Law* 525 (2004), 532; E. Bribosia, I. Rorive and J. Ringelheim, *supra* note 1, at 3.

14 See, for example, *Dewey*, 429 F.2d 324 (6th Cir. 1970); *Dewey* v. *Reynolds Metals Co.*, 402 US 689 (1971).

15 *Dewey*, 429 F.2d 324 (6th Cir. 1970).

16 *Dewey* v. *Reynolds Metals Co.*, 402 US 689 (1971).

17 *Public Law* No. 92-261, 28 Stat. 103 (1972), codified as Subchapter VI of Chapter 21 of 42 U.S.C. §2000e *et seq*. For more details regarding this legislative evolution, see R. Belton et al., *Employment Discrimination Law: Cases and Materials on Equality in the Workplace* (7th ed. Thomson/West 2004).

18 *Public Law* 101-336, 104 Stat. 327, enacted 26 July 1990, codified at 42 U.S.C. §12101—see E. Bribosia, I. Rorive and J. Ringelheim, *supra* note 1, at 3.

struggled with the exact meaning of the expressions "reasonable accommodation" and "undue hardship."[19] The US Supreme Court had the chance to clarify these concepts, as well as the limits to the employer's duty, in two decisions interpreting the "accommodation" provision of Title VII of the Civil Rights Act.

The 1977 *Hardison* decision involved an employee of Trans World Airlines who was fired because of his refusal to work on Saturdays after he converted to the "Worldwide Church of God" which required the observation of the Sabbath on Saturdays.[20] In order to function on a regular basis, the company had organized a rotating shift system based on the seniority of its employees which allowed Mr Hardison to avoid working on Saturdays for a period of time. However, after a number of years he was transferred to a new department in which his reduced seniority no longer allowed him to take his day off on Saturday. In spite of his requests for a solution, Mr Hardison was not exempted from the seniority system and was therefore fired for insubordination because of his refusal to work on Saturdays. In this case the employee was potentially the victim of "disparate impact discrimination," since the employment rule was facially neutral but nonetheless discriminated against persons belonging to specific religious beliefs. Indeed, Mr Hardison was fired not because his employer did not want to work with people with a specific religious belief but because a general rule applicable to all employees was incompatible with his religious practice. On this basis, the Civil Rights Act establishes the employer's duty of reasonable accommodation so as to prevent employees from becoming victims of similar discriminations.

The Court of Appeals decided in favor of Mr Hardison, since the airline had rejected three reasonable alternatives proposed by the employee which did not cause "undue hardship" to the company.[21] The US Supreme Court, however, reversed the decision, holding that the company had demonstrated sufficient efforts in trying to accommodate the employee's religious beliefs. More specifically, the Supreme Court found that there is "undue hardship" if the proposed accommodation requires the employer to bear more than a "*de minimis* cost."[22] The justices also held that an accommodation cannot be reasonable if it encroaches upon the rights of other employees because it would be discriminatory to force them to work on a weekend

19 See, for example, *Williams* v. *Southern Union Gas Co.*, 529 F.2d 483 (10th Cir. 1976); *Draper* v. *United States Pipe & Foundry Co.*, 527 F.2d 515 (6th Cir. 1975); *Cummins* v. *Parker Seal Co.*, 516 F.2d 544 (6th Cir. 1975), *aff'd by an equally divided Court*, 429 U.S. 65 (1976); *Johnson* v. *United States Postal Serv.*, 497 F.2d 128 (5th Cir. 1974); *Riley* v. *Bendix Corp.*, 464 F.2d 1113 (5th Cir. 1972); E. Zoller, "Les Rapports Entre Les Eglises et Les Etats aux Etats-Unis: Le Modèle Américain de Pluralisme Religieux Égalitaire," in *Laïcité, Liberté de Religion et Convention Européenne des Droits de L'Homme* (G. Gonzales, ed., Bruylant 2006), 40.

20 *Trans World Airlines, Inc.* v. *Hardison*, 432 US 63 (1977).

21 These three alternatives were: (1) to make somebody else work instead of him on Saturdays while he would work on Sundays instead of this person but with a normal salary; (2) to change departments; and (3) to depart minimally from the seniority system.

22 J. M. Oleske, *supra* note 13, at 533; 432 US 63, at 84.

only because—as opposed to their colleague—they do not observe a Saturday Sabbath. Moreover, the fact that the rotating shift system had been introduced by a collective bargaining agreement seemed sufficient in the eyes of the Supreme Court to demonstrate that a negotiation had been organized with the workers and that therefore an attempt at accommodation had been made.[23]

The Supreme Court's interpretation of the term "undue hardship" limits the possibilities for asking for reasonable accommodations under the Civil Rights Act and has been heavily criticized.[24] In their dissenting opinions, Justices Marshall and Brennan stressed that the "*de minimis* cost" criterion has almost made the duty of reasonable accommodation established by anti-discrimination legislation meaningless.[25] Nevertheless, this decision has determined the criteria according to which the Title VII duty should be applied. In fact, the Supreme Court explained how one has to proceed in assessing reasonable accommodation claims. First of all, the employee has to prove that a religious command in which he genuinely believes conflicts with an employment regulation, that he informed the employer of this situation and that he was sanctioned for not observing such a regulation. In such a case, the employee has demonstrated a prima facie case of discrimination. If the employer wants to avoid a liability, he in turn has to show either that he offered a reasonable accommodation which would allow the employee to follow his or her religious commands or, if no accommodation was offered, that such would amount to an "undue hardship."[26]

In the 1986 *Philbrook* decision, the Supreme Court further clarified the concept of "reasonable accommodation."[27] This case concerned a Connecticut school

---

23 It is interesting to note that the Canadian Supreme Court has explicitly rejected the "*de minimis* cost" criterion introduced in the United States, thus imposing a heavier "undue hardship" test on the employer. In the *Renaud* decision, involving facts similar to the *Hardison* case, the highest Canadian court held that it was not sufficient to invoke the existence of a collective bargaining agreement, which had introduced a rotating shift system based on seniority, in order to reject the demand from a Seventh Day Baptist not to work on Saturdays for religious grounds. The employer had to submit concrete and material proof of the "undue hardship" and of the risk of being flooded by accommodation demands caused by a snowball effect. Ultimately this meant that he could not avoid the duty of reasonable accommodation (*Central Okanagan School District No 23 c. Renaud*, [1992] 2 *R.C.S.* 984). See E. Bribosia, I. Rorive and J. Ringelheim, *supra* note 1, at 9–10.

24 K. Engle, "The Persistence of Neutrality: The Failure of the Religious Accommodation Provision to Redeem Title VII," 76 *Texas Law Review* 387 (1997), 387–406. This interpretation of the Court contrasts with the *Americans with Disabilities Act* which defines "undue hardship," regarding the duty of reasonable accommodation of disability, as a "significant difficulty or expense" (E. Bribosia, I. Rorive and J. Ringelheim, *supra* note 1, at 4).

25 R. T. Foltin and J. D. Standish, "Reconciling Faith and Livelihood: Religion in the Workplace and Title VII," 31 *Human Rights* 19 (2004).

26 R. L. Corrada, *supra* note 12, at 1413.

27 *Ansonia Board of Education* v. *Philbrook*, 479 US 60 (1986).

teacher who was a member of a church which asked its members to refrain from any secular work on the occasion of certain religious festivals. For this reason, each year Mr Philbrook missed approximately six days of school, whereas the collective bargaining agreement only allowed for an absence of three days a year for the observance of religious obligations.[28] Even though the alternatives suggested by Mr Philbrook were rejected by the school board, he was nevertheless offered the three necessary additional days off work, but without payment.[29] Not satisfied with this offer, Mr Philbrook went to court claiming a violation of Title VII of the Civil Rights Act. After his claim was rejected by the trial court the Court of Appeals reversed the decision, arguing that when an employer and an employee both propose a reasonable accommodation then the employer has the obligation to adopt the solution preferred by the *employee*, unless this represents an undue hardship. The Supreme Court did not share this viewpoint and stated that whatever reasonable accommodation proposed by the *employer* is sufficient to satisfy the requirements under the Civil Rights Act. In other words, the employer has fulfilled his obligation by proposing a reasonable accommodation without necessarily having to accept the solutions proposed by the employee.

By adopting a strict interpretation of the concept of reasonable accommodation under the Civil Rights Act, the Supreme Court's jurisprudence restricts its potential. Indeed, in his partial dissent Justice Marshall stressed that the solution to offer unpaid holidays did not seem satisfactory to him. He stated that it forced Mr Philbrook to "choose between following his religious precepts with a partial forfeiture of salary and violating these precepts for work with full pay."[30]

Following the *Philbrook* case, religious lobbies reacted to this restrictive interpretation. A number of bi-partisan bills were proposed in the US House of Representatives and in the US Senate. The latest one was dated 17 March 2005.[31] The Workplace Religious Freedom Act (WRFA) intends to strengthen the requirements imposed on employers pursuant to Title VII of the Civil Rights Act. The idea is to reinstall Congress' (alleged) original intent, which the Supreme Court is seen to have subverted substantially through interpretation. If adopted, this

28 E. Zoller, *supra* note 19, at 41.

29 S. A. Merriman, *Religion and the Law in America: An Encyclopedia of Personal Belief and Public Policy* (Abc-clio 2007), 129.

30 479 US 60, at 75.

31 However, this draft law is still pending. Indeed, because the US legislative process is relatively complex, many bills fail to become law, with many brought to the agenda of the House or Senate but not making it through the next step of the committee stage. For those which would be still subject to this review, the mere passivity of the committee is sufficient to permanently obstruct the adoption of the text (Ph. Lauvaux, *Les Grandes Démocraties Contemporaines* (PUF 2004), 302–303). Thus, it is likely that this latter proposal will remain blocked, like the previous ones, at an intermediate stage of the legislative process, and has in fact been introduced only for media-related purpose (*Id.* at 302). Indeed, this bill has already been introduced several times to Congress in recent years, without success (J. M. Oleske, *supra* note 13, at 536).

legislation would introduce a more restrictive interpretation of "undue hardship" because that term would no longer be limited by the *minimum cost* borne by the employer. Instead, the proposed bill limits that notion to a situation imposing a "*significant difficulty or expense*."[32] Hence, citizens would no longer be forced to choose between their beliefs and their salary if and when they are confronted with a professional requirement which stands in contrast to their religious obligations. In fact, in order for the employer to fulfill his duties, the WRFA establishes that the reasonable accommodation must put an end to the existing conflict between the employment rule and the religious beliefs of the employee. However, the bill tries to maintain a balance between demands from religious employees and employers by prohibiting any reasonable accommodation which would induce an employee into dodging his "essential functions."[33]

Even though numerous religious organizations support this legislative amendment, there is significant opposition to it as well. The critiques, raised mainly by the American Civil Liberties Union (ACLU),[34] denounce the risk of an encroachment upon the rights and freedoms of others. If a religious claimant demands a reasonable accommodation from his employer, the contrast with other rights or values generally leads courts to reject such a request. Opponents of the WRFA fear that with this amendment courts will no longer reject such demands and that this will threaten the rights and freedoms of others.[35] The federal District Courts and Courts of Appeals have so far rejected similar accommodations or demands to proselytize or engage in unwanted religious activities directed towards others. In the *Spratt* case, in order to avoid disrupting the county's religious neutrality policy, a federal District Court held that a county sheriff did not have to accommodate a social worker, hired to provide secular mental health counseling to prisoners, who used biblical readings proclaiming the famous "casting out of demons."[36] In the *Johnson* decision, a court rejected the accommodation invoked by an employee to be allowed to begin more statements on the job with the expression "In the name of Jesus Christ of Nazareth" because this might offend clients with other beliefs—or without any beliefs—with whom he entered into contact.[37] In *Chalmers*, another federal court determined that, due to the infringement of privacy, an employer had no duty to accommodate his employee's need to send letters to the homes of both

32 The legislator uses the same wording as the *Americans with Disabilities Act*, regarding reasonable accommodation of disability.

33 L. W. Murphy and C. E. Anders, "ACLU Letter on the Harmful Effect of S. 893, the Workplace Religious Freedom Act, on Critical Personal and Civil Rights," ACLU 2004, available at www.aclu.org.

34 This non-profit organization aims at defending and preserving rights and freedoms guaranteed to American citizens, primarily through legal proceedings or legislative lobbying—see www.aclu.org.

35 L. W. Murphy and C. E. Anders, *supra* note 33.

36 *Spratt* v. *County of Kent*, 621 F. Supp. 594 (W. D. Mich. 1985), *aff'd*, 810 F.2d 203 (6th Cir. 1986), *cert. denied*, 480 US 933 (1987).

37 *Johnson* v. *Halls Merchandising, Inc.*, 1989 WL 23201 (W. D. Mo. 1989).

a supervisor and a subordinate in which he criticized their private lives and urged religious solutions.[38] The opponents of the WRFA contend that these cases, where the federal jurisdictions so far have clearly rejected claims that threatened the rights and freedoms of others, could be decided differently because of the reinforcement of the employers' duty to accommodate.[39] Proponents, however, argue that this is an erroneous reading of the bill which only intends to impose a real duty of reasonable accommodation on the employer as was initially intended by Congress.[40]

Apart from the concepts of "reasonable accommodation" and "undue hardship," the Supreme Court also had to provide clarifications about what is intended by "religion" under Title VII of the Civil Rights Act. In fact, the anti-discrimination legislation only establishes a duty of reasonable accommodation in view of prohibiting discriminations on the grounds of "religion." The act states that for the purposes of Title VII the term "religion" means all aspects of religious observance and practice, as well as belief.[41] Philosophical beliefs are not covered. However, this has not prevented an evolution in the concept of "religion" through the Supreme Court's jurisprudence so as to include less traditional or non-theistic religious movements, such as Buddhism.[42] In *Seeger* and *Welsh*, the Supreme Court held that, with regards to the application of military service legislation establishing exemptions for conscientious objection, the definition of "religion" did not depend on the belief in a "Supreme Being." Since then, beliefs of a person are considered religious if they are sincere and occupy a place in the possessor's life parallel to that of God in traditional religions (the so-called "parallel belief" test).[43] The Supreme Court thus opted for a subjective approach to the concept of "religion" by granting more importance to the sincerity of the beliefs than to their content.[44]

Lower federal courts, or even state courts, have also provided very extensive interpretations of the concept of "religion" by including less traditional beliefs. In *Anderson*, a vegetarian bus driver sued his employer for being fired after refusing to distribute coupons for free hamburgers to passengers and won his case before

---

38 *Chalmers* v. *Tulon Co. of Richmond*, 101 F.3d 1012 (4th Cir. 1996).

39 L. W. Murphy and C. E. Anders, *supra* note 33.

40 R. T. Foltin and J. D. Standish, *supra* note 25, at 6.

41 Title VII of the Civil Rights Act of 1964 (Pub. L. 88-352), 42 U.S.C. §2000e, section 701(j).

42 In the *Torcaso* case, an *obiter dictum* attached to the opinion of Justice Black is often cited—although it is a statement "said by the way" which is not binding. This passage states that "[a]mong religions in this country which do not teach what would generally be considered a belief in the existence of God are Buddhism, Taoism, Ethical Culture, Secular Humanism and others"—*Torcaso* v. *Watkins*, 367 US 488 (1961).

43 *United States* v. *Seeger*, 380 US 163 (1965); *Welsh* v. *United States*, 398 US 333 (1970).

44 On this point, the US Supreme Court concurs with its Canadian counterpart, which also opted for a subjective approach in assessing the existence of a religious belief (*Syndicat Northcrest* v. *Amselem*, 2004 *CSC* 47, [2004] 2 *R.C.S.* 551)—see J. Woehrling, *supra* note 3, at 21–22.

a California court.[45] Thus, vegetarianism was recognized as a religious belief. In another case, a Wisconsin federal court recognized the "World Church of the Creator"—which espoused the supremacy of the white race—as a religion for the purposes of Title VII of the Civil Rights Act.[46] The facts of the case involved a member of that movement who was demoted by his employer out of the fear that he might treat his African American subordinates unequally. The court censured the employer's measure because it could not be based solely on the employee's religious beliefs if they were not acted upon. However, in other cases the courts' decisions were more restricted. The judges (re)emphasized that a religious conviction cannot be limited to a philosophy or a life style.[47] Thus, in *Slater* and *Swartzentruber*, the district court judges held that belonging to the Ku Klux Klan was not a religious belief for the purposes of the Civil Rights Act due to the mainly political and social nature of this movement.[48]

Sometimes judges do not directly address the delicate question of the existence of a "religion" under Title VII by denying the plaintiffs' claims on some other grounds. In *Cloutier* v. *Costco*, the employee of a big American retail chain store claimed the absence of a reasonable accommodation by her employer, even though she had informed the latter about the potential conflict between a professional rule and her religious beliefs. The "Church of Body Modification" required Ms Cloutier to keep her facial piercings visible, which conflicted with the dress code imposed by the company. The proper and professional image promoted by the American business prevailed over the "religious obligations" invoked by Ms Cloutier because an "undue hardship" in terms of the significant costs of the accommodation would have been caused. Without entering into the issue of the religious character of her beliefs the court stated that even if there had been "religion" the accommodation would not have been reasonable.[49]

Thus, in the US the Civil Rights Act forms a legal basis allowing individuals to obtain the recognition of their religious specificities in the workplace. Whereas Title VII of the Civil Rights Act is specifically concerned with the employment context, a second basis allows American citizens to require their employers to provide a reasonable accommodation on the grounds of the freedom of religion. Indeed, the Supreme Court has established a more general right to religious accommodation under the freedom of religion.

---

45 *Anderson* v. *Orange County Transit Authority*, Calif Super Ct, No 765255, 6/17/96. This decision issued by the Orange County Superior Court was preceded by a decision of the California Regional office of the EEOC, deciding in the same way (EEOC San Diego No. 345960598, 8/20/96).

46 *Peterson* v. *Wilmur Communications, Inc.*, 205 F. Supp. 2d 1014 (E.D. Wis. 2002).

47 *Smith* v. *Fair Employment and Housing Commission*, 12 Cal. 4th 1143 (1996).

48 *Swartzentruber* v. *Gunite Corp.*, 99 F. Supp. 2d 976 (N.D. Ind. 2000); *Slater* v. *King Soopers, Inc.*, 809 F. Supp. 809 (D. Colo. 1992).

49 *Cloutier* v. *Costco Wholesale Corp.*, 390 F.3d 126 (1st Cir. Mass. 2004).

B. Freedom of religion

Religious freedom is one of the first American constitutional freedoms recognized by the Founding Fathers. The importance of this right in the American legal system and the Supreme Court's interpretive work make it a fundamental instrument for the demands of reasonable accommodation of rules or policies established in the workplace as well.

1. Enshrining religious freedom

The First Amendment to the US Constitution provides that "[c]ongress shall make no law respecting an *establishment of religion*, or prohibiting the *free exercise* thereof."[50] This Amendment contains two clauses: the Establishment Clause prohibiting the establishment, assistance or funding of any religion, and the Free Exercise Clause establishing freedom of religion by prohibiting any restraint on the free exercise of religious activities.[51]

It is essential to take into account the interplay between the Establishment Clause and the Free Exercise Clause in order to better understand the protection that can be granted in the name of freedom of religion in the US.[52] Given that no religion can be preferred over another, public powers cannot protect or assist any religion if that would amount to the establishment of such religion.[53] Even though the Establishment Clause has been interpreted in a much less stringent way by the Supreme Court since the mid 1980s, it has been clear that freedom of religion is always understood—like most other American freedoms—as a negative freedom.[54] This means that the State cannot infringe upon religious freedom—i.e. a negative obligation *not to do something*—but it does not have to guarantee the effective exercise of such a freedom—i.e. a positive obligation *to do something*. In this aspect the American model distinguishes itself from the European approach, as enshrined in the case law of the European Court of Human Rights, where the

50 First Amendment to the US Constitution (author's emphasis).

51 This provision of the American Bill of Rights was initially only applicable to the United States' Congress, meaning only to the federal institutions. Only during the first half of the twentieth century were these two religious clauses "incorporated" into the Fourteenth Amendment, thus binding both federal and state powers. More specifically, as far as the Free Exercise Clause is concerned, its incorporation occurred by a 1940 decision of the Supreme Court which involved the rights of Jehovah's Witnesses to preach their beliefs on public streets (*Cantwell* v. *Connecticut*, 310 US 296 [1940])—see D. Laycock, "La Religion et l'Etat aux Etats-Unis: Affrontement des Théories et Changements Historiques," in *La Conception Américaine de la Laïcité* (E. Zoller, ed., Dalloz 2005), 38; E. Zoller, *supra* note 19, at 14.

52 K. Greenawalt, *Religion and the Constitution, Establishment and Fairness* (Princeton University Press 2006), 336.

53 E. Zoller, *supra* note 19, at 32.

54 *Id.* at 32.

State is a "neutral and impartial organizer of the exercise of various religions, faiths and beliefs."[55]

In the US the long tradition of religious individualism, as well as the tendency to consider all religious beliefs as having equal legitimacy, has allowed freedom of religion to be framed as a personal construction of the individual.[56] Everyone is a priori free to characterize as a "religion" any belief in an "afterlife" and to attach any right recognized by freedom of religion to that belief.[57] It seems nevertheless that the Free Exercise Clause only protects those "beliefs rooted in a religion."[58] Thus the problem is the absence of any definition by the Supreme Court of what constitutes "religion" for the purposes of the Free Exercise Clause. In the course of their jurisprudence, the justices have all the same accepted to include in this concept a number of less traditional religions, such as the Amish.[59]

2. The concept of religious accommodation under the Free Exercise Clause

Freedom of religion as established under the Free Exercise Clause constitutes a second legal basis for justifying a duty of reasonable accommodation of the rules, practices or policies infringing upon the religious beliefs of employees in the employment context. This second basis is relatively large because it applies both in the employment domain—where demands for accommodation have originated and for which the American legislator has already established a specific instrument—as well as in other contexts such as education or the provision of goods and services. Moreover, it allows an adaptation of rules and practices menacing the religious beliefs as put in place by individuals (such as a private employer) and by public powers (a public employer or the federal legislator or state legislator in the employment domain). However, in recent years the Supreme Court's case law has interpreted freedom of religion much less favorably by restricting the possibilities of invoking that freedom in vertical relationships, thus limiting the chances of obtaining a religious exemption from public authorities.[60]

In *Sherbert* v. *Verner* (1963), the Supreme Court took the step of establishing the obligation of a reasonable accommodation on the grounds of religious freedom with a decision concerning the employment context. Here the Supreme Court decided that the Free Exercise Clause only allows a government to refuse to exempt

55 ECtHR 26 September 1996, *Manoussakis and others* v. *Greece*, par. 47; ECtHR (Grand Chamber) 26 October 2000, *Hassan and Tchaouch* v. *Bulgaria*, par. 78; ECtHR (Grand Chamber) 13 February 2003, *Refah Partisi and Others* v. *Turkey*, par. 91; ECtHR (Grand Chamber) 10 November 2005, *Leyla Sahin* v. *Turkey*, par. 107.

56 E. Zoller, *supra* note 19, at 33.

57 *Id.* at 33.

58 *Thomas* v. *Review Board*, 450 US 707 (1981). Indeed it seems that in the United States atheism or agnosticism are not protected in a manner equivalent to currents which are "religious" in the strict sense of the word.

59 *Wisconsin* v. *Yoder*, 406 US 205 (1972).

60 F. M. Gedicks, "Exemptions Religieuses, Neutralité et Laïcité," in *La Conception Américaine de la Laïcité* (E. Zoller, ed., Dalloz 2005), 183.

religious believers from respecting a certain rule if it has demonstrated a compelling governmental interest behind a public rule which restricts a religious practice.[61] The case involved a Seventh-Day Adventist employee who had been laid off because she had refused to work on Saturdays for religious reasons. She was thereafter excluded from unemployment benefits because her refusal of Saturday work made it impossible to accept a suitable employment. Feeling that she had been treated wrongly by a public regulation which did not establish any exemption for individuals refusing certain jobs on religious grounds, she sued in the courts of South Carolina. After her claim was rejected at the state level she finally won her case before the US Supreme Court, which developed what is called the "Sherbert test."

According to that jurisprudence, a duty of religious accommodation on the basis of the Free Exercise Clause exists both for private and public actors when a practice, rule or legislation restricts the religious beliefs of a person. Hence, the duty to accommodate also concerns federal and state legislators, provided that certain conditions are met. The "Sherbert test" implies, in any case, that the person asking for a reasonable accommodation invokes a sincere religious belief and complains about a substantial burden on his or her ability to act upon that belief.[62] Whenever a demand for accommodation is addressed towards a public authority, the authority must demonstrate that it was pursuing a compelling state interest and that this objective was pursued in the manner least restrictive, or least burdensome, if it wants to avoid having to grant an exemption from the rule.[63]

What followed was a challenging jurisprudence by the Burger Court which, in accordance with *Sherbert*, facilitated the taking into account of religious identities in the employment area.[64] This increasingly favorable case law nevertheless became heavily criticized after the 1972 *Wisconsin* v. *Yoder* decision in the educational domain, which had allowed the Amish community to obtain an exemption from the Wisconsin state laws fixing the minimum compulsory school age at 16 years.[65] Some authors found that the Supreme Court had gone too far with the logic of reasonable accommodation. Then, between 1972 and 1990, the Supreme Court decided only in three cases in favor of demands for religious exemption. These

---

61 *Sherbert* v. *Verner*, 374 US 398 (1963)—see I. C. Lupu et al., "A Delicate Balance: the Free Exercise Clause and the Supreme Court," *Pew Forum on Religion and Public Life* (October 2007), 7–8; E. Zoller, *supra* note 19, at 35; D. Laycock, *supra* note 51, at 63; C. Froidevaux-Metterie, *Politique et Religion aux Etats-Unis* (La Découverte, 2009), 78.

62 Of course, the requirement of sincerity of belief does not involve demonstrating that beliefs whose free exercise is invoked represent the truth for the one who claims protection under the Free Exercise Clause. According to the Supreme Court, a jury or a judge does not have to intervene in this type of question—*United States* v. *Ballard*, 322 US 78 (1944).

63 K. Greenawalt, *Religion and the Constitution, Free Exercise and Fairness* (Princeton University Press 2006), 11.

64 Justice Burger, Chief Justice of the United States from 1969 to 1986, confirmed in many ways the progresses made under Chief Justice Warren.

65 *Wisconsin* v. *Yoder*, 406 US 205 (1972).

cases all involved the allocation of unemployment benefits, an issue to which the Supreme Court has always been particularly sensitive.[66]

The Supreme Court's limited enthusiasm for authorizing exemptions for employees who have been restricted in the exercise of their religious beliefs or practices by professional rules may be an indication that *Yoder* is only an isolated case which arose in a very specific context to which one must not attach too much importance. Proof of this are the numerous subsequent decisions in which the Supreme Court seemed much more timid with regards to the issue of religious exemptions on the basis of the Free Exercise Clause,[67] especially when it concerned vertical relationships.[68] All these cases indicate an apprehension by the courts to encourage citizens to claim a protected religion, which could then lead to requests for a religious exemption out of personal, secular reasons, and to a flood of demands for reasonable accommodation.[69] These considerations, as well as the change in the Supreme Court's composition,[70] have induced the justices to reconsider their reasonable accommodation-favorable jurisprudence. In fact, in the 1990 *Smith* decision, the Supreme Court held that a neutral measure of general applicability could not be subject to demands for accommodation and that a religious exemption could thus only be obtained from a public authority if the measure was neither neutral nor generally applicable and did not pursue a compelling governmental interest.[71] This case law was then confirmed in *Church of Lukumi*.[72]

66 *Thomas* v. *Review Board of the Indiana Employment Security Division*, 450 US 707 (1981); *Hobbie* v. *Unemployment Appeals Commission of Florida*, 480 US 136 (1987); *Frazee* v. *Illinois Department of Employment Security*, 489 US 829 (1989), all cited in I. C. Lupu et al., *supra* note 61, at 9.

67 *See United States* v. *Lee*, 455 US 252 (1982); *Goldman* v. *Weinberger*, 475 US 503 (1986); *O'lone* v. *Estate of Shabazz*, 482 US 342 (1987); *Lyng* v. *Northwest Indian CPA*, 485 US 439 (1988).

68 The situation is even more awkward for people invoking secular considerations, since atheism and agnosticism do not benefit from guarantees of free exercise of religion in the eyes of American courts—D. Laycock, *supra* note 51, at 69.

69 *Id.*, at 64.

70 Indeed, the Supreme Court decisions strongly depend on its members and their political and ideological preferences. Because of their nomination by the President of the United States, with the "advice and consent" of the Senate, they actually have both a political label—Republican or Democrat—and an ideological label—conservative or liberal. However, they are not bound by any allegiance towards the President. This is illustrated by the famous case *Brown* v. *Board of Education*, in which the Supreme Court ended the American segregationist doctrine in public schools, a very liberal decision carried by Chief Justice Warren, even though he was nominated by the Republican President Eisenhower—347 US 483 (1954).

71 *Employment Division, Department of Human Resources of Oregon* v. *Smith*, 494 US 872 (1990).

72 *Church of Lukumi Babalu Aye* v. *City of Hialeah*, 508 US 520 (1993).

Following this reduction in the protection of religious freedom, in 1993 Congress voted the Religious Freedom Restoration Act (RFRA) in order to reintroduce the "Sherbert test" in courts and tribunals whenever a violation of the Free Exercise Clause needs to be assessed.[73] Individual states decided to follow the federal example either by adopting legislation equivalent to the RFRA or by interpreting their Constitutions in a more religious freedom-favorable sense, thus converging with the *Sherbert–Yoder* line of cases rather than with the *Smith–Lukumi* precedents.[74] It seems therefore that the states were more attached to the Supreme Court's case law which favored reasonable accommodation on the basis of the Free Exercise Clause, even though few cases before state courts and tribunals show a real engagement in that direction.[75] One needs to note that in 1997 the federal RFRA was declared unconstitutional by the Supreme Court,[76] because Congress did not have the delegated powers to enact it.[77] However, the application of this interpretation was then limited by another Supreme Court decision in which the justices clarified that the RFRA was unconstitutional but only in as far as it applies to states and local powers.[78]

Hence, the *Smith* and *Lukumi* case law, which does not require (but allows) exemptions from non-discriminatory measures of general applicability, is limited to demands concerning vertical legislation at the state and local level. As far as the federal level is concerned, an exemption from measures that restrict religion, even though they are neutral and of general application, can always be invoked unless such measures pursue a compelling governmental interest. However, one needs to wonder about the real extent of the *Sherbert* test's application at the federal level given that most Supreme Court cases dealing with religious exemptions concerned state or local measures to which the *Smith* rule applies. Few are the cases where the reasonable accommodations for federal legislation or regulations are invoked. A small detour into the history of American federalism shows that the subdivision of competences between the federal authority and the states has rather worked in favor of the latter. In fact, American federalism is "centripetal" or "by association" and this has led to the attribution of specific competences to the central state. The single states, which had been independent and sovereign, kept the residual

73 *Religious Freedom Restoration Act* of 11 March 1993 (42 U.S.C. §2000bb *et seq.*).

74 Laycock cites more than twenty states as having passed state RFRAs or put similar provisions in their state constitution, not taking into account states whose courts have simply ignored *Smith* and states who have reserved the question whether to adopt *Smith*; D. Laycock, "Theology Scholarships, the Pledge of Allegiance, and Religious Liberty: Avoiding the Extremes but Missing the Liberty," 118 *Harvard Law Review* 155 (2004), 211–212.

75 D. Laycock, *supra* note 51, at 66.

76 *City of Boerne* v. *Flores*, 521 US 507 (1997); see E. Zoller, *Grands arrêts de la Cour suprême des Etats-Unis* (PUF 2000), 1247–1256.

77 J. M. Oleske, *supra* note 13, at 528; K. Greenawalt, *supra* note 63, at 32.

78 *Gonzales* v. *O Centro Espirita Beneficente União do Vegetal*, 546 US 418 (2006).

competences, which meant the larger part of such competences.[79] Therefore, it would seem that a majority of the demands for reasonable accommodation will rather concern measures taken at the state or local level rather than at the federal level. In that case, the *Smith* case law and its criteria of neutrality and general applicability will apply, unless the concerned state has adopted a "state RFRA" or a similar measure which reinstalled the *Sherbert* jurisprudence.

In sum, in the US there are therefore two bases allowing individuals to assert their religious identity in the employment context. On the one hand, the prohibition of discrimination on the grounds of religion is a first legal basis which is explicitly established in a legislative text of which the highest American Court has nevertheless adopted a limiting interpretation. This first possibility of religious exemption explicitly covers the employment context and applies both to private employers as well as public ones. On the other hand, accommodations on the basis of religious freedom can be regarded as judge-made law based on a constitutional provision. It allows individuals to demand the adjustment of a general rule entering into conflict with their religious beliefs in most aspects of social life in both horizontal and vertical relationships. Nevertheless, it may be noted that the demands for religious reasonable accommodation on the basis of this second ground towards public authorities nowadays have fewer chances of success at the state level. The public service employees at the local or state level—one of the most common hypotheses—are thus deprived of this second basis,[80] unless the relevant state has introduced a "state RFRA" or an equivalent mechanism. Otherwise, they need to turn to Title VII of the Civil Rights Act as long as their demand is deemed reasonable and does not constitute an "undue hardship" for the employer. Thus, it seems that in the US the guarantee of religious diversity in the employment context and the ensuing employee demands for recognition and adaption rely essentially on anti-discrimination legislation, while the right to freedom of religion is more relevant in other domains of social life.

II. Reasonable accommodations in France?

Even though the issue of reasonable accommodation as an instrument of religious diversity management in the employment context arose and developed on the North American continent, European countries are not untouched by questions relating to religious diversity and the right to equality. By advocating a "strict secularism," France could be expected to be the country perhaps least open to the

---

79 A. Alen, *Le Fédéralisme: Approches Politique,* Économique *et Juridique* (De Boeck-Wesmael 1994).

80 At least it will be more difficult for them to succeed on this basis since the *Smith* case has confined the scope of reasonable accommodation at the local and state level to measures not demonstrating a compelling government interest and not being a "neutral law of general applicability."

logic of accommodation of employees' religious rituals and beliefs. Nevertheless, a certain practice as well as some scattered provisions are indicative of a tendency to allow religious exemptions in the workplace in order to guarantee freedom of religion (A) or to respect the principle of equality and non-discrimination (B). Hence, it is interesting to ask whether France can progressively move from the favorable positions observable in practice and from a right to accommodation sometimes recognized in limited domains to a general right requiring the adaptation to the religious needs of employees of rules, measures or policies adopted in the professional domain. In fact, both classic foundations allowing the establishment of an employer's duty of reasonable accommodation, namely freedom of religion and the right to non-discrimination, also exist in France. However, one needs to analyze whether and, if so, in which way, these legal bases can be invoked so as to establish a right to religious accommodation in the employment context.

A. Accommodations on the basis of freedom of religion

As said, freedom of religion is a first possible basis for allowing the introduction of a right to reasonable accommodation enforceable against French employers. This fundamental right is guaranteed by a number of national and international instruments and has in fact been the first to be invoked in the employment context in order to obtain adjustments of rules, measures or policies restricting employees' religious beliefs or practices, whether in France or more generally in Europe.

Under French law, freedom of religion is guaranteed by the so-called Separation Act from 9 December 1905.[81] This piece of legislation not only establishes a true separation between the Churches and the State, thus instituting French secularism, but it also proclaims the freedom of religion. In its first Article, the Act provides that "the Republic ensures the freedom of conscience. It guarantees the free exercise of religion." Moreover, the 1789 Declaration of the Rights of Man and of the Citizen to which the Preamble of the current French Constitution refers,[82] establishes freedom of opinion, including religious opinions. The first Article of the French Constitution declares the respect of all beliefs. The use of the term "to respect" not only entails the negative obligation not to infringe upon different religious beliefs but also the positive obligation to help them develop.[83] This is the French and European idea of freedom of religion in contrast to the American one.[84] Besides the national instruments of protection of religious freedom, this

81 Law of 9 December 1905 concerning the Separation of the Churches and the State, in force from 1 January 1906.

82 Constitution of the Fifth Republic of 4 October 1958.

83 C. Haguenau-Moizard, *supra* note 5, at 51.

84 The European Court of Human Rights considers that as part of their margin of appreciation State Parties have "to secure true religious pluralism, an inherent feature of the notion of a democratic society" (ECtHR 26 September 1996, *Manoussakis and others* v. *Greece*, par. 44), and must thus play the role of "neutral and impartial organizer of the

fundamental right is enshrined in similar formulations at the European level in Article 9 of the European Convention of Human Rights (ECHR),[85] or in Article 10 of the Charter of Fundamental Rights of the European Union (EU Charter).[86]

The French secular tradition which pushes the separation of political power and religious organizations to its highest level seems to be in contrast with any idea of reasonable accommodation as a requirement of freedom of religion. However, in reality, for a number of years de facto accommodations, whether tacit or regulated by administrative circulars, have multiplied.[87] Indeed, the desire to respect everyone's freedom of religion has led private and public bodies to adjust provisions, measures or policies in domains such as education and employment. This informal system of de facto accommodations allows for some flexibility in the responses to religious demands but also places the individual claimant in the uncomfortable situation of total uncertainty. In fact, while the law does not expressly prohibit such practices, it remains silent with regards to the *duty* of public or private actors to accept someone's demands for accommodation. In the absence of any legislative or regulatory provision imposing its adoption, in practice religious exemptions are granted on a case-by-case basis.

As far as the employment domain is concerned, recent years have been marked by a number of religious demands by employees (i.e. concerning the wearing of religious signs, holidays for religious festivals or issues related to food restrictions or prayer time). Tensions between the respect of religious commands and the duty to adhere to professional requirements in the workplace have given birth to practices which de facto regulate these delicate issues and from which the legal domain remains excluded.[88] The practice of offering special menus within certain public services is a perfect example of this long bureaucratic tradition of taking religious identities in the public sector into account and responding positively to religious demands. Even though no legal text establishes any duty on the part of public powers to adapt the menus of public canteens to the religious beliefs of their users, demands of this type are generally accepted.[89] A similar practice can be observed in the private sector, where certain employers also provide religious

exercise of various religions, faiths and beliefs" (ECtHR (Grand Chamber) 13 February 2003, *Refah Partisi and others* v. *Turkey*, par. 91).

85 The Convention for the Protection of Human Rights and Fundamental Freedoms, signed in Rome on 4 November 1950 and entered into force on 3 September 1953, is a European source directly effective into national legal systems of State Parties, such as France.

86 The Charter of Fundamental Rights of the European Union, proclaimed in Nice on 7 December 2000, has full legal effect since the entry into force of the Treaty of Lisbon on 1 December 2009 (Article 6.1 of the Treaty on European Union).

87 Fr. Messner, P.-H. Prélot and J.-M. Woehrling (eds), *Traité de Droit Français des Religions* (Litec 2003), 446.

88 *Id.* at 446–447.

89 *Id.* at 478–479; A. Boyer, *Le Droit des Religions en France* (PUF 1993), 215.

accommodations in the form of company canteens that respect the religious meal requirements of certain employees.[90]

This system of "tacit" accommodations or exemptions depends entirely on the discretion of public and private employers, and this has a number of disadvantages. First, it does not fully guarantee everyone's freedom of religion. Second, these practices are not explicitly authorized by law. Moreover, it does not seem that this effort of accommodation is based on a large consensus, but is criticized by a number of people ranging from the most conforming secularists to the most convinced believers. This technique of de facto accommodation is thus heavily questioned nowadays. Hence, there is currently a trend among citizens to prefer addressing judges in order to find a balance between professional requirements and religious commands.[91]

In the educational domain, the issue of the wearing of religious signs in public schools was a perfect example of this trend towards litigation of religious demands, before the "Stasi" Act prohibited any kind of ostentatious religious sign in public schools.[92] In the employment context religious freedom has been invoked a number of times by employees desiring an adjustment of professional requirements in the workplace to their religious commands. In this sense, the lack of transparency and predictability of the informal system of de facto accommodation has induced many employees to turn towards the courts in order to obtain a favorable answer.[93]

It seems, however, that in the employment context—as in the educational one—the basis of freedom of religion is not sufficient to provide a legal basis for a general right to reasonable accommodation by public or private actors. Nevertheless, some authors hold that Article 1 of the Separation Act of 9 December 1905 could be the legal basis for a positive obligation of reasonable accommodation capable of guaranteeing the free exercise of religion,[94] and therefore of being invoked by

---

90 Association IMS-Entreprendre pour la Cité, *Gérer la Diversité Religieuse en Entreprise* (a practical guide published by a network of companies).

91 Fr. Messner, P.-H. Prélot and J.-M. Woehrling (eds), *supra* note 87, at 447.

92 Law No. 2004-228 of 15 March 2004 concerning through the application of the principle of "*laïcité*" the wearing of symbols or clothing demonstrating religious affiliation in state primary and secondary schools (*loi encadrant, en application du principe de laïcité, le port de signes ou de tenues manifestant une appartenance religieuse dans les* écoles, *collèges et lycées publics*). Note that the Committee of reflection on the application of the principle of "*laïcité*" in the Republic, known as the "Stasi" Committee, had made a proposal in its report to the President of 11 December 2003 to allow employers to regulate the wearing of symbols or clothing demonstrating religious affiliation for "imperatives pertaining to safety, consumer contact and internal social peace." However, the legislator did not follow this suggestion, although Mr Jean Glavany introduced a draft law incorporating this proposal of the "Stasi" Committee to the National Assembly on 7 February 2008 on behalf of the Socialist Group (*Proposition de loi No.710 du 7 février 2008 visant à promouvoir la laïcité dans la République*).

93 Fr. Messner, P.-H. Prélot and J.-M. Woehrling (eds), *supra* note 87, at 447.

94 See, for example, *Id.* at 447–448.

individuals in order to have their religious identity recognized in the workplace. So far, however, this position has neither been confirmed by courts at the national level nor at the European level. It is true that by committing to *ensuring* freedom of conscience and to *guaranteeing* the free exercise of religion, the French Republic intended to specify that it would not limit itself to a passive obligation not to interfere in any way with freedom of religion, but that it would also proactively intervene to implement that freedom. Thus, it seems logical to conclude that the public authorities must avoid drafting provisions which affect individual religious freedoms or, if that is the case, at least provide for an accommodation of that provision which ensures its respect without infringing the religious beliefs of citizens.[95] However, so far no French court has sanctioned a French public authority or a private actor for violating someone's religious freedom in the employment domain or any other context by not providing a reasonable accommodation of a rule, measure or policy.

With regards to the fulfillment of contractual duties, the French Cassation Court held that a Muslim employee who had worked for two years at the butchery of a supermarket where he was in contact with pork meat could not ask to be transferred to another service on the basis of his religious beliefs. According to the Court the religious beliefs of the employee are not part of the employment contract and the employee therefore has to perform the task for which he had been hired.[96]

As far as the freedom of expression, including religious expression, in the workplace is concerned, the French courts have repeatedly condemned any proselytizing behaviors in the public and private sector. For instance, the Versailles Administrative Court allowed the firing of a director of a municipal nursery who, during a discussion concerning Christmas, had urged two of her subordinates to join the Church Saint-Denis de la Chapelle by giving them a church leaflet.[97] The Toulouse Court of Appeals also held that an entertainer in a secular recreation center who had read from the Bible and distributed pamphlets in favor of his religion was guilty of proselytizing and had thus committed "gross misconduct" in violating the obligation of neutrality.[98]

With regards to religious signs or clothing, freedom of religion has also not been helpful in overcoming an employer's refusal to allow any clothing indicating a religious belief in both the public and private sector. In public services, the principle of neutrality applicable to civil servants has been interpreted so strictly by the administrative courts so as to thwart the right to manifest religious beliefs during the exercise of functions. For a civil servant to manifest his or her religious beliefs at work is considered a breach of a professional obligation justifying a

95 *Id.* at 448.

96 Cass. Fr., 24 March 1998, No. 95-44738.

97 T.A. Versailles, 7 March 2007, No. 0504207.

98 C.A. Toulouse, 9 June 1997, No. 09/97. See also C.A. Rouen, 25 March 1997, No. 95/04028; C.A. Basse-Terre, 6 November 2006, No. 06/00095.

temporary or definitive exclusion.[99] In order to determine the gravity of the breach of the principle of neutrality by a civil servant, the administrative judge will take all the circumstances of the case into consideration, in particular the nature and the ostentatious character of the religious manifestation as well as the nature of the civil servant's functions. For instance, the Paris Administrative Court confirmed the exclusion of a child caretaker in a municipal nursery wearing a Muslim headscarf, even though the woman exercised most of her functions in her home and wore the headscarf only in the presence of the pediatrician in charge of the monthly medical check-up.[100] Similarly, the Lyon Administrative Court of Appeals confirmed the decision by the Lyon Administrative Court, which had upheld the Regional Transportation and Housing Directorate's decision to suspend an employment auditor because she was wearing the Muslim headscarf during her service.[101] In a domain where the obligation of neutrality may seem less critical, the Toulouse Administrative Court rejected the demand of a doctoral candidate at the University of Toulouse who had been fired for wearing a Muslim headscarf, on the grounds that her status as a civil servant implied an obligation of discretion.[102]

With regards to the private sector, courts have been just as restrictive, generally allowing the dismissal of employees wearing the Muslim headscarf working in stores or commercial centers. According to the French courts, contact with customers requires a certain neutrality, or at least discretion, in the expression of personal opinions, especially if the employee did not wear any symbols manifesting a religious belief at the moment of hiring.[103]

On the contrary, as far as holidays to observe religious festivals are concerned, public and, increasingly, private employers allow this type of absence, as long as they are counted as personal days off. These adjustments are not legally required and imply that the employee uses his personal days off to observe his religious obligations.[104] Therefore, nothing prevents an employer from refusing similar absences. Indeed, the Cassation Court has already held that the absence of a Muslim employee to celebrate *Aid el-Kebir* against her employer's will could justify her dismissal.[105] With regards to the religiously required weekly day off, employee demands invoking freedom of religion in order to justify a reorganization of their working hours are rarely granted, whether in the public or in the private

99 C.A.A. Lyon, 27 November 2003, No. 03LY01392. See F. Dechavanne, "Actualité de la Question des Signes Religieux," Seminar *Islam et Laïcité* of 23 January 2009.

100 T.A. Paris, 22 February 2007, No. 0415268/5-2; see also C.A.A Versailles, 23 February 2006.

101 C.A.A. Lyon, 12 July 2005.

102 T.A. Toulouse, 18 April 2009.

103 C.A. Saint Denis de la Réunion, 9 September 1997, No. 97/703306; C.A. Paris, 16 March 2001; Conseil de Prud'hommes de Lyon, 16 January 2004. See F. Dechavanne, *supra* note 99; see also, however, the chapter by Rim-Sarah Alouane in this volume.

104 F. Dechavanne, *supra* note 99.

105 Cass. Fr., 16 December 1981.

sector. For instance, the Paris Administrative Court of Appeals confirmed the temporary exclusion of a Seventh-Day Adventist postal agent who observed the Sabbath and therefore was repeatedly absent on Saturdays.[106] Similarly, the Paris Administrative Tribunal allowed the dismissal of a nurse who refused to work on Saturdays because of her membership of the Seventh-Day Adventist Church.[107]

These different cases, in which freedom of religion has not helped plaintiffs to successfully claim or obtain a reasonable accommodation, illustrate how in France the logic of religious accommodation in the employment domain remains a favor granted on a case-by-case basis. Hence, as long as the employer does not abuse his powers, it falls within his discretion. With regards to civil service, the principles of secularism and neutrality stand in the way of a recognition of religious identities in the workplace even though a certain administrative practice tacitly and informally takes certain minor religious demands, such as special menus or holidays for religious festivals, into account. In the private sector these principles do not apply, but French employment law remains quite ambiguous with regards to religious practices. The French Employment Code only takes into account Christian religious festivals and days of rest by referring to Christmas, Easter, Pentecost and Sunday as the day of rest. However, sometimes the Employment Code allows permanent or temporary derogations from Sunday rest, when justified by "production and activity constraints or public needs," or if it concerns retail stores wishing to stay open on Sundays.[108] The Employment Code therefore only considers hypotheses of employers requiring their employees to work on Sundays for different reasons and not the situation of employees who for religious reasons wish to have a different day than Sunday off. Hence, it seems to be very difficult to establish a global policy on religious diversity within private companies. Some employers see the company as a "neutral, secular space where there can be no religious expressions,"[109] whereas others gladly accommodate their employees' religious demands, even when they seem exaggerated.[110]

It is clear that a company cannot require the removal of ostentatious religious symbols without any objective reason, simply prohibit the wearing of religious symbols in its internal regulations[111] or refuse a holiday for a religious festival without justifying it in terms of service reasons. The Employment Code provides that "employees have a right to direct and collective expression concerning the

---

106 C.A.A. Paris, 31 March 2009, No. 08PA01648.

107 T.A. Paris, 14 March 2002, No. 9919677/5.

108 C. Trav., art. L. 3132-12 *et seq*.

109 Association IMS-Entreprendre pour la Cité, *supra* note 90.

110 *Id.*

111 See an individual decision of 1 October 2004 of the Labor Relations Department of the French Ministry of Labor (*Direction des relations du travail du Ministère du travail*) in which it was considered that a general and absolute prohibition of all ostentatious religious or political symbols in a company's internal regulations was contrary to Article L. 1121-1 of the Employment Code.

conditions of exercise and organization of their work,"[112] and that "no one can restrict the rights and individual and collective freedoms of people without a justification based on the nature of the required task and proportionate to the envisaged aim."[113] However, even though an employee can theoretically assert his religious beliefs in a private company the employer can always thwart such demands by referring to the tasks for which the employee has been hired (e.g. the impossibility of a waiter refusing to serve a woman), to sanitary rules, to security or company regulations (e.g. the impossibility of avoiding the company's medical check-up), to the correct functioning of the company (e.g. the impossibility of abandoning one's tasks during prayer time),[114] or to the prohibition of proselytizing. Therefore, there is a certain absence of coordination in this domain, which strengthens the impression that the issue of religious accommodation in the workplace is today essentially a practice left to the employer's discretion, at least with regards to the legal basis of religious freedom.

There are, however, some scattered provisions in the French legislative landscape which reflect the idea of reasonable accommodation of individual religious rites or beliefs by explicitly establishing the possibility of religious exemptions. These religious exemptions are limited to a clearly circumscribed domain and one cannot derive from them a more general duty of reasonable accommodation of religious practices or beliefs of employees. In the employment context one can refer to conscientious objection in the medical domain. In fact, the French Public Health Code allows a doctor to refuse to perform an abortion.[115] Nor can a doctor be forced to perform a tubal ligation for birth control reasons.[116] It seems that in similar cases a doctor cannot be held liable for refusing medical assistance even if there is a danger for the woman.[117] The French Employment Code also contains a conscience clause allowing journalists to terminate their employment contract without notice if there is a "notable change in the character or orientation of the journal or newspaper" of a nature that threatens their moral interests.[118]

Apart from these specific provisions establishing exemptions from the application of professional rules on the basis of religious or conscientious grounds, it does not seem that in France there is a more general legal duty of reasonable accommodation in the employment context, which could be derived from the freedom of religion.

112 C. Trav., art. L. 2281-1.

113 C. Trav., art. L. 1121-1. Article L. 1321-3 of the Employment Code provides for the same obligation regarding a company's internal regulations.

114 See Cass., 29 May 1986 (the dismissal of a fundamentalist Muslim who refused to pass the annual medical check-up was held fair by the Court).

115 C. Santé Publ., art. L. 2212-8.

116 C. Santé Publ., art. L. 2123-1.

117 T. corr. Rouen, 9 July 1975, *D.*, 1976, p. 531; see Fr. Messner, P.-H. Prélot and J.-M. Woehrling (eds), *supra* note 87, at 466.

118 C. Trav., art. L. 7112-5.

B. Accommodations on the basis of the prohibition of religious discrimination in France and in Europe

The prohibition of treating people differently on the basis of their religion or beliefs has been established in a number of French, European as well as international legal instruments. In the absence of religious freedom as a viable legal basis for religious accommodations, the right not to be discriminated against because of one's religious beliefs or practices without justification could potentially constitute a legal basis in France for obtaining an adjustment of professional rules.

Article 1 of the French Constitution proclaims the equality of all citizens before the law without any distinction of origins, race or religion. The system of separation between Churches and the State introduced with the Separation Act also shows that religions have to be treated in the same way, since the State does not support any.[119] The Criminal and Employment Codes prohibit discrimination based on the fact of belonging or not belonging to a specific religion.[120] Article 14 of the ECHR also prohibits discrimination in the enjoyment of Convention rights and freedoms, including the right to religious freedom guaranteed in Article 9. Last but not least, Article 21 of the EU Charter prohibits any unequal treatment based on religion and belief without limiting itself to the rights contained in the Charter.[121]

Even though the French Republic is based on a legal proclamation of religious equality, the reality of the treatment of religions seems to contradict this statement.[122] Distinctions, albeit implicit, are being made between different religions. The choice of Sunday as a weekly day of rest is a perfect example. Even though the choice may seem legitimized by socio-historical justifications and by the fact that the public powers in codifying it in the Employment Code contributed to detaching it from its religious roots,[123] the measure still privileges Christianity over other religious beliefs.[124] The normalization of Sunday rest through its secular treatment does not facilitate demands of accommodation, in particular from Jews and Muslims with regards to the organization of working hours.[125] The same is true

119 P.-H. Prélot, "Les Religions et l'Égalité en Droit Français," 107 *RDP* 737 (2001), 738.

120 C. pén. fr., art. 225-1 *et seq.*; C. trav. fr., art. L122-45 *et seq.*

121 However, this provision only concerns "the institutions and bodies of the Union themselves, when exercising powers conferred under [the treaties], and … Member States only when they are implementing Union law" (Updated Explanations relating to the text of the Charter of Fundamental Rights of the European Union [Brussels, 18 July 2003, CONV 828/1/03 REV 1]).

122 P.-H. Prélot, *supra* note 119, at 739.

123 C. trav., art. L. 221-5. It is, however, possible to derogate from the rule of Sunday rest, but for reasons unrelated to any religious consideration.

124 K. Wojtyczek, "Les Religions et le Principe d'Égalité," 17 *Revue Européenne de Droit Publique* 117 (2005), 135.

125 In Islam, Friday is the day of public worship in mosques. In Judaism, Saturday is a day of rest when any form of work is prohibited.

with regards to official holidays in the secular calendar that usually coincide with Christian holidays.[126]

French law thus contains some different treatments between religions. Most of the time they are involuntary because they are a result of the historical French context and are not always easily detectable due to the maintenance of a formal equality facade.[127] In fact, these differentiations do not generally target directly one or more specific religious groups. For example, Sunday rest is a seemingly neutral rule that applies uniformly to all religious communities. However, the effects of this type of measure de facto disadvantage the members of specific religious groups privileging another weekly day of rest and thus create indirect discrimination towards other religious communities.[128] Yet, if a provision or general measure privileges certain religious groups, specific accommodations should be envisaged in favor of disadvantaged groups[129] in order to "somehow re-establish a situation of equality through compensation."[130]

In contrast to what was said about the basis of religious freedom, the right to equality could represent a more promising legal basis. Confronted with a measure which is applied equally to any believer but which has the de facto consequence of disadvantaging the believers of certain religions, some solutions could be found in the right to non-discrimination. In fact, besides the prohibition of direct discrimination, the concept of indirect discrimination also developed in order to guarantee more substantive equality when a rule, condition or practice, albeit generally applicable, has a disproportionately adverse impact on specific groups. An indirect discrimination can be justified if it responds to the classical criteria in the area of violations of fundamental rights: the pursuit of a legitimate purpose and a reasonable proportionality between that purpose and the litigious provision.[131] This proportionality control of the difference in treatment may raise the issue of reasonable accommodation, since it requires—while applied with a high level of scrutiny—that the concerned provision be implemented in the least restrictive way for fundamental rights. Thus, if there is a less restrictive way—namely by providing a reasonable accommodation—this might have to be taken in some instances.

---

126 A. Boyer, *supra* note 89, at 214–215. A "French-style" system of accommodations is, however, organized by Circular No. 2010-060 of 7 May 2010 providing for the few religious festivals of the calendar year 2010 for which leave permissions may be granted in the public sector. Nevertheless, only the Orthodox, Armenian, Muslim, Jewish and Buddhist religions benefit from this measure, only for certain specific religious festivals, and exclusively in the public sector.

127 However, by recognizing only certain groups as religious groups and by relegating other movements considered religious in other countries to the rank of sects, public authorities create voluntary differences of treatment.

128 K. Wojtyczek, *supra* note 124, at 134.

129 *Id.* at 135.

130 P.-H. Prélot, *supra* note 119, at 745.

131 E. Bribosia, I. Rorive and J. Ringelheim, *supra* note 1, at 18.

In Europe, the idea of indirect discrimination arose in the case law of the European Court of Justice (ECJ),[132] but it found its first confirmation in the religious domain thanks to the case law of the European Court of Human Rights (ECtHR) and in particular[133] in its famous *Thlimmenos* judgment (2000).[134] In that case, a Jehovah's Witness, previously convicted for his refusal to perform military service, was denied access to a position as a public accountant because under Greek law people guilty of a crime cannot become civil servants. Deeming himself a victim of discrimination on the grounds of religion,[135] he went all the way to the ECtHR. The judges declared that the Greek law, notwithstanding its general nature, is discriminatory if it does not establish "appropriate exceptions" for people convicted of a crime due to their religious beliefs. The State therefore has a positive obligation to adjust the general rule concerning access to civil service in order to prevent certain religious groups from becoming subject to discriminatory treatments.

Nevertheless, earlier decisions of the former European Commission of Human Rights concerning the issue of reasonable accommodation in the religious domain did not seem to adopt that type of reasoning.[136] The Commission rejected applications by employees or agents who claimed that their professional or contractual situations prevented them from practicing their religion. In the case *X* v. *United Kingdom*, the Commission rejected the application of a Muslim primary school teacher working in a London public school whose demand to accommodate his working hours in order to be able to go to pray on Friday afternoons had been

132 Named "Court of Justice of the European Union" since the entry into force of the Treaty of Lisbon on 1 December 2009. The main decisions in which the Court of Justice developed the concept of indirect discrimination are: Case C-152/73, *Sotgiu* v. *Deutsche Bundepost* [12 February 1974]; Case C-96/80, *Jenkins* v. *Kingsgate* [31 March 1981]; Case C-170/84, *Bilka-Kaufhaus GmbH* v. *Weber von Hartz* [13 May 1986]; Case C-237/94, *O'Flynn* v. *Adjudication Officer* [23 May 1996].

133 It is important to note that the ECJ could not develop the concept of indirect discrimination on the grounds of religion prior to the adoption of Employment Equality Directive in 2000 which implements this principle within EU law (in line with Article 13 of the Amsterdam Treaty, now Article 19 TFEU). For an overview of the case law of the European Court of Human Rights on religious discrimination, see R. De Gouttes, "Les Discriminations Religieuses et la Convention Européenne des Droits de l'Homme," in *La Liberté Religieuse et la Convention Européenne des Droits de l'Homme* (T. Massis and C. Pettiti, eds, Bruylant 2004), 81–96.

134 ECtHR 6 April 2000, *Thlimmenos* v. *Greece*, App. No. 34369/97; E. Bribosia, I. Rorive and J. Ringelheim, *supra* note 1, at 15; J. Ringelheim, *Diversité Culturelle et Droits de l'Homme: la Protection des Minorités par la Convention Européenne des Droits de l'Homme* (Bruylant 2006), 329–330.

135 Actually, the concept of indirect discrimination is only implicit in this ruling. It was clearly formalized later in the case *D.H. and Others* v. *the Czech Republic* (ECtHR [Grand Chamber] 13 November 2007).

136 See the chapter by Saïla Ouald Chaib in this volume discussing this case law in more detail.

rejected.[137] In the *Konttinen* decision, a Finnish Seventh-Day Adventist railway employee who had been fired for repeatedly leaving his job on Friday evenings in spite of his employer's refusal, lost his case.[138] In *Stedman*, the application by a British Christian employee working in a travel agency who had been fired because of her refusal to work on Sundays was also rejected.[139]

These three decisions, in the employment context, were handed down prior to *Thlimmenos* and could induce a belief that the ECtHR has since adopted a different jurisprudence. However, subsequent decisions seem to contradict *Thlimmenos*, which would rather indicate that it is an isolated decision in the ECtHR's jurisprudence. Thus, in the *Kosteski* judgment, the ECtHR sentenced a civil servant to a monetary penalty because he had abandoned work to celebrate a Muslim religious festival without authorization.[140] Here the ECtHR never even considered the issue of indirect discrimination and of its possible justification, but had simply left the State a wide margin of appreciation.[141] However, it seems that the European judges decided in this way because they found this case was mainly one involving the religious considerations raised by the applicant. Therefore, they essentially analyzed the case under Article 9 of the Convention, under which the ECtHR systematically grants States a wide margin of appreciation,[142] and almost completely avoided the reasoning based on Article 14. Moreover, it was an extreme case in which the employee had unilaterally and without the employer's consent decided to arrogate the right to be absent because he had to assist in a religious festival. Furthermore, it was also of concern that the employee had apparently declared himself Muslim in an opportunistic way in order to excuse his absence. It seems that it was essentially the employee's behavior which motivated the ECtHR's decision, holding that the freedom of religion did not discharge the employee from providing a justification for his absence. In different circumstances, if the Muslim faith of the employee had not been doubted and if he had suggested to his employer an accommodation of the working rules, and if the latter had refused to do so and the employee had clearly claimed discrimination on the grounds of religion before the ECtHR, perhaps the judges could have followed their jurisprudence in favor of religious accommodations in the workplace begun in the *Thlimmenos* judgment.

In any event, this type of case clearly shows that the ECtHR seems to be reluctant to derive a duty of reasonable accommodation in the employment

137 EComHR 12 March 1981, *X* v. *United Kingdom*, App. No. 8160/78.

138 EComHR 3 December 1996, *Konttinen* v. *Finland*, App. No. 24949/94.

139 EComHR 9 April 1997, *Stedman* v. *United Kingdom*, App. No. 29107/95.

140 ECtHR 13 April 2006, *Kosteski* v. *The Former Yugoslav Republic of Macedonia*, App. No. 55170/00.

141 See also ECtHR 11 January 2005, *Phull* v. *France*, App. No. 35753/03; ECtHR 4 March 2008, *El Morsli* v. *France*, App. No. 15585/06.

142 J.-Fr. Flauss, "Abattage Rituel et Liberté de Religion: le Défi de la Protection des Minorités au Sein des Communautés Religieuses," 45 *Revue Trimestrielle des Droits de l'Homme* 195 (2001), 204–205.

domain from the basis of religious freedom alone.[143] However, a foothold towards the admission of reasonable accommodation on the basis of religion has been opened since the *Thlimmenos* judgment.[144] Since this jurisprudence has not been confirmed yet as far as the religious domain is concerned, and more specifically in the employment context, we have to admit that for the moment a right to "religious accommodation" in the workplace is at its embryonic stage on the basis of the principle of non-discrimination.[145]

On the European Union side, the right to non-discrimination may also provide the cornerstone for the establishment of a right to religious accommodation in the workplace. The Employment Equality Directive[146] explicitly provides for a duty of reasonable accommodations in the employment context but only "in relation to persons with disabilities,"[147] and not for religious beliefs and practices. One can nevertheless identify the preconditions of a similar duty in the prohibition of indirect discriminations based on religion or beliefs.[148] This concept was in fact developed by ECJ case law concerning sex discrimination, but was also enshrined in the anti-discrimination directives.[149]

Under EU law and ECJ case law, the French Republic was obliged to introduce a type of reasoning which up to that moment was foreign to its system. Whereas the freedom of religion was never sufficiently strong to force France into introducing reasonable accommodation as an instrument to take religious identities into account in the workplace, the right to non-discrimination and the force which it has assumed during these last years has pushed the country into changing its way of addressing the issue. In fact, the anti-discrimination directives, including the concept of indirect discrimination, were implemented into the French legal

143 E. Bribosia, I. Rorive and J. Ringelheim, *supra* note 1, at 15.

144 *See Glor* case, which seems to fit more in the line with case law initiated by the *Thlimmenos* case, but concerning discrimination on the grounds of disability (ECtHR 30 April 2009, *Glor v. Switzerland*, App. No. 13444/04).

145 However, see *Jakobski* v. *Poland*, where the ECtHR held that there is "a positive duty on the State to take reasonable and appropriate measures to secure the applicant's rights under paragraph 1 of Article 9" of the Convention (ECtHR 7 December 2010, par. 47).

146 The Directive notably prohibits discrimination on the grounds of religion or belief in employment and occupation (Council Directive 2000/78/EC of 27 November 2000 establishing a general framework for equal treatment in employment and occupation, *O.J.* No. L 303, 2 December 2000, 0016-0022).

147 Directive 2000/78, art. 5.

148 See L. Vickers, "Religion and Belief Discrimination in Employment – The EU Law," *European Network of Legal Experts in the Non-discrimination Field*, European Commission, DG for Employment, Social Affairs and Equal Opportunities (2006), 20–22.

149 Directive 2000/78, art. 2 §2 (b); See, for example, the *Vivien Prais* case (Case C-130/75, *Vivien Prais* [27 October 1976], par. 18) demonstrating that the concept of reasonable accommodation on the grounds of religion was implicit in the European Union legal system even before the adoption of non-discrimination Directives (E. Bribosia, I. Rorive and J. Ringelheim, *supra* note 1, at 18).

order.[150] In 2004, the *Haute Autorité de lutte contre les discriminations et pour l'égalité* (HALDE—the French Equality Body) was created with the purpose of guaranteeing the effective implementation of the right to non-discrimination.[151] The HALDE has now been replaced by and incorporated in the *Défenseur des droits* starting May 2011, but its previous work remains relevant in this regard.

Indeed, in some recommendations,[152] the HALDE had a chance to highlight the discriminatory character of certain measures taken in the public sector or in private enterprises. With its intervention the HALDE had, at times, been able to persuade public or private actors to abandon some unequal measures towards certain religious beliefs.[153] Sometimes courts themselves followed the HALDE's conclusion by sentencing employers for their religiously discriminatory actions.[154] In spite of the non-legally-binding character of the HALDE's recommendations, thanks to their dissuasive effect on employers or through the importance which the courts attach to the HALDE's work, a certain consideration of religious identities in the workplace is being obtained.

As far as hiring is concerned, the HALDE had emphasized that private employers cannot ask job candidates about their religious beliefs and, in particular, about the meal rules prescribed by their religion.[155] The relevant case involved a children's entertainer whose job application had been rejected after he stated that he ate halal meat and therefore could not take part in meals with the children. With regards to certain internal guidelines with which private companies try to restrict their employee's religious freedoms by introducing clothing codes or regulating the wearing of religious signs, the HALDE provided some cornerstones. In its view, an employer can only limit religious practices in its internal regulations if the necessity of his decision is justified by objective and proportionate factors.

150 Law No. 2008-496 of 27 May 2008 concerning various provisions of adjustment to Community law on the prevention of discrimination, *O.J.*, 28 May 2008 (incorporating a definition of indirect discrimination in Article 1132-1 of the Labor Code).

151 Law No. 2004-1486 of 30 December 2004 establishing a High Authority to combat discrimination and promote equality, *O.J.*, 31 December 2004.

152 Even if the HALDE translates the French word "délibération" by the English word "deliberation" in the English version of its website, it seems more appropriate to use the English word "recommendation."

153 See, for example, in the domain of vocational training, the HALDE's recommendations in which it pointed out the discriminatory character of the prohibition of trainees wearing the Muslim headscarf from following internships taking place in public schools (Recommendations No. 2008-121 of 2 June 2008, No. 2008-167 and 168, 1 September 2008, No. 2009-234, 235, 236 and 238 of 8 June 2009, and recommendations No. 2008-167 and 168, 1 September 2008).

154 This approach was confirmed by the Administrative Tribunal which ordered the director of a training center to reinstate a trainee whose registration had been canceled because she was wearing the Muslim headscarf (T.A., 27 April 2009, *Salma Saïd c. GRETA Top Formation*, No. 0905233/9).

155 Recommendation No. 2008-10, 14 January 2008.

For instance, employers could refer to the nature of the position or the performed tasks. However, the formulation should be as precise as possible in order to avoid a general and absolute prohibition, and the modalities of the restriction should be discussed with the people concerned in order to reconcile their beliefs and the company's interests. Moreover, the employment rule should remain proportional to the envisaged purpose and should be assessed on a case-by-case basis by taking into account the concrete situation of each employee.[156] Thus, in a January 2009 deliberation, the HALDE deemed that a private company could not refer to the principle of neutrality of the workplace in its internal guidelines in order to restrict religious signs, considering that no legislation or French case established that principle in the private sector, except for the case of proselytizing.[157] And the French Council of State considered that the wearing of religious signs such as the Muslim headscarf cannot be in itself characterized as proselytizing.[158] Following these deliberations in which the HALDE reminds employers which are the good practices with regards to religious diversity management, the latter often follow those recommendations and sometimes they even directly address the independent authority to obtain an opinion before adopting certain measures.

Sometimes the French courts themselves develop a reasoning influenced by European law and thus envisage accommodations of certain religious beliefs in the workplace. For example, the Paris Appeals Court did not consider the statements of a public official concerning the non-exploitation of a restaurant owned by a Muslim during the period of Ramadan.[159] That same court also decided that a private employer who wants to restrict the religious practices of his employees needs to show that the reasons for doing so are objective and not discriminatory. The French judge therefore appealed to the right to non-discrimination and ordered the re-integration of a female employee working in a call center who had been fired because she wore the Muslim headscarf.[160] The employee had been hired with the headscarf, which at that time did not seem to pose any problems to the employer given that she was doing surveys and polls. As soon as she was transferred to the company seat where she had direct client contact, the employer required that she take off the headscarf. The employee refused to do so and was fired. In the eyes of the court the mere fact of having direct client contact was not a sufficiently legitimate justification to allow for a restriction of the employee's freedom of religion. It was still necessary to provide a case-by-case justification of the pertinence and proportionality of the restriction with regards to the concretely assigned tasks and the context of their performance. However, in that case, the employer had raised none of these issues in connection with the wearing of the headscarf by the employee. This important decision shows an evolution in the way French judges approach religious identities in the workplace,

156 Recommendation No. 2009-107, 6 April 2009.

157 Recommendations No. 2009-22, 26 January 2009 and No. 2008-32, 3 March 2008.

158 C.E., 27 November 1996, *M. et Mme Jeouit*.

159 C.A. Paris, 20 December 2007, *Ghoufali c. SCI Immobess*, No. 07/00211.

160 C.A. Paris, 19 June 2003, No. 03/30212.

thanks to the recent developments in anti-discrimination law. Indeed, before they seemed to allow the dismissal of employees in private enterprises when the former had direct client contact.[161]

Nevertheless, the cases in which the French judges pronounced themselves in favor of an adaptation of the applicable rules in the professional context to the employees' religious beliefs are in general not directly based on the right to non-discrimination on the grounds of religion. The judges prefer to mask their reasoning.[162] There is still a lingering hesitance to distance oneself from the classical formalist approach to equality law. This jurisprudence therefore remains laconic and often badly motivated.[163]

In any case, thanks to the recent developments of anti-discrimination law the French legal landscape looks much more receptive to the admission of a general right to reasonable accommodation on religious grounds in the employment context, rather than having to rely on informal practices or isolated recognitions in different pieces of legislation or scattered case law. However, in order to really be able to speak about a right to religious accommodation in the workplace this recent evolution still needs to be fully integrated into the French legal system. This may either occur by means of a legislative provision establishing it explicitly as a general principle,[164] as was done in the Civil Rights Act in the United States, or by establishing precedents that recognize reasonable accommodation on the grounds of religion, as was done by the US Supreme Court on the basis of the Free Exercise Clause. However, the concrete adjustments made in practice never rose to the status of a right, and even less so to that of a fundamental right.[165] Therefore, we need to observe that if a right to reasonable accommodation is currently still at its embryonic stage at the European level, it is even more so in the French legal order.

Conclusion

Faced with a society which is increasingly marked by religious diversity and with the demands of recognition which this entails, Western countries have searched for solutions responding to the new challenges posed in all sorts of domains. One of the areas where the religious demands have been most visible is the employment context, since this concerns individuals in their everyday life.

---

161 See, for example, C.A. Saint Denis de la Réunion, 9 September 1997, No. 97/703306.

162 F. Ast, "L'Apport du Droit à la Non-Discrimination à la Protection du Pluralisme Religieux: Regards Croisés des Juridictions et de la HALDE," *Article des actes du colloque "Manifester Sa Religion: Droit et Limites"* (l'Harmattan 2010), 24.

163 *Id.* at 21.

164 However, no such proposal has as yet been introduced.

165 F. Ast, *supra* note 162, at 25.

In this context, the US has developed an interesting technique which allows taking religious identities in the workplace into account: reasonable accommodation. By mobilizing fundamental rights such as freedom of religion and the principle of equality and non-discrimination, they were able to develop a balanced system which ensures that public and private employers have to take religious pluralism into account. Employment rules, measures or policies need to be adapted to the religious beliefs of employees, but this accommodation is only possible if it does not question the system established for the majority. The success of this technique therefore depends on the correct balancing of the concerned interests. Reasonable accommodation thus encompasses the idea of a constant negotiation between the religious claimant and the respondent public or private employer, which ensures some flexibility. It can also occur in different forms. Sometimes it is the result of a friendly negotiation between the parties, and sometimes of a court order. In some cases, the issue will be to grant an exemption from the application of a rule (e.g. a derogation of work hours); in other cases it will be to provide certain infrastructures to the employee or to grant him certain advantages (e.g. specific menus offered in public service canteens or in private companies).[166] The flexibility reasonable accommodation offers and the different forms it can take are thus likely to make this instrument attractive for other legal systems.

In the US, it is principally the prohibition of discriminations and its legislative establishment in the Civil Rights Act which have constituted the basis for religious accommodations in the workplace. Freedom of religion and its judicial interpretation complemented this first legal basis, essentially in order to extend these religious exemptions to other domains of social life. Even though the issue of religious accommodation was first developed by judges, it was the legislator who allowed this principle to become fully operative in the specific employment context. Therefore, the American legal system nowadays possesses an instrument allowing for the recognition of religious specificities in an important domain of social life, which could not leave the European powers indifferent in as much as they themselves were dealing with these new issues.

With regard to France, the two legal grounds which allowed taking religious pluralism into account in the American sphere are also recognized. It seems that also in France the prohibition of discrimination on the grounds of religion is the more promising basis on which to ask for an adjustment of working rules to employees' religious beliefs. In turn, freedom of religion has not led to an introduction to the French legal environment of the idea of religious accommodation of rules in social life, and especially in employment.

Whereas from a legal point of view only the right to non-discrimination seems to be able to permit the application of religious accommodation in the French professional sphere, one still needs to wonder in practice about the feasibility and the desirability of a similar concept given the specific French context. It is true that with regards to the employment domain, especially in the private sector,

166 K. Greenawalt, *supra* note 52, at 336.

the issue is still very unclear and that the solutions adopted by employers could not be more different, apart from being somehow unpredictable. Nevertheless, it seems that the explicit legislative introduction of religious accommodation in the employment context would be symbolically too charged. The de facto practices were in the past shaped by the intervention of the HALDE, and it remains to be seen how the *Défenseur des droits* will continue this role. An intervention of the legislator, introducing a formal concept of reasonable accommodation, asks too much from a country with a secular, Republican tradition,[167] even if this principle had to meet certain conditions and was limited to the employment context. It seems that an evolution towards a formalization of these already existing practices of accommodation would have a counterproductive effect since it would mean less flexibility and lead to more controversies. From a practical and theoretical point of view, the most adequate solution for the moment appears to be the technique of "concerted adjustment." This procedure is very similar to reasonable accommodation but differs because it does not benefit from a legal foundation but rather falls into the citizen sphere. A friendly negotiation amongst concerned parties, possibly framed by a broader intervention by other citizens,[168] best corresponds to the French tradition. Since the civil law tradition does not grant as much importance to case law as to legislative acts, in case of a failure of such negotiations, as a last resort, a case-by-case approach by the courts seems to be more appropriate than a legislative intervention like the American example, notwithstanding that a certain consistency of the jurisprudence is desirable.

It will therefore be interesting to see whether the French political representatives will start reflecting on this issue, by transforming already existing practices of religious accommodation in the workplace from unspoken and arbitrary into transparent and predictable without, however, amending the legal system which, for the time being, seems unready to welcome such changes.

167 This is true for the private sector. In contrast, in the public sector a legislative intervention in the direction of the non-consideration of religious identities in the workplace does not seem symbolically too charged.

168 Actions pursued by the former HALDE provide for some indicators of how such negotiations might be conducted.

Chapter 13

A Perspective from Across the Atlantic: "The Faith at Work" Movement in the United States. A New Management Model for Religious Diversity in the European Workplace?

Amandine Barb

Introduction

"Faith is coming out of the closet at work."[1] With this statement, Princeton University professor David Miller emphasized the importance and visibility gained by religion in the American workplace over the past two decades. Indeed, long ignored by the secular corporate world and traditionally confined to employees' private lives, faith has risen to new prominence in many American companies confronted with a diversification of their workforce and with growing claims from assertive religious groups. To respond more effectively to those new challenges, some employers are increasingly changing the way they deal with religion. From *passive* attention to their employees' beliefs and practices, under anti-discriminatory or even accommodationist policies, they are moving towards a more *proactive* recognition of religious diversity in order to take advantage of the multi-faith work environment and to avoid costly conflicts. In other words, the objective of the so-called "faith at work" movement, a term coined by Miller,[2] is to actively assert the place and value of faith in secular American companies through a more *positive* engagement with the diverse religious identities of employees.

This chapter discusses how religion, an element traditionally overlooked by employers compared to other forms of diversity, has progressively been integrated into the diversity management policies of a growing number of American businesses. It will analyze the various forms taken by this assertive engagement of faith as well as some of the problems it has raised. At a time when the European

1 M. Dollarhide, "When God Goes to the Office," *CNN*, 10 March 2008, available at www.cnn.com.

2 D. Miller, *God at Work. The History and Promise of the "Faith at Work" Movement* (Oxford University Press 2006).

Commission is launching a project entitled "Promoting Diversity Management at the Workplace" to encourage employers across Europe to give proper attention to diversity management in their business strategies, this chapter asks to what extent similar policies as applied by the "faith at work" movement have been—or could be—adopted by European companies, also confronted with an increasingly multi-religious workforce. The question is whether and how the more positive approach to religion could be a relevant and efficient model for the management of religious diversity in the European workplace.

1. Structural changes in US society paving the way

The trend towards a more active engagement with religious diversity in American businesses started in the 1990s, mainly as a reaction to several structural changes in American society that had significant repercussions in the workplace—the growing diversification of the religious landscape, the presence of more assertive minorities and evangelical Christians and, more generally, a greater public visibility of faith.

Religion in the workplace has become a much discussed and controversial issue in the US over the last three or four decades, mainly as a result of changes in the religious make-up of American society, which significantly evolved in the second half of the twentieth century. Following the 1965 Immigration and Nationality Act, which notably contributed to removing restrictions on immigration from Asia, non-Christian religious minorities such as Muslims, Hindus, Sikhs, Jains and Buddhists have increased in size and in proportion in the US, especially in urban areas.[3] Beyond the growing presence of minority faiths, since the 1970s there has also been a well-documented rise in the number of evangelical Christians, who today represent 26.3% of the US population.[4] To a lesser extent, an increasing percentage of Americans also say that they belong to so-called "new religious movements," i.e. marginal religious or spiritual groups whose tenets and practices are often difficult to categorize (Wicca, a neo-pagan religion which relies on witchcraft, is one typical example).

Over the decades, this religious diversification of American society has been reflected in companies throughout the country. And as the number of individuals with different beliefs and practices has become more significant in US businesses, so have the demands for accommodations with established workplace rules from employees arguing that the requirements of their faith should be better taken into consideration and their right to religious expression better respected. Hence more

3 A 2008 survey from the *Pew Forum on Religion and Public Life* reported that about 21.5% of the US population did not identify as Christians. 91% of Americans considered themselves as Christians in 1948, 82% in 1989 and 84% in 1999.

4 X, "US Religious Landscape Survey," *Pew Forum on Religion and Public Life*, February 2008, available at religions.pewforum.org.

and more conflicts between employers and employees, on problems related to dietary restrictions, clothing, observance of holy days, prayers in the office, etc. have arisen. The issue has become particularly salient in today's multi-faith America, as the Equal Employment Opportunity Commission (EEOC), the federal agency in charge of enforcing employment discrimination laws, recently reported that religious bias complaints in the workplace have increased 69% over the last ten years.[5]

2. Interplay between the law and the "faith at work" movement in the US

Since the end of the 1960s, several federal laws and directives have been adopted in the US in order to help companies deal with these new challenges and, more particularly, to regulate employees' right to religious expression and to fight against religious discriminations. In line with the constitutional protection of freedom of religious exercise contained in the First Amendment,[6] the US Congress institutionalized decades ago, through federal law, the principle of "reasonable accommodations" in the workplace. In 1972, Title VII of the 1964 Civil Rights Act, which already prohibited discrimination based on religion, was amended to require all medium and large companies to "reasonably accommodate an employee's religious observance or practice, unless doing so would cause them an undue hardship." This duty to reasonably accommodate was interpreted by the Supreme Court in *TWA* v. *Hardison*,[7] and *Ansonia Board of Education* v. *Philbrook*,[8] in which it held that "undue hardship" meant only "more than a minimal burden" imposed on employers, thus giving them more legitimate reasons to refuse accommodations.[9] In reaction to those decisions, Congressmen, supported by various faith-based organizations, have attempted for more than a decade to challenge the Court's jurisprudence and to reinstate through legislation a strong accommodationist standard in the workplace, which would ultimately oblige employers to be more sensitive and considerate towards their employees' beliefs and practices. The Workplace Religious Freedom Bill, for instance, a federal bipartisan bill backed by a coalition of forty religious groups, has been precisely designed to "restore the level of protection that religious freedom deserves" by extending the criteria defining an "undue hardship," which would make it more complicated for companies to reject employees' claims for religious accommodations. But opposed by secularist organizations and by the chambers of commerce, the various versions of the bill

---

5 "Religion and Corporate Culture. Accommodating Religious Diversity in the Workplace," The Tanenbaum Center for Interreligious Understanding, 2008; "Religion-Based Charges. 1997–2010," US Equal Employment Opportunity Commission, 2010.

6 The *First Amendment* states that "Congress shall make no law respecting an establishment of religion or prohibiting the free exercise thereof."

7 *Trans World Airlines, Inc.* v. *Hardison*, 432 US 63 (1977).

8 *Ansonia Board of Education* v. *Philbrook*, 479 US 60 (1986).

9 See also the chapter by Gabrielle Caceres in this volume.

introduced since 1995 have all failed to pass so far (a new version was proposed in May 2010).[10] Therefore, the principles of anti-discrimination and of reasonable accommodations, even though they protect employees' freedom of conscience and allow them to negotiate potential compromises with their employers, have been perceived by many as enabling only a passive and limited acknowledgment of religion, and thus have been considered as an unsatisfactory and insufficient answer to the problems raised by religious diversity in the workplace.

This issue has been all the more complicated and sensitive for US companies, which apart from federal regulations did not have real management tools to properly deal with an increasingly multi-faith working environment. Indeed, although diversity policies had long been implemented in American businesses, notably to avoid discriminations based on race, ethnicity, gender and sexual orientation, religion was often missing on managers' agendas. Employers were, for instance, reluctant to accept the creation of faith-based affinity networks, whereas groups representing ethnic minorities (African-Americans, Latinos, Asians) or disabled workers were encouraged. Religion was commonly regarded as an issue that was too "touchy," if not taboo, best left on the margins of the secular workplace. This situation appeared in deep contradiction with the historically strong attachment of Americans to religion (about 90% still declare they believe in God),[11] as well as with the important public visibility gained by faith in the US since the end of the 1970s and the growing influence of conservative evangelical Christians in society and politics.

3. Faith enters the workplace

It was precisely in order to adapt corporate management strategies to the evolution of the workforce and the challenges raised by religious diversity that, starting in the 1990s, new tactics and policies were imagined by companies to more directly and positively address the issue of faith in the workplace. Some employers argued that a multi-religious environment should not be perceived as a constraint, but rather as a strength, and thus companies had to "embrace religion rather than to reject it."[12] For businesses, the best way to deal with the religious diversification of their workforce was not to neglect faith, but rather to engage it. Managers had to adopt an active approach towards religion in order to take advantage of the diversity, and to make it

10 Some states, such as Oregon, Massachusetts and New York, have chosen from the beginning of the 2000s to enact their own "mini" Workplace Religious Freedom Acts. See, for instance, G. Hamilton, "Oregon House of Representatives Passes Workplace Religious Freedom Act," *ReligiousLiberty.TV*, 1 June 2009, available at www.religiousliberty.tv.

11 F. Newport, "Belief In God Far Lower in Western U.S.," *Gallup.com*, 28 July 2008, available at www.gallup.com.

12 David Miller, quoted in N. Banerjee, "At Bosses' Invitation, Chaplains Come Into Workplace and Onto Payroll," *The New York Times*, 4 December 2006.

a positive and productive element for employees as well as for the whole company. The main objective was not to change existing laws, but to suggest new corporate strategies that could be applied by employers within the daily organization of the office, in order to better recognize and value religious diversity.[13]

These principles and the basis of what would later be called the "faith at work" movement were already emphasized at the end of the 1990s in the Federal Guidelines on Religious Exercise and Religious Expression in the Federal Workplace published by the Clinton administration.[14] Although these guidelines remained consistent with the Supreme Court's interpretation of Title VII and did not create any new rights for public employees, they were significant in that they insisted particularly on the right to religious expression in the workplace and explicitly encouraged federal employers to better respect and value the multiple beliefs and practices of their workforce. While reaffirming that in some circumstances the government's interests could outweigh the free exercise of religion, the directives also made clear that "[f]ederal employees may engage in personal religious expression to the greatest extent possible" and that in most cases managers had to avoid "restricting" or "regulating" the private exercise of their faith. The accompanying memorandum sent to Federal Departments and Agencies similarly pointed out the necessity to "ensure that the Federal workplace is generous to followers of all religions, as well as to followers of none." Therefore, these guidelines already aimed not only at reinforcing the protection of the free exercise of religion in public institutions, but also, more generally, at giving more legitimacy to faith within the American workplace. The objective was to make public employers less reluctant and suspicious towards the expression of faith in the office, as well as make employees more comfortable with it. These regulations, even if they did not change the established laws regarding discrimination and accommodation on the basis of religion in the American workplace, nonetheless clearly emphasized the necessity for managers to be more aware of the various beliefs and practices of the individuals working in their offices.

4. The "faith-friendly" company: proactively managing religion

4.1. Diversity management

More generally, the growing preoccupation with religion in the American workplace has progressively led, over the last two decades, to the implementation of new religious diversity management strategies in a variety of US companies

---

13 J. E. King Jr., M. P. Bell, E. Lawrence, "Religion as an Aspect of Workplace Diversity: An Examination of the US Context and a Call for International Research," 6 *Journal of Management, Spirituality and Religion* 43 (2009), 43–57.

14 *Federal Guidelines on Religious Exercise and Religious Expression in the Federal Workplace*, 14 August 1997, available at clinton2.nara.gov/WH/New/html/19970819-3275.html.

willing to adapt their corporate culture to the evolution of society in order to create a more receptive environment for their employees of faith. The businesses which decide to establish policies to actively engage the diversity of their workforce have been labeled "faith-friendly" in the US—an expression first coined by Miller and now used by companies themselves as well as by media and academics. Different from "faith-based" companies, which affirm a specific—often Christian—religious identity,[15] "faith-friendly" businesses do not intend to advance or identify with one particular religion, but rather aim at acknowledging their employees' diverse religious beliefs and practices. Therefore, as Miller argues, whereas "faith-based" can often be perceived as "discriminatory and problematic," the term "faith-friendly" is more "consensual and positive," and gives the impression that everyone is "welcome to the table," which in turn helps to "legitimize" the presence of religion in the workplace.[16]

"Faith-friendly" employers in particular often provide ideological and ethical justifications for their new approach to religion. They defend their initiatives by insisting on the *social* dimension and impact of the policies they implement. Their attempts at giving greater visibility, importance and legitimacy to religion in the daily life of the office are efficient ways to fulfill what sociologist Eck calls the ideal of religious pluralism, that is "the energetic engagement with [religious] diversity," which requires "recognizing [differences] rather than hiding them" as well as active "participation," "engagement" and "exchange."[17] Hicks, in his *Religion and the Workplace: Pluralism, Spirituality, Leadership*, suggests that US companies should commit themselves precisely to the construction of a "moral framework" to transform workplaces that are characterized by religious diversity into workplaces governed by the spirit of "respectful pluralism," which supposes an engagement of religious values and an active promotion of religious expression in the office.[18] "Faith-focused" businesses echo Hicks when they present themselves as contributing to the "acceptance" and "inclusion" of all employees of faith, and thus to the protection and advancement of religious understanding in the whole society, by raising public awareness of religious diversity and by encouraging "healthy manifestations of faith."[19]

---

15 The fast food chain *Chick-fil-A*, whose official purpose is to "glorify God by being a faithful steward of all that is entrusted to us [and] to have a positive influence on all who come in contact with [us]," can be considered an example of a "faith-based" company in the US.

16 "Taking God to Work," *Homiletics*, July–August 2007, available at www.homileticsonline.com.

17 D. Eck, "What is Pluralism?" *The Pluralism Project*, available at pluralism.org.

18 D. A. Hicks, *Religion and the Workplace: Pluralism, Spirituality, Leadership* (Cambridge University Press 2003), 195.

19 R. Grossman, "Religion at Work: Many Employers are Weaving Religion and Spirituality Into Company Cultures," *Human Resources Magazine*, December 2008.

4.2. Strategies

The new strategies adopted by executives to create a more pluralist work environment have been diverse and depend on the choices made by the faith-friendly company. These measures range from the systematic official acknowledgment of religious holy days, the opening of office rooms for prayers, and the establishment of employees' faith-based groups to more daring initiatives, such as the hiring of "corporate chaplains" to deliver "pastoral care" to employees.

One of the main steps taken by "faith-focused" companies has been to encourage workers to create their own religious affinity groups, on the model of existing ethnic or gender-based networks. In 2001, for example, Ford Motor Company established the Ford Interfaith Network (hereafter "Interfaith Network"), in order to enable employees with diverse religious affiliations to meet regularly and be able to express and share their religious opinions within the workplace.[20] The first Interfaith Network was created in the Ford headquarters of Dearborn, Michigan, where a significant proportion of the employees are Muslim. The launch of this initiative was an official way for managers to better take into account the growing diversity of their workers and to avoid frustration and conflicts by valuing, instead of ignoring, their various religious identities.[21] Ford praises the Interfaith Network as a tool enabling "employees of all religions to come together and express their faith in appropriate and meaningful ways in the workplace and to build bridges to the community."[22] Indeed, beyond dealing with requests for accommodations such as prayer and ritual ablution facilities or kosher food in the cafeteria, the religious groups that compose the Interfaith Network also aim to give religion a more visible, legitimate and "normalized" status within the company.[23] Their first goal is therefore educational: they hold Bible/Talmudic study groups, celebrate their various holy days, teach "Faith 101s"—i.e. short presentations intended to increase awareness of their beliefs and practices among employees—invite religious speakers and organize a company-wide event for the National Day of Prayer.[24] Through this type of initiative, Ford has established itself as a model of a "faith-friendly" corporation, whose aim is to foster understanding between its employees and to promote a genuine "religious pluralism" in the office. In the media, the Interfaith Network is often highlighted as a prime example of the "faith

20 X, "Ford Interfaith Network," *The Pluralism Project*, 2005, available at pluralism.org.

21 Quoted in T. Henneman, "A New Approach to Faith at Work," *Workforce Management*, 2004, available at www.intheworkplace.com.

22 See corporate.ford.com/dynamic/metatags/article-detail/ergs-442p.

23 "Employee Resource Groups are Finding Support in ECD," *Ford Communications Network*, 19 February 2001, available at fordglobe.org.

24 See M. Gunther, "Finding God at Work," *Fortune*, 17 January 2007, available at money.cnn.com/2007/01/16/news/companies/faithfriendly_companies.fortune/?postversion=2007011707. The National Day of Prayer is officially proclaimed by the President of the US every year on the first Thursday of May. It was established by Congress in 1952.

at work" movement, although similar encouraging policies towards religion have been implemented in other major American firms, such as American Airlines, Intel and Texas Instruments, since the beginning of the 2000s.[25]

4.3. Risky business: being too friendly with faith?

Nevertheless, the active engagement of religion in the workplace has also proven to be potentially risky for "faith-friendly" businesses. Sometimes it is hard to draw precisely the boundary between the right to religious expression, valued and encouraged by "faith-friendly" policies, and the unlawful religious harassment of other (non-religious) employees. In particular, a more active approach to religion in the workplace could help trigger harassment cases. In recent years, there has been an increase in the number of proselytizing court cases in the US, often because of Christian employees attacking their co-workers on their sexual orientation and lifestyles or displaying their faith in ways felt as oppressive.[26] Hence, the necessity exists for managers to supervise "faith-friendly" policies and to be able to balance various competing interests, that is the spiritual demands of some of their employees and the right to privacy of others, as well as the basic corporate and financial objectives of the company. That might be one explanation for why religious affinity networks are strictly regulated by employers: they are usually only allowed to meet, on a voluntary basis, after work hours or during the lunch break, so that expressions of faith can be better controlled, and excesses and problems avoided. These networks also have to be officially authorized by the company, which could be criticized, since it tends to favor mainstream religions to the detriment of employees from less prominent religious or spiritual groups: Ford's Interfaith Network, for instance, can only be composed of representatives from religions which have at least 350 million adherents worldwide, which automatically excludes more marginal faiths.[27]

Yet, despite those challenges, some companies have even gone further in the integration of faith in the workplace, notably by hiring professional chaplains at their employees' request. Workplace chaplaincies, organized on the model of those existing in the military or in prisons, have indeed multiplied over the past few

---

25 L. Fenner, "Religion-Based Employee Groups Enhance Culture of Inclusion," *America.gov*, 29 November 2007, available at www.america.gov. Texas Instruments notably invites employees to create their own religious groups, with the explicit goal of fostering mutual "respect and understanding."

26 E. Volokh, "Freedom of Speech, Religious Harassment Law, and Religious Accommodation Law," 33 *Loyola University Chicago Law Journal* 57 (2001), 57–69; D. N. Kaminer, "When Religious Expression Creates a Hostile Work Environment: The Challenge of Balancing Competing Fundamental Rights," 4 *New York University Journal of Legislation and Public Policy* 81 (2000), 81–142.

27 There are currently eight religions represented in the *Ford Interfaith Network*: Buddhism, Catholicism, Evangelical Christianity, Hinduism, Islam, Judaism, Mormonism and Orthodox Christianity.

years in the US,[28] as an answer to a growing demand from companies, which progressively led to the establishment of several professional organizations of corporate ministers, such as Workplace Chaplains and Marketplace Ministries. The leading group in the country, Corporate Chaplains in America, founded in 1996 in order to "provide genuine caring in the workplace," today employs more than 1,500 chaplains, who intervene in local companies to advise a worker confronted with a difficult personal situation or to help resolve a conflict.[29] Most workplace chaplains in the US are Christians, but it is possible for employers to hire Jewish, Muslim or even interfaith ministers.

In the same way, and in order to make their diversity management more efficient, US corporations are increasingly searching for "culturally competent" managers, that is individuals who are able to deal with the cultural, ethnic and religious diversity of the workforce. Since the 1990s there has been a significant rise in the number of books, articles and websites designed to help employers be more sensitive to their employees' beliefs and practices. From the 1995 book *Workplace Diversity: A Manager's Guide to Solving Problems and Turning Diversity into a Competitive Advantage* to *Religion and Corporate Culture: Accommodating Religious Diversity in the Workplace* published in 2010, to websites such as *diversityincbestpractices.com*, American employers now have at their disposal a wide range of resources to be "culturally competent" and to engage with religion in an efficient and productive way.

But in order to acquire solid "religio-cultural" competencies, American companies can also resort to new consulting firms especially created to advise employers on how to positively manage their diverse workforce. The Tanenbaum Center for Interreligious Understanding, founded in 1992 and based in New York, is certainly the most prominent of those organizations. Its official objectives are to "combat religious bias in the workplace" and "change how companies view religion." In order to fulfill these goals, the Center provides corporations with "tools to manage religious diversity."[30] Besides intervening directly with managers and staff, the Tanenbaum Center offers several online resources—from information about world religions to case studies of court decisions and "interactive quizzes for self-assessment"—to help companies "prepare to handle the complexities of modern organizational life" and "create respectful and productive environments." For instance, an online "religious diversity checklist" enables businesses to assess whether they sufficiently and effectively take into consideration the diverse faiths of their workforce, through various categories such as holidays/time off, dress, food, employee networks, office space, etc.[31] According to a 2008 survey from the Tanenbaum Center, half of companies in the US now require their managers

28 N. Banerjee, *supra* note 12.

29 See www.chaplain.org.

30 See www.tanenbaum.org.

31 "Religious Diversity Checklist," available at www.tanenbaum.org/resources/workplace-tools/religious-diversity-checklist.

to be trained in religious diversity issues.[32] This data, as well as the emergence of consulting firms solely dedicated to the management of religion in the workplace, clearly testifies to the growing appeal and institutionalization of the "faith at work" movement in American society. Religion, long neglected in offices, is progressively finding a niche in US corporate culture.

This evolution is also confirmed by new developments in the academic world. A group on "Management, Spirituality and Religion" has, for example, been established within the Academy of Management, the main national professional association for scholars working on management and organizations in the US. More recently, the Center for the Study of Religion at Princeton University launched a research program entitled the "Faith & Work Initiative," whose main goal is not only to methodologically analyze the treatment of religious diversity in US companies, but also to overtly advance a more proactive approach to religion in the office.[33] The program proposes courses for undergraduate students and regularly sponsors conferences on the topic of work and religion, in the US and abroad. The existence of such an initiative and the creation of similar research projects at other American universities, e.g. the Yale Center for Faith and Culture,[34] emphasize all the more the growing interest in the management of religious diversity in the workplace.

Finally, and although it is a more marginal trend within the "faith at work" movement, it is worth noting that, since the end of the 1990s, besides the implementation of policies designed to deal with demands from an increasingly diverse workforce, a whole new discourse on "spirituality" has also emerged in the American corporate world.[35] Very vaguely defined, "spirituality" is described in this case as a universal quality, present in every human being, and as more neutral and less divisive than religion, from which it is often distinguished. Beyond the acknowledgment of the multiple religious beliefs and practices represented in the office, some companies now try to appeal to the "spiritual dimension" of their employees, whether they are traditional believers or not, in order to foster a more inclusive, sensitive and ethical workplace. Through the organization of spiritual retreats or meditation sessions, the goal is to create a more "holistic" and "integrative" work environment, where each individual can bring their "whole self," which could contribute to material as well as spiritual well-being.[36] This new discourse on spirituality is part of a broader interest in the "spiritual" within American society

32 The Tanenbaum Center for Interreligious Understanding, 2008.

33 See faithandwork.princeton.edu/index.php. This center is hosted by both the Yale Divinity School and the Yale School of Management.

34 See www.yale.edu/faith/about/abou.htm.

35 A. McLaughlin, "Seeking Spirituality … At Work," *Christian Science Monitor*, 16 March 1998, available at csmonitor.com.

36 See, for instance, R. Fuller, *Spiritual, but not Religious: Understanding Unchurched America* (Oxford University Press 2001); W. C. Roof, *Spiritual Marketplace: Baby Boomers and the Remaking of American Religion* (Princeton University Press 2001).

in general, and seems to correspond to what Lioger describes as the "signifying spiritualization" (*spiritualisation signifiante*) of social activities in contemporary western societies, that is the search for a superior, almost sacred, meaning to our daily occupations.[37] In any case, the "spirit at work" movement, as it is often labeled in the media, has become increasingly popular in the US corporate world over the past few years. Since the beginning of the 2000s, numerous books, with catchy titles such as *Your Soul at Work* and *A Spiritual Audit of Corporate America*, have been published about the relationship between business and spirituality. Moreover, several American universities[38] now have courses on the topic of spirituality in the workplace in order to train future managers and employers on this issue.

But this new movement has also been criticized in American society, notably by secularists and non-believers, who fear that such a vague emphasis on the "spiritual" in a secular workplace might dangerously blur the line between spheres that should remain separate, and could represent disguised attempts by some employers at creating a "faith-based" working environment. They also argue that such a discourse on "spirituality" in the everyday life of the office could ultimately give the impression that a good, moral and trustworthy employee necessarily needs to be overtly "spiritual," which would risk marginalizing and isolating those who have no faith or refuse to identify as either spiritual or religious.

4.4. Religion as a "business tool" for US companies

For many businesses, those recent initiatives have been a way to deal with concrete problems raised by the growing diversity of their workforce. Nevertheless, even though employers often justify them as an ethical and social necessity in a multicultural company—and more broadly in a multicultural society—it appears that those "faith-friendly" management policy rhetorics also serve more basic strategic interests for American corporations. Indeed, better consideration of employees' various beliefs and practices and promotion of a multi-faith working environment are not only considered by companies as efficient ways to prevent conflicts, to enrich individuals' work experiences or to foster religious pluralism. American executives are also aware that those initiatives could enable them to fulfill more pragmatic financial objectives, notably by giving their company a value-added profile in a very competitive market. The development of religious diversity management in US businesses—as the development of other diversity policies based on ethnicity, gender, sexual orientation or disability—is therefore

37 R. Lioger, "L'individuo-globalisme, nouvelle culture croyante des sociétés industrielles avancées," 16 *Revue Internationale de Politique Comparée* 135 (2009), 135–154.

38 Stanford University's Business School organized a seminar entitled "The Business World: Moral and Spiritual Inquiry Through Literature," while the Yale Center for "Faith and Culture" mentioned above launched a special program on "Ethics and Spirituality in the Workplace," whose main goal is to "promote efforts to align business practice with authentic human flourishing and the global common good."

also closely tied to the strategic goals pursued by employers. Ford's Interfaith Network's official mission is, for instance, not only "to assist the company in becoming a worldwide corporate leader in promoting religious tolerance," but also to "help management increase and maintain religious diversity, attract, develop, and retain talented employees of faith and be more aware of religious consumers' and investors' needs." A Ford representative confirmed that the company's policies towards religion, beyond being ideologically driven, were also "good for business," since, he argued, engaging diversity was for a corporation a "competitive advantage in a global economy."[39] The promise of an open, inclusive or even holistic work environment, where employees would be able to live and express their faith more freely, could be particularly appealing to some workers, which would make the company more attractive on the market. More generally, "faith-friendly" policies could also contribute to the reinforcement of broader corporate strategies designed to give a more positive image of businesses which are increasingly perceived today as lacking an "ethos," if not a "soul." By presenting themselves as concerned with "spirituality" and the "whole individual" and as more focused on immaterial values such as the protection of freedom of conscience and the defense of religious tolerance, American corporations are certainly also hoping to gain a social credibility and thus a new moral legitimacy in the eyes of society.

5. Religious diversity management in Europe: Is the "faith at work" movement exportable?

5.1. Contrasting lines

Like their American counterparts, companies in Europe have been confronted with a growing religious diversification of their workforce over the last few decades, notably because of the arrival of immigrants from Africa and Asia.[40] Hence, similar questions exist on this side of the Atlantic, on how to properly and effectively handle an increasingly multi-faith working environment to more positively engage with employees' religious identities and to minimize potential tensions and conflicts. In recent years, a few initiatives which resemble American "faith-friendly" policies, albeit much less elaborate, have been taken by some European institutions and companies seeking to better acknowledge the diverse religious identities of their employees.

Since the beginning of the 2000s, the European Commission has played a prominent role in advocating a more active approach to (religious) diversity in the workplace, beyond the mere respect for anti-discrimination laws. Besides conducting a study in 2005 entitled "The Business Case for Diversity—Good Practices in

39 *The Pluralism Project*, 2005.

40 See, for instance, L. Vickers, *Religious Freedom, Religious Discrimination and the Workplace* (Hart Publishing 2008).

the Workplace" in order to foster the "advancement of diversity management in companies," the Commission has launched a series of projects to convince employers within the EU to better "recognize and value" the differences in their workforce, that is to hire and include women and men of different ages, abilities, ethnic origins, sexual orientations and religions. Through several initiatives such as the development of a diversity benchmarking system for businesses and the implementation of a "European Diversity award" in the workplace, the Commission explicitly intends to "encourage employers to put diversity management more firmly on their strategic business agendas." In 2007, during the European Year of Equal Opportunities for All, the Commission published a "Training Manual for Diversity Management" directed at businesses all over the EU which contained advice and case studies. Therefore, like their American counterparts, European companies are increasingly invited to take the multiple identities of their employees into consideration and to actively foster a pluralist work environment, where differences are not hidden or neglected, but valued and positively engaged. It is precisely to achieve this ideal that the Directorate General for Employment, Social Affairs and Equal Opportunities of the European Commission asked Member States to make companies located in their countries sign a "Diversity Charter," through which they commit themselves to the implementation of several measures in order to "promote diversity and equal opportunities in the workplace."[41] As of September 2010, the Charter has been accepted by 144 companies in Belgium, 365 in Spain, 870 in Germany, and 2,895 in France, where the first workplace diversity programs were implemented in 2004.[42]

Nevertheless, the "faith-friendly" measures taken by corporations within the European Union have only been one—often marginal—aspect of broader diversity policies aiming at engaging various types of differences in the workforce. Indeed, in the diversity agenda of European companies, religion has certainly remained the most neglected—or the least targeted—element. As is clear in the 2005 report "The Business Case for Diversity" mentioned above, most of the companies which signed the "Diversity Charter" proposed by the European Commission, and which have indeed proved very active in developing pluralist and inclusive corporate policies, have mainly focused on fighting discriminations related to sexual orientation, disability, ethnicity and age. Of the 19 companies highlighted in the study, only four—British Telecommunications, Coco-Mat, Ford and Tesco—explicitly made the engagement of religious diversity one of their main priorities and areas of action. It seems therefore, as a recent comparative report on diversity management in Europe and the US pointed out, that for European businesses, contrary to their American counterparts, "religious diversity has (traditionally) been regarded as a lesser issue" than, for example, gender or ethnic diversity.[43]

41 European Commission, Directorate-General for Employment, Social Affairs and Equal Opportunities, available at ec.europa.eu/social/main.jsp?catId=915&langId=en.

42 *Id.*

43 "Diversity in a Global Environment. Is a Global Diversity-Inclusion Strategy a US-Centric Concept?" *Insights*, April 2007, available at www.bridgepartnersllc.com.

One possible explanation for this situation may be the suspicion and skepticism with which religion is often regarded in Western European societies, especially in countries such as France with a long history of separation between church and state. The widely shared assumption that religious beliefs and practices have long lost their relevance in the public space and should only be confined to the private sphere of individuals may dissuade many European managers and scholars from actually considering the engagement and the management of religion in the workplace as important issues that need to be addressed. It also probably makes it difficult for companies to be comfortable overtly acknowledging the religious identities of their employees or encouraging a greater religious expression in the office.

In that sense, the important place of religion in American history and contemporary society (although sometimes exaggerated), also certainly explains the popularity gained by "faith-friendly" policies in the US. The fact that religious beliefs and practices are usually perceived as strong social and civic values, and as evidence of both private and public morality,[44] probably helped convince American employers that giving a greater visibility to religion in the workplace could be a positive and desirable management strategy.

5.2. Experimental "faith-friendly" policies in European companies

Yet, as European societies are inexorably growing more and more religiously diverse, and as this evolution is being increasingly felt in the workplace, notably through demands for accommodations arising from minorities, some companies are progressively starting to "break the taboo" and to adjust their diversity management policies to the multi-religious reality of the office. The few experimental "faith-friendly" initiatives taken since the beginning of the 2000s, mainly in the United Kingdom, testify to a greater sensitivity of employers towards religion. Following the model of American businesses, some British companies have indeed launched their own awareness campaigns and diversity training programs on religious diversity.

One of the most comprehensive and ambitious "faith-friendly" management strategies in Europe was established in 2004 by British Telecommunications and ten other UK corporations, including Barclays, The Royal Bank of Scotland and the BBC. Realizing that "despite progress in developing policies to address issues of disability, age, gender and ethnicity, there had been little guidance on issues of belief for businesses," these companies decided to found the "Employer's Forum on Belief" ("Forum"), to "share good practice on religion … in order to make the most of their diverse workforces."[45] Over the years, the Forum has taken several initiatives to promote a more positive engagement of religious diversity in the whole

44 See, for instance, P. Edgell, J. Gerteis, D. Hartmann, "Atheist as 'Other': Moral Boundaries and Cultural Membership in American Society," 71 *American Sociological Review* 211 (2006), 211–234.

45 X, "Employers Forum on Belief Launches at the BT Centre," Employer's Forum on Belief (2005), available at www.efbelief.org.uk/news.php/23/employers-forum-on-

British corporate world—some very similar to those existing in US companies, such as holiday celebrations, faith-based affinity groups, corporate seminars (entitled "Taste of Religion"), etc. In 2010, the Forum reinforced its advocacy campaign with the creation of an award meant to compensate local public institutions and private businesses for being particularly active in the advancement of a pluralist workplace.

Tesco, a British grocery retailer, can be considered as another model of a European "faith-friendly" company. In 2006, executives issued a "cultural and religious fact-book" through the "Everyone is welcomed at Tesco" program. The toolkit, which included a calendar with the main holy days and festivals of major world religions as well as information on religious diet, prayers and dress, was distributed to the company's staff throughout the UK with the explicit purpose of having managers and employees learn about their co-workers' diverse beliefs and practices. Emphasizing the pluralist objective of this "faith-friendly" gesture, Tesco's website explains that the fact-book will enable employees "to understand and support people from all backgrounds and faiths."[46] More recently, the company also provided its managers with a special "support pack" for Ramadan, designed to help them more effectively "manage" the potential demands from Muslim employees and customers during that period of the year.

Even though the scope and impact of those initiatives are still too limited to evoke the beginning of an actual "faith at work" movement in Europe, they nonetheless already reveal that the ideal of a "respectful religious pluralism" may be slowly permeating the European corporate culture. Therefore, if it seems very unlikely that concerns for spirituality in the workplace could easily travel to this side of the Atlantic, it is yet possible to argue that the US model of the "faith-friendly" company can be to some extent appealing to an increasingly diverse Europe in search of new effective ways to deal with the problematic issue of religion at work.

5.3. National context matters

Nevertheless, in the case of Europe, the feasibility and desirability of "faith-friendly" policies will also certainly depend on each national context and, more particularly, on the historical relations between the state and religious groups in each country, as well as on the dominant popular perception towards the place and role of religion in the public sphere.

According to this logic, it is not surprising that most of the recent religious diversity management policies in Europe have been implemented in the "multicultural" UK, where the state—although officially Anglican—already recognizes in many ways various religious groups. Therefore, the fact that

belief-launches-at-the-bt-centre. The other companies are Land Registry, Accenture, B&Q, The Cooperative Group, Race for Opportunity, Shell and London Underground.

46 X, "Everyone is welcome at Tesco," Tesco, available at everyonewelcomeattesco.com; D. Thomas, "Tesco Vows to Distribute Religious Knowledge to UK Workforce," *Personnel Today*, 24 April 2006, available at www.personneltoday.com.

religious communities and citizens are recognized and often accommodated in the UK makes it certainly easier for British managers to take religious diversity into account within their corporate culture. Being used to a multicultural approach to religion in the broader society, they are also probably more likely to accept a greater visibility (and expression) of various beliefs and practices in the workplace.[47]

On the contrary, the development of "faith-friendly" policies seems more improbable in a country such as France, where for more than a century there has been a strict separation between church and state, and where a majority of the population is deeply attached to the ideal of *laïcité*. The commonly held assumption that religious beliefs and practices should be strictly relegated to the private sphere of individuals—because they could only have a dangerous, divisive influence in the public space—makes it difficult to imagine that such an active engagement of religion could be possible in the French workplace, at least without raising many protests, concerns and worries. Given this context, and although an office is not strictly speaking a "public space," it seems doubtful that French managers would actually think of religious diversity management strategies as necessary, useful or appropriate. It even seems today that more and more French people would agree with the idea that the principle of a strict *laïcité* should also apply to the workplace, as exemplified in recent controversies over the wearing of the veil by Muslim employees in kindergartens.[48] Concerned with the ideal of separation, and wary of multiculturalism, most French would feel uncomfortable with "faith-friendly" policies or with assertive forms of religious expression in the workplace, which they believe in the end would certainly lead to more tensions among employees, and thus would appear as counter-productive in the context. This is the reason why, in a European country such as France, a "faith at work" movement is unlikely to gain much credibility.[49]

---

47 Some of the new religious diversity management strategies have nevertheless also been criticized in Great Britain, mostly by secularist organizations such as the National Secular Society, which campaigns for a complete disestablishment of the Church of England and for the implementation of a separation of church and state based on the French model of "*laïcité*." In the case of the workplace, they defend the idea that British offices should remain strictly secular spaces, "where religion plays no part," and is best left at the door every morning. These secularist activists have particularly targeted the "Employer's Forum on Belief" initiative mentioned above. They notably argue that some of these experiments have already led to more conflicts between employees and to more lawsuits in the recent years. And, as a counter-example, they often invoke the US, where, according to them, the main consequence of "faith-friendly" policies was a dramatic rise in the number of religious discrimination complaints.

48 C. Gabizon, "Voile islamique: malaise dans les entreprises" ["Islamic Veil: Embarrassment in Companies"], *Le Figaro*, 7 February 2011, available at www.lefigaro.fr.

49 Even though new consulting groups focusing on religion in the workplace have recently set up there. See "Cultes & Cultures Consulting" available at www.cultesetcultures-consulting.com.

Conclusion

The "faith at work" movement that has emerged in the US over the last two decades has progressively placed religion at the center of the diversity management policies of an increasing number of American companies. These companies are willing to better acknowledge and value the various confessional identities of their employees and to avoid the conflicts often triggered by the confrontation between work requirements and demands of faith. Although they have raised several concerns, notably about religious harassment and proselytizing, "faith-friendly" strategies appear today appealing to a growing number of managers in the US. And their scope seems to expand all the more as they have also started to influence the way some European companies actually deal with the religious diversification of their own workforce. Traditionally focused on ethnicity, age, disability or sexual orientations, the US diversity agenda is slowly broadening as companies now also tend to take religion into account. Even though the impact of such policies is deemed to be limited in the European Union due to different national contexts, experimental "faith-friendly" initiatives in the workplace nevertheless already testify to a greater awareness, sensibility and openness of European employers towards the evolving reality of the religious landscape.

Chapter 14
Religion, Diversity and the Workplace: What Role for the Law?

Julie Ringelheim*

Introduction

The question of religious diversity in the workplace touches upon two crucial and much debated issues in contemporary Europe: religion and labor relations. The place of religion in European societies and its relations with the secular state in a context of growing religious pluralism are the object of vivid controversies. The handling of religious diversity in liberal democracies raises a range of challenges which have become familiar themes in political theory discussions and in the public debate in general: does equality mean that people always have to be treated identically? Should religious differences be taken into account by legislators and policy-makers in some circumstances? What sort of religion-based demands can be accommodated in a liberal democracy and which ones cannot?

Since the 1990s, controversies on these issues have been raging intensely among multiculturalists,[1] liberals,[2] feminists,[3] or French-type

---

* This paper was written while I was a Visiting Fellow at the Centre for the Study of Human Rights of the London School of Economics. I wish to thank the Centre for its support and assistance. I also thank Ilke Adam, Emmanuelle Bribosia, Daniel Dumont, Isabelle Rorive and Andrea Rea for stimulating discussions on the subject of this chapter.

1 Prominent proponents of multiculturalism include W. Kymlicka, *Multicultural Citizenship* (Oxford University Press 1996) (advocating multiculturalism from a liberal perspective); B. Parekh, *Rethinking Multiculturalism: Cultural Diversity and Political Theory* (Macmillan 2000); T. Modood, *Multiculturalism* (Polity Press 2007) and *Still Not Easy Being British—Struggles for a Multicultural Citizenship* (Trentham Books 2010); J. Carens, *Culture, Citizenship, and Community—A Contextual Exploration of Justice as Evenhandedness* (Oxford University Press 2000).

2 For liberal critiques of multiculturalism, see in particular B. Barry, *Culture and Equality—An Egalitarian Critique of Multiculturalism* (Harvard University Press 2001) and J. Waldron, "Minority Cultures and the Cosmopolitan Alternative," in *The Rights of Minority Cultures* (W. Kymlicka, ed., Oxford University Press 1995), 93–122.

3 S. Okin, "Is Multiculturalism Bad for Women?" in *Is Multiculturalism Bad for Women? Susan Moller Okin with Respondents* (J. Cohen, M. Howard and M. C. Nussbaum, eds, Princeton University Press 1999), 9–24 (criticizing multiculturalism from a feminist

Republicans.[4] As for labor relations, they have been profoundly affected by the move from a Fordist to a post-Fordist economy, in which the notion of flexibility becomes central, along with the growth of mass unemployment and precarious and atypical forms of work. Furthermore, the problem of discrimination in employment against ethnic minorities, which are often also *religious* minorities, is a rising concern across the European Union.

It is in this wider context that the legal issues posed by religious diversity in the work sphere must be situated. Account must also be taken of the specificity of the workplace. The latter is characterized by a peculiar mix of freedom and constraint: the worker who enters into a work contract accepts being subject to the authority of the employer; she agrees to work under its direction, to receive instructions, to have imposed certain tasks in exchange for a wage. Formally, everyone is free to take a job or not. In practice, working is a necessity for most people. At the same time, people enjoy a certain degree of freedom to choose what type of work to do. Against this background, the legal questions religious diversity raises are threefold: first, are workers entitled to observe their religion at work in the first place? Second, can they claim to have their work conditions adapted in case of conflict with their religious beliefs? Third, and conversely, can an employer prohibit religious expression in the workplace or refuse to accommodate religious needs and, if so, for what motive? To be sure, if practicing one's religion at work were not recognized as a right, this does not mean that employers may not, on their own initiative, allow their workers to express their beliefs or adjust their work conditions to their religious practice. However, where the employer refuses to do so, the worker has no means of redress. In other words, the central concern from a legal viewpoint is whether respecting and/or accommodating religion at work is—or should be—left to the *discretion* of employers or whether it is—or should be—a matter of *legal obligation* and, if so, what are its scope and limits.

This chapter seeks to explore where European law stands and what direction it could take in this regard. In order to put the legal discussion into perspective, section I, drawing on social science studies, examines the social and economic developments which form the background against which the issue of religion in employment arises in contemporary Europe. This will set the ground for the analysis of the possible legal responses to religious claims in the European workplace, which will be the focus of section II. Both EU law and the European Convention on Human Rights (ECHR) will be considered. Two legal concepts will retain our

---

perspective). See also A. Phillips, *Multiculturalism without Culture* (Princeton University Press 2007); S. Benhabib, *The Claims of Culture—Equality and Diversity in the Global Era* (Princeton University Press 2002) (both proposing avenues for reconciling respect for diversity and women's rights).

4 On the French-type Republican model, see, for example, D. Schnapper, *Qu'est-ce que la citoyenneté?* (Gallimard 2000). For a critical account of the French Republican model, see C. Laborde, *Critical Republicanism—The Hijab Controversy and Political Philosophy* (Oxford University Press 2008).

attention: the right to religious freedom, guaranteed under Article 9 of the ECHR, and the right not to be discriminated against, protected under EU law and Article 14 of the ECHR. The adoption of EU directive 2000/78/EC[5] has significantly extended the protection provided in EU countries against discrimination based on religion or belief in the employment sphere. Yet, as will be seen, current European law does not provide a straightforward answer as to what extent either of these notions protect religious interests in the work context. In particular, the question is not yet settled as to whether an obligation to accommodate religious beliefs at work—similar to the duty of reasonable accommodation of religious needs of workers which has been recognized in Canada and in the US—can be derived from the norms of religious freedom or non-discrimination as guaranteed under European law. Two approaches can be discerned in European case law: the first one, which will be termed the "freedom of contract" approach, insists that the terms of a work contract, which workers freely agree to, can limit the latter's freedom to manifest their religion. By contrast, the second conception, here called the "social inclusion" approach, is concerned with promoting the participation of all groups in social and economic life. Accordingly, it attaches special importance to the elimination of indirect barriers to the professional integration of certain groups such as religious minorities. It will be argued in section II that with the development of non-discrimination in EU law, this second perspective is increasingly gaining ground.

This chapter is concerned with religious practice by *workers*. Of course, the opposite situation also exists: sometimes, religious claims in the work sphere are advanced by employers. This is the case where religious organizations act as employers and wish to impose special obligations based on their spiritual convictions on their employees. A specific exception to the prohibition of discrimination based on religion has been inserted in this regard in Directive 2000/78/EC for so-called "ethos-based organisations."[6] The questions raised by this provision, however, are of a different nature than those relating to religious expression by workers. For reasons of space and consistency, this chapter only addresses this latter situation, which is by far the most frequent.

I. Religious diversity and work relations: The wider context

Understanding the social dynamics that underpin the issue of religious diversity in the workplace and how it is dealt with in contemporary Europe requires considering two questions. First, it is noteworthy that these discussions are especially focused

5 Council Directive 2000/78/EC of 27 November 2000 Establishing a General Framework for Equal Treatment in Employment and Occupation, OJ 303 L, 2/12/2000, 16–22 ("Employment Equality Directive").

6 Article 4(2) of The Employment Equality Directive; see in particular the chapter by Yves Stox in this volume.

on *minority* religions. The expression of minority faiths in the workplace thus appears as one instance of a broader phenomenon, that is the new visibility of religious minorities in Europe, which has contributed to renewing controversies about the relations between religions and the secular state (1). Second, the questions raised by religious pluralism in the employment context must also be viewed against the background of the more general evolution of the employment market and labor relations (2).

1. Religious minorities and the renewal of the debate on secularism

Judging by the case law discussed in various chapters in this volume, disputes relating to the religious practice of workers seem to concern primarily, although not exclusively, *minority* faiths. Muslims, who constitute the largest religious minority in Western Europe—they are estimated to represent four to seven percent of the current population in France, Germany, Great Britain and the Netherlands[7]—are especially present in these discussions. In Belgium, a study carried out in 2009–2010 found that the most frequent requests for accommodation of religious beliefs reported by the employers interviewed concern Muslims.[8] In the United Kingdom, according to a 2007 inquiry commissioned by the Home Office, Sikh, Muslim and Hindu organizations were almost twice as likely as Christian organizations to report unfair treatment experienced by their members in employment.[9] The latter included dress restrictions, working on religious days, lack of respect for religious customs as well as application and recruitment practices. Among them, Muslims were the most likely to indicate that this unfair treatment was frequent rather than occasional.

It could be tempting to interpret the over-representation of minorities in contestations relating to religion at work as the sign of a rising religiosity among them which would contrast with the decline of religious practice in the majority populations. The supposed growing religiousness among Muslims and the threat it is said to pose to the European tradition of secularity have indeed become a common narrative in European media.[10] Yet such reading overlooks other important factors to be taken into account when considering the position of

7 J. Césari, *When Islam and Democracy Meets: Muslims in Europe and the United States* (Palgrave 2006), 9. The author, however, notes that it is difficult to obtain accurate statistics in this regard as in most European countries religious affiliation is not asked in population censuses.

8 I. Adam and A. Rea (eds), *La diversité culturelle sur le lieu de travail. Pratiques d'aménagements raisonnables*, Research commissioned by the Centre for Equal Opportunities and the Fight against Racism, September 2010, 132.

9 P. Weller, A. Feldman and K. Purdam, *Religious Discrimination in England and Wales* (Home Office Research Study 220, 2007), 51–64.

10 See J. Cesari, "Introduction," in *European Muslims and the Secular State* (J. Cesari and S. McLoughlin, eds, Ashgate 2005), 4; Ph. Connors, "Contexts of Immigrant Receptivity and Immigrant Religious Outcomes: The Case of Muslims in Western Europe," 33 *Ethnic and Racial Studies* 376 (2010), 380.

religious minorities in the workplace. First and foremost, despite the high degree of secularization of Western European societies, the traditionally dominant religion still to some extent informs the legal organization of employment. This is most evident regarding the official days of rest, which in large part reflect Christian holidays. In relation to this, it is interesting to note that according to the findings of the aforementioned Belgian study, the most frequent request for accommodation reported by employers concerns the possibility of taking a day off for religious reasons. Another example of Christian influence on employment regulation is the fact that European legislations legalizing abortion usually recognize a right to conscientious objection for doctors and nurses.[11] Whatever the actual level of religiosity among the majority population, the fact that Christian religious traditions are implicitly taken into account in the norms that structure the work sphere means that observant Christians can remain *invisible* in the workplace. By contrast, this state of affairs heightens the visibility of minority religions insofar as their followers have to make special requests if they want to have their work conditions adapted to their religious practice.

Another factor that helps put into perspective the idea of a rise in religious demands at work lies with the evolution of the situation of minority religious communities in the socio-economic sphere. The first generation of migrant workers from Muslim countries who arrived in West European states in the 1950s–1960s—as part of guest-worker programs in the case of Belgium, France, Germany and the Netherlands[12]—were confined to specific, unskilled, sectors of the economy. However, the second and third generations, who grew up in Europe, are accessing wider and more diversified employment areas. Minority workers are now present in sectors where they were previously absent. Accordingly, some employers are confronted today with a religious diversity that was practically nonexistent thirty years ago and that they have not been used to dealing with. It has also been suggested that as descendants of immigrants have acquired citizenship, they have become more confident and assertive in their demands for cultural and religious recognition.[13] If such requests are becoming more common this would be the sign that young minority workers feel that they are part of the country they live in and are therefore entitled to have their religious traditions respected, whereas their parents tended to adopt a low profile.

Meanwhile, the public assertion of the Muslim (or other minority) religion and identity contradicts what has long been a common assumption in Europe, namely that modernity would inevitably bring in its wake the decline and marginalization of religion.[14] The secularization theory, which has long been dominant in

---

11 See, for instance, the French legislation: Article 2212-8 of the Public Health Code (*Code de santé publique*) (Loi No. 2001-588 of 4 July 2001, *J.O.* 7 July 2001).

12 J. Césari, *When Islam and Democracy Meet*, *supra* note 7, 13.

13 I. Adam and A. Rea, *supra* note 8, 136.

14 J. Cesari, "Introduction," in *European Muslims and the Secular State* (J. Cesari and S. McLoughlin, eds, Ashgate 2005), 2.

social sciences, has popularized the idea that faith was to become increasingly irrelevant in modern societies and would retreat to a strictly private sphere. As Casanova points out, the secularization thesis, in its classic version, claims that societal modernization entails not only the "structural differentiation," that is the autonomization of the secular spheres—the state, the economy, science—from religion, but also the fading away and privatization of religion.[15] This process was seen as indispensable to modernity: in order for a society to be modern, it had to privatize faith, to relegate it to non-public and non-political spaces.[16] Yet since the 1960s this theory has been subject to intense debates and critical reappraisals.[17] Empirical research has highlighted that outside Europe, modernity did not necessarily entail the decline of religiosity and the marginalization of religion.[18] In Europe itself, which is considered the most secularized region in the world, the secularization process took different forms and attained different levels of intensity, depending on the dominant religious tradition and the history of State–Church relations.[19] Moreover, from a normative viewpoint, a number of authors have argued that, provided certain conditions are met, religions may enter the public sphere and assume the role of civil society actors without endangering individuals' freedom and modern differentiated structures.[20]

The rise of religious pluralism in contemporary Europe has also contributed to renewed discussions about the meaning and implications of *secularism*, that is the political-legal doctrine which posits the separation of state and religion as a necessary component of liberal democracies. This notion has translated into various institutional models across Europe, ranging from strict separation or *laïcité* in France to mild forms of separation in Germany, the Netherlands or Belgium. But in theoretical literature on secularism, the French *laïcité* and the

---

15 J. Casanova, *Public Religions in the Modern World* (University of Chicago Press 1994). On the concept and theory of secularization, see also D. Martin, *On Secularization—Towards a Revised General Theory* (Ashgate 2005); R. Wallis and S. Bruce, "Secularization—The Orthodox Model" in *Religion and Modernization: Sociologists and Historians Debate the Secularization Thesis* (S. Bruce, ed., Clarendon Press 1992), 12; B. Wilson, "Reflections on a Many Sided Controversy," in *Religion and Modernization: Sociologists and historians debate the secularization thesis* (S. Bruce, ed., Clarendon Press 1992), 195.

16 J. Casanova, *supra* note 15, 38–39 and 63–66; T. Asad, "Secularism, Nation-State, Religion," in *Formations of the Secular—Christianity, Islam, Modernity* (Stanford University Press 2003), 181–201, at 181.

17 See inter alia the collection of articles in J. A. Beckford and Th. Luckmann (eds), *The Changing Face of Religion*, (Sage 1989) and S. Bruce (ed.), *Religion and Modernization: Sociologists and historians debate the secularization thesis* (Clarendon Press 1992).

18 P. Berger (ed.), *The Desecularization of the World: Resurgent Religion and World Politics* (Eerdmans 1999).

19 See D. Martin, *supra* note 15; R. Wallis and S. Bruce, *supra* note 15, at 15–17. For an inquiry into religious practice in the different parts of Europe, see A. M. Greeley, *Religion in Europe at the End of the Second Millenium* (Transaction Publishers 2003).

20 See, in particular, J. Casanova, *supra* note 15, esp. at 55–58 and 211–234.

American disestablishment clause, both based on a strict conception of separation, have tended to be viewed as the paradigmatic forms of secularism.[21] Yet, in recent years, various authors have argued that secularism, properly understood, is not incompatible with the state accommodating religious practice of citizens nor with individuals expressing their faith in the public sphere.[22]

The workplace occupies a peculiar position in these debates. These debates are indeed largely structured around the distinction between the public and private spheres. But depending on what definition of these notions is adopted, the workplace can fall on either side of this dichotomy. Under one approach, very present in feminist literature, the public square is understood as comprising all domains external to the family. From this perspective, the employment sphere, like market relations in general, is part of the *public* realm.[23] For other scholars, the public refers to state institutions as opposed to civil society, which includes the family, the market and private associations of citizens.[24] Here, the workplace will be seen as part of the *private* sphere, at least as far as private employment is concerned. Yet civil servants who are employed in state institutions fall within the public sphere. Hence, in many European states, the question arises whether the notion that the state should be neutral towards the various religions and beliefs entails special obligations for public servants, in particular in relation to the wearing of religious symbols while at work. As illustrated by several chapters in this book, there is no consensus on this issue in Europe. The positions taken by the various states on this matter reflect the conception of secularism prevailing in their legal and political traditions. Additionally, even if employment in the private sector is considered as part of the private sphere, it is nevertheless highly regulated by the state: the way the relations between state and religions are conceived may thus impact how religious expression at work is dealt with in both public and private employment.

---

21 On the importance of the American constitutional model in theoretical discussions about secularism, see in particular V. Bader, "Religion and States. A New Typology and a Plea for Non-Constitutional Pluralism," 6(1) *Ethical Theory and Moral Practice* 55 (2003).

22 See, among others, L. Zucca, "Crucifix in the Classroom: The Grand Chamber Decision in Lautsi," *International Journal of Constitutional Law* 2011 (forthcoming) and L. Zucca, "Law vs. Religion," in *Law, State and Religion in the New Europe: Debate and Dilemmas* (C. Ungureanu and L. Zucca, eds, Cambridge University Press 2012); C. Laborde, *Critical Republicanism. The Hijab Controversy and Political Philosophy* (Oxford University Press, 2008) (writing from a Republican perspective); T. Modood, *Multiculturalism: A Civic Idea* (Polity 2007) (writing from a multiculturalist perspective); R. Bhargava, "States, Religious Diversity, and the Crisis of Secularism," *Open Democracy*, available at www.democracy.net (arguing for a conception of secularism inspired by the Indian model).

23 See, for instance, the classic article by F. Olsen, "The Family and the Market," 96 *Harvard Law Review* 1497 (1983). On the different understandings of the public and private spheres in political theory, see J. Weintraub, "The Theory and Politics of the Public/Private Distinction," in *Public and Private Thought and Practice—Perspectives on a Grand Dichotomy* (J. Weintraub and K. Kumar, eds, The University of Chicago Press, 1997), 1.

24 J. Weintraub, *supra* note 23.

2. The evolution of work relations

As emphasized by Adam and Rea, the question of how religious diversity is managed in the work sphere must also be viewed in the light of the profound evolutions labor relations have undergone in Europe in the last forty years.[25] It is generally considered that European societies have moved from a fordist to a post-fordist economy. In the fordist system, the economy was dominated by large industrial enterprises engaged in the mass production of cheap standardized goods, based on a high specialization of tasks and a pyramidal structure of management. Labor relations were characterized by a hierarchical organization of work and uniform collective norms regulating large sectors of the industry. In the post-fordist model, by contrast, the service industry holds a central place while workplace governance is marked by increasing heterogenization and individualization of work modalities. Flexibility and autonomy become key words.[26]

More empirical research is needed to assess how these changes impact on the way religious pluralism is dealt with in the workplace. However, it is possible to surmise that their impact is ambivalent: in some respects, current changes could facilitate the taking into account of religious specificities in the workplace. But in other regards, these processes increase the vulnerability of certain categories of workers, hence making it more difficult for them to insist on having their religious beliefs accommodated.

Adam and Rea suggest that as a general matter, the trend towards heterogenization and flexibilization of labor organization leaves more room than old-style rigid regulations for adaptations of work conditions to personal circumstances of various types, including religious practice.[27] In fact, one striking indication arising from their inquiry into the accommodation of cultural and religious diversity in the workplace is that requests for adjustments of work modalities are by no means limited to religious motives. Such demands are described as a recurring issue in the day-to-day life of companies. The most frequent requests according to interviewees relate not to religion but to family situations: they concern in particular parents who have alternate guardianship arrangements for their children and wish to have their working time adapted accordingly.[28] More generally, it has been pointed out that the individualization of work conditions is part of a larger

25 I. Adam and A. Rea, *supra* note 8, 136.

26 For an overview of this transformation and how it affects labour relations in the EU, see A. Supiot (ed.), *Au-delà de l'emploi—Transformations du travail et devenir du droit du travail en Europe* (Flammarion 1999). See also H. Collins, *Employment Law* (2nd ed.) (Oxford University Press 2010), 101–105.

27 I. Adam and A. Rea, *supra* note 8, 136.

28 I. Adam and A. Rea, *supra* note 8, 48–49. See also E. Bribosia, A. Rea, J. Ringelheim and I. Rorive, "Reasonable Accommodation of Religious Diversity in Europe and in Belgium: Law and Practice," in *The Others in Europe* (S. Bonjour, A. Rea and D. Jacobs, eds, Editions de l'Université de Bruxelles 2011), 91 and 107–108.

process of diversification of aspirations, expectations and lifestyles in European societies which is inevitably reflected in the work sphere.[29] Thus, relations between religious beliefs and employment must be situated in the broader debate about how to enable all workers, and especially women, to better reconcile the various aspects of their lives: paid work, unpaid work, family life, leisure, rest, etc.;[30] in other words, how to implement the "general principle of adapting work to the worker," to which the EU Council Directive 93/104/EC refers.[31] For Collins the "problem of achieving a balance between work and other aspects of the life cycle is surely one of the most complex facing society today."[32]

Yet other trends in the European labor market seem likely to make accommodation of minorities' religious specificities more difficult. Adam and Rea highlight that some categories of workers, especially those employed in low-skilled jobs, are still subject to tightened control and have little autonomy.[33] In fact, for the most precarious workers, the weight of subordination to the employer has increased: in their respect, the employer does not only enjoy the authority normally attached to employment relations, he also has the power not to renew the contract which, in a time of mass unemployment, is a particularly daunting prospect.[34] Generally, compared to the 1960s, the socio-economic condition of the most vulnerable categories of the workforce has worsened. Unemployment has become structural. Job insecurity has risen. While in the Fordist period, a full-time employment contract of indefinite duration was the norm, in the post-Fordist era, the employment status of workers becomes more unstable and fluctuating. Temporary work, casual work and part-time work have become much more common.[35] For many workers, the flexibilization of work conditions requires their adjustment to the company needs rather than to their own aspirations.[36] At

29 This process is especially manifest in the evolution of working time management: whereas the fordist model was based on uniform, standardized and stable working schedules, nowadays, timetables are increasingly heterogeneous and individualized. The number of workers who have the same timetable every day and every week has significantly decreased in Europe. See A. Supiot (ed.), *Au-delà de l'emploi—Transformations du travail et devenir du droit du travail en Europe* (Flammarion 1999), 93–137.

30 See H. Collins, *Employment Law* (2nd ed.) (Oxford University Press 2010), 77–97.

31 EU Council Directive 93/104/EC of 23 November 1993 concerning certain aspects of the organization of working time, *OJ 307 L*, 13/12/1998, 18. See also A. Supiot (ed.), *supra* note 29, 127.

32 H. Collins, *supra* note 30, 12. See also H. Collins, "The Right to Flexibility," in *Labour Law, Work and Family: Critical and Comparative Perspectives* (J. Conaghan and K. Rittich, eds, Oxford University Press 2005).

33 I. Adam and A. Rea, *supra* note 8, 132.

34 A. Supiot (ed.), *supra* note 29, 37.

35 R. Castel, *Les métamorphoses de la question sociale. Une chronique du salariat* (Gallimard 1995), 645–675; A. Supiot (ed.), *supra* note 29, 53–92; H. Collins, *supra* note 30, 38.

36 R. Castel, *supra* note 35, 649–650. See also A. Supiot (ed.), *supra* note 29, 261–263.

the same time, employers have become more demanding in the level and variety of skills they require from their employees: in line with the new management methods, individuals are expected to bring to the company not only their technical competences but also personal and social abilities, such as adaptability, autonomy, reactivity, communication skills or creativity.[37] The development of these new selection criteria has contributed to the gradual exclusion from stable employment of the least-qualified, the least "adaptable" to the new work organization models.[38]

Among the groups that are especially harmed by these evolutions lie immigrants and their descendants. Their unemployment rate is generally consistently higher than the national average. In addition, they tend to be concentrated in low-paid and low-level jobs.[39] Although this is not the only factor that explains this situation, the existence of discrimination is widely documented.[40] This phenomenon particularly affects migrants from Muslim countries, including second generations. In the United Kingdom, the first triennial review published by the Equality and Human Rights Commission in 2010,[41] highlights that compared to the other religious and conviction groups, Muslims have the lowest rates of employment: male Muslim unemployment is nine percent while the national average is five percent.[42] The British labor market, moreover, is characterized by a high level of occupational

37 See L. Boltanski and E. Chiapello, *The New Spirit of Capitalism* (Verso 2007), 90–91 (original title: *Le nouvel esprit du capitalisme*, Gallimard 1999).

38 L. Boltanski and E. Chiapello, *supra* note 37, 82–98 and 240–242; R. Castel, *supra* note 35, 651–655.

39 A. Heath, "Crossnational Patterns and Processes of Ethnic Disadvantage," in *Unequal Chances, Ethnic minorities in Western Labour Markets* (H. Anthony and Ch. Sin Yi, eds, Oxford University Press 2007), 639–695.

40 See in particular the studies on discrimination against migrant workers conducted in various European countries based on situation-testing: E. Cediey and F. Foroni (ISM-CORUM), "Les Discriminations à raison de 'l'origine' dans les embauches en France. Une enquête nationale par tests de discrimination selon la méthode du BIT," Bureau International du Travail, 2006 (published in 2007); E. Allasino, E. Reyneri, A. Venturini, and G. Zincone, "Labour market discrimination against migrant workers in Italy," 67 *International Migration Papers* (International Labour Office 2004); R. Zegers de Beijl, "Documenting Discrimination against Migrants Workers in the Labour Market. A comparative study of four European countries," International Labour Organization, 2000; P. Arrijn, S. Feld and A. Nayer, "Discrimination in access to employment on grounds of foreign origin: the case of Belgium," 23 *International Migration Papers* (International Labour Office 1998); W. Actis, M. Angel de Prada and C. Pereda, "Labour market discrimination against migrant workers in Spain," 9 *International Migration Papers* (International Labour Office 1996); Fr. Bovenkerk, M. J. I. Gras and D. Ramsoedh, "Discrimination against migrant workers and ethnic minorities in access to employment in the Netherlands," 4 *International Migration Papers* (International Labour Office 1995).

41 Equality and Human Rights Commission, *How Fair is Britain? Equality, Human Rights and Good Relations in 2010, The First Triennial Review* (2010), available at www.equalityhumanrights.com/key-projects/how-fair-is-britain.

42 *Id.*, 405.

segregation. Muslims are less likely than any other religious group to be in better paying, higher status positions. Instead, they are found to a greater extent in plant and machinery factory work and unskilled jobs.[43] Similarly, in Belgium studies have shown a process of "ethno-stratification" of the labor market which penalizes in particular people with Moroccan and Turkish backgrounds, regardless of whether they have acquired Belgian nationality: they are more likely than the majority population to be unemployed and remain largely concentrated in less skilled and low status jobs.[44] Such a phenomenon of "ethnic penalty" has also been observed in the case of second-generation Maghrebins in France[45] and Turkish and Moroccan migrants in the Netherlands.[46]

Coming back to the issue of religious diversity at work, given the vulnerable positions of many minority workers, and especially Muslims, in the labor market, they are likely to have little bargaining power if the employer refuses to accommodate their religious beliefs. In view of the difficulties they experience in the labor market, it can be hypothesized that they will often not be in a position to negotiate or contest the employer's decision.[47]

A last factor that proves significant for how religious diversity is dealt with in the workplace is the importance taken by the relation between companies and

---

43 *Id.*, 429.

44 See K. Phalet, "Down and Out: The Children of Migrant Workers in the Belgian Labour Market," in *Unequal Chances, Ethnic Minorities in Western Labour Markets* (H. Anthony and Ch. Sin Yi, eds, Oxford University Press 2007), 143–180; S. Vertommen, A. Martens and N. Ouali, "Topography of the Belgian Labour Market—Employment: Gender, Age and Origin," *Research within the framework of the Interuniversitary Consortium on Immigration and Integration, Koning Boudenwijnstichting/Fondation Roi Beaudouin,* June 2006, available at www.kbs-frb.be; A. Martens, N. Ouali, M. Van de Maele, S. Vertommen, Ph. Dryon and H. Verhoeven, "Discriminations des étrangers et des personnes d'origine étrangère sur le marché du travail de la Région de Bruxelles-Capitale," *Recherche dans le cadre du Pacte social pour l'emploi à Bruxelles, Rapport de synthèse*, January 2005.

45 R. Silberman and I. Fournier, "Is French Society Truly Assimilative? Immigrant Parents and Offspring on the French Labour Market," in *Unequal Chances, Ethnic Minorities in Western Labour Markets* (H. Anthony and Ch. Sin Yi, eds, Oxford University Press 2007), 221–268.

46 P. Tesser and J. Dronkers, "Equal Opportunities or Social Closure in the Netherlands?" in *Unequal Chances, Ethnic Minorities in Western Labour Markets* (H. Anthony and Ch. Sin Yi, eds, Oxford University Press 2007), 359–401.

47 I. Adam and A. Rea observe, however, that the fact that religious minorities are concentrated in certain sectors may in some cases facilitate the accommodation of their religious needs, such as the adaptation of canteen meals to dietary requirements: for pragmatic reasons, employers may tend to respond positively to such requests when they are supported by a large part of the workforce. But some demands, in contrast, may be more difficult to satisfy where minorities' members are numerous: where Muslims represent the majority of employees, it might not be possible for a company or institution to allow them all at the same time to take a day off for a religious holiday or to leave work earlier during Ramadan. On this point, see the findings of I. Adam and A. Rea, *supra* note 8.

the general public in a service-based economy. Indeed, in service companies, the work relation does not only involve the employer and the workers: the client—her preferences, attitudes, expectations—acquires a crucial place. This, in some European countries, appears to have a determining impact on how *visible* religious practice, primarily the wearing of a headscarf by female employees, is handled by employers. The French and Belgian case law analyzed by Alouane and Alidadi in their contributions to this volume provides various examples of situations where the wearing of a headscarf is deemed problematic by the employer as soon as the employee has to be in contact with the public. By the same token, the Belgian study on accommodation of religion in the workplace suggests that it is a common practice for private companies in Belgium to base their policy regarding the headscarf on a distinction between front-office and back-office work, prohibiting it in the first case, allowing it in the second.[48] The supposed negative attitudes of the general public towards certain types of religious manifestations thus permeate the work relationship and directly influence how some forms of religious diversity are managed by employers.

II. Religious diversity and work relations: What role for the law?

The concrete questions religious diversity may raise in the sphere of labor relations are varied and numerous, for the forms the practice of a religion may take are themselves very diverse. In some cases, the issue is simply whether a worker can express her religious beliefs while at work, for instance, through the wearing of specific clothes like a headscarf or through the act of praying. Here, the question is whether the employer, in virtue of its general authority, can prohibit this sort of behavior in the work sphere. In other circumstances, the problem is whether an employee can have his work conditions adjusted to allow him to observe his faith either *within* or *outside* the workplace, for example, being allowed to take a day off for a religious holiday, having canteen meals adapted to dietary requirements or being exempted from performing certain tasks, like having contact with pork meat, serving alcohol or contributing to the production of arms. In this situation, a pre-existing norm applicable in a specific work context—the list of holiday days, the composition of canteen menus, the definition of tasks to be carried out by the staff—conflicts with a worker's religious practice: the problem is thus whether the latter can obtain an adaptation of this rule in order to solve the conflict. Of course, in practice the distinction between these two types of cases is not clear-cut: more often than not, where an employer's decision to forbid one religious manifestation at work (e.g. the wearing of a headscarf) is contested, the employer will try to justify it by claiming that this behavior clashes with some work rule or requirement (e.g. safety conditions or the image the company wants to convey

48 I. Adam and A. Rea, *supra* note 8, esp. at 94–95.

to the public). This may spark a second discussion on whether this rule can be adjusted to accommodate a worker's religious needs.

The starting point of any legal analysis of these questions is that employment is based on a contract: it is "a consensual relation between two parties involving an exchange."[49] Workers sell their labor power—their time, efforts and skill—in return for pay.[50] Furthermore, the distinctive trait of the employment contract is the element of subordination it involves: by taking a job, the employee consents to being subject to the authority of the employer. The employer acquires the right to direct the worker to perform a range of tasks according to his instructions. Formally, each contracting party is supposed to be free and equal. In reality, in most of the cases, the employer is in a much stronger position than the employee. This permits the employer to fix the terms of the contract to his advantage. The initial inequality of power is compounded by the authority the employer enjoys over its employees in virtue of the contract. There is thus a clear risk that the employer might abuse the factual and legal power it holds. This danger has long been recognized by the law: the tension between freedom to contract and subordination lies precisely at the heart of employment law as it has developed in European countries.[51] In the words of Supiot, "the question of power is at the core of labour law."[52] Despite differences of legal traditions in Europe,[53] the main object of employment law has everywhere been "to be a countervailing force to counteract the inequality of bargaining power which is inherent and must be inherent in the employment relationship."[54] Labor law thus aims at framing the exercise of its power by the employer: by introducing mandatory rules and procedures, it seeks to secure a minimum level of safety and fairness for workers and to prevent potential abuse of managerial authority.[55]

Employment law has typically been concerned with safeguarding the safety and health of workers, protecting them against termination of contract without just cause, regulating working hours and, in most industrialized countries, guaranteeing a minimum wage. Yet, traditionally, it does not deal with the place of religion at work. Accordingly, the question arises whether authorizing religious expression and/or accommodating spiritual beliefs in the workplace is left to the discretion of employers—meaning that they can allow it or not without having to provide justification for doing so and that workers who do not conform with their decision can be disciplined—or whether workers can derive from some existing legal

49 H. Collins, *supra* note 30, 6.

50 *Id.*, 3.

51 A. Supiot, *Critique du droit du travail* (2nd ed.) (P.U.F. 2007), 110.

52 *Id.*, 109 (my translation).

53 For an overview of the different traditions of labor law in Western Europe: A. Supiot, *supra* note 51, 13–33.

54 P. Davies and M. Freedland, *Kahn-Freund's Labour and the Law* (3rd ed) (Stevens 1983), 18, quoted by H. Collins, *supra* note 30, 6.

55 H. Collins, *supra* note 30, 11; A. Supiot, *supra* note 51, 111.

provision a right in this regard which could be enforced through judicial action. In European law, there are two possible foundations for such a right: the right to religious freedom, protected under Article 9 of the ECHR, and the prohibition of religious discrimination, laid down by the European Convention but also by EU law. While Article 14 of the ECHR precludes discrimination in the enjoyment of the rights enshrined in the ECHR, the Employment Equality Directive, adopted in 2000, outlaws discrimination in employment and occupation based inter alia on religion or belief.[56]

Traditionally, two different responses have coexisted to the question whether religious freedom or anti-discrimination can protect religious interests at work. These two approaches fundamentally rest on different understandings of the relationship between market processes and anti-discrimination as well as, more generally, between freedom to contract and human rights. The first approach gives primary importance to contractual freedom. It will be termed here the "freedom of contract" approach (1). The second, alternative, conception can be labeled the "social inclusion" approach as it recognizes a central place for the objective of achieving social and professional inclusion of all groups, and especially the most disadvantaged (2). Recent developments in EU anti-discrimination law have clearly reinforced this second approach. Yet the extent to which employers could be required, based on the non-discrimination norm, to accommodate religious beliefs of their workers remains uncertain.

1. The freedom of contract approach

The issue of religion in the workplace can be viewed as one instance of a broader problem which employment relations give rise to, that is the potential tension between contractual freedom and human rights. The terms of a labor contract, or the requirements made by employers based on their managerial authority, may involve restrictions to the fundamental rights of workers, for example, where they are required to wear a uniform which excludes the wearing of a headscarf. But similar questions can arise in relation to other rights: to take one example among many, when an employer prohibits employees from speaking to the press about the company without prior authorization, it limits the employees' freedom of speech. The general question this raises is to what extent human rights are applicable to the work sphere. According to the first approach, contractual freedom must be given primary importance. Under this view, private parties should be left as free as possible to define the terms and conditions of the contract as best suits their economic interests, including where this implies departing from certain human rights. Employers cannot be required to accept certain conditions or behaviors if they were not provided for in the contract. In view of the authority conferred

56 Council Directive 2000/78/EC of 27 November 2000 Establishing a General Framework for Equal Treatment in Employment and Occupation, *OJ 303 L*, 2/12/2000, 16–22.

to them by the contract, to which the worker has consented, they should be able to decide at their own discretion whether the religious practice of a worker is compatible with business interests. The worker's right to religious freedom is guaranteed insofar as by virtue of his contractual freedom he is free not to take a job or to resign if the conditions conflict with his religious beliefs.

As noted by De Schutter, this approach looks with suspicion at any attempt by the state to intervene in market processes and impose certain obligations on employers.[57] Accordingly, it restrictively interprets the obligations stemming from the prohibition to discriminate. On this account, non-discrimination only entails that employers cannot disadvantage certain individuals in decisions on recruitment, promotion, access to training, etc. based on characteristics such as their religion or belief, race, ethnicity, gender, disability, sexual orientation or age; they can only have regard to criteria which have a direct and genuine link with the position to be provided. But businesses cannot be required to go beyond this and contribute to the wider societal goal of promoting the social and professional inclusion of groups disadvantaged on the labor market, such as ethnic or religious minorities, through measures such as adapting the organization of work to their religious needs.[58] The observance of a (minority) religion is seen as a choice, the consequences of which must be assumed by the individual worker, in case his religious practice does not fit with the current organization of the workplace. Non-discrimination here is regarded as an instrument in the service of the market: it contributes to the good functioning of economic processes by eliminating irrational decisions by employers that are based on characteristics unrelated to work performance. But it does not justify imposing rules that deviate from market norms and aim at remedying exclusionary effects produced by the market itself.[59]

This view is reflected in the 24 March 1998 decision of the French Cassation Court: in the case of a supermarket employee of Muslim faith who had asked to be transferred from the butchery to another service in order not to be in contact with pork, the Court ruled that absent any express contractual clause, religious convictions of workers are not part of the labor contract. Hence, the employer does not commit any fault by asking the employee to execute the task for which he was hired.[60] In other words, the employer is free to ignore religious requests by

---

57 O. De Schutter, *Discriminations et marché du travail. Liberté et* égalité *dans les rapports d'emploi* (P.I.E.-Peter Lang 2001).

58 For a discussion of this first conception of non-discrimination, see O. De Schutter, *supra* note 57, esp. at 24–28.

59 *Id.*, at 203–204.

60 Cass. soc., 24 mars 1998, No. 95-44.738, *M. Azad c. Chamsidine*. On this case, see the chapter by Rim-Sarah Alouane in this volume. See also O. De Schutter, *supra* note 57, at 51.

employees without having to provide any justification for it. Freedom to contract overrides the right to religious freedom.[61]

A similar conception underlies the approach of the former European Commission of Human Rights to cases involving requests for accommodation of work schedules for religious reasons. In the famous *X.* v. *United Kingdom* decision, where a Muslim teacher complained that the London state school in which he worked had refused to arrange his timetable so as to enable him to take forty-five minutes off on Friday to attend the prayer at the mosque, the European Commission of Human Rights found no interference with his right under Article 9.[62] Determining in its opinion was the fact that he had voluntarily accepted teaching obligations under his contract with the school and remained free to resign if he found that these duties clashed with his religious beliefs.[63] The Commission, therefore, did not require the state to demonstrate that satisfying the applicant's demand would not have been possible for reasons related to work performance: in its view, the mere fact that workers are free to leave their job is sufficient to protect their religious freedom. The Commission also rejected the discrimination claim. The applicant pointed out that Christian workers had no difficulty reconciling their working obligations with their religious observance as general official holidays reflect Christian traditions. To this, the Commission simply replied that he has not shown to have been treated less favorably than individuals placed in comparable situations, that is "teachers belonging to religious minorities."[64] The Commission thus considered as self-evident that the applicant's situation can only be compared to that of other minority workers and not to that of employees practicing the *majority* religion. It added that "in most countries, only the religious holidays of the majority of the population are celebrated as public holidays."[65] The Commission thereby suggested, without any further explanation, that it is only natural that the norm of the workplace corresponds to the norm of the majority and that adepts of minority faiths must adapt to it or resign. The European Court has never directly addressed the issue, but in *Kosteski* v. *the Former Yugoslav Republic of Macedonia* (2006), it incidentally endorsed the Commission's jurisprudence on work schedule and religious holidays.[66] In particular, it expressed doubts that taking a day off to

61 More generally, on the relations between labor law and individual human rights in French law, see A. Supiot, *supra* note 51, at 160–164.

62 ECommHR, 12 March 1981, *X.* v. *United Kingdom*, App. No. 8160/78, *D.R.* 22, 27.

63 *Id.*, par. 9 and 15. This is restated in ECommHR, 3 December 1996, *Konttinen* v. *Finland*, App. No. 24949/94, *D.R.* 87-B, 68; see the chapter by Saïla Ouald Chaib in this volume for a discussion of this and related case law.

64 *X.* v. *United Kingdom*, par. 27.

65 *Id.*, par. 28.

66 ECtHR, 13 April 2006, *Kosteski* v. *The Former Yugoslav Republic of Macedonia*, par. 37. In the country concerned, citizens of Muslim faith were allowed, under the Constitution, to take a day off on Muslim-recognized public holidays. The problem at

celebrate a religious feast is a manifestation of religious beliefs protected under Article 9 of the ECHR.[67]

2. The social inclusion approach

The "freedom of contract" approach presents several problems. By postulating that the two parties to the contract are free and equal, it neglects the reality of power relations in which they are located. In practice, workers are usually not in a position to negotiate the terms and conditions of the contract. Job contracts are generally offered on a "take it or leave it" basis by employers.[68] Further, by stating that the employees' right to freedom of religion is not affected as long as they remain free to resign, it overlooks the importance of the sacrifice required from individuals to be able to practice their religion.[69] For most people, employment is their main source of income. Beyond economic necessity, work is also "the medium through which many people gain self-respect and a sense of participation and inclusion in society."[70] In addition, at least as far as days of rest are concerned, it disregards the fact, discussed above (see section 1.1), that in most European countries the majority religion is implicitly taken into account in current regulation of the workplace.

The alternative approach to the issue of religious diversity in the work sphere acknowledges the importance of employment for individuals' well-being as well as for social cohesion and seeks to achieve a balance between freedom to contract and the objective of social inclusion. It rests on a different vision of the relations between the work sphere and human rights. Under this view, human rights would be of limited utility if individuals could only exercise them at the cost of being excluded from the labor market. Thus, where a person is refused a job or fired because she wishes to manifest her faith in the workplace, this should count as a restriction to religious freedom. This does not mean that there cannot be situations in which an employer has valid reasons to limit religious practice at work or reject requests of accommodation. But the legitimacy of such interference should be assessed according to the criteria set forth in Article 9(2): while having a legal basis, it must be necessary in a democratic society to achieve one of the legitimate

---

stake was that the authorities contested that the applicant was truly Muslim, since he had previously celebrated Christian holidays.

67 *Id.*, par. 38.

68 H. Collins, *supra* note 30, 7.

69 In this sense, see the critique of the European Commission's case law: C. Evans, *Freedom of Religion under the European Convention on Human Rights* (Oxford University Press 2001), 130–131, and J. Velaers and M.-C. Foblets, "L'appréhension du fait religieux par le droit—A propos des minorités religieuses," 30 *Revue trimestrielle des droits de l'homme* 273 (1997), at 293.

70 L. Vickers, *Religious Freedom, Religious Discrimination and the Workplace* (Hart Publishing 2008), 47. See also H. Collins, *supra* note 30, at 3–4.

aims listed. It cannot be assumed that merely because a person is bound by a contract, any restriction to her rights decided by the employer is justified. State authorities have a positive obligation to protect individuals against violations of their rights committed by private parties like employers.[71] According to Collins, this conception of the relationship between employment and human rights is increasingly gaining ground:

> the former sharp contrast between the public sphere of rights and the private sphere of market relations in which civil liberties had no application is increasingly questioned. It is no longer accepted that workers leave their rights of citizenship at the doors to the workplace. The question is rather how far civil liberties should be protected against an employer's exercise of market power.[72]

Collins argues that the best reconciliation between the rights guaranteed under the ECHR and employment contracts "would be to require the employer to justify the contractual restriction by reference to a test of proportionality, so that the employer would be required to demonstrate that the terms represented a business need of the employer that could not satisfactorily be met by any lesser restriction on the Convention right."[73] In the same vein, Vickers claims that any legal regulation of the relations between work and religion should seek to find "some compromise whereby religious individuals can work where to do so does not disproportionately interfere with the rights of others."[74] The right to resign should only be considered as a residual protection where accommodation of religious practice is inappropriate because it conflicts with the rights of others or places too much of a cost on the employer.[75]

The development of EU anti-discrimination law clearly reinforces this approach. Social inclusion is one of the declared aims of this body of law. The Employment Equality Directive, the first EU instrument prohibiting discrimination based on religion or belief in employment, states in its Preamble that it is designed inter alia to foster a labor market favorable to social integration, to guarantee equal opportunities for all, and to promote the full participation of citizens in economic, cultural and social life.[76] Now, as emphasized by De Schutter, merely prohibiting employers from taking certain characteristics into account in

---

71 See inter alia D. Spielmann, "Obligations positives et effet horizontal des dispositions de la Convention," in *L'interprétation de la Convention européenne des droits de l'homme* (F. Sudre, ed., Nemesis-Bruylant 1998), 133–174.

72 H. Collins, *supra* note 30, 25 and 209–234.

73 *Id.*, 217.

74 L. Vickers, *supra* note 70, 10.

75 *Id.*, at 52–53.

76 Preamble, Recitals 8 and 9 Employment Equality Directive. See also H. Collins, "Discrimination, Equality and Social Inclusion," 66 *The Modern Law Review* 16 (2003) and O. De Schutter, *supra* note 57, at 57.

decisions on recruitment, promotion or firing is not sufficient to achieve social and professional integration of those who are excluded from the employment market. This is because the structure of the workplace itself produces exclusionary effects on certain groups. Thus, under this second approach, companies can be asked to do more than abstain from paying regard to certain features: they can be required to some extent to contribute to the objective of social inclusion through various measures, including transforming the work environment or organization in order to eliminate barriers to employment opportunities for certain disadvantaged groups, like religious minorities.[77] In other words, the company can be asked to assume a social responsibility. This can be justified by the fact that businesses benefit from multiple advantages that are present in the environment in which they operate and that are provided by the collectivity, such as material infrastructures, public services and a legal framework.[78]

In this relation, it is important to highlight that the Employment Equality Directive outlaws both direct and indirect discrimination. While direct discrimination occurs where a person is treated less favorably than another is, has been or would be treated in a comparable situation based on a prohibited ground,[79] indirect discrimination occurs where a norm that is neutral on its face, because it does not formally distinguish between individuals based for example on religion or belief, but nonetheless puts persons with a given religion or belief at a particular disadvantage compared with other persons.[80] This entails that a policy which is not deliberately designed to harm a protected group but which has this effect in practice can, potentially, be deemed discriminatory. By raising attention to the adverse impact certain norms have on specific categories of persons, the notion of indirect discrimination enables the questioning of the apparent neutrality of the environment.[81] Hence, a rule which disadvantages workers practicing a certain religion, such as dress requirements excluding the possibility of wearing a headscarf or the setting of uniform days of holidays which does not permit minority workers to take a day off for important religious celebrations, could be contested based on the prohibition of indirect religious discrimination. To be sure, not each and every practice resulting in disadvantage is prohibited under non-discrimination law: a measure having such impact will not be deemed discriminatory if it is proved to rest on a legitimate aim and to constitute a proportionate mean to achieve this objective.[82] Nonetheless,

77 O. De Schutter, *supra* note 57, at 25–28.

78 O. De Schutter, *supra* note 57, at 27.

79 Article 2(1)(a) of the Employment Equality Directive.

80 Article 2(1)(b) of The Employment Equality Directive. Note that the European Court of Human Rights has endorsed the notion of indirect discrimination: ECtHR, 13 November 2007, *D.H. and Others* v. *Czech Republic*.

81 O. De Schutter, "Interdiction de discriminer envers les étrangers et obligation d'intégration par le droit," in *Le droit et la diversité culturelle* (J. Ringelheim, ed., Bruylant 2011).

82 Article 2(1)(b) of The Employment Equality Directive.

the prohibition of indirect discrimination implies that where a work requirement penalizes workers observing a certain religion, the employers can be asked to justify this rule and this justification can be subject to judicial review. In effect, how judges will assess what constitutes a legitimate objective and proportionate means will be crucial in determining to what extent the prohibition of indirect discrimination protects religious interests in the work sphere.[83]

Canada and the US have gone one step further: in both countries, the law expressly recognizes a right to *reasonable accommodation* of religious beliefs in the work sphere.[84] The specificity of reasonable accommodation compared to indirect discrimination is to promote individualized solutions to conflicts between work rules and the religious practice of workers: where a norm is shown to have a detrimental effect on a person practicing a certain religion, it is not enough to establish that it is justified by a legitimate objective. The employer must also verify whether in the specific circumstances at stake it cannot be adapted to the situation of the individual affected.[85] This obligation, however, only exists as long as the accommodation is reasonable: the employer will be discharged of its duty to accommodate if it can prove that it took all necessary means to find a solution but any adjustment would have entailed undue hardship and would therefore have been unreasonable, because it would have impaired on the rights of others,

83 On the justification of indirect discrimination, see generally D. Schiek, L. Waddington and M. Bell (eds), *Cases, Materials and Texts on National, Supranational and International Discrimination Law, Ius Commune Casebooks for the Common Law of Europe* (Hart Publishing 2007), at 435–471.

84 In the US, following an amendment inserted in 1972, Title VII of the 1964 Civil Rights Act places a duty on private and public employers "to reasonably accommodate to an employee's or prospective employee's religious observance or practice without undue hardship on the conduct of the employer's business." (*Civil Rights Act of 1964*, CRA, Title VII, 42 US Code Chapter 21, §701 (j)). On this provision and related case law, see Ch. L. Eisgruber and L. Sager, *Religious Freedom and the Constitution* (Harvard University Press 2007), 87–108, and J. M. Oleske, Jr., "Federalism, Free Exercise, and Title VII: Reconsidering Reasonable Accommodation," 6 *University of Pennsylvania Journal of Constitutional Law* 525 (2004). In Canada, the obligation to provide reasonable accommodation was derived by the Courts from the equality and non-discrimination principles (see *Ontario Human Rights Commission and O'Malley* v. *Simpsons-Sears Ltd*, [1985] 2 *S.C.R.* 536). Moreover, the right to reasonable accommodation under Canadian law is not limited to employment, it also applies to the supply of goods and services. See P. Bosset, "Les fondements juridiques et l'évolution de l'obligation d'accommodement raisonnable," in *Les accommodements raisonnables: quoi, comment, jusqu'où? Des outils pour tous* (M. Jézéquiel, ed., éd. Yvon Blais 2007), 3–28, and P. Bouchard and Ch. Taylor, "Building the Future—A Time for Reconciliation," Consultation Commission on Accommodation Practices Related to Cultural Differences, Government of Quebec (2008), available at www.accommodements.qc.ca.

85 O. De Schutter, *supra* note 81. On this notion, see also L. Vickers, *supra* note 70, 223–225.

involved disproportionate cost or hampered the efficiency of the company.[86] Based on this notion, employers have been required for instance to allow exceptions to dress requirements, changes in working timetables or selected absences for religious festivals.[87] In the view of Vickers, such a duty to accommodate where to do so does not cause undue hardship can "create an adequate level of protection for religious interests, whilst giving space to employers to find an appropriate and proportionate balance between the competing rights at work."[88]

Under EU law, a right to reasonable accommodation in employment has been expressly recognized only in favor of disabled workers.[89] Yet various authors argue that the prohibition of indirect discrimination based on religion or belief in employment may implicitly entail an obligation to reasonably accommodate religious practice. In order to satisfy the requirement of proportionality, a rule having a detrimental effect on a protected group must be the least restrictive means to achieve the legitimate aim sought. This can be interpreted as requiring that before implementing such a rule, the employer considers alternatives to it, including the possibility of allowing individual exceptions in order to avoid disadvantaging persons with a particular religion.[90] For instance, imposing the wearing of a uniform may be justified by reasons of hygiene and safety or communication strategy. But refusing to adapt this dress code in order to allow the wearing of a headscarf, where doing so would not impair these objectives, could be deemed disproportionate. On this account, the approach taken in disability discrimination should be considered as the expression of a more general principle, namely that employers should make allowance for the different needs of socially excluded groups and contribute to fostering their social and professional integration.[91]

---

86 Note that the notion of "undue hardship" has been interpreted differently by Canadian and U.S. Courts. U.S. Courts accept more easily that an accommodation is unreasonable. See E. Bribosia, J. Ringelheim & I. Rorive, "Reasonable Accommodation for Religious Minorities: A Promising Concept for European Antidiscrimination Law?," 17 *Maastricht Journal of European and Comparative Law* 137 (2010), at 140 and 148.

87 *Id.*, 140–150.

88 L. Vickers, *supra* note 70, 223.

89 Article 5 of The Employment Equality Directive provides: "In order to guarantee compliance with the principle of equal treatment in relation to persons with disabilities, reasonable accommodation shall be provided. This means that employers shall take appropriate measures, where needed in a particular case, to enable a person with a disability to have access to, participate in, or advance in employment, or to undergo training, unless such measures would impose a disproportionate burden on the employer. This burden shall not be disproportionate when it is sufficiently remedied by measures existing within the framework of the disability policy of the Member State concerned."

90 See H. Collins, *supra* note 30, 73; L. Vickers, *supra* note 70, 223; and E. Bribosia, J. Ringelheim and I. Rorive, *supra* note 86, 157–158.

91 See, in particular, H. Collins, *supra* note 30, at 73–74. See also O. De Schutter, *supra* note 57, 205.

It remains to be seen whether the European Court of Justice will validate this interpretation of the Employment Equality Directive.[92] The European Court of Human Rights in the *Thlimmenos* v. *Greece* ruling (2000)[93] has already seemed to endorse the principle on which the concept of reasonable accommodation rests. The applicant was a Jehovah's Witness whom the Greek authorities had refused to appoint as a chartered accountant on the ground that he had been convicted of a serious crime five years earlier for having refused to serve in the military due to religious reasons. This decision was based on existing legislation barring the profession of chartered accountant to any person convicted of a crime. The Government insisted that since the legislation has general application, no exemption could be provided. But the Court rejected this argument, stating that the right not to be discriminated against under Article 14 of the ECHR is not only violated when states treat differently persons in analogous situations, but also *when they fail to treat differently* persons whose situations are significantly different, without objective and reasonable justification.[94] In the case at stake, while the legislation was based on a legitimate objective, namely to prevent dishonest or untrustworthy people from this profession, its application to Mr Thlimmenos lacked any reasonable justification: his conviction did not imply any dishonesty or moral turpitude likely to undermine his ability to work as a chartered accountant.[95] Hence, "by failing to introduce appropriate exceptions to the rule barring persons convicted of a serious crime from the profession of chartered accountants," Greece

92 So far, only in the 1976 *Vivien Prais* case (Case C-130/75 *Vivien Prais* [1976] ECR 1589), decided well before the adoption of the Directive, has the ECJ implicitly touched upon the issue. The applicant had presented her candidacy for a competition organized by the Council of the European Communities to hire translators. She complained about the fact that the Council had rejected her request to take part in the written test on another date based on the ground that the date set coincided with an important Jewish holiday. She claimed that the Council had violated the clause in the Staff Regulation according to which candidates are chosen without distinction of race, religion or sex. Whilst rejecting her claim, the Court admitted that it is "desirable that an appointing authority informs itself in a general way of dates which might be unsuitable for religious reasons, and seeks to avoid fixing such dates for tests" (par. 18). But given that a written test must take place under the same conditions for all candidates, the appointing authority must not accommodate other dates for the test unless it has been notified before the other candidates have been invited (par. 13). Although this terminology is not used, this ruling seems to endorse to some extent the logic underpinning the notion of reasonable accommodation. See also the chapter by Titia Loenen in this volume (discussing a number of difficult choices the ECJ will have to make if and when called upon to decide a religious discrimination case under the EU non-discrimination directives).

93 ECtHR 6 April 2000, *Thlimmenos* v. *Greece*, par. 44.

94 *Id.*, para. 44.

95 *Id.*, par. 47.

violated his right not to be discriminated against on the grounds of his religion.[96] Since then, however, the European Court has not made any other application of this principle, at least in the employment sphere.[97]

Conclusion

Debates sparked by the management of spiritual diversity in the workplace include several different and interrelated dimensions. First, they reflect the more general queries and tensions generated by the pluralization of the religious landscape in European societies. From this perspective, they are part and parcel of wider controversies about the relations between religions and the secular state. Second, from another viewpoint, they echo the growing discussions about how to allow workers to better reconcile their professional activity with their personal or family life. This problem takes particular significance in a context marked by the rise of individualization and flexibilization of work organization as well as the "precarization" of labor conditions of the most vulnerable categories of workers. One major challenge in this regard is how to ensure that flexibility does not merely serve the interests of employers but also meets the aspirations and needs of employees. Third, and more fundamentally perhaps, religion in employment touches upon the vaster problem of how to define the relations between work, law and human rights. At stake here is the task of determining what in labor relations should be regulated by the state and what should be left to private parties to decide, based on their contractual freedom, having regard to the inequality of power between employers and workers. The development of EU anti-discrimination law is likely to have a crucial impact on the way this question is dealt with across Europe. The emphasis it places on the objective of social inclusion, and the prohibition of indirect discrimination it includes, give further strength to the view that freedom of contract is not in itself a sufficient justification for restricting religious freedom at work, and that employers can be required to contribute to the elimination of indirect barriers to the professional integration of minority religious groups.

96 *Id.*, par. 48. For a discussion of this ruling, see L. Vickers, *supra* note 70, at 115–116, and E. Bribosia, J. Ringelheim and I. Rorive, *supra* note 86, 153–154.

97 In *Jakobski* v. *Poland*, the Court holds that refusing to accommodate dietary requirements of a detainee based on his religious beliefs constitutes a violation of the right to freedom of religion under Article 9 of the ECHR. While not using this terminology, the Court in substance acknowledges an obligation for state authorities to reasonably accommodate religious beliefs of individuals where they find themselves in closed public institutions, like prisons. See ECtHR 7 December 2010, *Jakobski* v. *Poland*. See also the chapter by Saïla Ouald Chaib in this volume (drawing inspiration from this case and others to suggest ways to improve the reasoning of the Court in religious accommodation cases).

Index

For Product Safety Concerns and Information please contact our EU representative GPSR@taylorandfrancis.com
Taylor & Francis Verlag GmbH, Kaufingerstraße 24, 80331 München, Germany

www.ingramcontent.com/pod-product-compliance
Ingram Content Group UK Ltd.
Pitfield, Milton Keynes, MK11 3LW, UK
UKHW022008180926
475701UK00003B/248
* 9 7 8 1 1 3 8 2 5 6 0 5 7 *